The Beginnings of
Brunel
University

The Beginnings of Brunel University

*From Technical College
to University*

JAMES TOPPING

OXFORD UNIVERSITY PRESS
1981

Oxford University Press, Walton Street, Oxford OX2 6DP
London Glasgow New York Toronto
Delhi Bombay Calcutta Madras Karachi
Kuala Lumpur Singapore Hong Kong Tokyo
Nairobi Dar Es Salaam Cape Town
Melbourne Wellington

and associate companies in
Beirut Berlin Ibadan Mexico City

Published in the United States
by Oxford University Press, New York

© James Topping, 1981

British Library Cataloguing in Publication Data

Topping, James
The beginnings of Brunel University
1. Brunel University—History
I. Title
378.421'83   LF449.B/   80-41452

ISBN 0-19-920116-1

Printed in Great Britain
at the University Press, Oxford
by Eric Buckley
Printer to the University

*To my colleagues
at Brunel University,
particularly those
who were at Acton
Technical College,
and to the lay
members of Brunel
College Governing
Body and of the
University Council*

Preface

Two of the outstanding events that marked the development of higher technological education in the middle of the twentieth century were the creation of the colleges of advanced technology in 1956 and their transformation a decade later into technological universities. An authoritative account of these happenings has been provided by the late Sir Peter Venables in his *Higher Education Developments: The Technological Universities 1956–76* (London, Faber, 1978). Brunel College was the last CAT to be designated (in 1962) and became Brunel University in 1966. It grew out of a very different institution, Acton Technical College, and some account of the growth of that college is therefore given in the first few chapters of this book.

I was helped considerably in writing about these early beginnings by J. T. Fielding, formerly in the education department of the Middlesex County Council and later Principal of Kilburn Technical College. I am also indebted to several members of the university staff, notably Professor S. C. Bevan and G. R. Halcrow, whose recollections of 'Acton days' were invaluable.

Professor Bevan was kind enough to read and comment on the whole of the typescript and to him and Professor John Burnett I owe much. My debt is greatest to Professor George Jackson and Professor S. A. Urry who provided me with material and assistance of many kinds; even more, their informed criticism and kindly encouragement as the writing proceeded helped guide the book into its present form.

I am glad to express my thanks to Professor John Crank, B. H. Winstanley, E. R. Chandler, C. E. N. Childs, Robert Adlington and many other members of staff of the university who helped me in various ways. And to those who willingly undertook the typing, particularly my former secretary, Miss S. T. E. Sherratt, whose critical mind improved much of the writing, I am greatly indebted. Others gave generously of their time and skill; Tom Lewis of the London College of Printing helped with some of the figures, and Peter Humphrey of the Audio Visual Centre of the University provided a fine collection of photographs from which most of the plates have been selected.

Whatever is included in this account of the beginnings of the University no doubt reflects my own close involvement, but I have been at pains to present a balanced view. I am very much aware that some aspects of the University's development have received inadequate attention; I regret in particular that too little is included about the contribution of the Students' Union to the growing life of the University. My attempts to find a way through the scant documentation and to gather information from old students were fruitless; it proved an impossible task with the resources I had available.

As it is the writing has taken much longer than originally planned. Long ago in 1972 the Research Awards Advisory Committee of the Leverhulme Trust Fund awarded me an Emeritus Fellowship which helped me to make a start and I would like to express my gratitude for their timely assistance. It made the end result, belated as it is, possible.

JAMES TOPPING

Contents

PREFACE   vii

LIST OF ILLUSTRATIONS   xi

1. The Beginnings at Acton   1
2. The Formative Years   24
3. The Governance of Acton Technical College   44
4. How to Educate Technologists, 1944–54   58
5. Acton Technical College, 1955–7   72
6. Brunel College of Technology, 1957–9   111
7. Other Building Plans (Phases II and III)   132
8. Brunel College of Technology, 1959–61   143
9. Some Educational Ideas   160
10. College of Advanced Technology   180
11. Planning the Move to Uxbridge   195
12. The Years 1962–4   204
13. The Charter of the University   231
14. Buildings at Uxbridge—Phase One   249
15. Finance   272
16. The Years 1964–6   286
17. Brunel University—the First Two Years   308
18. The University Buildings, 1968   337
19. The Years of Separation, 1968–71   354
20. Developments on Site One   383
21. The Quinquennium 1972–7   394
22. Retrospect   406

APPENDICES   428

INDEX   439

List of Illustrations

FIGURES

2.1. Total Number of Students in the Universities of Great
Britain, 1948–57   39

2.2. (a) Development of work in all Establishments
(b) Development of work in Acton Technical College   41

11.1. The University Sites   199

12.1. Plan of Brunel College showing huts and Woodlands
Annexe   209

18.1. First Floor of Lecture Centre   343

18.2. Plan of Engineering Centre   345

18.3. Plan of the University in 1969   351

20.1. The BIOSS building and the Cleveland Road entrance
to the University   383

PLATES

1. Acton Technical College   *facing p.* 52

2. Brunel College, Acton   ,, 53

3. Model of Brunel College as planned in 1959   ,, 84

4. Model of Phase One, Uxbridge   ,, 84

5. Engineering Centre, Uxbridge   ,, 85

6. Two of the Engineering Towers   ,, 85

7. Administration Building   ,, 148

8. Communal Building, as later modified. Renamed
Refectory Building   ,, 148

9. Lecture Centre from the south-west   ,, 149

10. Lecture Centre from the south-east   ,, 180

11. Mathematics Building   ,, 181

12. Biology and Chemistry Building   *facing p.* 244
13. Physics Building   ,,   245
14. Bridge over the Pinn, with Lecture Centre and
    Mathematics Building   ,,   276
15. Sports Centre   ,,   276
16. Library   ,,   277
17. Buildings in 1968   ,,   340
18. General view in 1971   ,,   341
19. General view in 1975   ,,   341
20. First Hall of Residence (Clifton)   ,,   372
21. Second Hall of Residence (Saltash)   ,,   372
22. Third Hall of Residence (Chepstow)   ,,   373
23. Some student flatlets on Site One   ,,   373

CHAPTER 1

The Beginnings at Acton

THE growth of technical education in Britain from the middle of the twentieth century was extraordinary by any standards. The war years, 1939-45, were followed by such changes both in outlook and provision as to mark the beginning of a new era. This was no less true of education in all its varied forms than it was of many other areas of our national life but was specially true of the changes in technical education. 'Further education in this country is passing through a revolution' commented the Ministry of Education report for 1948.

To catch a glimpse of the scene before the war it might be recalled that in 1938 there were nearly 400 colleges in England and Wales providing further education of some kind. Many of them, like Acton Technical College, were fairly recent foundations. Acton was opened in 1928, and several other colleges were built in Middlesex in the next decade. There was similar growth elsewhere. The colleges were variously named polytechnics, technical colleges or institutes, colleges of further education, colleges of commerce, colleges or schools of art, and were officially referred to as major establishments, partly to distinguish them from the evening institutes which, as their name implied, conducted classes in the evenings only and had no day work whatsoever. In fact these evening institutes usually had no premises of their own and were to be found accommodated in a school (a chapel was not unknown) or some other institution; there were about 6,000 of them in 1938. Around Acton Technical College at that time were several Evening Institutes housed in schools.

Together these colleges and institutes provided a range of courses of rich variety, which had been developed in response to the needs or demands of many different groups of students, most of whom having left school comparatively early had gone into industry or commerce and were moved in whatever time they could make available to continue their education or to acquire some new skill or to procure some additional qualification. They were certainly motivated variously and in differing measure. In the early days of technical colleges all the courses had been conducted as evening classes, but in time more and more classes were held during the day, some organized as full-time courses and others on a part-time basis. Some firms allowed their apprentices and other workers to attend classes during the day, an arrangement usually referred to as 'part-time day release'.

By 1938 the demand and provision for further education had so grown that there were about 1.2 million students attending evening classes in the various institutions (excluding Art Schools and Art Classes[1]) in England and Wales. At that time, it should be remembered, about 90 per cent of the nation's children left school at 14; legislation had been passed in 1936 to raise the school-leaving age to 15, but little was achieved until after the war. Of the students attending evening classes less than a quarter, some 265,000, were in the Colleges of Further Education; the others were in the Evening Institutes.

The number of part-time day students was very much smaller, and had reached in 1938 around 51,000; about 42,000 of them were on part-time day release. 'We are exceedingly glad to be able to record an appreciable increase in the number of these students' commented the Board of Education report for 1938. 'At the same time it remains true to say that the number benefiting by day release still form only a very small proportion of those who attend in their own time in the evenings, and of course a still smaller proportion of the total number of young workers in industry and commerce.'

Of the 51,000 part-time day students nearly 20,000 were in Day Continuation Schools, which offered a general education, with or without a vocational bias, for part-time students up to the age of 18. The Education Act of 1918 had made provision for compulsory Day Continuation Schools but for various reasons,

---

[1] If little is included here about Art Education, this is not to underestimate its importance in Further Education.

mainly financial, the attempt to establish them was abandoned except in one place (Rugby). Thereafter some were maintained on a voluntary basis, and pupils in employment attended by arrangement with their employers.

The other part-time day students, nearly 32,000 of them, were in the colleges following one or other of two main groups of courses, termed Technical Day Classes and Senior full-time courses. These were also attended by full-time day students, numbering 4,584 and 9,143 respectively. The Senior full-time courses included those in preparation for university inter- mediate and final degree examinations. There were therefore some 13,700 full-time day students in all, but not every college had full-time students; in fact only 81 of the 208 major establishments provided senior full-time courses. Some 27 of the colleges—of which 10 were in the London area—provided full- time higher technological courses of as much as three years' duration.[2]

Table 1.1, extracted from the *Education in 1938* Report, shows the distribution of students amongst the various groups of courses.

TABLE 1.1

Numbers of Students in Further Education Establishments 1937–8 (England and Wales)[3]

	Evening	Part-time Day	Full-time Day
Evening Institutes	913,706	—	—
Colleges of Further Education	265,157	(a)29,675	(a) 4,584
		(b) 1,972	(b) 9,143
Day Continuation Schools	—	19,629	—
Total Number of Students	1,178,863	51,276	13,727

(a) Technical Day Classes.   (b) Senior Full-time Courses.

The number of pupils in the Junior Technical and other Junior full-time schools was 29,036, more than double the number of full-time students in the Colleges of Further Education where the schools were normally housed.

The demand for evening classes at a time when such a large proportion of the nation's children left school before the age of

[2] Percy Report, *Higher Technological Education*, HMSO, 1945, 7.
[3] Excluding Art Schools and Art Classes.

15 or 16 is readily comprehensible, but it might be asked how and why arrangements for full-time education developed in Colleges of Further Education outside or alongside the main educational provision in schools and universities, a social phenomenon of some complexity and worthy of deeper study than it has yet received. This duality has been the subject of some political controversy in recent years, particularly since C. A. R. Crosland,[4] as Minister of Education, made his 'Woolwich Speech'. It is less than fair to label him as the creator of what is often referred to as the 'binary system' of higher education. He inherited it and of course tried to remould it, but social forces had been at work for nearly a century. Whatever resulted could not, in any case, be called a system. Rather could it be said 'that further education has grown up as the handmaiden of employment', and as the Crowther report[5] added 'English further education cannot be understood without realising that virtually everything that exists in it has come into existence as the conscious answer to a demand arising from industry or from individual workers. Where something does not exist, it is because no effective demand for it has been expressed.'

The inadequacy of this as a philosophy of further education is obvious enough; it merely provides a general description of the way in which courses in the many institutions multiplied in response to changing social patterns. Something more is needed, however, to account for the differential growth of further education in various localities and in different institutions. The development of new industries, the movement of population, the active interest of some firms, the initiative and foresight of education committees and administrators, and the vision of the policy makers in the colleges were all contributing factors.

At a time of very limited educational opportunity it would not be surprising to find that the demand from individuals had outstripped that from firms. Lord Eustace Percy[6] wrote in 1930 'the weakness of technical colleges has been that they have been built up too much in response to a demand from below and not enough in response to a demand from above. The demand has

[4] Woolwich Polytechnic, April 1965.
[5] *Report of the Central Advisory Council for Education (England)*, 15 to 18, Volume 1, HMSO, 1959, 333 (Crowther Report).
[6] *Education at the Crossroads*, Evans, 1930.

been the demand of individual young men and women engaged in commerce and industry to continue their education. . . . It has not been the demand made by industry itself for a high standard of training for its workers.' Cotgrove[7] later claimed that 'there is no evidence of any pressure by industry before the 1930's for any extension of technical education. The demands of industry for trained manpower were fully met by existing provision, though this had increased little above the level achieved twenty-five years earlier in 1905.'

It should be remembered, however, that there were some important changes and movements in the nineteen-twenties. Notably the introduction in 1921 of national certificates, sponsored by the Board of Education and professional institutions, so that some ten years later about 2,000 ordinary certificates and 750 higher certificates had been awarded—not large numbers but not insignificant. Further the interest of a few industrial firms, unusual in their devotion to education and training, had led to the formation of the Association for the Advancement of Education in Industry and Commerce (AEIC) in 1919, which later merged into a bigger body, BACIE, the British Association for Commercial and Industrial Education. Government too played a part, in which Lord Eustace Percy, as President of the Board of Education (1924-29), was the moving spirit. He initiated a number of enquiries into education for industry and commerce. One of these, known as the Malcolm Committee, was asked 'to enquire into and advise upon the public system of education in relation to the requirements of trade and industry'. Its approach to the development of full-time technical education was very cautious; there was no evidence, it suggested, 'of an unsatisfied demand on the part of industry for the product of a full-time system. It would be deplorable if any such development as has been suggested should result in the output of a substantial number of highly-trained young men whom industry was unable to absorb.'[8] Rather was it the part-time 'senior and advanced courses in Technical Schools' which were of most immediate and obvious interest to trade and industry, and these courses appeared to be

[7] S. F. Cotgrove, *Technical Education and Social Change*, London, George Allen and Unwin, 1958, 81.

[8] *Report of the Committee on Education and Industry (England and Wales)*, Second Part, 1928.

quite adequate 'in relation at any rate to expressed needs'. The main cause of concern was the 'disquieting indifference on the part of many employers to the desirability of securing the best possible training for young workers at least up to the age of 21'. The employers' organizations in giving evidence to the Committee had confessed, sadly no doubt, that although they were in a position to state a collective view on the raising of the Elementary School leaving age and the establishment of a system of compulsory Day Continuation Schools, they were not able to present such a view on Technical Schools and Colleges 'due largely to lack of knowledge of the system and to lack of practical experience of its working'. The Committee recommended, not surprisingly, that closer co-operation between Technical Schools and industry was urgently needed. It questioned too whether the educational outlook in the Technical Schools was sufficiently practical, and implied that there should be some reappraisal of the roles of the Schools and the firms in the purposes of education and training; these roles overlapped and should not be too rigidly defined. 'We record our strong opinion that the only really satisfactory method of arranging for the technical education of apprentices and other young learners is by means of part-time attendance during working hours. This may take the form of what is called the sandwich system. . . .' The term sandwich, as will be explained more fully later, was applied to arrangements whereby a period of attendance at college was followed by a similar period in an industrial firm, an alternation of learning and training that usually continued throughout the whole length of the course.

Technological changes in industry were influencing ideas about practical training, and the newer industries felt the need for change more urgently. The introduction of new industrial techniques demanded differently skilled craftsmen and technicians and more semi-skilled operatives. Technical Colleges, it was pleaded, should be more involved in their training. Previously there had been little or no relatedness between what was taught in the schools and colleges and what the students did at work. The current philosophy was that the function of technical institutions was to teach the principles underlying the practice of any particular trade or technology, and not to provide training in the industrial processes. The latter was industry's responsibility, and in some strange way theory and practice became separated. But a different view gradually gained acceptance. The Board of Education Report for 1937 pointed to

the growing realisation that there is a problem of training for industry and commerce towards the solution of which the technical and commercial schools can make a definite contribution. Under present-day conditions it is less easy for the works to furnish in the daily round the general training that once could be given. Yet the growth of mechanisation has in no sense diminished the need for skill and resourcefulness. There is, therefore, a growing belief that the old apprentice training confined to the works can probably best be replaced, at least in certain ranges, by a system of training in which the works and technical school collaborate and each play their part.

It went on to press the case for part-time day release; it might also have extolled the merits of sandwich courses.

If views about training were changing only slowly few doubted that new colleges had to be built and new policies and courses devised. The Middlesex County Council, for example, faced with an unprecedented influx of industry and population after the 1914–18 war, adopted a far-reaching scheme to expand and modernize technical education in the county. Seven new technical institutes were planned, of which those at Acton and Southall were opened in 1928 and devoted to engineering and building, followed in January 1929 by that at Ealing which was to be a main centre for arts and crafts and commerce. The 1931 financial crisis gave rise to some retrenchment, but Willesden Technical College was opened by 1934, and a year or so later a long-term building programme for technical, commercial and art education was sanctioned involving an expenditure of nearly one million pounds. So by the outbreak of war large colleges had been completed at Twickenham (1937) and at Hendon (1939), and one at Enfield was partially finished when hostilities started. Sites had been acquired too for other colleges. The sensitivity of the Middlesex County Council to the need for a well-planned system of technical colleges in the County during those crucial and difficult years was commendable. An Assistant Secretary for Technical Education was appointed in 1931, and in 1933 a new sub-committee was constituted with special responsibility for technical education.[9]

[9] Given the title, The Further Education Sub-Committee, in 1945.

The real beginnings of technical education in Middlesex, however, occurred many years earlier in the last decade of the nineteenth century, a period which saw major developments in, if not the effective start of, technical education throughout Britain.[10] It was in 1892 following the important legislation of 1889-90 that the County Council established a Technical Education Committee and, interestingly enough, appointed in 1898 an Organising Inspector of Technical Education.

By 1901 three Polytechnics, as they were then called, had been established at Chiswick, Kilburn and Tottenham, and ten years later each had been enlarged and supplemented by smaller Technical Institutes at Harrow (1907), Ponders End, Enfield (1911) and Edmonton (1912). However, since Middlesex at that time was largely rural and residential the County Council was somewhat cautious in its attitude to additional provision, favouring the erection of combined County Schools and Evening Institutes of which three were built at Ealing, Enfield and Twickenham.

Caution was also evident in their handling of the possible development of advanced work in the Middlesex Polytechnics, an attitude reflected in a report of the Secretary to the Education Committee in 1915: 'Middlesex not being to any large extent a manufacturing district cannot attempt to provide itself with this higher technical training, but it would be well to have scholarships which would enable suitable boys who have received a good general education to go to the Technical Institutes of London'—and many did, for many years thereafter until the Middlesex Technical Colleges were fully developed. There was the vexed question of out-county fees[11]—the higher fees paid by a student attending a technical college in a county other than the one in which he resided—which bedevilled technical education for many years.

Within Middlesex each Polytechnic contributed to the early development of other technical colleges. Chiswick Polytechnic (earlier named the Acton and Chiswick Polytechnic) is perhaps

[10] Mechanics Institutes started in Glasgow in 1823 and quickly spread to the industrial areas of the north. One in London opened in 1824 became Birkbeck College.

[11] In the 1930s a student residing outside the Administrative County of Middlesex paid treble the ordinary fees, unless he worked in Middlesex in which case double the ordinary fees were payable. There were special arrangements for students who lived in London.

the best example. Having started as a private School of Arts and Crafts, it was acquired by the County Council in 1899, renamed a Polytechnic, with the intention that it should be the central institution serving the west of the County. It was progressively enlarged. In the reorganization of 1928, however, not only was its Junior Technical School for Engineering transferred to start the new Acton Technical College but some evening classes in engineering were moved too. Few at that time could have realized how the new college was destined to outgrow its parent. As other colleges were built, other courses were dispersed from Chiswick. Some classes in commerce were transferred to Ealing Technical College in 1930, and art and printing classes were moved to Twickenham on the opening of the new technical institute there in 1937. In fact the Junior Art School was moved to Twickenham at that time in the same way as the Junior Technical School for Engineering had been transferred to start Acton Technical College nine years earlier. Chiswick Polytechnic continued as a major centre for business studies, home economics, health and nursing courses, but suffered a severe setback during the 1939–45 war when it was extensively damaged. Its remaining Junior School, a Commercial School, was then transferred to Twickenham. The Polytechnic was later rebuilt on the same site, and extended its work considerably to include courses in commerce and management studies, and provision for general and adult education.

It is evident that junior schools were an important feature of the Middlesex scheme of technical education; in fact most of the Technical Institutes or Colleges had such schools associated with them. The Southall Institute started (in 1928) as a Trade School with an entry of 52 boys, and in addition there were part-time classes mainly in the evening for older boys. By 1931 the School had about 180 pupils, and the Institute some 90 students attending part-time day classes as well as over 400 evening students; the Institute was recognized for Ordinary National Certificates in Mechanical Engineering, Electrical Engineering and Building. The next year recognition of Higher National Certificate courses followed; the Institute was renamed Southall Technical College and in 1934 the first extensions to the College were opened. At Ealing the Technical Institute and School of Arts and Crafts, to use its full title, also grew quickly; it had two junior schools at the start, an Art School and a School for Salesmanship for Retail Distribution.

The growth of the Acton, Southall and Ealing Technical Colleges and of their Junior Schools, was closely linked with the development of new industries in West London which marked the nineteen-twenties and thirties. Many workers were attracted from the depressed areas in the North of England and South Wales where unemployment was high; a general migration of population to the south-east of the country took place, but in addition there was a considerable movement of people out of London into Middlesex. The population of the county which in 1921 was 1,253,000, expanded to around 1,638,000 by 1931. It reached 2,248,000 in 1947. The development of transport contributed to the change, for centres of population grew up along the extensions of the railways, in particular the Piccadilly line, and the new road system. Through Acton two great arterial roads, the Great West Road and Western Avenue, were constructed and along them industry and housing proliferated. 'Even a generation ago Middlesex was a dormitory' wrote the H.M. Inspectors in their report on the Acton and Chiswick Polytechnic in 1928; 'now large portions of it are being transformed into workshops, and nowhere is the process taking place more rapidly than in the western districts, until recently devoted to market gardens, orchards and pasture.'

Acton once presumably fair with oak trees took on a very different aspect, particularly the northern part of the borough which has been described as 'a horrid example of the twentieth century doing its worst'.[12] Known for its numerous laundries and locally called 'Soap Suds Island', Acton became a centre of light engineering and other industries. Some engineering firms had established themselves earlier, notably D. Napier and Son, Engineers, Ltd., which in 1903 moved from Lambeth to Acton, 'just down the road' from where the College was later built.

By 1904—so greatly had the business recovered since 1895—about five hundred men were employed, more than there ever had been at Lambeth in its best days. Many of them were tradesmen—fitters or machinists—trained by apprenticeship within the factory, and skilled in many operations which were still done by hand. They worked a 54-hour week, in two shifts of five hours each in a full working day

---

[12] M. Robbins, *Middlesex*, Collins, 1953, 219.

(seven in the morning till mid-day; one o'clock to six), and the young men studied in the evening, at their own expense, at the Regent Street or Chelsea Polytechnic. The first pre-occupation at the new factory was Napier's most important contribution to the technical progress of the motor car—the first commercially successful six-cylinder engine.[13]

By 1906 the new works at Acton employed 1,000 men, many of whom must have been highly skilled, for each car was still an individual piece of engineering and not an assemblage of components.[14] In the first war 1914-18 the firm became involved in the design and manufacture of engines for the early aeroplanes, and by 1918 its business had so changed no cars were made at all. 'On the other hand, during that year orders placed by the Government for aircraft engines and parts—including an order for 100 of Napier's own engines—were worth nearly £2½ million.' Montague Napier decided after the war that the firm's policy should be to concentrate on aero-engines and by 1927 production at Acton was about fifty a month. The difficult years of the depression were weathered, business improved with the adoption of re-armament by the Government and before the end of 1938 the firm was discussing with the Air Ministry 'the possibility of building 1,000 *Sabres* a year, and to do that they would need a new factory'. A new works was in fact built at Liverpool where there was still considerable unemployment, and the first Sabre was produced there in February 1942; production had of course started at Acton much earlier.

Napier's had close relations with Acton Technical College from its very beginning, and some of the firm's engineers and technical staff contributed much to the College's development. Other firms contributed too, including many of those more recently established in the area. Amongst them were the London General Omnibus Company (later the London Passenger Transport Board), CAV, Hoover, EMI, Metal Box, Kodak, Guinness, Glaxo, Rotax, Ultra Electronics, Glacier Metal, Wilkinson Sword, Rootes, Gillette, Sperry Gyroscope, Firestone Tyre Co., Mond Nickel, Heinz, Beecham and many others. Some of them were very near the College, others were further afield. Electrical and Musical Industries (EMI), for

[13] C. Wilson and W. Reader, *Men and Machines*, Weidenfeld and Nicholson, 1958.
[14] A. J. P. Taylor, *English History, 1914-1945*, Oxford, 183. 'In 1913 there were 198 different models of motor-cars being produced, all by hand one at a time.'

instance, had factories at Hayes, some seven miles away. This company was established in 1931 as a result of a merger of two giant talking-machine companies, Gramophone and Columbia. As far back as 1907 the Gramophone Company had built its first premises at Hayes on eleven acres of open land, admirably placed for transport purposes between the canal, which gave direct access to the London docks, and Brunel's Great Western Railway, alongside which sidings were later constructed that linked the works with the main line. With the coming of 'wireless' the company became involved in the design and manufacture of receivers and radiograms, and the associated equipment, as well as cabinets. By 1931 the number of employees had risen to 15,000, and Hayes had grown from a village of 2,000 people to a developing urban area with a population of about 12,000.[15] It was in 1931 that the Company became interested in the development of television, and Isaac Shoenberg assembled around him an exceptional team of physicists and engineers whose work culminated in the EMI-Marconi system of television transmission adopted by the BBC for regular public reception in Britain in 1936–7. The Company was increasingly involved in the education and training of craftsmen, technicians, technologists and managers, and it developed links not only with Acton Technical College but with many other institutions and other local technical colleges as these were established, particularly Southall.

Of the many firms associated with Acton Technical College mention might be made of CAV; their factory in the older industrial area near Napier's establishment in Acton Vale was established in 1902. This is now one of several CAV product centres devoted to diesel fuel injection systems and other vehicle equipment, and the Company is a member of the Joseph Lucas industrial Group. Their Research and Engineering Headquarters are at Acton, a new research laboratory having been opened there in 1959. Another company which moved to Acton in the early years of the century was the Wilkinson Sword Company. It transferred from Chelsea to larger premises at Southfield Road, Acton, in 1903 and became increasingly involved with the manufacture of razors and later with razor-blades and a range of cutting tools.

[15] The population of Hayes and Harlington in 1931 was 23,649.

Other firms were in the Park Royal area in North Acton. Development there

first occurred during the war (1914-18), when it was used for Government purposes. . . . By the end of 1918 only 18 factories had been established in the Park Royal area and most of these were the result of the special demand at that time for war material. At the present time (1937) there are some 230 factories in the area, of which (excluding branch factories) one third have been transferred from the County of London. The greater part of the development has occurred in recent years, particularly in 1932 and 1933. Many of the factories are small, employing under a hundred persons, although some few employ a considerable number of workers.[16]

One of the bigger concerns was Guinness, which built a large complex at Park Royal in 1936, an attractive group of industrial buildings designed by Sir Giles Gilbert Scott. Writing in 1933, D. H. Smith in his interesting book *The Industries of Greater London* stated, 'one can safely assume that this district may ultimately prove to be the largest single centre of industrial activity in the south-east of England'. It was later described as the greatest concentration of industry south of Birmingham, a development that was aided by the building of the North Circular Road in 1923-34. The Glacier Metal Company had been established in this area as far back as 1899 for the manufacture of anti-friction materials. During and after the first World War it developed quickly, becoming involved in the manufacture of bearings for the motor-car industry; larger premises became necessary and the factory was moved in 1923 to its present location in Alperton. It went through difficult times during the depression, the labour force falling to about 250 in 1933. It was reorganized as a public company in 1935, and Wilfred Brown (later Lord Brown) was made Managing Director in 1939. He guided the growth of the firm during the war years, 1939-45, when the numbers employed rose to 3,000 and he was particularly responsible for the development of a novel type of factory organization and a new managerial structure, for which the firm is perhaps best known.[17]

Further afield in the clean atmosphere of Harrow Kodak

[16] London Passenger Transport Board, Fourth Annual Report, 1937.
[17] See Elliott Jaques, *The Changing Culture of a Factory*, Tavistock Publications, 1951, and Wilfred Brown, *Explorations in Management*, Heinemann, 1960.

built a factory as early as 1891 on a site of about three acres. By
the early nineteen-seventies there were over 100 buildings on a
55-acre site with a staff of some 5,000. The Engineering division
employed a good number of professional engineers and of course
many more technicians, whilst the Research Laboratory, which
was started in 1928, had by then a staff of about 300.

Amongst the more recent factories were those of Hoovers in
Western Avenue, and of the Firestone Tyre and Rubber Co. and
of Gillette Ltd. in the Great West Road, typical of the industrial
growth along these roadways but also outstanding as examples
of new industrial buildings in the nineteen thirties. The Gillette
factory was completed in 1937 and its clock-tower is now a well-
known landmark. The Firestone Tyre Company's works alongside were equally striking; they were built in 1928 and started the
development, very soon after the completion of the Middlesex
section of the Great West Road in 1925. 'The Great West Road
provides an outstanding example of industrial development on
an arterial road', commented one report[18] at the time; 'within a
two-mile stretch there are no less than 53 factories, all of them
new, employing about 11,000 workers. The road has in fact
become one of the principal industrial centres of outer London.'
The other new highway, Western Avenue, of which the Acton-
Greenford section was constructed over the period 1921-9, saw
similar expansion. One of the earliest buildings along it was that
of Hoovers, which was built in 1932 and became the headquarters of the British Hoover organization; housing a training
centre concerned with all aspects of company training, as well as
a school for apprentices. The Metal Box Company also built a
factory in this Perivale area, just off Western Avenue, for the
manufacture of their own machinery used in producing tin plate
cans and plastic containers. Originally at Worcester this
engineering unit was moved to the company's Acton works
before being finally established at Perivale in 1946. The Acton
works had been built earlier in 1930,[18] and it was there that the
main research department was housed as were the important
activities associated with food technology.

These firms were typical of the widespread and rapid
expansion of industry in West London; they are chosen not only

[18] London Passenger Transport Board, Fourth Annual Report, 1937.
[19] For the British Can Company, which was later purchased by Metal Box.

because they were in varying measure associated with Acton Technical College, but because they exemplify the technological and scientific basis of much of this industrial development, which demanded more and more facilities for technical education for a rapidly increasing number of craftsmen, technicians and technical staff. It is little wonder that as soon as a new technical college was opened, it was inadequate for the demand; educational planners, in this field particularly, faced a sisyphean task.

When Acton Technical College came into being in 1928 the accommodation comprised 10 classrooms, 2 drawing offices, 5 laboratories, an assembly hall (fitted up as a gymnasium), machine shop with tool store and forge, plumber's shop, woodworking machine shop, joiner's and carpenter's shop, and dining hall.[20] The cost was about £50,000. How this accommodation was used in the first year was tellingly described in the brochure published at the formal opening of the College (first called a Technical Institute) on 23 February 1929:

The buildings are used by the Junior Technical School for Engineering during the hours 9 a.m. to 4 p.m. Thereafter, until 9.30 p.m., it is used by about 250 apprentices of the General Post Office Engineering Department, 60 apprentices of the London General Omnibus Company, and 900[21] other students, distributed over five evenings per week. It is anticipated that the number of students will be greatly increased next session.

This latter forecast was amply fulfilled.

The Junior Technical School, the JTS as it was called, accepted boys at the age of 13; they stayed in the school for about three years and followed a technically-biased secondary school course. The curriculum, which was fairly broad-based included technical drawing, woodwork and engineering workshop practice (even pattern-making); moreover the boys had access to the college's facilities and equipment. The school had its own teachers and headmaster but all the members of the Technical College staff had some teaching duties in the school. It was not until 1951 that a lecturer was appointed in the College, who was not assigned duties[22] in the school.

[20] Usually called the canteen, and it accommodated 200.

[21] Some doubt must be expressed about this figure, as the total enrolment for the session 1928–29 is usually given in later reports as 973, excluding the JTS.

[22] Duties, one member of staff remembers, included lunch supervision, attendance at morning prayers, playground supervision and 'marching in'.

Similar arrangements obtained in other colleges and were widely regarded as a potent justification of Junior Technical Schools generally. Not everybody agreed; indeed some went so far as to say 'the view that its past success (of the JTS) is due to its pupils being taught by the same instructors as for senior students is, on examination, scarcely tenable.'[23] What perhaps is more important is that there was increasing recognition of the success of the schools. The Malcolm Committee[24] in 1928 commented: 'we have heard very warm praise of the work of the Junior Technical Schools which, although they are a comparatively recent creation, have for some time past won the approval of employers and educationists alike'.

Some teachers considered that the age-range of pupils in the schools was too narrow, and pleaded that the age of admission should be lowered to 11 and the leaving age extended beyond 16 so that the schools could have sizeable sixth forms. Such a policy, with its considerable educational merits, had to await the 1944 Education Act; in any case it was incapable of realisation at Acton within the buildings available; there was a continuing and growing competition for classrooms and workshops as the day work of the College expanded and the School tried to develop. The symbiotic relationship which existed between the College and the School, with whatever advantages and disadvantages that flowed from it, was dictated by their joint use of the buildings and facilities.

The School founded in 1910 had been transferred, as mentioned above, from Chiswick to Acton in 1928; it started at Acton with 240 boys. Initially it offered a two-year course but from 1930 onwards this was extended to three years, so the number of boys increased accordingly. There were 357 boys in 1935–6. The School was mainly intended for those who proposed to enter industry as skilled craftsmen, particularly in engineering, building and allied trades. The H.M. Inspectors who inspected the College and the School in 1934 noted the occupations taken up by boys who left the School for employment, and found that over the years 1929–33 at least 90 per cent of them went into engineering and building trades thus 'completely fulfilling its [the School's] purpose of providing recruits for these trades'. However, the curriculum in the third year was so devised that pupils of adequate performance could proceed to the senior engineering classes in the College and take an Ordinary National Certificate or Ordinary National Diploma. A certificate was awarded after the successful completion of a part-time course of three years' duration, and a diploma after a full-time course which lasted two years.

In this way a good number of boys qualified as technicians and some in due course became technologists. The School Report for 1938/9 records:

> During the year 19 past students have gained national certificates in either mechanical or electrical engineering, and 8 Junior Technical School boys in the matriculation course passed that examination; 15 students obtained diplomas in engineering. One outstanding success has been obtained this year by S. J. Watson, who passed through the J.T.S. in 1931–3 and the Day Diploma Course in 1933–5. He has since attended the College courses. He has been awarded a Whitworth Scholarship, being placed first on the list of candidates.

The reputation of the school locally, amongst employers and parents, was very high.

The College also developed rapidly and even in its second year the buildings were 'filled to capacity'. It became necessary to hold some of the evening classes outside and the old Acton County School came into use, the first of a number of buildings into which the College expanded. This school was usually referred to as the Woodlands Building or Annexe, as it adjoined a very small public space, known as Woodlands Park, where a few trees survived. Quite soon an extension to the College was built, consisting of a large science laboratory, two drawing offices and an advanced physics laboratory. The science laboratory was designed for building science, as at that time the College had classes in building construction, and higher national certificate courses in building were developed later, but all the classes in building were subsequently transferred to the Willesden and Twickenham Technical Colleges.

These new facilities were ready for use at the beginning of the 1932/3 session. Even at this early stage, the College had outgrown the policy of its founders, for though it was built to cater for the needs of students up to the level of the Ordinary National Certificate in engineering, by 1930 Higher National Certificate classes had been started and the following session saw the beginnings of B.Sc. classes. So rapid was the growth of the College that the new Principal (R. W. MacAdam, appointed in 1931 to succeed G. A. Robinson) was able to announce in his first report that 'the London County Council have agreed that classes leading to the degree of B.Sc. External of London University in Pure and Engineering Science be held at Acton'. He went on to explain 'that tentative arrangements have been made to provide classes for Matriculation, Intermediate and Final degree work for Pure and Engineering Science. The final courses will extend over two years being put into operation in September (1931).' These were all evening classes. In the light of later developments, it is of some interest to note that the degree classes evoked little enthusiasm from the H.M. Inspectors who wrote in 1934: 'recently[25] classes have been started for the Final examinations of the B.Sc. Engineering degree of London University. This is a new departure and should be watched with care on various grounds. The teaching is satisfactory and the energy and determination of the students very praiseworthy but concentration on University work is apt to have undesirable consequences in a technical college.' And as to the science degree classes the comment was 'it is open to doubt whether the degree syllabuses are really suited to evening students.'

Full-time courses for matriculation were introduced in 1932 as well as a full-time two year National Diploma course in Mechanical Engineering, which was followed by a similar course in electrical engineering in 1937. The Board of Education sanctioned in August, 1932, the establishment of a Senior Day Department in the College. By that time there were about 1,900 students in all and student-hours totalled over 211,000.

A picture of the College is provided by the notice which appeared in the prospectus of the Ealing Technical College in 1934. It is reproduced below, for it not only summarizes all the courses but exemplifies how Technical Colleges then presented themselves to the public. The educational arrangements in the College were typical of British Further Education at that time. About 90 per cent of the students were in evening classes, and were in the main technicians, craftsmen and others who worked in the industries in the localities around the College. There was

[25] September 1933.

also some provision for adults, in particular women's classes in housecraft and domestic science.

ACTON TECHNICAL COLLEGE

Principal—ROBT. W. MacADAM, B.Sc. (Hon.) A.M.I.Mech.E.

The Acton Technical College is situated in the High Street, Acton, opposite to the Public Library. The College provides organised courses in the various branches of Science and Technology.

Excellently-equipped laboratories and workshops provide for full instruction in the various branches.

The College comprises the following departments:—

1. SENIOR DAY COURSES. Full-time Day Courses, 9 a.m. to 4 p.m.

   (*a*) London University Matriculation.
   (*b*) National Diploma in Mechanical Engineering (2 years' course).

2. JUNIOR TECHNICAL SCHOOL. (Engineering), 9 a.m. to 4 p.m.

3. PART-TIME DAY COURSES.

   (*a*) For Engineers.
   (*b*) For Pharmaceutical Apprentices preparing for the examinations of the Pharmaceutical Society of Great Britain.

4. EVENING CLASSES.

   (*a*) Organised classes and courses in connection with the following branches of study:—
   Matriculation.
   Inter. B.Sc., Pure and Engineering.
   Final B.Sc., Pure and Engineering.
   Ordinary and Higher National Certificate Courses in:—
   Mechanical Engineering.
   Electrical Engineering.
   Building Construction.
   Chemistry.
   Classes in:—
   Production Engineering.
   Land Surveying and Levelling.
   Carpentry and Joinery.
   Plumbing.
   Pattern Making.

Economics.
Electric and Oxy Welding.
Physical Culture, etc.

(*b*) The Technical Annexe. County School, Woodlands Road.
Classes in Technical subjects and handicrafts.

(*c*) The Women's Institute. Acton Central School. Classes
in Industrial and Domestic Subjects, Arts and Crafts.
Teachers' Course in Cookery. First Aid, Vocal Music,
Elocution, etc.

(*d*) The Commercial Annexe. Priory School, Acton. Classes and
courses in Commercial Subjects, French, Geography, etc.
These courses lead to the more advanced work in Chiswick
Polytechnic.

Further information with regard to these schemes may be
obtained from the Principal.

The pattern did not change much over the next five years, but
numbers of students rose steadily and reached 2,800[26] in the
session 1938–9; student hours were 355,000. The main change
was the expansion of day courses, both part-time and full-time.

The chief full-time activities were still centred in the
Engineering Departments with their Ordinary National
Diploma courses, and in the Science Department with classes in
mathematics, physics and chemistry for the matriculation and
intermediate science and engineering examinations of the
University of London. The part-time day classes in engineering
and science covered a wide range to University degree level.

The number of full-time students was about 160, and there
were another 150 students attending part-time day classes. The
range of activities of the College is indicated by the examination
successes of 1939 which included 6 university degrees (3 special
Chemistry, 2 special Physics and 1 B.Sc. General), 23 passes
in Intermediate Science and Engineering, 13 Matriculation
passes, 42 ordinary national certificates, 31 higher national
certificates and 15 ordinary national diplomas in engineering,
8 ordinary and 2 higher national certificates in building, and 4
ordinary national certificates in chemistry. There were also
about 340 passes in the technological examinations of the City
and Guilds of London Institute, 12 students gaining a full

[26] This number of students is quoted in later reports but is inconsistent with other
figures given in 1938–9 and 1944–5 reports of the College.

technological certificate, and some 24 successes in women's subjects.

To many not familiar with Further Education, these numbers may not seem high in a College with some 2,800 students, many of whom were following courses of two or three years' duration, but by standards at that time they were good. The so-called wastage rate, or drop-out rate, of students in evening classes in *all* Technical Colleges was high, much higher of course than the failure-rate in the examinations, for many students who started the courses did not complete them. Some twenty years later the Crowther Committee[27] examined carefully the success and wastage rates in some technical courses and found that in the five-stage courses rather more than a quarter of the original students acquired either an Ordinary National Certificate or a City and Guilds Intermediate Certificate and 10 per cent or less a Higher or Final. The Acton results in 1938 were likely to have followed a similar pattern.

The College then had four main departments, as well as the Junior Technical School; they were Mechanical Engineering, Electrical Engineering, Science and Women's Work. There was also a Department of Industrial Administration and Business Management which had been created two years earlier in 1936. Heads of the Engineering and Science departments had been formally recognized by the Middlesex County Council as late as September 1938, and the Principal was no longer, directly at least, in charge of all the departments of the College as he had been earlier. To relieve the Principal even further a Vice-Principal, R. W. Broadbent, was appointed with the status and rank of a Head of Department, and he was also Headmaster of the Junior Technical School. Other Heads were G. H. Rice (Mechanical Engineering), W. F. Giddings (Electrical Engineering) and R. S. Anderton (Science).

The Engineering and Science Departments had gained some recognition of their advanced work by external examining bodies. The University of London inspected the College in December 1933, before any students had completed the courses leading to the degree of B.Sc. Engineering, and recommended that 'tentative recognition should be granted to this College and that it be inspected again in two years' time' and in 1935 the

[27] Crowther Report p. 355.

University intimated its continued recognition of the College. To meet some of the criticisms concerning accommodation and equipment additions to the building were made; these included a new Heat Engines and Hydraulics laboratory which was completed in 1938 and 'brought the equipment of the College up to the standard required by the London University'. It was at this time that recognition was granted to the College for another five years, and nine special subjects in the B.Sc. Engineering Part II examinations were specified which included Mechanics of Fluids and Applied Thermodynamics.

Recognition by the Royal Institute of Chemistry of some of the classes in chemistry in the Science Department came in July 1938. An earlier application to the Institute in 1934 had not been successful, presumably because of the restricted nature of the laboratories and other accommodation, but this was improved in 1937 by the addition of 'an advanced physical chemistry laboratory, a research laboratory and a classroom'.

In 1939 another addition followed, consisting of an engineering workshop, library and students' common room, but these 'were not fully equipped or furnished' until considerably later.

The Women's classes were housed outside the College; as far back as 1930 this work had been removed to the so-called Annexe and a part-time 'lady superintendent' appointed to take charge. In 1936 another move was made, this time to a school building in East Acton Lane which was rented by the Middlesex County Council from the Acton Education Committee, and for the first time since its commencement the women's section had the full use of a building adapted to its special needs, but even then it had to use accommodation in other Acton schools as well. The need for a full-time Head, responsible for all the Women's classes, became increasingly apparent; the H.M. Inspectors commented on this in their 1934 report, and in 1935 'a full-time Lady Superintendent' was appointed; she became known as the Head of the Women's Institute.

And so the first ten years of the College were marked by a steady continuous development, a growth from a School with some evening classes to a Technical College with a wide spectrum of part-time day and evening activities fostering a School within it, and responding more and more to the needs of the adult population fast growing around it.

All this was seemingly shattered by the outbreak of war in
1939. The senior and junior students were evacuated early in
September to Ivybridge in Devon, but as there were no facilities
in the village for technical education the Board of Education
agreed that the Junior Technical School be moved to Wolverton
and it was transferred there in November 1939. The Senior day
students however returned to Acton where the College re-
started its activities; in fact evening classes had re-opened there
in October 1939 and continued in spite of the black-out and the
travelling difficulties; enrolments were inevitably reduced
but reached about one half of the previous session's numbers.
The Junior Technical School re-opened in Acton in January
1940.

The College became involved almost immediately in the
training of workers for local engineering firms, but in that
strange first year of the war with more evacuees returning to
London it was able to maintain and in some ways develop its
full-time and part-time day programmes. It was, nevertheless,
as the annual report recorded 'an exceptionally trying and
difficult year'. There were even more difficult years ahead.

CHAPTER 2

The Formative Years

THE special work which Acton Technical College took up
during the 1939-45 war was mainly concerned with the training
of technicians and craftsmen but it involved other groups as
well; in all about 2,300 men and women were in the College
between 1939 and 1945 following specially devised full-time
training programmes. Some were civilians who went into local
firms; others were army tradesmen, including electricians,
fitters, turners, machinists and welders, about 1,200 of them, on
courses lasting 8 to 16 weeks. There were also some 800 members
of the Women's Services (ATS, WAAF and WRNS) trained as
clerks, domestics or cooks on short courses of 2 to 4 weeks, and
another 200 women were given some basic technical instruction.
A course of a very different kind was that for engineering cadets,
42 in number, who attended a two-year course of degree
standard.

The arrangements in other technical colleges followed a
similar pattern. The colleges accepted a training function which
earlier had been left to industry, and they thereby became more
aware of the needs and problems of training alongside those of
education in an academic institution. If the colleges were in
great measure diverted from their normal activities to train
workers and soldiers, this did not mean that part-time day and
evening classes stopped; on the contrary they were continued
often in modified form under very difficult conditions. Some
were held during the day at the week-ends. Full-time courses
were even expanded, in some of the senior colleges in response to
a request from Government to train cadets for the armed forces,
a development which prepared the way for major changes later.
It profoundly influenced the contribution a few colleges were
able to make to higher education subsequently.

Some reference, hardly adequate, was made to this war-time use of technical college resources in the report of the Ministry of Education, entitled *Education in 1947*, which was presented to Parliament in 1948 and was the first to appear after the war. It recorded that

The last Report presented by the Board of Education covered the calendar year 1938 and was published in May, 1939. The preparation of formal Reports was suspended during the war years owing to the paramount need for economy in manpower and use of paper. The present Report is, therefore, the first Annual Report to be presented by a Minister of Education for England and Wales.

It went on to make a brief mention of the contribution of the education service during the war years, and noted 'the special training provided for nearly 300,000 men and women in the armed forces and industry by technical colleges and other institutions for further education; [and] the system of state bursaries which helped to supply the needs of the services and of industry for technical personnel at the university level'. The other items referred to, though outside our main concern, were remarkable and included the establishment of the youth service as a direct responsibility of the central department and of local education authorities and the foundation of the Council for the Encouragement of Music and the Arts (later to become the Arts Council of Great Britain). Above all the Report noted that at the end of 1942 Mr R. A. Butler 'had begun the long series of discussions and negotiations with the various interests concerned which culminated in the publication of the government's White Paper "Educational Reconstruction" in July 1943. The Education Bill, based mainly on proposals made in the White Paper, was published in December of that year and became law on 4th August, 1944.'

The 1943 White Paper had stated:

Plans were in hand immediately before the war to increase the provision of technical, commercial and art colleges and to expand and bring up to date, where necessary, those already in existence. For this purpose a programme of capital expenditure of some £12,000,000 was contemplated. The post-war cost of such a programme will inevitably be higher, but it will be of the first importance that these plans should be revised and expanded to meet new requirements, and as soon as possible, carried into effect. Provision will accordingly be made to place a duty on Education Authorities to provide adequate facilities for technical, commercial and art education, both full-time and part-time. This general duty will be translated into concrete terms by requiring Authorities to submit schemes for further education which, when approved by the Board, Authorities will be required to put into effect by such stages as the Board may determine.

This in fact the 1944 Education Act did, and in March 1947 local authorities were asked 'to prepare, in consultation with industry, neighbouring authorities, universities and voluntary bodies, comprehensive schemes of further education, including the county colleges which will provide for the compulsory part-time education of young people under 18 who have left school'.

By the end of 1949 nearly all local education authorities had submitted their schemes and plans for county colleges; together these provided almost for the first time a comprehensive description of further education in Britain. The Middlesex Scheme of Further Education was approved by the Minister of Education in July 1953. It detailed the building projects completed between 1934 and 1939, totalling in costs £714,470 for sites and buildings and £107,000 for apparatus and equipment; it reviewed the post-war changes up to about 1950, surveyed the work of the Technical Colleges and Schools of Art, and indicated the sort of policy the County Council would wish to pursue in the years immediately ahead. It pointed out of course that any scheme of development of further education had to take account of how soon the Junior Technical, Commercial and Art Schools could be absorbed into the reorganized system of secondary education, and in particular of how quickly they could be housed in new schools and so release accommodation in the Colleges which was urgently needed for more senior classes and especially for part-time day release classes. The most important post-war change, the County Council stated, 'in relation to the provision of further education of a professional or vocational nature is the rapidly growing demand from employers for facilities for part-time day instruction for their employees in place of evening classes.' If the 4,295 pupils in attendance in the Junior Schools in the County during the 1949–50 session could be transferred to other premises, some 20,000 part-time day students could be accommodated in the

Colleges for one day per week. That year the number of part-time day students in the 12 Middlesex Technical Colleges stood at 7,800, and there were about 1,150 full-time students.

If in addition the demand for some of the courses provided in Technical Colleges, such as matriculation, preparatory professional, one year commercial and some catering courses which admitted students at the age of 16, were to decline because of the changes in secondary school provision outlined in the Council's Development Plan, even more accommodation would be freed in the Technical Colleges. Changes in fact were slow. The Junior Technical and other schools were ultimately squeezed out, but Technical Colleges in Middlesex as in other counties clung tenaciously to their O-level and A-level classes. This was a difficult area of contending interests, which strained the relations between the Colleges and the Secondary Schools. Nevertheless it has to be said that the College provision satisfied the needs of many boys and girls who found continued attendance at schools irksome and the freedom and independence in the Colleges attractive. It was too a contribution to the thinking and practice that made Sixth Form Colleges possible later. The County Council Scheme expected some extension of ordinary national diploma type courses, which are roughly of A-level standard, and it is noteworthy that it foresaw some of these courses might be based 'on the sandwich system under which periods of study and employment alternate'. Certain Colleges were named at which diploma courses in engineering and building might be started.

In setting out possible programmes of development for each of the colleges, the County Scheme said of Acton Technical College 'with regard to full-time courses of instruction there is little doubt that the County of Middlesex should provide at least two centres (at present Acton and Enfield[1]) for degree or comparable courses in science and technology', and reflecting current educational discussions, it went on

These courses in time may be converted into courses in preparation for a Diploma in Technology or any other equivalent qualification which may become recognised. The teaching staff, accommodation, equipment and amenities for sports and social activities in these

[1] Enfield Technical College later became part of one of the new Polytechnics, the Middlesex Polytechnic, designated in January 1973.

centres should be in keeping with the status of the colleges concerned. The students will be non-residential but with only two centres in the County some students will have long journeys and in the long term policy the provision of some residential accommodation may be worthy of consideration.

Less cautious was the statement concerning the proposed building programme at Acton designed to enable some such developments to take place: 'it has been found necessary to replan the whole of the Woodlands site to accommodate all advanced work, i.e. higher national certificate, final degree courses or work of comparable standard, in new buildings offering the most up-to-date facilities for higher technological education.' The County Architect had already prepared a site plan.

By 1948-9 Acton Technical College had some 4,500 students of whom 385 were following full-time courses, and 1,270 were in part-time day classes. (These numbers are taken from the Annual Report for 1948-9, but different figures appear in other places.) The number of student-hours, an ubiquitous technical college statistic, is often a better guide to the actual growth of work in the college. In 1948-9 the number of student-hours was 1,075,616, a three-fold growth from 1938-9 when it was 355,005. Some of the full-time students were in the School of Catering, a catering course having been started in 1947; another group was in the Engineering Departments taking the Ordinary National Diploma courses in Mechanical and Electrical Engineering which dated from 1932, but the majority of full-time students were in the Science Departments preparing for the Matriculation examination and the Intermediate Science and Engineering Examinations of the University of London. There was little day work in the College above Intermediate (GCE A level) standard but some degree courses, which had started earlier as part-time classes, were beginning to be held full-time.

Part-time day courses for the B.Sc. Engineering degree were introduced in 1945 in the Mechanical Engineering and Electrical Engineering departments, followed by full-time courses in 1946. Similar full-time degree courses in Chemistry and Physics were started in 1948. The numbers were never large, but along with the more numerous part-time students in the day and in evening classes the load on the Departments was considerable. The report of the Department of Electrical Engineering for

1948-9 recorded 'the fine results obtained from our first venture into full-time Engineering Degree Courses', and the Department of Chemistry and Biology remarked on the 'increased demand for degree courses' and noted that a student from the full-time B.Sc. Chemistry class had been awarded a research scholarship tenable at Imperial College. Most of the advanced classes in the College however were held in the evenings, but some were organised on a part-time day basis and besides degree courses included higher national certificate courses in mechanical, electrical and production engineering, as well as chemistry, with applied physics added later (1951).

The number of successes in the higher national certificate examinations in 1948-9 was 86 and another 136 students gained an ordinary national certificate; in addition 13 full-time students passed the Ordinary National Diploma examinations. Some 35 students (part-time and full-time) were successful in the University of London external degree examinations: 14 in Engineering, 10 in Special Chemistry, 3 in Special Physics and 8 gained the General Degree. In addition about 100 students (again part-time and full-time) passed the Intermediate examination and 22 the Matriculation examination. Since the start of degree courses in 1932, just over 200 students had by this time graduated from the College. Some were very outstanding students who for various reasons acquired a degree the hard way. Unfortunately the records are very incomplete but old students include a professor of mathematics, two professors of physics, and some holding responsible positions in industry. In the other fields of the College's activities the aggregated examination successes showed by 1948-9 about 550 higher national certificates, about 1,200 ordinary national certificates and diplomas, and over 4,500 passes in the technological examinations of the City and Guilds of London Institute.

The combined College and Secondary School staff of full-time teachers had grown to 83, about 60 of them in the College. 'The status of a college academically' wrote the Principal, 'can be judged by the number of senior assistants on the college establishment. For the session 1948/49 the Acton Technical College is entitled to 17 senior assistants.' Of these 17, three were in 1973 on the staff of Brunel University, one of them being a Professor; of the others one was a Director of one of the New

Polytechnics, one a Head of Department in another of the New Polytechnics, and one a Professor at another university. Others had retired after long service with Brunel College/University.

As to the Junior Technical School, it was 'one of the largest in the country with a normal enrolment of approximately 350'. It was becoming an embarrassment to the expansion of the College. The Principal of the College (R. W. MacAdam), who incidentally had supported the development of the School with great devotion, complained in a report to the Governors at the end of 1948 that 'this school does not come under Further Education and should be found accommodation elsewhere. The Secondary School is occupying accommodation which should be used for Further Education. The numbers admitted to the part-time day courses and full-time senior courses have to be seriously restricted because of the presence of the Secondary School in the building.'

Accommodation difficulties had been present almost from the start. But after the first addition to the buildings in 1932, further extensions were completed in 1937, 1938 and 1939, to which reference has been made earlier. Accommodation outside the main building also became available, for happily the new Acton County School for boys was opened in 1939 and the old County School buildings, known as Woodlands, were taken over by the College and altered in various ways to house some of the work of the Women's Department and to provide much-needed accommodation for some of the science classes.

Further alterations and additions to the Woodlands buildings followed after the war. A block of four classrooms was erected in the old school playground and came into use in September 1950, and modifications were made to the old buildings to provide a biology laboratory where work up to degree standard could be carried out. Some primitive provision of a laboratory and workshop for Plastics Technology was also made in the basement of the building, giving support to work in plastics that had started so promisingly. What were named 'higher technological courses' in the Chemistry and Technology of Plastics together with Plastics Machines and Mould Design were introduced in 1948–9, and a course for the Associateship of the Plastics Institute had also been started. Four of the five candidates who entered for the Associateship examination from the College in

June 1950 were successful; it was the first examination of that kind held by the Institute.

Another growing-point was the Women's Department and particularly the courses in catering. In 1950-1 there were 86 full-time and 137 part-time catering students on the roll. To provide for some of the specialist needs of the Hotel and Catering School a single-storey building was erected on the Woodlands site, alongside the old school gymnasium, and completed in 1950; it included a kitchen and a room used as a restaurant where meals were served by the students—an important educational addition, but also invaluable to the College and to others in Acton, for it was open in a limited way to the public as a place where a civilized meal could be enjoyed. The College had a canteen in the main building, but to provide a mid-day meal for pupils of the School and students of the College was an increasingly difficult problem. Staff could take lunch in one of the classrooms adjoining the canteen; they paid 1s. for lunch and 1d. (old money) for a cup of tea!

To the original main buildings further additions were impossible because of the restricted nature of the site; modifications were made, however, to some of the existing rooms to keep pace with changes in the courses and in particular to cater for the advanced classes in science and engineering. For instance the Department of Physics and Mathematics, which in December 1948 had been created by dividing the Science Department into two parts, partitioned rooms to provide small laboratories for high vacuum technology and advanced optics, and to house its first electron microscope—an old model, of course, bought second-hand but useful none the less. The other part of the Science Department, named Chemistry and Biology, acquired a small physical chemistry laboratory by a similar division of rooms.

By continuous improvisation, modifications of existing rooms, use of more and more halls and schools outside, and the shedding of more elementary courses to other Colleges, an increasing volume of advanced work was accommodated. New buildings were desperately needed. Some of the temporary accommodation was woefully inadequate. The evening classes in Management Studies, for instance, were held in the Priory School, a secondary modern school near the College, with furniture suitable for children—a more uncongenial setting for adults can hardly be imagined.[2] 'It has been necessary to continue the use of the Church Halls to accommodate many of our day classes' wrote the Principal in 1952; 'classes are held in the Churchfield Road Congregational Church, Church Road Baptist Church and Newton Avenue Baptist Church.' The Co-operative Hall was also used; the provision as in the other Halls was primitive and a member of staff remembers waiting on the pavement outside to borrow a match from a passer-by to light the gas-fire! Other accommodation was more appropriate; in particular, the new Acton County School was used more and more for evening classes and the Headmaster, G. T. C. Giles, was helpful and sympathetic. What was known as the Technical Annexe to the College was housed in the County School; it had its own Head-master or Responsible Master and conducted preliminary courses, mainly in science and mathematics, for those, including some older students, who wished to qualify to enter one or other of the senior courses in the College.

'The only real and lasting solution of the accommodation question is the provision of a new building, planned and equipped to undertake instruction of university degree standard, as well as applied research in various branches of technology. Such a building has been planned for erection on the Woodlands site.' So read the Annual Report for 1948–9; it continued,

The first phase is to build a self-contained block to house the follow-ing departments—Chemistry and Biology, Physics and Mathematics, Industrial Administration and Management. The next phase will be to add the Administrative Offices, Staff and Students' rooms, Examination Hall, Library and Refectories etc. The final phase of the plan will be to provide for the Women's Department and the Engineering Departments with the necessary laboratories and work-shops. It is hoped that a start will be made to build this new addition to the College in 1950.

The initial planning seemed to go expeditiously, for the Annual Report of the following year, 1949–50, recorded that 'The building has been designed not to exceed an expenditure in amount agreed by the Ministry of Education . . . The starting

[2] C. Sofer and G. Hutton, *New Ways in Management Training*. Tavistock Publications, 1958, 24.

date for the new building is the first quarter of 1951 when a start will be made with the foundations and sub-structure.' A year later, 1950-1, there was further progress to report: 'work has now commenced on the new building and the foundation and sub-structure is nearing completion. It is hoped that work on the superstructure will commence early in 1952.' The steel framework was 'nearly complete' by the end of 1952, but construction slowed up and there were many sad accounts of a severe unclad steel frame standing gauntly against the skies, evidence of the economic disorders and national shortages of the time. The Annual Report of 1952-3 was encouraging: 'steady progress is being made with the erection of the new Science Block at Woodlands. . . . The work of completing the building is now well under way, but' it added sadly 'it will be some time before the building can be used for educational purposes. The accommodation which will become available in the new block is urgently needed now.' Indeed it was, but even after another year (in 1954) there were no signs 'of the possibility of using some of the accommodation'. The building ultimately came into use in September 1957, but before that date major changes in the organization of the College had been made and to the events leading to these we will turn later.

The restrictions and limitations of the College's accommodation were, of course, a subject of comment by the group of H.M. Inspectors who visited the College in November 1952 to make the first inspection since that of 1934. Every Department was affected, although the Mechanical and Electrical Engineering Departments seemed to be less harassed by shortages than the others. The Department of Management and Production Engineering on the other hand was severely handicapped. It had been created as a separate Department in 1949, responsible for the Higher National Certificate courses in Production Engineering earlier organized within the Department of Mechanical Engineering, and also for the various management courses that had been developed attractively since the end of the war. The College could be regarded, the Inspectors suggested, as one of the pioneer establishments in 'this comparatively fresh field of study'; the achievements had been remarkable in many respects—'in the breadth of their scope since they range from classes for foremen to classes for top executives; the extent of their appeal, since students are drawn from all parts of Britain and some come from overseas; and the degree of recognition they are accorded from commerce and industry, as shown by the extensive list of firms who have sponsored students.' All this was being done with the scantiest of amenities, the Methods Engineering courses, for instance, being limited within one room, and the other side of the Department's work, in production engineering, was similarly circumscribed by inadequate laboratories and limited equipment.

The Science Departments with equally promising programmes were subject to similar restraints. 'The accommodation for the Chemistry and Biology Department is insufficient and largely unsuitable. The pressure on both Intermediate and Advanced laboratories is so great, as they are used almost continuously from 9 a.m. to 9.30 p.m. and on Saturday mornings, that servicing is difficult . . . At the Annexe (Woodlands) the conditions are slightly better, partly because the practical work there is confined to the more elementary stages of Chemistry, but the provision for Biology leaves a good deal to be desired' — a polite understatement.

Some of the mathematics classes were held in Church Halls, and the Inspectors' comment was 'The Congregational Church Hall at the rear of the main building is not suitable for classes'. And as to physics 'the accommodation for all course work at the College and Annexe and for research and development work in Physics is inadequate and little can be done until the new Science Block is completed. All laboratories are in constant use and are congested most of the time.'

The College had had to manage without a library until 1949. 'In 1946–48 the Science Library consisted of one book-case of pre-war books in the Head's room and a tea-chest full of dusty journals under the stairs'—so a member of staff recalls. The extension at the back of the main buildings which had been built just before the war in 1939 reverted ten years later to its original purpose. The library was at last furnished and brought into use, and limited though it was provided the College with an essential facility. Its value as well as its inadequacy were quickly apparent and the H.M. Inspectors suggested in 1952 that 'more accommodation is urgently needed for housing books and to provide more reading spaces in the Library'. They also referred

to the urgent need for a library for the students of Catering, as
the main library held no books in that field, the only provision
being a collection of books in the Staff Room for use by the
teachers—a comment that could have been made on most
departments, not merely Catering, in most technical colleges.

Social facilities for the students were minimal, and the
Students' Union was

greatly hampered by the paucity of accommodation which is available
for its use. Occasional use is possible of classrooms, halls and the gymnasium for recreation, dances, dramatic shows and other activities.
Nevertheless it has a sound organisation which covers a large number
of activities. A large measure of success has been achieved as a result
of the personal enthusiasm of the students in such activities as
mountaineering, swimming and squash, although no special facilities
are available.

The H.M. Inspectors noted particularly the urgent need for
students' common rooms; 'those originally planned as such are
in full use as class-rooms'. A small room was made available to
the Students' Union in the library extension; it had to serve
a multitude of purposes.

It would be misleading to give the impression that Acton was
unusual amongst technical colleges in having overcrowded
buildings. With little or no new building during the war, with
the damage some colleges suffered at that time, and above all
with the increased demand for further education that mani-
fested itself after the war all Colleges were over-full and
struggling with unprecedented accommodation problems. The
Ministry of Education report for 1949 made clear that four years
after the end of the war[3] the conditions of work continued in
many areas to be extremely bad and quoted H.M. Inspectors'
reports to the effect that 'every hole and corner in the colleges
has to be used for teaching purposes. During the past year classes
have been seen in main halls, dressing rooms, staff rooms, stores,
etc.' The facilities of technical colleges generally were 'taxed
almost beyond reason but not, to their credit, beyond their
powers of ingenuity and improvisation'.[4] This is not to justify
the state of affairs, but to probe more deeply would force us to
ask questions as to why further education had remained the

[3] The nation's economic difficulties in 1949 were grave. The pound was devalued in
1949. [4] *Education in 1949*, HMSO, 5.

36 *The Formative Years*

cinderella of the education service for so long before the war. 'Technical education in this country has never received the attention it deserves' wrote the McNair Committee[5] in 1944.

Standards of achievement throughout further education in these difficult years somehow or other remained high, and teaching was in large measure good; technical teaching demanded and received in some special way great devotion. 'In the technical and commercial colleges and schools are to be found some of the best teachers in the whole of the educational field' was the comment of the McNair Committee, but it added 'nevertheless, all our evidence, and not least that of the keenest and most competent teachers themselves, shows that the professional equipment of technical teachers as a whole is not satisfactory, and that the full benefits of technical education are not being realised because, for one reason or another, the teaching is not as good as it ought to be.' Soon afterwards, in 1946–7, the first Training Colleges for Technical Teachers were established and some impact has since been made on a complex and wide-ranging problem.

The 1952 Inspectors' Report on Acton Technical College made the comment 'the teaching is of a high order and the examination results are excellent. Excluding the London Colleges whose students take the internal degree, Acton obtained more external degrees in the session 1951–2 than any other technical college in the country.' Of course, in some respects the teaching was too good, in that it could be said the staff combined with the students to defeat the examiners of the University of London—a basic criticism of the London University system of external degrees, whatever other good features it might have had or still has. The Inspectors, one suspects, were hinting at this when they added to their general commendation a postscript:

points, however, which should be seriously considered, especially in relation to the degree courses, are (i) the prevalence of the formal academic type of lecture, and (ii) the heavy load of lectures which the degree students have to attend each week. The question arises as to whether the type of student in this College, normally one who has failed to secure University entrance, would not profit from a more liberal method of approach. It was felt that too much was done for the student, that he did not have enough time to read and think for himself.

[5] *Teachers and Youth Leaders*, HMSO, 1944, 108, 113.

Not enough breadth, as well as not enough time, were common criticisms, and still are, of technical education generally. But some improvement has been achieved in both respects in recent years.

The growth of degree courses in the College is worthy of further mention, as one example of a remarkable development of university degree courses in some technical colleges in many parts of Britain. The Ministry of Education Report for 1950, in surveying the progress of education in the first half of the twentieth century, noted the growth of degree courses outside the university sector. It pointed out that in 1949 some 8,772 technical college students were undertaking university degree work (mostly external degrees of the University of London) on a full-time basis, and 11,295 on a part-time basis, and 'to these must be added a large number of students taking university degree courses by means of part-time evening study'. It was not an insignificant contribution to higher education, particularly at a time when the number of students in the universities was around 85,000, and of these over 11,000 were doing work beyond first-degree level.

The involvement of Acton Technical College in degree courses had grown considerably after the war. The numbers[6] of first degrees obtained by students of the College over the period 1948–55 are given in Table 2.1; they include full-time and part-time students. Unfortunately the records do not show the numbers of full-time students separately. The growth and decline of these numbers were much in keeping with the national pattern at that particular time. One of several factors contributing to these changes was the release of men from the armed forces who continued their education under the Further Education and Training Scheme (FETS).

This had been introduced in 1943 to 'secure a supply of men and women to occupy posts of importance in the professions, industry and commerce and to enable those whose educational training had been interrupted by war service to resume it without hardship'. The Department of Education made awards to those who wished to attend universities and other institutions

---

[6] These numbers are taken from the Annual Reports published by the College. The aggregated numbers of B.Sc. successes in these reports are not consistent with the annual figures.

of higher education, and by the end of 1947 over 52,000 awards had been granted. Over a third of the students in the universities at that time were in receipt of such grants. By 1949 the number of awards had risen to over 83,000 but the scheme had then

TABLE 2.1

First Degree Successes[7]

Year	Engineering	Special Chemistry	Special Physics	B.Sc. General	Total
1948–9	14	10	3	8	35
1949–50	13	9	4	20	46
1950–1	20	25	7	30	82
1951–2	13	17	10	36	76
1952–3	11	15	7	22	55
1953–4	10	11	8	19	48 (52*)
1954–5	10	10	18	12	50 (52†)
Total	91	97	57	147	392 (398)

* Including 2 Special Botany and 2 Special Zoology degrees.
† Including 1 Special Botany and 1 Special Zoology degrees.

passed its peak. Inevitably not all the ex-service men who wished to go to a university were able to find places there; in fact only just over one-half of the award holders went to universities. Many others went to technical colleges where the university degree classes expanded in response to the demand and the number of full-time degree students was higher than at any other time. But following the first flood immediately after the war the flow receded, and it was around 1951–2 that the number of students graduating from technical colleges was at its highest. The Acton figures reflect this pattern.

How the total number of students in the universities began to fall is shown in Figure 2.1. The student numbers reached 85,421 in 1949–50 which proved to be the post-war peak, but by the end of the quinquennium (1952) they had fallen to 83,458. The decrease was not the same in all faculties; the number of technology students fell a little but the number of students taking science continued to increase.

How the numbers of full-time students in the faculties of pure

[7] For the period 1932–48 the total number of students who graduated from the College was about 170.

science and technology in the universities[8] changed over the period 1948 to 1957 is shown in Table 2.2. The figures for 1938–9 are given for comparison.

TABLE 2.2

Full-time Students in Universities

Year	Pure Science	Technology
1938–9	7,767	5,288
1948–9	16,099	10,884
1949–50	16,917	10,933
1950–1	17,168	10,591
1951–2	17,053	10,215
1952–3	17,601	9,993
1953–4	16,971	10,036
1954–5	17,327	10,586
1955–6	18,133	11,379
1956–7	19,899	12,496

The factors that were influencing university student numbers were more complex than was at first appreciated; the impact of the cessation of the Further Education and Training Scheme

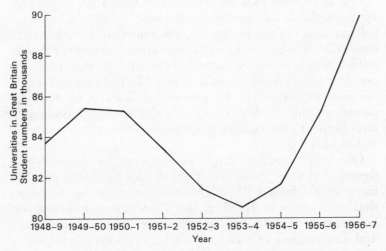

Fig. 2.1. Total number of Students in the Universities of Great Britain, 1948–57.

[8] *University Development, 1947–52*, HMSO, 58.

was obvious enough but it was off-set by other social trends which only became clear later. In technical colleges, with all the variety of their provision, it was the degree courses that were most seriously and immediately affected. In fact the numbers of full-time students in technical colleges increased a little over the period 1950–3, but this masked a considerable fall in the number of students taking university degree courses. Table 2.3. shows the number of full-time students in Major Establishments (other than Art) in England and Wales,[9] and also the number taking university courses in each of the four years.

TABLE 2.3

Full-time Students in Major Establishments (other than Art) in England and Wales

Session	Total Number	Number taking University Courses
1950–1	39,809	5,436
1951–2	40,821	5,309
1952–3	44,739	4,736
1953–4	48,202	3,825

It is interesting that the Ministry of Education Report for 1952 noted that the numbers of full-time students in technical colleges rose slightly in 1951–2 and commented, rather optimistically, 'Since the Further Education and Training Schemes (which greatly increased the number of full-time students in the post-war years) is now coming to an end, the slight increase in numbers suggests that the permanent demand for full-time courses is rising slightly.' However valid that conclusion might have been for some courses, it did not apply to degree courses in technical colleges.

One other comment might be made on the Acton degree figures shown in Table 2.1. They do not fully represent the increased teaching responsibilities with respect to degree courses that the College accepted, as the Table does not include the large numbers of students who took the Intermediate Science and Engineering examinations, many of whom went on to universities or other institutions to complete degree courses. Also some of the students who took the B.Sc. Engineering Part I

[9] *Education in 1951, 1952, 1953, 1954*, HMSO.

examination at the College went on elsewhere for Part II, usually because the College could not offer the special subjects they required.

To illustrate the growth of the College as a whole, the lower part of Figure 2.2. indicates the development of the evening, part-time day and full-time day classes over the years 1947–52, with the corresponding data for 1937–8 to serve as a basis of

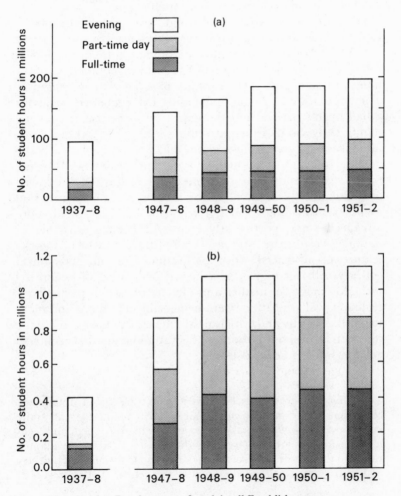

FIG. 2.2. (*a*) Development of work in all Establishments.
(*b*) Development of work in Acton Technical College.

comparison, and to put these changes in the national setting the
upper part of Figure 2.2 shows the development in all Further
Education Establishments in England and Wales.[10]

There can be no doubt that the College had travelled a long
way in its first twenty-five years to become 'one of the more
important major technical colleges in Greater London', as the
Inspectors' Report of 1952 described it. 'In the first ten years of
its existence the College earned for itself a place of considerable
importance in the educational and industrial circles of the
County. This position has now (1952) been firmly consolidated.'

It had followed a development common to many technical
colleges but the speed of growth had been exceptional, a reflection in some degree of the rapidity of social changes round it.
The population of Acton and Ealing had increased by about
a half in this period, and the industrial pattern had changed
significantly. So had the pattern of social needs and demands,
not only in Acton but throughout the country, particularly the
demands of many individuals for a continued education directed
to vocational ends. The response of the College had followed
orthodox lines, a shedding of the more elementary instruction
to other institutions and a purposeful building-up of more
advanced work, particularly courses associated with higher
national certificates and university degrees, which were a
feature of advanced work programmes in other technical
colleges. All this had been achieved over a period when the
orthodox modes of further and higher education, particularly
technological education, were being subjected more and more
to public scrutiny and criticism. Much new thinking marked the
nineteen forties, but it did not affect Acton and other technical
colleges until some years later.

In 1939 it could be written:[11]

Technical Education itself is in a state of transition. It retains the
characters of its palaeotechnic[12] origin. Attendance is still quite
voluntary; pre-occupational courses are hardly developed, and technical institutions are still largely 'night schools'. Courses are adapted
rather to the requirements of the students than to the needs of industry
and instruction is still predominantly theoretical. Yet neotechnic[12]

[10] *Compare Education in 1949*, HMSO, 32.
[11] W. A. Richardson, *The Technical College*, OUP, 1939, 11.
[12] Terms used by Lewis Mumford in *Technics and Civilisation*, London, 1934.

developments are not without their effect. Employers of industry are more willing to become partners in the work of the Colleges and more and more are granting educational privileges to their employees. . . . Industry is now looking to the technical institutions to undertake more thoroughly a pre-apprenticeship and even an apprenticeship training. Once more those concerned with technical education are looking to the Continent for inspiration and ideas just as they did after the days of the Great Exhibition.

Britain had a very different involvement with the Continent over the next few years, and the war provided compelling reasons for a re-examination of the education and the training that technical colleges should offer. The opportunity was taken by many official and unofficial groups to set out new plans and to provide new vision and new hope. By the time the centenary of the Great Exhibition came round in 1951 winds of change were blowing through the colleges, or at least through some of them.

CHAPTER 3

The Governance of
Acton Technical College

THE responsibility of the Middlesex County Council during the nineteen-fifties for the provision and maintenance of the technical colleges and schools of art in its area derived from national arrangements whereby the Education Acts passed by government were administered by bodies known as Local Education Authorities (LEAs).

The Act of 1902 (the Balfour Act) established these authorities; it abolished the school boards and technical instruction committees and placed the national provision for education (elementary and higher) under the administration of some 300 Authorities, mainly County Councils and County Borough Councils; other Councils responsible for elementary education only were known as Part III authorities.

Although the Authorities had a statutory duty to provide elementary education, they were merely given permissive powers to provide 'education other than elementary'. Consequently the provision of technical colleges and schools of art was far from uniform over the country, but wherever they were developed the cost was shared equally by the State and the LEA in each area and although the mode of sharing has changed over the years for some items of expenditure, a significant part of the cost of these institutions continues to be borne by the local rates. The other part is met by grants from Government.

The technical colleges and schools of art are in this way firmly set in 'the public sector of education' and the Local Education Authorities are deeply involved in their administration and control as well as in their financing. Some of this control is delegated for each college to a Committee or Governing Body

appointed by the Local Education Authority and usually
including representatives of local interests, particularly industry
and commerce. The degree of control which a Governing Body
can exercise is limited and is laid down in what are usually
known as the Articles of Government. For Middlesex Colleges
these were naturally revised by the County Council from time to
time in the light of new legislation and changing ideas about
college governance.

When Acton Technical College opened in 1928 the Fisher
Education Act of 1918 applied, subject to a good number of
amendments and modifications. It has been described[1] as 'one of
the finest education acts that had appeared on the statute book
of any country', but many of its intentions remained unfulfilled.
It is best remembered in the world of further education for the
worthy attempt to introduce compulsory Day Continuation
Schools,[2] which along with other provisions in the Act were
dropped, mainly because of economy measures resulting from
the industrial depression in the early nineteen twenties. There
was also a lack of enthusiasm for these schools among some
employers and some parents. It was the Fisher Act however that
rationalised the system of grants for educational purposes and
introduced two main grants, one paid to all education authorities for elementary education, and the other to those education
authorities responsible for higher education. The latter was
fixed at 50 per cent of approved net expenditure, including the
cost of new buildings.

The first Governing Body at Acton Technical College was a
Committee formed of members appointed by the Middlesex
County Council and by the Borough of Acton Local Higher
Education Committee; there were also some representatives
of the Borough of Brentford and Chiswick and some repre-
sentatives of local industrial firms.

Alderman W. Palmer was the first Chairman of the Governing Body and he served until his death in September 1939; he
was succeeded by the Revd. C. V. Camplin Cogan, Rector of
Acton, who had been a member of the Governing Body since
1931, and he continued as Chairman until 1948, when with
the passing of a new Education Act certain changes in educational administration in the County came into force. The 1944

---

[1] W. A. Richardson, *The Technical College*, OUP, 1939, 62.   [2] See page 2.

Education Act was a well-prepared measure, the culmination of a long period of careful planning and wide consultation. It removed some of the untidiness in the national system of education, provided for a unitary system of primary, secondary and further education, and reduced the number of Local Education Authorities by more than a half. Those that remained were given modified functions; in particular instead of 'powers' of providing facilities for secondary and further education they were accorded 'duties'. Further Education was defined as meaning all forms of education, except secondary and university education, for persons over compulsory school age.

The old Part III authorities responsible for elementary education (a term no longer used) became redundant. Middlesex, like all county authorities, was required to partition the county into 'divisions' and to set up 'divisional executives' which would exercise on behalf of the county certain specified functions relating to primary and secondary education, and in certain circumstances further education. The only powers that could not be delegated were those of raising a rate or borrowing money. Acton became one such divisional executive and, although its responsibilities did not include the Technical College, it maintained as did the Borough generally a lively interest in the College's affairs.

Some of the repercussions of the 1944 Act on further education and on the secondary technical schools in particular were referred to in Chapter 2; there were other consequences. The Acton Technical College Governing Body was reconstituted and given wider powers; new Articles of Government were formulated by the Middlesex Education Committee, and accepted in July 1948. They had regard to the views of the Minister outlined in Circular 98 of April 1946. 'The Minister is of the opinion that consideration should be given to the constitution of the Governing Bodies of all major colleges of Further Education.' The Circular suggested 'there is room for ensuring a closer and more adequate association of industry, commerce, the professions and the Universities on the management of these institutions,' and added, 'No less important is that Governing Bodies so constituted should be given all reasonable freedom of action in directing the affairs of the College, including the power to incur expenditure within the heads of estimates submitted to and approved by the providing authority.'

The new Acton Governing Body held its first meeting on 13 January 1949. It had twenty members; the Chairman of the Education Committee of the County Council and the Chairman of the Further Education Sub-Committee were ex-officio Governors; six were appointed by the County Council from members of the Council or of its Education Committee, and six others were appointed 'in such proportion as the County Council may from time to time determine, by the Divisional Executives and District Sub Committees of the County Districts, which in the opinion of the County Council are mainly served by the College'. The remaining six members were appointed by the County Council and 'so chosen as to give adequate representation of the important industrial and commercial interests and, where necessary, of the Universities.'

This was long before the days of staff and student participation in College government. Even the Principal was not a member; he could however attend all meetings of the Governing Body 'except on such occasions or for such times as the Governing Body may for good cause otherwise determine'. And Heads of Departments could be asked to attend as required. The Chief Education Officer of the Council or his representative (usually the Assistant Education Officer for Further Education) was entitled to attend all meetings. The Chief Education Officer at the time was T. B. Wheeler. The Clerk of the Governing Body, appointed by the County Council, was Dr J. Ewart Smart, Borough Education Officer of Acton, who had served as Clerk of the Governing Body since the College was opened.

The Governing Body retired every third year, coinciding with the triennial election of County Councillors, and changes in the political party in power could be reflected in the composition of the Governing Body. Also the political allegiance of the members from the County Council might be different from that of the members appointed by the local Divisional Executives which included Acton, Ealing, Harrow and Brentford and Chiswick. The arrangement worked reasonably well but not without occasional conflict.

The industrial members in 1949 were Wilfred Brown (Glacier Metal Co.), G. F. Shrigley (British Light Steel Pressings), Major

C. Johnson (Mond Nickel Co.), W. Lee and John S. Paget (Napiers). Dr David Heron was nominated by the University of London. Wilfred Brown was appointed Chairman, an unusual distinction for a new member, and Alderman C. O'Day was the first Vice Chairman; he was an Alderman of the Borough of Acton and well known locally. W. Lee was succeeded the following year by Walter Puckey (formerly of Hoovers and the Ministry of Supply).

The College had to be conducted in accordance with the Education Acts 1944 to 1948, and any relevant regulations made by the Minister of Education; the Articles of Government and other regulations made by the County Council also applied. The Governing Body was a sub-committee of the County Education Committee, submitting reports through the Further Education Sub-Committee.

The functions of the Governing Body were set down as follows:

(a) The Governing Body shall have the general supervision of the College, including the buildings, playing fields, grounds, furniture and equipment thereof, and shall inform the County Council of repairs, alterations or additions necessary to maintain the same in proper condition.

(b) The Governing Body shall carry out schemes of instruction approved by the County Council.

(c) The Governing Body shall submit to the County Council an annual estimate of income and expenditure required for the purposes of the College for each ensuing financial year, in such form and at such time as the County Council may require.

(d) The County Council may approve such estimates with such variations, if any, as they may think fit to make.
The Governing Body shall only incur expenditure within the estimate as approved by the County Council and in particular such expenditure shall not exceed the amount approved by the County Council under each head of the estimate in any year.

(e) The Governing Body may authorise the purchase of books, apparatus, materials, stationery and furniture to the extent to which provision has been made under the appropriate head in the approved estimates for the financial year; all such purchases shall be made in accordance with arrangements made by the County Council from time to time and notified to the Governors.

(f) The Governing Body shall set up the necessary courses and classes of instruction consistent with the general educational character of the College as determined by the County Council from time to time.

The Governing Body was however given new responsibilities concerning the appointment of staff. The Principal and Heads of Departments remained essentially County Council appointments, but the Governing Body had the right to nominate one third of the members of the Joint Committee that interviewed candidates for these posts and made a recommendation to the County Council.

All the other teaching staff appointments were made by the Governing Body in consultation with the Principal, subject to confirmation by the County Council. But the posts were advertised by the County Council, and the Chief Education Officer in due course sent the forms of application to the College! The appointments had to be within the limits of the establishment of staff laid down by the County Council for the current year. This latter procedure was fairly lengthy, starting with discussions between the Heads of Departments and the Principal about the staffing needs of the College for the following year; these were then discussed at a meeting of the Principal and Assistant Education Officer when there was some inevitable bargaining, and ultimately the Education Officer made submissions to the County Council Further Education Sub-Committee for all the Colleges in the County. His recommendations were usually accepted by the Committee, but by the time the County Council's agreement was transmitted back to the College its staffing needs had often changed—one of the penalties paid for the processes of democracy.

Similar arrangements applied to the appointment of non teaching staff; they were appointed by the Governing Body 'except that employees who will be in receipt of remuneration exceeding £550 per annum inclusive on the basis of full time service or such higher amount as may be prescribed by the County Council from time to time shall be appointed by the County Council'. This proviso was indicative of the difficulties that attended any proposal concerning more senior administrative posts in the College, including the post of librarian and the appointment of more senior laboratory staff. This problem increased in difficulty as the College expanded, for although its needs differed from those of other Colleges in the County it became in one sense a pace-maker for the others, and every decision became a precedent. Non-teaching staff establishment in technical colleges often seemed to fit awkwardly into the categories used or devised by the Establishments Committee of the County Council, and the decisions of the Committee respecting requests from Colleges sometimes appeared not to be fully in accord with educational needs and developments.

There was more freedom in the appointment of part-time teaching staff, but the following extract from the Articles of Government reads as if the restrictions were considerable.

The Governing Body is empowered to authorise the opening or re-opening of classes in subjects which have been approved by the County Council and to engage or re-engage sessional part-time teachers for subjects for which they have been approved. Posts for part-time teachers may be advertised in such journals as may be deemed appropriate and the Governing Body shall take such steps as may be necessary to ensure that suitable persons are engaged by them. In cases of urgency the Principal may be authorised provisionally to engage part-time staff, provided such action is reported by the Principal to the Governing Body who shall then decide whether to approve the person engaged.

Steps should be taken to build up a panel of qualified teachers for part-time posts and the Principal may be given, subject to subsequent confirmation by the Governing Body, authority to appoint teachers from the panel to fill vacancies.

All the teaching staff of the College were in the service of the County Council; the conditions of service were those adopted by the County Council for all its Colleges, and the salaries were in accordance with the regulations made by the Minister of Education so that the national Burnham salary scales applied.

The Principal was in a position of considerable authority. His responsibilities and duties were described as follows:

(a) The Principal shall control the internal organisation, management and discipline of all Departments of the College, and shall exercise supervision over the teaching and non-teaching staff including Canteen Staff.

(b) The Principal shall have the power of suspending a student from attendance for any cause which he considers adequate, but on suspending any student he shall forthwith report the case

to the Chairman of the Governing Body if the student is attending part-time classes, or to the Governing Body if the student is
in full time attendance and in the latter case the Governing
Body shall consult the County Council before confirming or
removing the suspension.

(c) The Principal shall take steps to ensure that students are
admitted only to such courses or classes by which they will
benefit and on prior payment of the fee prescribed by the
County Council provided that the Governing Body may remit
or partially remit fees in case of financial hardship in accordance with regulations made by the County Council and may
award in accordance with regulations made by the County
Council allowances to students ordinarily resident in the
County and attending the College.

(d) There shall be full consultation at all times between the
Principal and the Chairman of the Governing Body.
Suitable arrangements shall be made for enabling Heads of
Departments and teaching staff to submit their views or
proposals to the Governing Body through the Principal.

(e) All proposals and reports affecting the conduct and curriculum
of a College shall be submitted formally to the Governing Body.
The Chief Education Officer or his representative shall be
informed of such reports and proposals and be furnished with a
copy thereof at least seven days before they are to be considered.

(f) There shall be free consultation and co-operation between the
Principal and the Chief Education Officer on matters affecting
the Welfare of the College.

There was no Academic Board or Board of Studies; the
Principal was expected to formulate educational policy, which
he did after discussions with Heads of Departments and consultations with the County Assistant Education Officer. One
innovation that followed the establishment of the new Governing Body in 1949 was the setting up of three Advisory Committees, one for engineering including management, a second
for the science courses, and a third for catering and hotel courses
and women's work. They were asked:

(i) to advise on the conduct of existing courses and, when
considered necessary, to advise on the inauguration of new
courses to meet the demands of industry in the area served by
the College;

(ii) to advise on the staffing, accommodation, and equipment
necessary for the conduct of existing and new courses;

(iii) to meet as required by the Governing Body, and submit reports and recommendations to the Governing Body.

Each Advisory Committee consisted of nine members; three from the Governing Body, three from the management side of industry and three representing employees in industry. Neither the Principal nor Heads of Departments were members, but they invariably attended meetings of the Committees; indeed Heads of Departments were responsible for servicing the Committees in almost every detail. Meetings were held two or three times a year and the minutes went to the Governing Body where recommendations were considered. It provided an effective procedure whereby the Principal and Heads of Departments could bring particular matters to the notice of the Governors.

The College served two masters—the Ministry of Education and the Middlesex County Council. Contacts with the County Council were mainly through the Chief Education Officer and his staff, but there was an awareness in the College of the hierarchy of committees through which the County Council conducted its business—the Further Education Sub-Committee and the Education Committee in particular, but also the extremely powerful Finance and Establishment Committees. The College was aware too that there were direct contacts and negotiations between the County Education Committee and the Ministry of Education; its own contacts with the Ministry however were almost entirely through Her Majesty's Inspectors, who served as the instrument by which the Ministry exercised a fair measure of control over the educational work of the College. Inspectors advised on new developments; new courses had to be approved; the provision of equipment was scrutinised and other capital expenditure, particularly that on new buildings, was subject to detailed examination. It has to be said that the Inspectors carried through this work with understanding and tact and their influence was generally good. They were frequent visitors to the Colleges; each Inspector served as a specialist for a particular subject or group of subjects and paid special visits to the Department concerned. At rather long intervals each College was subject to a full inspection, an occasion when a group of Inspectors spent a week or more at the College and examined in some detail its facilities, programme of work, the

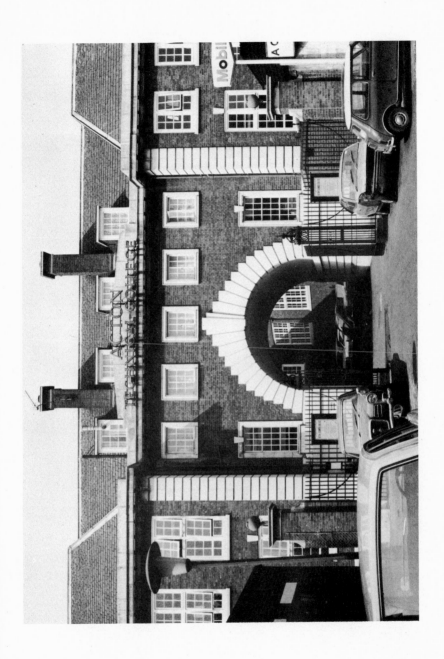

1. Acton
Technical
College

2. Brunel College,
Acton

quality of the teaching and its general policy. Acton Technical College had a full inspection in 1934; the next one did not take place until 1952, delayed perhaps because of the disturbances of the war years. The Reports of these two inspections have already been referred to and the second one is mentioned again in Chapter 5; they mark interesting stages in the history of the College. Middlesex did not have its own inspectorate as some other authorities like London did, and so a greater burden was shouldered by the staff of the Chief Education Officer, some of whom came to know the colleges well; great store was placed upon direct contact with the colleges and particularly on direct consultation between the Assistant Education Officer and the Principals.

This admirable arrangement, fully acceptable to the colleges, did not however ensure that the various submissions which Governing Bodies had to make to the County Council would be dealt with speedily; some were but others were slow, and the variations imposed by the County Council were occasionally annoying. The report of H.M. Inspectors on Acton Technical College in 1952 noted 'the long delays between the submission of equipment requirements and the issue of the authorisation to place the orders' and added that 'a sense of frustration is some-times felt by the Governing Body because its recommendations are subject to amendment by the County committees which are not in such close touch with the College'. In fairness it has to be added there were slow procedures in the Ministry of Education too, and Inspectors invariably seemed overwhelmed with too many files; added to this were the further time-consuming processes involved in gaining approval of courses by the Regional Advisory Council. LEA, Ministry, Regional Advisory Council were a formidable combination of hurdles that each College had to jump and of course in the right sequence. The first two derived from the dual control of the Colleges, whilst the third reflected the recognition that many courses served regional interests and needs, and were of import to an area wider than that of the LEA responsible for the particular college concerned.

The rapid expansion of Technical Colleges which were locally controlled had led, not surprisingly, to unnecessary duplication of courses in some regions, and as far back as 1928 a Regional

Council, representative of both educational and industrial interests, was established in Yorkshire. Nearly twenty years later the Percy Committee[3] recommended that Regional Advisory Councils should be set up in England and Wales 'concerned with the coordination of technological studies in Universities, Colleges of Technology and the other Technical Colleges in the Region'. Percy's vision was only partially realized, particularly as far as the universities were concerned. But the Minister of Education[4] 'took steps in 1946 to establish Regional Advisory Councils and regional academic boards for the whole of the country', and by the following year nine of these councils had been set up in England and the Welsh Joint Education Committee had taken over the responsibility for Wales. Associated with the Regional Advisory Councils were Regional Academic Boards, which had as one of their duties a general regard for the development of graduate courses in technology in universities and technical colleges. Over the years they have in fact had little or no effect on courses in universities, but the Boards have taken cognisance of the courses already established in universities when deciding whether new courses of degree standard should be started in technical colleges. Although individual professors and other members of university staffs have made their own personal contributions to the work of the Regional Advisory Councils and Academic Boards, there has been no effective participation of universities at the level of policy and planning.

Local Education Authorities on the other hand have been very much involved and well aware of the importance of representation on the Regional Advisory Councils. For example, the Chairman of the Middlesex Further Education Sub-Committee (Mr. T. N. Graham) was in 1949 elected Chairman of the Regional Advisory Council for London and the Home Counties; the Chief Education Officer was also a member of the Council, and various Principals and Heads of Departments of Middlesex Technical Colleges served from time to time on the Council or the Academic Board or on one of the many Committees of the Council. This measure of participation was not unusual.

Procedures had to be developed to facilitate the participation of Local Education Authorities, Regional Advisory Councils and the Ministry of Education in the approval of courses in

---

[3] Percy Report, 13.   [4] *Education in 1947*, HMSO, 28.

technical colleges. A very complex structure evolved, although attempts were made to simplify it or remove redundant members from time to time. Colleges applied to the RAC through their LEA (which implied that Authority's approval) for permission to run a new course. The application was usually considered first by a specialist advisory committee of the RAC and secondly by its Approval of Courses Committee, and if the Council finally agreed the support of the Minister of Education was sought, usually through the Regional Staff Inspector. (In some cases the recommendation of the RAC was overruled by the Inspector.) Approval having been granted, the course could be started but could only continue if more than a certain specified number of students had been enrolled. Should the course lead to a professional qualification, such as a Higher National Certificate, the approval of the Joint Committee and therefore of the appropriate professional body, say the Institute of Physics or the Royal Institute of Chemistry, was required. This approval itself depended on an 'inspection' of the College by a visiting party and an assessment of its staff, facilities and equipment. 'If the virtue of further education is that it is as flexible as a rubber hose, and highly sensitive to social demand, the corresponding vice is that it is also a maze, through which only the old and experienced are likely to find their way without error.'[5]

To all these problems was added the even more intricate one of finance, in which the Regional Advisory Councils played no part; it was the preserve of Local Education Authorities and the Ministry. In the constitution of any RAC would be found such words as 'any recommendation involving expenditure charge-able to national, county or county borough funds shall be addressed to or stand referred to the authority primarily concerned with the expenditure.'

Acton Technical College was financed by Middlesex County Council, but at least 50 per cent of the total expenditure was covered by grants from the Ministry of Education. The percentage grant system had its critics, as a 'money spending device', but it continued until 1959–60 when new arrangements were introduced whereby a number of specific grants to local authorities, including grants for education, were replaced by

[5] *Education in Great Britain and Ireland*, Open University, 183.

a general grant. This in turn was changed in 1967. The various apportionments of the national and county council financial responsibilities for education changed little, if at all, the arrangements within the colleges or the relations between the colleges and the County Council; the appropriate clauses in the Articles of Government remained operative and had to be followed. Requests from the College to the Chief Education Officer went first to the Further Education Sub-Committee and later to the Education Committee, which would make a recommendation to the County Council in such terms as: 'that subject to the approval of the Ministry of Education, the purchase of 200 tubular steel stacking chairs for Acton Technical College at an estimated cost of £480 be approved.' Or a list of equipment for several colleges might be approved together; the Minute would read: 'Provision was made in the financial estimates for the purchase of the following machinery and equipment for uses in Technical Colleges. The approval of the Ministry of Education has been received. Your Committee recommends that approval be given to the purchase of the equipment as detailed in the Report now submitted at an estimated cost of £2,105.'

Occasionally the decision of the Ministry of Education would be known beforehand, as in the case of the re-grading[6] of the Departments of the College in 1948. The Minute of the Education Committee reads:

During recent visits to Acton Technical College Her Majesty's Inspector has discussed with the Principal the organisation of the College Departments in view of the continuing development of the more advanced work. The Ministry of Education now intimates that approval would be given to the following arrangements under Section 7(e) of the Burnham Further Education Report 1948, as from 1st September, 1948.

There follows the proposed new gradings of all the departments (including two that were new), and the recommendation to the County Council that 'as from 1st September, 1948 and until further notice the work of Acton Technical College be organised in five Departments as detailed in the Report now submitted. . . . The Finance Committee has been requested to submit an estimate of £1950 being the estimated total salaries

[6] See page 31.

for a whole year for the two additional appointments of Heads of Departments.'

This illustrates not only the County Council procedures, but the role of the Inspectors in controlling College policy and arrangements. In the nineteen fifties the grading of departments was left to the Local Education Authority, and in Middlesex regular reviews became the rule.

A major project like the building of the Science Block (page 32) concerned not only the Ministry of Education but the Ministry of Health, which had to be asked to approve the application for a loan to cover the sum involved. Also at that time special building permits had to be obtained. The Minute of the Education Committee in July 1950 reads:

> Your Committee recommended that, subject to the approval of the Ministry of Education, the consent of the Ministry of the Health to the raising of a loan and the grant of a licence and planning permit, the County Council approves the erection of a science block at the Woodlands Annexe of the Acton Technical College at the total estimated cost of £699,800 (including a sum of £16,100 to meet Quantity Surveyor's fees, salary of Clerk of Works and other expenses), and that tenders for the work be invited from firms on the appropriate selected list of contractors designated by the Chairman of the Education Committee, and that the Chairman of the Education Committee, with the concurrence of the Chairman of the Finance Committee, be authorised to accept the lowest tender if satisfactory, or with the concurrence of the General Purposes Committee, any other tender in circumstances referred to in Standing Order 130, the work to be carried out under the supervision of the County Architect.

Just over seven years later the Science Block was officially opened.

CHAPTER 4

How to Educate Technologists
(1944-54)

THE widespread questioning of the role of technical colleges in the country's educational arrangements, and particularly in higher education was not merely a post-war phenomenon. A deeper consideration and reappraisal had started before the war and continued throughout the war years, but the decade immediately following the war was marked by continual discussion and debate in which more and more individuals, institutions and organizations became involved.

The Ministry of Education Report for 1949 referred to 'an intensification of the educational activities of many industrial and professional organisations' and also to the 'determination by all those concerned to re-examine the basic problems involved in the organisation of technological education at its higher levels'. It might be added that the multiplicity of counsels and the seeming indecision were often frustrating for many of those intimately concerned with technical education.

Perhaps the outstanding event in this field during the war was the setting up of a special committee 'to consider the needs of higher technological education in England and Wales and the respective contribution to be made thereto by Universities and Technical Colleges'. It was appointed in April 1944 by R. A. Butler, then Minister of Education, and was linked with the new policies for technical education outlined in the 1944 Education Act. The Chairman of the Committee was Lord Eustace Percy, then Rector of the Newcastle Division of the University of Durham; the Committee came to be known as the Percy Committee. It was to have regard to the requirements of industry and to make recommendations as to the means of maintaining appropriate collaboration between Universities and Technical Colleges.

The Committee looked particularly at the country's use of and need for mechanical, electrical and civil engineers. The national output of professionally qualified engineers had in 1943 reached about 3,000, and of these some 1,250 were educated at Universities and university colleges and closely associated institutions like the Manchester College of Technology and the London Polytechnics; the others were mainly from Technical Colleges where the majority of them had followed part-time courses leading to a Higher National Certificate; a few had taken a London external degree. The figure of 3,000 needed to be maintained, so it was suggested, for at least the next ten years, and not merely were engineers required in such numbers but their quality must be changed too.

It is specially a demand for men fitted for executive responsibility, and for men capable, not only of research, but of applying the results of research to development. In both respects, therefore, it is a demand for special qualities and for a high grade both of ability and character. At present the demand is not being met; and the whole reputation of our national system of higher education in this field depends upon the extent to which it can be met in future.[1]

The Technical Colleges should continue, the Committee suggested, to be responsible for training about one half of the 3,000 engineers[2] needed annually, but to do this the evening and part-time day arrangements must be reformed and the Colleges emancipated from the external degree system of London University. 'It is probably right that, for perhaps two-thirds of the engineering students in technical colleges, academic study and works practice should be strictly concurrent. But even for them, evening classes alone, which absorbed four-fifths of all the candidates for Higher National Certificates in 1937-8 are wholly inappropriate to higher studies so exacting as those demanded of the modern engineer.' For the other third, some 500 annually, the Committee recommended 'a course of higher technological education which will require continuous full-time study over substantial periods'. The courses should combine full-time study and works practice, and although the exact

---

[1] *Higher Technological Education*, HMSO, 1945, 9.

[2] In fact the technical colleges were sending out 4,000 engineers by 1955.

length of the study periods was left open their aggregate length should, the Committee recommended, be comparable with the total length of a university degree course and 'the remainder of the student's working year should be occupied by a planned course of works practice'. If the term 'sandwich course' was not specifically used, the Committee must have had such courses in mind. They made clear that 'university degrees should not be granted only on examinations, or in respect of courses conducted solely in the evening or on the basis of part-time day release', and that new full-time courses should be specially planned.

We would insist that such courses, whatever their length and arrangement, should be directed to the development to the highest level of the teaching of the art of technology, based on sufficient scientific foundation. Such courses should have a status in no way inferior to the university type of course; they should require equal ability in the student; and they should afford a preparation for the most advanced post-graduate studies. They will be different from University courses; and their development should not, therefore, be hindered or deflected by University affiliations or by arrangements for the grant of University degrees whether by existing Universities—or as some of our witnesses have suggested to us—by some new national technological University created purely for purposes of examinations and standardisation.

The Committee went on to stress how important it was that the institutions should have freedom to develop new courses and new teaching: 'such freedom implies not only freedom to plan their own syllabuses, but freedom also to award their own qualifications. This freedom of a teaching community to adapt its examinations to its teaching is now the characteristic mark of a University: it should equally be the characteristic mark of the institutions to which is to be entrusted the development of a type of higher technological education which is, for the most part, new to this country.' These recommendations enshrined much of the thinking of reformers at the time, who often turned to the Institutes of Technology in America or the German Technische Hochschulen as models.[3] A strictly limited number of technical

---

[3] See for example *Nature*, Vol. 152, 1943; *Scientific Research and the Universities in post-war Britain*, Parliamentary and Scientific Committee, Oct. 1943; H. Lowery, *Memorandum on Post-War Education and Training of Physicists*, Institute of Physics, May 1942.

colleges would have to be selected to undertake this special task of developing these newly designed technological courses. For engineering up to six colleges, exclusive of any in the Greater London area,[4] might be needed to start with. These colleges would have a wide range of responsibilities and activities.

A very important function of these Colleges would be the provision of post-graduate courses in special branches of technology; these courses might be either full-time or part-time, and would be intended for their own graduates or for graduates from Universities and for men who had been in industry for some time. We are of the opinion that far too little attention has been paid in the past to refresher courses, and 'new development' courses, both of which would come into this category.

A major difficulty the Percy Committee faced related to the type of award that students following the new courses would gain; should it be a degree or a diploma, and should the Colleges award their own qualifications or should some national body be created that would amongst other things guarantee the standard of the awards? The Committee, unanimous in all their other recommendations, failed to agree on the degree-diploma issue and the two arguments for the award of a degree, B.Tech., and for a Diploma in Technology were set out in their Report. These were arguments, it might be said, that re-echoed with little variation for a decade at least. But whatever the title of the new award a National Council of Technology should be established empowered to confer degrees or diplomas in approved colleges. This Council would act through an Academic Board representing the Colleges of Technology but containing also independent members. It would, however, not act as an external examining body. 'It should not prescribe syllabuses or set examination papers, but should approve and moderate courses of study leading to its awards, should suggest standards of staffing and equipment, and should ensure an adequate examination standard by selecting or approving the external examiners to be associated with the academic staff of a College in the conduct of final examinations.'

Lord Eustace Percy, in view of the conflicting proposals of the Committee, felt constrained to offer the Minister of Education

[4] This area presented special problems which the Committee outlined.

'independent advice' and proposed that the selected colleges should be given the title of the Royal Colleges of Technology and that, for the present, each should be given power, subject to moderation by the Academic Board of the National Council of Technology, to confer at the graduating stage an Associateship of the Royal Colleges of Technology and at the post-graduate stage a Fellowship. It was a praiseworthy attempt at compromise which did not receive strong support, although the same or similar proposals appeared in the recommendations of other groups later. Interestingly enough Lord Eustace Percy at a public lecture[5] some five years later confessed:

The report which commonly bears my name recommended, five years ago, the selection of a few Technical Colleges for development into institutions of Higher Technology and I added to the report a personal note suggesting, as a title of these institutions, the Royal Colleges of Technology. But I did not have the courage in that note to say what I then believed, and now know, to be true: that no such development can be hoped for so long as Technical Colleges are owned and administered by Local Education Authorities. A Royal College of Technology may be a state institution, like the Scottish Central Colleges, or it may be an independent institution like an English University College; but it cannot be administered by a municipal committee. And, in fact, the recommendations of the Percy Committee have fallen flat owing to the obstinate reluctance of the Ministry of Education and the L.E.A.'s to do anything so 'undemocratic' as to select one institution from among others for special development, or to allow an independent governing body to spend the money of the rate-payers. So long as this continues, it is hardly too much to say that half our assets for experiment and development in higher technological education are immobilised in a blocked account.

The Ministry of Education responded to the Percy Report by setting up a special working party which reported in December, 1947, followed by the establishment of a National Advisory Council on Education for Industry and Commerce which held its first meeting in June 1948. Sir Ronald M. Weeks had accepted the Minister's invitation to serve as Chairman and there were 72 members. The Council tackled the thorny question, amongst others, as to 'what award can be given to

[5] Delivered at a meeting of the Education Group of the Institute of Physics, 25 Oct. 1950.

students in technical colleges at the end of a course of study in technology which shall be comparable in prestige and status to a university degree, having in mind that the course of study will in most cases be different in kind from a university course, though equivalent in standard.'[6] They fairly quickly published an interim draft report which was submitted for comment to the universities, local education authorities, professional institutions, technical colleges, industry and interested government departments, 145 different bodies in all, and in their final report published in 1950 they came down in favour of a diploma rather than a degree, on the grounds that a degree 'would not receive the support of the universities and would not provide technological education with its own hall-mark'.[7] The Council stated that *all* the university bodies consulted opposed the proposal that certain selected colleges should be empowered to award their own degree. Another proposal[8] of a national 'Technical University' granting degrees and approving and moderating courses in certain colleges was also frowned on; 'most universities have made it perfectly clear that any attempt to establish a national degree-awarding body which did not have the full characteristics of a university would meet with their strong opposition'. The Council was driven to suggest the establishment of a national body with the title Royal College of Technologists, which would grant an Associateship as the first award available to students who had followed approved courses, with Membership and Fellowship as higher awards.

The statement of government policy[9] issued subsequently accepted this and many others of the Council's recommendations. The College of Technologists, without at first the right to use the title 'Royal', was to be established, and proposals for making improved financial assistance available for selected colleges and courses were to be announced very shortly. 'The Government accept the view,' the White Paper stated, 'that for its technological posts industry needs recruits of a wide range of

---

[6] *Education in 1949*, 29.

[7] *The Future Development of Higher Technological Education.* HMSO, 1950, 23.

[8] This proposal of the National Advisory Council was too far ahead of its time, and had to wait until 1963-4 for acceptance and implementation.

[9] *Higher Technological Education*, Statement of Government Policy for the Development of Higher Technological Education in Great Britain, Sept. 1951. There was however a General Election in Oct. 1951, followed by a change of Government.

types and with many differences in outlook and experience, and that these varied demands can be met only by a suitably varied educational provision under which higher technological educa- tion similar in age-range, length and standard, and serving the same professions should be provided both in universities and in a number of selected technical colleges.' There was no doubt about the dual provision, a view from which the University Grants Committee did not dissent;[10] they asserted that the aspects of technology appropriate to universities and technical colleges were not the same though they might overlap to some extent, but they left the line of demarcation unclear. The definition of these different roles continued to worry many in education and industry; the Percy Committee had tackled the problem, with partial success, and other groups and committees spent much time trying to clarify it.

There were, of course, other difficulties and other problems, not only in technological education but in science, commerce and art. The Lord President of the Council in December 1945, only a few months after the publication of the Percy Report, asked a Committee, presided over by Sir Alan Barlow, 'to con- sider the policies which should govern the use and development of our scientific man-power and resources during the next ten years'. It reported[11] in May 1946 and gave its approval to many of the recommendations of the Percy Report. It did more; it tackled the problem of trying to estimate with the meagre information and slender guides at its disposal the nation's need for scientists: 'we are satisfied that the immediate aim should be to double the present output, giving us roughly 5,000 newly qualified scientists per annum at the earliest possible moment.' The Committee was clear that there were ample reserves of intelligence in the country to allow a doubling of the numbers of students in the Universities, and that such an increase would in any case still leave us behind some European countries and the United States of America in the provision we made for higher education. They were in no doubt that 'the nation will be genuinely short of scientists in 1950 and that without heroic efforts it is unlikely that supply will have finally overtaken demand even five years later'.

[10] *A Note on Technology in Universities*, UGC, HMSO, 1950, 4.
[11] *Scientific Man-power*, HMSO, 1946 (Barlow Report).

The Committee stressed the contribution the Universities should make to the education and training of engineers and technologists; though they welcomed the Percy proposal that new technological courses should be developed in selected Technical Colleges, they emphasised that this 'will not absolve the Universities from their responsibility for training a high proportion of the nation's first-class technologists.' They implied that the Percy Committee had under-estimated the country's need for technologists and the universities' contribution; they affirmed 'certainly the expansion in the number of students in technology at the Universities should not be less than that which we recommend in the case of pure science'. In fact, as noted earlier, the universities succeeded in doubling the number of students of technology in two, not ten, years for by 1948-9 there were 10,884 such students compared with 5,288 in 1938-9. The theme about quality was reiterated: 'in order to provide technologists of the highest possible quality, we think that urgent consideration should be given to the development of two or three Institutes of Technology, preferably in University Cities, whose aim should be to provide graduate and postgraduate courses and to conduct research at least equal to that demanded of candidates for doctorate degrees in the Universities'—a proposal repeated with some variation by the Robbins Committee[12] nearly twenty years later. They (the Barlow Committee) also suggested that consideration should be given to the foundation of at least one new university, which perhaps facilitated the establishment of the new University College at Keele in 1949.

Educational arrangements in two other fields, commerce and management, were the subject of separate enquiries initiated in 1946. One Committee under the chairmanship of Sir Alexander Carr-Saunders was asked 'to consider the provision which should be made for education for commerce and for the professions relating to it, and the respective contributions to be made by universities and by colleges and departments of commerce in England and Wales.' It reported[13] in December 1949, and among many recommendations proposed that there should

[12] They suggested five SISTERS (Special Institutions for Scientific and Technological Education and Research).
[13] *Report of a Special Committee on Education for Commerce*, HMSO, 1949.

be a new qualification in commerce of a standard equivalent to
that of a university degree which would meet the needs of those
engaged in the mercantile as distinct from the professional side
of commerce. The courses for such an award would normally be
provided on a 'sandwich' basis, that is 'full-time attendance at a
technical college for six months a year coupled with service in
business for the remaining part of the year'.[14] The Committee
left the decision about the type of award, whether degree or
diploma, to the National Advisory Council on Education for
Industry and Commerce. Another Committee reported earlier
in 1947; it was the Urwick Committee on Education for
Management[15] whose recommendations greatly influenced the
introduction in 1951 of national certificates and diplomas in
management studies. The Percy Committee had underlined the
importance of including such studies both at the undergraduate
and post-graduate stage: all students of technology, whether
at universities or colleges of technology, should be introduced
to these subjects. Even more, at least one institution should be
selected as a centre of post-graduate study of industrial administration. All this was reinforced later by various reports of the
teams[16] that visited America sent by the Anglo-American
Council on Productivity. And other groups added their support.

The plethora of reports from professional institutions and
other bodies was indicative of the general concern about, and
wide interest in, technological education, a concern which in
large measure led to the setting-up by Government of numerous
official committees to some of which reference has been made.
But their many recommendations neither satisfied the interest
nor quenched the concern. There would be little point however
in summarizing more of these reports; enough to state that they
had much in common, that they repeated a theme with variations expressing the special interests of the body concerned. One
report might emphasize the university contribution to technological education, another might stress the importance of
creating a few special colleges of technology, and yet another
the need to upgrade technical education generally, but there
was wide agreement about the need for more and better

---

[14] *Education in 1949*, 35.   [15] *Education for Management*, HMSO, 1947.
[16] R. W. MacAdam, Principal of Acton Technical College, was a member of one of
the teams.

technologists and about the dependence of the British economy on developing and improving our technological output.

Whilst all this educational discussion was going on, social and industrial needs did not stand still, and universities and colleges of technology had to improvise policies to meet the changing demands. There was political change too; in particular the Attlee Government which had initiated many of the enquiries was succeeded, in October 1951, by a Conservative administration. It is common now for commentators to look back on the year 1951 as the watershed of change. But the Korean War which started in 1950 was still going on and continued until 1953; defence spending was heavy and economic and financial problems paramount. Housing policy, enshrined in the slogan of 300,000 houses a year, was a main concern of the new Government, and it was a difficult time in which to press for major educational changes involving significant increases in expenditure. The Government was involved, in any case, in large educational spending on primary schools because of the high birth rates just after the war. And from 1953 the needs of the additional children in the secondary schools had to be met.[17] Economic affairs began to improve if somewhat slowly; 'in 1953 for the first time since the war an odd-numbered year passed without an economic crisis,'[18] and by the end of 1954 rationing and most controls had been removed.

It was in January 1952 that the new Government began to formulate its policy on higher technological education; it did not follow the earlier Government which had accepted the recommendation of the National Advisory Council on Education for Industry and Commerce concerning the establishment of a College of Technologists, but it did accept another of the Council's recommendations in favour of increased financial assistance for selected technical colleges and courses. The rate of grant to local education authorities from central funds for certain types of advanced work and research was raised from the standard rate of 60 per cent to 75 per cent,[19] and this increased rate was to apply to capital as well as maintenance expenditure

[17] The number of primary pupils rose from 3.7 m in 1945 to 4.6 m in 1955 while the number of secondary pupils rose from 1.1 m to 2.0 m. See J. Vaizey and J. Sheehan, *Resources for Education*, Allen and Unwin, 1968, 18.

[18] C. M. Woodhouse, *Post-War Britain*, The Bodley Head, 1966.

[19] Circular 255, *Advanced Technology*, Ministry of Education, July 1952.

and therefore to new buildings and equipment for advanced technological work. Though perhaps only a small beginning, colleges were glad to take advantage of the increased grants and about 500 approved courses in 24 colleges (of which Acton Technical College was one) were reported by the end of 1954. By that time the Minister was able to announce the removal of particular restrictions on technical college buildings and a substantial expansion in the size of annual building programmes for technical education generally; he also expressed his anxiety 'that certain major colleges should be able to shed their lower grade work and have more freedom to provide for advanced technology and research', which seemed to contain a promise of things to come.

The Government was also involved in decisions concerning the provision for technological and scientific education in the universities, and in January 1953 announced its intention of enabling the Imperial College of Science and Technology to carry out a major expansion over the next five years, and to raise the number of its full-time students from 1,650 to 3,000. There was a further promise that resources for developments in other parts of the country would also be made available, and in fact major developments were sanctioned later (December 1954) at the Universities of Glasgow, Manchester, Leeds and Birmingham, as well as more specialized provision in other centres. The capital grants amounted to about £5 million, as well as £15 million for the Imperial College project. This was a direct response to recommendations from the University Grants Committee concerning the 'building up of one or more institutions of university rank devoted predominantly to the teaching and study of the various forms of technology.'[20] The Committee in its report had noted, as mentioned earlier in chapter 2, the fall in the number of students taking technology in the universities, but in putting forward plans for further development it assumed that 'in the course of the next few years the problem of recruiting technological students will have to be solved'. More than that, it agreed that the number of those taking technology should be increased, and advocated a policy of expansion in those universities where the numbers of technology students were already high. No immediate expansion of the total university population

[20] *University Development, 1947–52*, HMSO, 59.

was anticipated, on the contrary, there might be 'some slight fall over the next few years'. Outside the UGC however and outside Government the discussion continued. Some current views on universities and their possible development were expressed by the Parliamentary and Scientific Committee in a memorandum[21] issued in July 1954; the Committee noted that the expansion recommended by the Barlow Committee had been achieved, and was so bold as to assert that 'for the time being there is no need to envisage any further *major* expansion of the university student population in this country'. It went further: 'the arbitrary dictum of the Barlow Committee that the number of arts students in the Universities should be doubled, as well as the number of science students, should now be abandoned. The University Grants Committee should give increasing attention to the problem of ensuring that the Universities will provide the country with an increasing number of scientists and technologists within the overall student population.'

The Committee also expressed its belief that further Government action in support of the development of higher technological education was urgently needed, and argued that certain selected technical colleges should be enabled to make their special contribution. 'A few Colleges of Technology should be selected and granted a Royal Charter, under which they would be described as Chartered Colleges of Technology.' The Committee grasped the degree-diploma nettle, deciding in favour of a Bachelor of Technology, and suggested that the Colleges should be given powers to examine and make their own awards, subject to the appointment of external examiners—a fundamentally different proposal from the Royal College of Technologists put forward a few years earlier.

Such colleges would have to be given more academic freedom; 'there would be great advantages' it was suggested, 'in giving the Royal Chartered Colleges complete financial independence in the same way as the universities on a quinquennial basis.' Their roles would no longer be consonant with 'single local authority finances, administration and control'. This vexed question was the main issue faced by the Association of Principals of Technical Institutions (APTI) and the Association of

[21] *Memorandum on Higher Technological Education*, Parliamentary and Scientific Committee, July 1954.

Technical Institutions (ATI) at their joint meeting in June
1954, when they considered a 'Report on the Development of
Higher Technological Education' drafted by their Joint Policy
Committee. The culmination of a long period of discussion and
disagreement, the Report advocated the selection and recognition of a strictly limited number of Regional Colleges, about
fifteen to twenty, each serving a region rather than the area
of a particular LEA. How should they be selected, and how
financed? What particular administrative structure was needed
to serve a region? 'Central Government sources should contribute not less than 75 per cent of the grant and the remainder
should be provided by Local Education Authorities.' Further
'the selection of Regional Colleges and the award to them of
central government grants should preferably be undertaken by
a Regional Colleges Grants Committee or, failing the establishment of such a body, by the Ministry of Education'.

But there was even more uncertainty, or less agreement,
about the title of the award, except that 'a Regional College
should be in a position to confer its own distinctive award upon
successful students'. But what should it be? A Diploma in
Technology would be inappropriate, because of the seeming
impossibility of finding suitable nomenclature for awards higher
than a diploma. The Regional Colleges when established must
resolve this matter themselves—a tame conclusion! If the
Government was waiting for a consensus, however, this was the
nearest to one that the technical college world was likely to
reach. Was there much point in delaying further?

When the Parliamentary and Scientific Committee's Report
was debated in the House of Lords in December 1954, it was
made clear, so *Education in 1954* records, 'that the Government
preferred evolutionary progress to revolutionary changes; that
some thirty colleges had been planned to develop ultimately
into advanced regional colleges; that local education authorities
had done excellent work in linking local industries with their
colleges; and that in the Government's view it would be a mistake to remove the colleges from the control of the authorities.'

The Minister (Sir David Eccles) was obviously not ready to
announce his policy; he had only been in office a few months,
having succeeded Miss Florence Horsburgh in October 1954.
The National Advisory Council on Education for Industry and

Commerce had been trying once more to find an acceptable solution to the old problem of what sort of award colleges of technology should be enabled to make; 'much of the Council's time (in 1954) was spent on preparing revised proposals for a national award in advanced technology. These were presented to the Minister in September, and were still under consideration at the end of the year.'[22] The recommendations turned out to be somewhat different from those the Council made in their first main report in 1950, and in their new form were accepted, after wide consultation, by the Government. Major policy decisions were foreshadowed in the Queen's Speech in June 1955, and the following month the Minister announced the appointment of Lord Hives as Chairman of the new National Council for Technological Awards (NCTA).

At last the years of indecision and frustration seemed to be at an end. There was a sense of relief that the report-writing and the argumentation would now stop. The new policies, inevitably a composite of many elements that had been hammered on the anvil of public discussion for a decade, were not universally acceptable, but in fact they ushered in developments in technical colleges which far exceeded the most sanguine expectations of many closely involved. To these changes, and Acton Technical College's involvement in them, we now turn.

[22] *Education in 1954*, 22.

CHAPTER 5

Acton Technical College, 1955-7

R. W. MACADAM resigned from the Principalship of Acton
Technical College in 1954; he had been appointed in 1931, had
directed the College from its early beginnings and steered its
growth into the major technical institution in Middlesex. 'The
volume of high level and high quality work which is being done
is largely due to his inspiration, guidance and unremitting hard
work', wrote the H.M. Inspectors in 1952. He had become well
known and respected in Acton, and his considerable contribution to technical education in the County was widely recognised. He decided to retire early, and for family reasons to go out
to New Zealand. There he quickly became involved again in
educational matters, and was appointed to the staff of the
Ministry of Education in Wellington where he served as an
adviser for many years, one of his special interests being the
development of national certificate type courses in that country.

Anyone succeeding MacAdam, as I[1] did on 1 January 1955,
would have taken over the College at a very interesting stage of
its development and at a critical time in the history of technical
education. There were problems inevitably, some deriving from
the very success of the College and in particular its rapid growth
within buildings that had become grossly inadequate. Others
were inherent in the social and political conditions of the time,
the slowness of the economic recovery of the country after the
war and the accompanying delay in the formulation of national
policy for higher technological education. The College had
six departments; Chemistry and Biology, Physics and Mathematics, Mechanical Engineering, Electrical Engineering,
Management and Production Engineering, and a combined

---

[1] It seems impossible to do other than use the first person singular from this point
onward.

Women's Department and Hotel Catering School. All of them were over-crowded. The full time staff numbered about 90 and there were also more than 200 part-time teachers. The student population had reached 4,600 and a little over half were evening students; some 530 attended full time. The Secondary Technical School, the former JTS, though by this time independent and likely to be moved into other premises,[2] still occupied some of the rooms during the day; there were nearly 400 on the roll and boys seemed to swarm everywhere.

The overcrowding was oppressive; cupboards full of apparatus and other academic aids clogged every corridor; students emerged from one chemistry laboratory through a hole rather than a door; the old Woodlands building, even though extra classrooms had been built around it, seemed to be bursting at the seams, and four or five Church Halls (some quite unsuitable) were used for classes, as were some neighbouring schools in the evenings.

The new building called the Science Block[3] was still incomplete; with such slow progress it was little wonder that the staff and students referred to it with a mixture of unbelief and despair. In the High Street buildings there was one common room for *all* teaching staff, full-time and part-time; the Governing Body had to meet sitting at students' desks or tables in a classroom which was specially cleared on each occasion and the evening[4] students despatched elsewhere. Advisory Committees met in the Principal's room or in one of the Heads of Department's rooms; not that every Head of Department had his own room; the Heads of two large Departments, Chemistry and Biology and Physics and Mathematics, shared a room, as did the Heads of the Electrical and Mechanical Engineering Departments. Members of the teaching staff found a corner where they could. Research, inevitably limited, somehow got a few square feet of bench space in a crowded laboratory. The Library strangely enough seemed comparatively spacious, even though only a handful of students could work there (there were 28 seats)

---

[2] The ultimate decision was to close the Secondary Technical School; no further pupils were admitted after September 1959.

[3] We could not drop the habit of using the unfortunate term 'block'.

[4] The Governors always met in the evenings, taking a hasty sandwich and a cup of tea or coffee beforehand. In contrast, at Guildford, where I served earlier, the Governors met in the afternoon and had afternoon tea—a reflection of the different social milieu.

and it was sometimes full of secondary technical school boys. It was nevertheless an oasis, a simple room in the extension at the back of the buildings away from the noise and clamour where the Librarian had assembled a small but good stock of books and periodicals. Nearby was a so-called Students' Common room, very small indeed, which had to serve many of the purposes of the Students' Union. 'An effort was made to try and improve the Common Room' wrote the President of the Union in the Annual Report for 1954–5, 'but it is obviously far from ideal. It has to be used by all students, and the overcrowding, particularly during the lunch breaks, emphasises the need for a Common Room at Woodlands.'

Acton was in these and other respects not very different from many other technical colleges. It had however some special features. The most unusual Department was that named Management and Production Engineering, a rare combination of disciplines, which brought together on its teaching staff a small group of production engineers and social scientists (psychologists, in the main). Its Head of Department, Robert Harcourt, had graduated in English at Cambridge and after the war had returned to take a second degree in psychology. He was an unusual technical college Head of Department, both in regard to his education and experience and his general outlook. I grew to appreciate his unconventional approach to most problems, though I found his seeming disregard of agreed policies and time-tables more and more disconcerting. His capacity for thinking through a new problem however was striking and helpful; I could expect from him as from no one else a novel point of view.

He took up the post of Head of Department on 1 January 1953, succeeding Winston Rodgers through whose efforts the College had gained a reputation for its Management Courses.[5] Harcourt was immediately involved in a research investigation into the functioning of his department, evidence indeed of his unusual approach. He had applied successfully to the Joint Committee on Human Relations in Industry (set up by the Department of Scientific and Industrial Research and the Medical Research Council in 1953) for funds to carry out a

---

[5] The Department had earlier been named the Department of Industrial Engineering (page 33).

project of which the objectives were described as: (i) to examine the function and possibilities of a department of Management and Production Engineering in servicing industry; (ii) to examine with that department its services and structure; (iii) to establish the most effective feed-back mechanism from industry to the department. The original intention was to have a research team engaged by the College itself but this proved untenable for it was necessary to ensure that the research workers had adequate freedom and independence, while on the other hand the Middlesex County Council wished to guard 'against the disturbance of existing arrangements by irresponsible criticism'. A year elapsed before a way out was found, and it was as late as March 1954 that the County Council invited the Tavistock Institute (which had been called in to help resolve the difficulties) to undertake the investigation.

The proposed study though fully accepted by the staff of the Department gave rise to some heart-searching among staff of other departments of the College. At the first meeting of the Staff Association at which the project was considered a motion was proposed recommending that the staff should not co-operate, but it was defeated. Cautiously they decided to note that the project was to be started and that they 'would welcome the opportunity to study the full results and implications'. The Governing Body was cautious too but finally agreed to sanction the research. The ultimate decision lay of course with the County Council and they at last approved the plan that emerged from the lengthy negotiations. It is noteworthy that 'the decision of the County Council, after careful consideration and clarifications, to accept the opportunity to have an outside organization examine and help change one of its operating units, was probably without precedent among British local authorities'.[6] A liaison Committee of the County Council, the College and the Tavistock Institute was formed with the purpose of keeping the progress of the project under review, on the understanding that the project could stop at any time if any one of the parties wished to withdraw. The study started on 1st June 1954, with Dr C. Sofer and G. Hutton as the field workers, and with Dr A. T. M. Wilson, Chairman of the Management

---

[6] C. Sofer and G. Hutton, *New Ways in Management Training*. Tavistock Publications, Ltd., 1958, 104.

Committee of the Tavistock Institute, responsible for the overall plan; it continued for two years.

When I arrived at the College in January 1955, some if not all of the initial difficulties had been overcome and the main style of the investigation decided. I was never intimately involved in it, but went to many of the meetings, an interested observer increasingly intrigued by the methods the social scientists used in such 'collaborative research'. I read the interim reports which appeared at six-monthly intervals with more interest in the techniques than concern for the contents; not that the contents were unimportant, but they lacked (for me at least) novelty. I appreciated their function in keeping the College and the County Council in touch with emerging research findings and 'in paving the way towards a final public report'. The final report was published in 1958.

It was difficult to assess how the on-going study was affecting the College; some staff dismissed it uninterestedly, a few feared it might lead to a more general 'inquisition', others felt it was valuable even if its consequences were likely to be minimal, and a small group reacted more positively. Certainly it fully engaged the Head and the Staff of the Department and must have influenced for good their thinking about courses, teaching methods and relations with industry.

These latter aspects of the study interested me most for I felt compelled to concentrate on working out an educational policy for the College, appropriate to the circumstances of the time. The main problem was the advanced courses for which enrolments were small; there was seemingly no difficulty in continuing to fill GCE advanced level classes or in expanding the various part-time classes, and no lack of support for evening classes leading to ordinary and higher national certificates in engineering and science and in preparation for the technological examinations of the City and Guilds Institute. But a programme of activity limited to classes which were well supported would have left the College undistinguished from other technical colleges in the County and many further afield; nor would it have used the College's resources and in particular the abilities and experience of its teaching staff to the full.

The significant questions were clear enough; what was to replace the full-time degree courses to which very few students were being recruited, and indeed what was to be the College's contribution to higher technological education which was still being debated nationally and about which Government had not announced a policy? In the absence of such a policy what should the College do? Too many people and colleges were just waiting. In the Annual Report of the College for 1954-5, the first for which I was responsible, I wrote

The demand for part-time courses shows no abatement and indeed cannot fully be met, but the pattern of full-time enrolment is changing, particularly for degree courses. There continue to be large numbers of students who wish to attend the more elementary full-time courses, in preparation for the General Certificate of Education examinations at the Advanced Level. Most of these students, however, do not stay at the College but, after passing their examinations, move on to the Universities and into the professions. The number of students wishing to attend degree courses is steadily falling, for reasons which are fairly obvious. Immediately after the war the Universities were not able to cope with the large numbers of returned ex-service men, and consequently the larger Technical Colleges were called upon to educate and train many of them. It was always apparent that this was a temporary phenomenon and, especially in view of the expansion of University departments, that the numbers would fall steeply as they have done since 1952. The majority of Technical Colleges undertaking work of this standard now have seriously reduced numbers, and many of the full-time degree courses are likely to disappear.

The Annual Report provided an opportunity of bringing to the notice of the Governors, the Staff of the College and a wider public some features of the changing educational scene, both within and without the College. Only tardily did I realise the importance of such an agency and all too slowly tried to transform it from a pedestrian collection of statistics high-lighting successes and student-hours. What I now find interesting in the above extract from the 1954-5 Report is that it reflects my growing concern about GCE Advanced Level Classes in Technical Colleges in the sense that I was increasingly dissatisfied with what was essentially ambulance work for those who had failed A Levels at school; if it were done at all should it not have at least a special Technical College flavour and at best express a Technical College philosophy of education? Secondly the use of the phrase 'educate and train' was deliberate; partly a reaction against the common use of the words 'the *training* of scientists and engineers' and partly an indication of my main interest in trying to combine education and training in some positive way. Thirdly, I was convinced that full-time degree courses would, because of the falling demand, disappear from Technical College programmes; I was even more certain that they *should* be replaced for I felt strongly that external degree courses prevented Technical Colleges from making their own special contribution to higher education. I hardly need add that I appreciated the qualities of the students on such courses for I had taught them for many years; they were worthy of better opportunities.

The strength of Technical Colleges was in their links with industry; could not these be made even stronger and used to develop a mode of education in which an appeal to practical things would be fully exploited? Teachers with industrial experience, and there were many on the staff of technical colleges, could surely help to do this and be stimulated by such an approach, but it was also clear that if the teaching were to be really effective the students themselves would need to be able to appreciate the practical situation that was being described or analysed in the classroom. How could they be given, even at the student stage, a practical background? Part-time day release, with which Technical Colleges had had long experience, was not the answer. In such arrangements the works element and the College element were out of balance, and more important were often unrelated. How could one achieve a proper balance and a satisfactory measure of relatedness? What criteria did one apply to these and other aspects of linked education and training?

Some Technical Colleges in various parts of the country had over the years, going back at least half a century,[7] organized what became known as sandwich courses, to describe the alternation of a study period in college and a training period in industry. The term, unattractive as it is, continues to be used although some prefer to call them integrated courses, whilst in America they are referred to as cooperative courses— integrated in the sense that some real attempt is made to relate the college and industrial phases of the student's experience, and

[7] Glasgow in 1888; Sunderland in 1903.

cooperative in that college and industry combine to provide the education and training.

Before going to Acton I had become convinced that if Colleges of Technology had a special place or a place at all in technological education it was not through courses of the traditional university type, even if emancipation from the London external system were somehow granted, but it was to be achieved by making use of the colleges' special relationship with industry and by combining education and training in a carefully organized way. It seemed to me that sandwich courses, re-fashioned to meet current developments in education and technology, were the special contribution colleges could and should offer. My appointment at Acton gave me the opportunity to put these ideas into practice. I was concerned that the contribution should be different from that of the Universities; there was no point in trying to reproduce the university pattern but I soon found, not surprisingly, that others regarded different as synonymous with inferior and consequently unacceptable. The innovator's task, especially in education, is always difficult.

However, I was able to write in the Annual Report for 1954-5:

much thought has been given to the future educational policy of the College, and plans have been made to introduce in the session 1955-56 a series of sandwich courses in Applied Science and Engineering. These may well transform the work of the college. Their success depends greatly on the support of industry, so we are specially glad to be assured of the help and cooperation of many local firms. A brochure describing the Sandwich Courses has been prepared and distributed widely.

This was only about six or seven months after taking up the post of Principal; I was clearly in a hurry. But action was urgent, for admissions to the full-time degree courses were very low and the Middlesex County Council was not likely to tolerate much longer the small classes. It was accepted practice that special permission had to be obtained through the Chief Education Officer to continue classes with admissions below certain specified numbers.

Moreover the H.M. Inspectors who visited the College in

1952 had commented on the Mechanical Engineering Department as follows:

There are 10 students enrolled for the full-time course for B.Sc. Part I first year, 8 for Part I second year, and 8 for Part II. These numbers in Part I include students going on to electrical engineering subjects in Part II. The numbers in Part I may be considered to be reasonable, since all the students take all the subjects of the two years. The numbers for Part II are too small for economic provision as 8 subjects in Mechanical and Civil and 5 in Electrical Engineering are offered, from which only 4 have to be chosen. At the time of the Inspection there was one class of one student, 3 classes of 2 students, 7 classes of 3 students, one class of 5 students and one class of 8 students. The numbers in the part-time classes which cover three years' work are also small. In some cases two stages of a subject are combined to make a class of reasonable numbers. This situation needs careful consideration in view of the proximity of similar courses in London. If the number of students in the classes cannot be increased, continuation of the classes can hardly be justified.

A like comment was made on the Part II degree classes in the Department of Electrical Engineering: 'each of the four senior members of the staff spends about half of his teaching hours with these classes of only three students.' The full-time degree courses in Science were better attended but the fall had started, as shown by the small numbers in the first and second years. There were however still large enrolments for the part-time day degree classes, some 300 in all.

The College set out its new policy in the sandwich course brochure, published first in the summer of 1955; by way of introduction it was explained that

Many groups of industrialists and educationists have considered, particularly during the last ten years, the education and training of the scientists and the technologists whom industry and Government service need. Consequently many reports have been published and much has been written on the policies that should be adopted, and in particular on the special contributions the Universities and Technical Colleges should separately make. This brochure does not discuss the problems again, but tries to explain what one Technical College, aware of the needs and impressed by the importance of a new approach to technical education, proposes to attempt.

There followed some comment on the courses which Technical Colleges should inaugurate and develop; it went on 'Technical Colleges and industrial firms have been close partners for many years, and one field of successful collaboration has been in what have become known as sandwich courses of education. They have hitherto been mainly for the training of engineers. It is now proposed to extend their scope so as to include physicists, applied mathematicians, chemists, biologists and metallurgists.' The courses were to range over the work of all the departments of the College and to follow a common plan—four-year courses, with six months in college and six months in industry each year. They were to have new features too, which were described in broad terms.

For admission students should have gained an Ordinary National Certificate at a high standard or a General Certificate of Education with two A-level passes. The courses were 'works-based' in that the students were apprentices sponsored by their firms, but 'college-based' students could 'equally well be accepted'.

The brochure continued:

The College is aware that with the freedom to design these courses, to frame the syllabuses and to set the examinations, subject only to the approval of External Examiners appointed by the College, it has a great opportunity. It has also the considerable responsibility of keeping well in mind its educational aims. It realises that students should not merely be aided to learn certain techniques, and to acquire a knowledge of science and technology and of some of the industrial applications of science. They should be helped to appreciate the scientific approach to a problem, how the scientist tackles the new and unknown, and how he expresses an answer to a question. This is difficult to achieve; it cannot be enshrined in a syllabus but it should permeate all the teaching. Further, the students should be introduced to the wider world, so profoundly affected by science and technology, and confronted with some of the problems which men face today. One of the aims therefore will be to liberalise the curriculum as far as possible, not merely by introducing additional subjects, important as these may be, but by making full use of the technological courses. It needs to be recognised that the subjects of science and engineering can be the means to a liberal education if wisely and properly used. However, besides teaching these subjects in a broader way an attempt will be made to deal with some of the aspects of science, including its history, method and philosophy, which often do not find a place in lecture-courses. These are referred to later as the 'fundamentals of science'. English and Social Studies will also be included.

The College was thus involved in its first early attempts at 'liberal studies', for which it later achieved a lively reputation. My own concerns were to make scientists (and engineers) more articulate, to help them understand their science better, particularly to comprehend what scientific method is and to understand something of the social interactions of science, to be aware of its social function. I addressed the staff on these topics[8] at a meeting in the College on 6 July 1956. A good discussion followed and a panel of eight staff members was asked to draft a syllabus for a course with the title 'Fundamentals of Science'. Other staff members became involved in the subsequent debate. Fruitfully it triggered off the highly original work of John Isaac, lecturer in physics in the College, to which reference is made later.

I was also concerned about the overloading of syllabuses and students' time-tables. The brochure went on:

> However, the accumulation of knowledge is not the paramount aim. Too often are students overloaded with facts and so fail to comprehend the basic principles or the general framework. Consequently in a new situation they seldom know how to proceed. An emphasis will therefore be placed on the understanding of scientific principles, and students will be trained throughout the course in the application of these principles to the solution of new problems. They will thus experience, in some measure, the discipline and the excitement of working on the frontiers of knowledge.

Laboratory courses would need to be overhauled; and indeed the project which each student would undertake in his final year would confront him with a 'real' situation; he would need to work out his own method of solution and devise the equipment required. It would be an exercise in problem-solving. 'In these ways the College will attempt to help the student to be able to apply his learning to a series of industrial situations. But his education in the College must be supplemented by his experience, in the firm, of technical tasks and of the patterns of

[8] J. Topping and A. J. Woodall, 'Scientific Method', *Bulletin of the Institute of Physics*, Apr. 1959, 73–6.

behaviour used in undertaking them. This is one of the great
advantages of a sandwich course.'

There was no major difficulty in gaining the support of the
Chief Education Officer of Middlesex County Council, Dr C. E.
Gurr,[9] for the change-over to sandwich courses, and there was
stronger support from Dr C. Whitworth, who at that time was
Assistant Education Officer of the County Council. He was later
appointed Principal of the College of Advanced Technology at
Salford, and when it became the University of Salford was its
first Vice-Chancellor; he was closely associated with the Middlesex Technical Colleges in the nineteen-fifties. In March 1955 he
called a meeting at the Middlesex County Council headquarters
with the intention of developing courses of the sandwich type
leading to a Middlesex diploma, starting with a course in
applied physics and mathematics. He hoped that the Ministry of
Supply, Admiralty Research and Department of Scientific and
Industrial Research laboratories would support such a scheme,
and though unsuccessful in the County generally his interest
gave a fillip to the proposed developments at Acton.

Fortunately too the Staff Inspector (Engineering) at the
Ministry of Education at the time was C. R. English (later Sir
Cyril) who supported strongly the Acton proposals. He had
been involved at Salford with the Principal of the Royal
Technical College, Dr P. F. R. Venables (later Sir Peter), in
starting sandwich courses there. These had been introduced
in 1950 in co-operation with Metropolitan Vickers Electrical
Co. Ltd., and were greatly helped forward by Dr Willis (later
Lord) Jackson who in 1953 was appointed Director of Education and Research of the firm.[10] It is interesting that it was
another electrical firm, the General Electric Co. Ltd., that
supported a similar sandwich course development about the
same time at Birmingham College of Technology, where Mr
J. J. Gracie, a Director of G.E.C., was also Chairman of the
Governing Body of the College. All the students in the first
sandwich course, which was in electrical engineering and
started in 1954, were employees of this Company. Dr Venables
moved from Salford to Birmingham in 1956. Although I was not

[9] He succeeded T. B. Wheeler in 1951, and was also Secretary to the Middlesex
Education Committee.
[10] See P. F. R. Venables, *Sandwich Courses*, Max Parrish, 1959.

closely in touch with these important pioneering developments at Salford and Birmingham, I was aware of them and particularly of those at Birmingham through my professional contacts in the Institute of Physics with Dr M. R. Gavin, who was then (1950–5) Head of the Department of Physics and Mathematics in the College and Vice-Principal. His support of these courses encouraged me.

I was also encouraged in the ways of educational innovation by Mr Wilfred (later Lord) Brown, Chairman of the Governing Body of Acton Technical College, who, I suspect, had been influential in my appointment as Principal. As Managing Director of a local firm, the Glacier Metal Company, he was brought in and made Chairman when the Governing Body was re-constituted in 1949. To him major changes in technical education were highly desirable and he welcomed sandwich courses as a contribution to a fundamental re-shaping of the whole structure. These views were his own, and not shared by some other members of the Governing Body or by the County Council Further Education Committee. For this and other reasons there were often noisy arguments in meetings of the Governing Body; the Chairman thrived on controversy, and he was also ever ready to press for changes in official policy towards Acton and other Middlesex Technical Colleges, which seemed to bring him into recurring opposition to the County Council. To me as Principal he gave strong support, all the more valuable and reassuring at a time of rapid change when difficulties abounded and new situations demanded new thinking and new organizational structures. He may have seemed to some guilty of trying to apply indiscriminately to education ideas and concepts that were derived from the Glacier experiment, but he was too discerning to make such a simple transfer.

For a new Principal there was a web of personal relationships to create, extend and sometimes repair—with the staff, students, Governors and members of advisory committees, County Council Education Officers and Architects, Her Majesty's Inspectors, officers of the Borough of Acton, heads of firms, personnel and education officers, local headmasters and headmistresses, the press, principals of other Colleges, officers of professional institutions, the Regional Advisory Council, the Association of Technical Institutions and many other bodies.

3. Model of Brunel College as planned in 1959

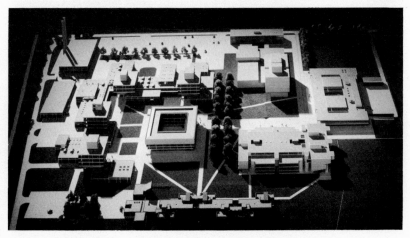

4. Model of Phase One, Uxbridge

5. Engineering Centre, Uxbridge

6. Two of the Engineering Towers

There was a seemingly endless succession of committees, internal and external. My contacts with students were limited to the officers of the Students' Union, and to get to know the students better I decided to give a course of lectures in the Physics and Mathematics Department, an unusual step for a Principal and difficult to fit into an overburdened diary. I deliberately spent much time with Heads of Departments and encouraged them to consult with me often and regularly for earlier in my career I had suffered as a Head of Department from seeing the Principal only rarely, perhaps twice a term. The staff as a body I met very occasionally and as it turned out too seldom; only slowly was this repaired. I had naturally many casual contacts with staff individually.

The reaction of the teaching staff of the College to the introduction of sandwich courses was mixed. Heads of Department responded enthusiastically and I assumed mistakenly that most of the staff were of the same mind. There was in fact some caution, conservatism perhaps, in response to what must have seemed another disturbing influence, all too soon after and too similar to the Tavistock Study in the Department of Management and Production Engineering. Other staff feared that to do away with external degree courses was to depreciate the very element in the College's growth over the past decade on which they prided themselves; it was also to remove a great buttress to technical education which had enabled some of them (and many others outside the College, particularly some of their best students) to gain a university degree. All this was understandable and needed discussion. What was much more troublesome was that the sandwich courses unfortunately became linked with another change that I tried to introduce at the same time which some of the staff strongly opposed. In retrospect it is clear enough that I tried to make this change too quickly and with too little staff consultation.

In those days Principals of Colleges saw little of their staff, except at second-hand through Heads of Departments. When I went to Acton I found that the Principal addressed the Staff at 9 a.m. on the first morning of each new term, a practice I continued for a while, when new members of staff were welcomed and special announcements made. No other formal contacts existed. There was a Staff Association, whose officers made representations to the Principal on behalf of the staff from time to time, as did on other occasions the officers of the College branch of the Association of Teachers in Technical Institutions, the ATTI. The lines of demarcation had not been strictly assigned by the two Associations but there was no conflict, only some occasional confusion. At least I found it confusing initially.

A practice had grown up whereby nearly all the staff were fully engaged on teaching duties during the day, for ten sessions as the phrase went, and in addition they taught evening classes on two evenings a week for which they received additional pay—overtime. They were grossly over-worked; no educational advance was possible until the teaching hours were reduced. As a first step the College should accept, I pleaded, the arrangements common in many colleges, notably the London Polytechnics, where the staff had their total teaching duties distributed over ten sessions a week which usually *included* two sessions in the evenings with corresponding relief from teaching on two sessions during the day. I had worked such a scheme for so many years at the Polytechnic, Regent Street, that I could not understand the opposition its proposed introduction at Acton evoked; of course the staff were reluctant to lose the additional pay the 'overtime' provided, and some had become dependent upon it. I suggested that where financial difficulties arose the change should be introduced gradually, but the problem remained a contentious one and strained relations between 'the new Principal' and the leaders of the Staff Association. It availed little to point out that the H.M. Inspectors had stated in their report on the College in November 1952: 'the system of filling the time-tables of the full-time staff with day work should be reconsidered. A large proportion of evening work is done by the full-time staff as overtime. Evening work should generally be a part of normal duty. Suggested reductions in the number of day lecture periods per week and the combination of small classes for laboratory work might allow this to be done without any increase in full-time staff.'

I was more concerned to relieve the staff of some of the heavy teaching responsibilities many of them carried, and to provide opportunities for planning new courses and initiating new teaching methods. Not only did the staff have no time to think, but the students had no time either—the full-time students followed a succession of lectures, laboratories and other classes *throughout* each day of a five-day week, and sometimes on Saturday mornings. Part-time day release students were even more sorely tried, for they spent a full day in the College, followed usually by an evening class often three hours in length, as well as another full evening in the week. Evening students customarily spent three full evenings in the College, and much of their other evenings doing 'homework'. These were common practices, which applied in most other technical colleges.

'If we were confined to one comment and one recommendation about English further education, it would be this' wrote the Crowther Committee[11] in 1959. 'At every stage and every level, the need is more time, for less pressure on both staff and students.' Where pressure could be reduced was in the full-time courses, but these were so often linked with part-time arrangements or dominated by a further education outlook, that little was done either to liberate or liberalize them. There was too little recognition that, in this area in particular, colleges need not wait for changes in policy but could solve some of the problems themselves.

In an article published in the Bulletin of the Institute of Physics in June 1955, I wrote,

It has become increasingly clear to many Technical College Teachers that the remedy lies in their own hands—they must put their own house in order; they must inaugurate new courses and new methods of training which their experience and knowledge of industrial needs specially qualify them to undertake. For too long have they waited, for too long have they been tied to the external University degree, for too long have they waited for a new status. But status as one of the Institute's reports wisely says, 'will depend on the extent to which the Colleges fulfil what is regarded as their essential function and will not be acquired by comparatively minor changes or organisation or of the nomenclature of awards'. In recent months a few Technical Colleges have quite independently put forward new schemes of training for physicists, but suitable for adaptation for technologists generally. They are firmly based on Technical College experience and therefore old in concept but yet they mark a new era in technical education. These Colleges propose to introduce sandwich courses, allowing for six months' college training followed by six months in industry, over a period of four years.

[11] *15 to 18*, Ministry of Education, HMSO, 1959, 367.

The first sandwich course introduced at Acton Technical College was in Applied Physics; it started in January, 1956 with nine students. Six of the students were industry-based, that is, they were sponsored by firms—Kodak, D. Napier & Son, E.M.I., Telegraph Condenser Co., National Coal Board and the Electrical Research Association. The other three were College-based, having enrolled for the B.Sc. Special Physics Course which had had to be closed; they were not connected with any particular firm and the College was responsible for placing them for industrial training. These three students were accepted by the G.E.C. Research laboratories at Wembley and the English Electric Valve Company for their first period of training. The College was greatly encouraged by such a measure of support, particularly as the only award the College could offer successful students was its own Associateship, specially devised for the purpose. The students had however some assurance of its degree-equivalence in that the Institute of Physics had agreed to grant successful students complete exemption from the Graduateship Examination of the Institute; it was therefore professionally acceptable from the start. The support of the Institute was not only timely but invaluable, and was critical in getting the course accepted by firms and students alike. As to the Associateship it was in fact never awarded, the course later becoming recognized for the award of the Diploma in Technology.

Other sandwich courses 'leading to the Associateship' were being actively planned in Applied Chemistry, Applied Biology, Metallurgy, Mathematics and Electrical and Mechanical Engineering, and the award for these was also subsequently changed to the Diploma in Technology. One innovation in January 1956 was a sandwich course leading to the degree of B.Sc. Engineering of the University of London; it had to be arranged over five years, not four, to fit in with the Part I, Part II and Part III examinations of the University which were held in June each year, and to allow for four periods of industrial training amounting to two years in all. Such a course satisfied some of the members of the Staff of the engineering departments who were still uncertain about an 'associateship'; I was prepared, albeit with some hesitation, to make the experiment for though the disadvantages of an external course were still present it did offer valuable experience with a sandwich course strongly supported by a local firm.

All the twenty students in the first year of the course were from Napiers and were equally divided between mechanical and electrical engineering. The support of Napiers to Acton Technical College with these sandwich course experiments was as weighty and as valuable as that of Metropolitan Vickers to Salford College of Technology and of the General Electric Company to Birmingham College of Technology. J. S. (later Sir John) Paget, Manager at the firm and a member of the Governing Body of the College, was greatly interested in the new educational arrangements as was J. F. A. Radford, Manager of Personnel Services in the firm. To them both the College owed much; they not only supported the College by sending their student apprentices to the new sandwich courses but contributed much to its educational thinking and particularly to ideas about industrial training. It was through Radford that we developed the ideas associated with an 'industrial tutor' and coined the term before it was adopted by other firms and colleges.

Publication of the Government's White Paper on Technical Education came in February 1956. It caused much excitement in the College as indeed it did elsewhere. Acton was listed amongst the twenty-four colleges in England and Wales which were receiving 75 per cent grant[12] for certain of their advanced courses. 'The Government now wish', the Paper continued, 'to see the proportion of advanced work at these colleges vigorously increased, so that as many of them as possible may develop speedily into colleges of advanced technology.' In this way the intention to create Colleges of Advanced Technology was made public. It was too readily assumed by many that some twenty colleges would be so designated, but in fact only eight were included in the first list that was announced in the House of Commons by the Minister on 21 June, 1956. The same day Circular 305 was issued by the Ministry; it introduced a new nomenclature to distinguish the three major types of technical college to be known as local, area and regional colleges; to these had been added a fourth—Colleges of Advanced Technology,

[12] Circular 255, Ministry of Education. There were over 30 such recognised courses at Acton.

and the Circular defined these colleges more fully and set down the conditions governing their recognition.

Acton Technical College was not included in the provisional list of Colleges of Advanced Technology, nor did it seem likely that it would be among any additions in the foreseeable future; it was by definition (Circular 305) a Regional College. The Minister had expressed the hope that two more colleges of advanced technology would be designated later, 'one in the south-west at Bristol and the other in the north-east, where no existing college was immediately suitable for designation.' This was followed by a statement early in 1957, after a personal visit of the Minister to the North-East, 'that while no existing college seemed to him suitable for designation, he would be prepared to designate the Rutherford Technical College, Newcastle, as a college of advanced technology when the advanced work at that college had developed sufficiently.'[13] In fact the College was not so designated but much later, in 1970, became one of the new Polytechnics.

There was some disappointment at Acton and local patriotism expressed itself in terms of 'no advanced college in Middlesex but three in London'. If however only seven colleges were to be selected from the list of 24 could one really complain about the choice? The seven were the major technical colleges at Birmingham, Bradford, Salford and Cardiff, and three Polytechnics in London—Battersea, Chelsea and Northampton. Loughborough, by then a direct-grant institution, was the eighth. It was perhaps stretching the term College of Advanced Technology far to include a college almost entirely devoted to science, like Chelsea, though no one questioned its eminence amongst the colleges. Some years later it seemed destined to be transformed into a technological university and be moved to Hertfordshire, but other ideas prevailed. It became a School of the University of London, and in 1972, as Chelsea College, was granted a Royal Charter of Incorporation as a School of the University. Looking back this decision now seems almost inevitable.

In 1956, however, the future was not easily discernible. What were the Government's intentions? Did the phrase in the White Paper 'as many of them as possible' mean that other colleges

[13] *Education in 1957*, HMSO, 30.

amongst the 24 would be designated as Colleges of Advanced Technology—soon or at some time in the future? Whatever the answer, and increasingly one got the impression that it was in the negative, there was one sentence in the White Paper that lifted the spirits of many at Acton; it read 'the Government believe that for the highest technological qualifications sandwich courses will become more and more appropriate'. This sentence was blazoned across the next edition of the brochure published by the College on 'Sandwich Courses in Applied Science and Engineering.' This support for the introduction of sandwich courses brought more than a measure of assurance to the Staff that the College, having anticipated national policy, was on the right lines. There was no real alternative to pressing on with the College's educational schemes. 'We are hopeful' I wrote in the Annual Report for 1955–6, 'that when our projected developments, both in buildings and academic policy, are nearer achievement they will be appropriately recognised.' The work of planning and starting new sandwich courses continued unabated; some were introduced hurriedly, and perhaps their innovational elements suffered; others were so novel, like the course in Production Technology, that a long time was needed to launch them. The course in Applied Chemistry started in October 1956, followed by courses in Electrical Engineering and Mechanical Engineering in January 1957. The Department of Mechanical Engineering also started a sandwich course leading to a Higher National Diploma. 'These new sandwich courses began in January 1957, with twenty-seven students in the Diploma in Technology course and eighteen in the Higher National Diploma course' ran its entry in the Report for 1956–7; 'The first College phases of these courses were very satisfactory, but it is clear that some changes in the structure and content of the courses might well be made. The sandwich courses leading to the degree of B.Sc. Engineering attracted twenty-three students in the first year and twenty continued in the second year.' The Department of Electrical Engineering was able to report that there were ten students in the first year of the sandwich course in electrical engineering.

The demands on the staff, and in particular on Heads of Departments, were considerable; new courses had to be devised long before curriculum development had achieved its present-day acceptance; new teaching methods had to be tried, new associations with industry started, and industrial training thought through anew. 'All this has involved the College in a fundamental re-consideration of its educational aims', I wrote in the College Annual Report for 1955–6;

Contents of courses and teaching methods have come under review and the Staff have collectively examined and discussed many of the problems. In connection with the sandwich courses a tutorial system has been introduced; some members of the full-time staff have been appointed as tutors, each responsible for a few students. Tutors visit the students in their firms, and the students come back to the College to talk to their tutors and to discuss with them academic, industrial or personal matters. The College has received much help from many individual industrialists and from many firms.

These new responsibilities were faced by many of the staff with an interest which grew with experience into something bordering on enthusiasm; others found them searching and difficult. But there was a general feeling of pioneering in a novel mode of education and training; the College read the Report on Sandwich Training and Education by the National Advisory Council on Education for Industry and Commerce, which was published as an appendix to the White Paper, with an assurance of being abreast of developments. There was no doubt as to the measure of support for sandwich courses which the National Advisory Council proffered. 'Regional Advisory Councils have been consulted and discussions have been held with representatives of industry and everywhere the Council finds support for its view that all necessary steps should be taken for the development of sandwich courses and particularly of those leading to a high standard of professional training.' The preparation of this report on sandwich courses, it might be added, had been a main pre-occupation of the National Advisory Council during 1954, an indication of the striking revival of interest in these courses. Not only had a number of technical colleges started new courses, mainly in mechanical and electrical engineering, but some of the largest firms had lent active support. 'The number of sandwich courses increased in 1955 from 70 to 100,' noted *Education* in 1955. 'It is expected that many of these new sandwich courses will aim at the standards likely to be required

by the National Council for Technological Awards.' In fact few
of the courses at that time were of this standard. Most of them
prepared students for a Higher National Diploma or a College
Diploma; in 1955–6 only 52 students were in sandwich courses
leading to a degree. There were however nearly 1400 students in
Higher National Diploma[14] sandwich courses, and these were
commonly regarded as of university pass degree standard. Very
few technical colleges were involved, perhaps between 40 and
50, but this was double the number two years earlier. A list
published in 1953 showed only about 40 sandwich courses in 24
technical colleges in England and Wales.[15]

The main recommendations of the National Advisory
Council, however, were concerned not with the type of course,
but with the nature of the award and the character of the new
Council that would be responsible for it. The Minister accepted
the National Advisory Council's proposals and in July 1955
announced the establishment of the National Council for
Technological Awards, with Lord Hives as its first Chairman.
By November the members of this Council and of the two Boards
of Studies had been appointed and the first meetings were held
in December 1955. The Council had eleven members, including
five persons appointed by the Minister; 'four were selected for
their distinction as technologists and one for his knowledge of
local education authority administration'. One of the technologists, Sir Harold Roxbee Cox (later Lord Kings Norton), was
elected vice-Chairman. Of the six members who were nominated
by the Boards of Studies three were teachers from technical
colleges and three were from professional institutions. It was
made very clear that 'all the members of the Council and the
Boards serve as individuals and not as representatives of particular organisations'. I had been nominated by the APTI to
serve on the Board of Studies for technologies other than
engineering and at one of the early meetings was elected vice-
Chairman. As the Chairman, vice-Chairman and one other
member of each Board of Studies were asked to sit on the
Council I found myself a member of the Council from the
very start, and as matters turned out continued as a member

---

[14] *Education in 1958*, HMSO, 43.
[15] H. V. Field, *Sandwich courses* (a) *Educational Standpoint*, Association of Technical
Institutions (ATI), Feb. 1953.

throughout the whole life of the Council—until 1964. It was an experience that served me well in my work at Acton; by the same token my contribution to the work of the Council was grounded in the activities of a College fully committed to sandwich courses.

The Council had been set up as an independent body with the task of creating and administering academic awards gained by students in technical colleges who successfully completed courses approved by the Council. These awards were to be comparable with a university first degree. The Council was not an examining body, although it would necessarily be concerned with the standards of the examinations and the approval of external examiners. As the White Paper explained:

> At the moment, the only national qualification of sufficiently high level for many of the best students attending technical colleges is the London External Degree. This suffers from the disadvantages inherent in external control and is limited to a few technologies. It was therefore considered to be unsuitable as a permanent qualification for colleges of advanced technology. In the National Advisory Council's view the best way of overcoming the difficulty was to create a new qualification of high standing which would allow the colleges freedom to plan their own courses in consultation with industry and the professional bodies and to conduct their own examinations.

The Council (NCTA) got to work quickly, even though F. R. Hornby who was appointed as Secretary in May 1956 was unable to take up his duties until the following September. In the meantime F. G. Ward of the Ministry of Education acted as Secretary and by May 1956 the Council had issued its first memorandum (NCTA 1), announcing that for the time being it would make a first award only, to be called Diploma in Technology or Diploma in Technology (Engineering). The Council had no power to award anything other than a diploma; simply the freedom to choose the diploma's title.

Colleges were naturally interested in, and perhaps somewhat anxious about, the conditions the Council set down for the recognition of courses leading to the new Diploma. Besides the general condition 'the Colleges as a whole will be expected to provide a substantial programme of advanced studies; in particular, the subjects constituting the course must be conducted in an environment where advanced studies are the main preoccupation of the Staff', there were other more particular desiderata.

The College will be expected to provide good library facilities and good social amenities. It is desirable for the College to have residential facilities. The absence of such facilities will not prevent courses being recognised at the moment. It is intended, however, to make this a condition as soon as possible. There must be adequate accommodation and equipment for the course. Facilities should be available for private study. The staff common rooms should be separate from the staff work rooms.

These were stringent demands, having in mind the facilities in technical colleges, even in major institutions, at that period. But the Council was assured that the new Diploma would not gain acceptance alongside a university honours degree, if from the very beginning standards of accommodation, teaching and examining were not high. There can be no doubt that the policy was wise.

As to the award itself there would be two honours classes, first class and second class, and much discussion centred upon the statement 'a student who successfully completes the course will normally reach the level of second class honours.' Also the decision that 'those who do not reach this standard [second class honours] may be considered for the award of the Diploma at the pass level' gave rise to misunderstanding and some mis-representation. But no great harm was done and colleges dealt with the associated problems very sensibly. This was only a small part of the re-orientation they were called upon to make in changing to a system of internal examinations after years immersed in the processes of external degrees and the assessment procedures of national certificates and diplomas. When the Memorandum was republished in revised form, NCTA 1 (revised), in 1961 however the phrasing was changed and included the simple statement: 'there are three classes, first class honours, second class honours, and pass'. Although much of the original document was retained the new version embodied experience of the Council in dealing with courses and colleges, to which reference had already been made in the Council's Annual Reports.[16]

[16] See for instance Report of NCTA for the period Dec. 1955 to July 1957, 5-9.

Following the issue of the Council's first memorandum some colleges quickly submitted applications for the recognition of courses, and the two Boards of Studies became involved in devising procedures for their consideration. Visits to colleges were arranged, as novel an experience for the staff of the colleges as it was for members of the visiting parties, but the arrangements speedily acquired a form that was efficient and at the same time acceptable to colleges. If the courses themselves, their structure and content, often raised difficult educational or academic questions, the facilities of an individual college, its aims, general standards and potential, were sometimes even more difficult to assess and consequently led to a disparity of judgements among the members involved. Few if any of the colleges reached the standards the Council had outlined in its Memorandum; nevertheless colleges and courses were recognized, sometimes subject to certain conditions. Such a policy was justified in that it allowed colleges to run their new courses whilst their amenities were being improved, as they almost invariably were in response to recommendations by the Council's visiting parties. The Report of the Council for the period December 1955 to July 1957 commented,

No single College visited has accommodation which satisfies fully the Council's requirements and in some cases good work is being done in singularly unsuitable accommodation. The most common deficiencies are in respect of accommodation for project work and private study, staff work rooms, laboratories for research by staff, libraries and amenities for students' social activities, but the substantial amount of new building either now in progress, or planned to start in the immediate future, gives firm promise that the majority of these deficiencies will have been met by the time that the renewal of recognition of courses is considered in five years time.

Acton Technical College was among the first colleges to be visited by members of NCTA. The visit took place on 10 January 1957 and following this the College was approved by the Council and four of its sandwich courses—applied physics, applied chemistry, electrical engineering and mechanical engineering—were recognized for the award of the Diploma in Technology. Applied Physics was given retrospective recognition in that the course had started in January 1956 and the

second year was recognized from January 1957. Members of the
visiting party were understandably critical of the accommodation and facilities the College then had, but it was possible to
explain that its new buildings on the Woodlands site were
nearing completion and would assuredly be in use at the
beginning of the following session, in September 1957.

The letter from F. R. Hornby, Secretary of NCTA, intimat-
ing the approval of the Council, dated 7 March 1957 reads as
follows:

The Council's approval is given on the assumption that plans for the
new building as outlined by you will be implemented with all possible
speed.

I am also asked to invite the attention of the College to the following
points:

1. It is suggested that some foreign technical publications should be
   provided in the library and that a microfilm reader might help to
   overcome the present shortage of space.
2. There is an immediate need for more reading room for students
   and this should receive attention by the College. The visiting
   party were informed that the proposed Reading Room in
   Phase II of the new building provides a minimum of 50 places
   and the Council consider that this should be increased if possible.
3. It is hoped that in view of their anticipated rapid growth all
   possible steps will be taken to help Engineering Departments by
   placing at their disposal accommodation in the existing building
   vacated by departments moving to the new building.
4. On form NCTA 3 you stated that the Local Education Authority
   is considering the provision of a hostel and new playing fields, but
   no further information on these matters was given to the visiting
   party. The Council hope that both these matters will receive
   attention.

As to the last point, the Chief Education Officer reported to the
Governing Body a few months later (May 1957) as follows: 'The
College will for the present continue to use the playing fields
of Southall Technical College but negotiations are in progress
for playing fields with suitable dressing accommodation to be
acquired by the College, and it is hoped that a hostel may be
provided adjacent to the proposed playing fields.' These particular plans did not materialize, being overtaken by other
developments. The playing fields of Southall Technical College

however served the Students' Union well; in the Report of the College for 1956–7 the Speaker of the Students' Union wrote: 'The Union obtained the use of a sports field at Warren Park, Hayes, and this together with the excellent pavilion at the grounds was a great boost to the Football and Cricket Clubs, both of which had successful seasons. The Union is, however, still having to hire courts for its Squash, Tennis and Badminton Clubs.'

I had been able to announce to the NCTA visiting party that a new college was to be created. In the Annual Report for 1955–6 some months earlier I had written: 'These developments make it inevitable that, sooner or later, a division into two colleges will have to be made: a College of Technology at Woodlands devoted to the education of technologists and a Technical College (in the new terminology an Area College), occupying the present High Street Buildings and undertaking, in the main, Ordinary National Certificate and craft courses for the training of technicians and craftsmen.' This division in fact took place in September 1957. Two Colleges were established; one retained the old name of Acton Technical College and remained in the old buildings (where it still is), while the other took the name of the distinguished engineer I. K. Brunel, became known as Brunel College of Technology and used the new buildings as its headquarters. Two engineering departments of the new College, mechanical and electrical, had to stay in the old buildings and share them with the Technical College and the Secondary Technical School.

The County Council had it in mind at one time to name the new College the Middlesex College of Technology, or even West Middlesex as another such regional college might be established later elsewhere in the County, possibly at Enfield. In pleading against such a title I suggested the College be given the name of a well-known person, preferably an engineer or scientist, associated in some way with Middlesex or Acton. Besides Brunel a number of names were considered. The chemist, W. H. Perkin, had opened a dye-factory in Greenford in 1856, just after his discovery of the first aniline dye, Tyrian purple or mauve; it was the first factory in that area and the research laboratory he built opposite was still in use in 1957. Another name was Sir Frank Dyson, FRS, a former Astronomer-Royal. Much earlier, in the late sixteenth century, Francis Bacon had lived at Twickenham Park a few miles from the site of the College, but the title of Bacon College of Technology was hardly acceptable (I suggested to the Chairman of the Education Committee), especially for a College which specialised in sandwich courses. However, the decision was with the County Council and they agreed finally (March 1957) to name the College after Brunel. He had been associated with Acton when he built the Great Western Railway through the area in the eighteen thirties,[17] and his magnificent viaduct over the Brent at Hanwell was not far away. The naming of the College did not perhaps seem very important at the time, but the choice of Brunel acquired more and more significance as the years passed. It was a good choice.

To facilitate the creation of the two Colleges I was asked to serve as Principal of both institutions on the understanding that a Principal of Acton Technical College would be appointed later. It was also decided to transfer the Hotel and Catering School to Ealing Technical College which could provide supporting departments, such as Business Administration and General Studies, around which this School was likely to grow and flourish. Likewise some of the Women's work was to be moved to Chiswick Polytechnic. Before the Hotel and Catering School moved the Head had been prevailed upon to start a sandwich course in Catering (a title always likely to raise a smile) on the same pattern as other courses in the College but at a lower level. It was surprising such a course had not been introduced earlier for the changing load of activity in the hotel industry between summer and winter seemed to fit well with the sandwich course educational structure. The catering course made a good start in September 1956, 'the first course of this character to be offered in the field of catering education in this country'.

The session 1956-7 certainly marked the end of an epoch; it was a critical year in many ways and onerous too. Not only was there all the new educational activity associated with the sandwich courses but preparations had to be made to move into new buildings, involving the transfer of much apparatus and equipment. Dr J. H. Skellon, the Head of the Department of

---

[17] The first section of the railway to be completed, that between Paddington and Taplow, was opened to the public on 4 June 1838.

Chemistry and Biology, had devoted much of his time over several years to these buildings, working closely with the County Architects, and many details owed much to him, particularly the services in the laboratories. Planned merely as a 'Science Block' the buildings needed some modifications to serve the new purposes, but little could be done at such a late stage except to partition a few rooms and change some lecture-rooms and laboratories to different uses. During the later stages of the construction a number of small alterations were effected, including the provision of rooms for the Principal and the administrative staff of the College. Laboratories described as intermediate laboratories for chemistry, physics, botany and geology, and intended for large GCE A-level classes, had to be diverted to more advanced work and appropriate modifications made.[18] The situation was made no easier by an earlier decision, dictated by restrictions on expenditure, to omit the top floor of the building—only four of the five floors were completed in the first stage and the temporary roof remained starkly bare with obvious evidences of incompletion. It was strange, at first uncanny, to take the lift to this floor and step out to an open space. One recalls too that although two lifts were originally planned only one was finally allowed; however, two lift-shafts were built—one unused, and there is only one lift even today.

The students were of course greatly interested in the new buildings, not merely because of the new teaching facilities which they awaited with eagerness and impatience, but they had high hopes that some provision would be made for the Students' Union. Indeed one good consequence of the omission of the top floor was the opportunity it presented to replan the floor in accordance with the new needs, and instead of additional classrooms to substitute a students' common-room, students' refectory and kitchen, as well as a staff common-room and staff dining-room. The original intention had been to provide refectories in association with the new accommodation for the Hotel and Catering Department in the next phase of the building programme, but the decision to transfer that Department to Ealing Technical College necessitated a change of plan. Moreover the need for refectories had become urgent.

The Annual Report for 1956-7 recorded that a start on the

[18] See Minute of Middlesex Education Committee, July 1956.

building of the top floor was imminent, and even more important 'the plans for Phase II of the building programme were also carried a stage further during the year'. The intention was to build alongside 'the Science Block' provision for the Engineering Departments so that the whole College could be assembled on one campus and the High Street buildings left for the sole use of Acton Technical College. 'The schedule of accommodation for the Mechanical, Electrical and Chemical Engineering Departments', the Annual Report continued 'was approved by the Ministry of Education, and it is hoped that the building of the Engineering Block will commence in 1958'—a hope that was not realized.

Meanwhile preparations for the occupation of the new buildings in September 1957 went on apace. Of great importance for the future of the two Colleges were decisions concerning the Heads of Departments; five Acton Heads had to be placed and there were several posts available in one College or the other. How could one satisfy the aspirations of the Heads and contribute most effectively to the development of the Colleges? The outcome was that Dr J. H. Skellon was transferred to Brunel College as Head of the Department of Chemistry and Biology (including Metallurgy), and R. A. F. Harcourt as Head of the Department of Management and Production Engineering. The other three Heads were selected to guide the development of Acton Technical College in its new form, W. F. Giddings as Acting or Deputy Principal, J. Atchison as Head of the Science Department and N. O. Spink as Head of the Engineering Department. Perhaps Atchison was the most disappointed person—and with some justification; he had hoped to be offered the Headship of the Physics Department in Brunel for he had built up the work in physics at Acton over many years, and had also devoted a good deal of time to the planning of the physics laboratories in the new building. The seeming harshness of the decision could only be justified in terms of the critical role of Heads of Departments in the future development of the new College. Giddings on the other hand was happy about his new post especially as it was expected to lead to his appointment as Principal which in fact it did. Spink had been Head of the Mechanical Engineering Department for a very short time (since 1955) and could hardly have expected the Headship of a major department in a College such as Brunel was likely to become, but his zeal and organizing ability were outstanding and I felt confident that he would be appointed to the Principal-ship of a Technical College in due course.

Similar problems arose in selecting teaching staff for the two Colleges. Some staff were specially fitted by qualifications and experience to stay at Acton Technical College and were happy to do so. For others who had been associated mainly with advanced work in the College the decision to transfer them to Brunel College was straightforward, but there were a few whose work straddled the activities of both Colleges and in their case the decision was more difficult; some of them may have had mixed feelings about being asked to stay at Acton Technical College. If so they were able, as some did, to apply later for posts at Brunel as that College expanded and its teaching staff increased. Of the 89 members of staff at the time 55 were transferred to Brunel.

The educational activities within the College since 1955, the growing relations with firms and schools, the planning of new courses and of the associated industrial training had in large measure made manifest the interests of the teaching staff and given some indication of the contribution they were likely to make in the future. The choice of those who were to remain at Acton Technical College was also important, for the success of that College in its new role had to be assured. In May 1957 the Education Committee recorded that they had 'authorised the Chairman of the Further Education Sub-Committee to consider and to make appropriate arrangements for the re-distribution of existing staff within the proposed establishments in consultation with the present Chairman and the Principal of Acton Tech-nical College. No promotion or demotions are anticipated, and it is not anticipated that any staff will be left redundant.' In fact the total establishment of full-time teaching staff was increased by ten and vacancies remained to be filled—about 15 vacancies at Brunel, where the approved establishment was 30 Senior Lecturers, 33 Lecturers and 8 Assistants Grade B. At Acton Technical College the establishment was 7 lecturers, 19 Assist-ants Grade B and 2 Assistants Grade A, as well as two Heads of Departments (Grade III) and the Deputy-Principal.

The County Council offered new contracts of service to those members of staff who joined Brunel College, on the understanding that they could remain on the old terms if they so desired. Some of the staff cautiously chose the latter but fairly soon afterwards accepted the new terms.

In those early days sandwich courses certainly had to be sold; the old further education outlook[19] of waiting for the demand for courses to express itself was neither appropriate nor adequate; firms had to be told what the College could offer; schools and potential students (and their parents) had to be similarly informed. To this end meetings of Headmasters and Headmistresses were held in the College, groups of education and personnel officers from firms joining in the discussions, and members of staff became involved in visiting firms and schools. These were early attempts to cultivate a living relationship between the College and the society around it, starting with industry and schools. 'During the year more industrial firms became closely associated with the work of the College', the Annual Report for 1956-7 records; 'of special interest was the formation of the Development Panel in the Department of Management and Production Engineering which may well serve as a pattern of college–industry collaboration in the future.' This Panel grew out of the Tavistock Study[20] in the Department; members of the teaching staff and some representatives of local firms met monthly and considered such topics as the pattern of local industry and industrial training needs, the attachment of College staff to firms and of employees of firms to the College, as well as possible research associated with these problems. The Panel also discussed in great detail the sandwich course in Production Technology which the Department hoped to offer; it was undoubtedly the College course to which industry made the greatest contribution, and was also the most original. The gestation period too was the longest and ironically its originality made its passage through the Subject Board of NCTA slow and difficult.

Other Departments were involved in the outward-looking activity. The Department of Mechanical Engineering recorded:[21] 'the College is indebted to representatives of local

[19] Page 4.
[20] See *New Ways in Management Training*, 80-3.
[21] *Annual Report*, Acton Technical College, 1956-7, 11.

industry, and to headmasters of grammar and secondary modern schools for the active interest which they have taken in the work of the Department, and especially for the help they have given at the many meetings they have attended at the College.'

The extended contacts outside the College were a reflection of the activity within. Meetings of staff were held at which various aspects of the sandwich courses were discussed. Freeing Wednesday afternoons of classes of all kinds, with the dual aim of relieving the students' overloaded time-tables and of fostering Students' Union activities, gave the added bounty of providing a time when the staff were free. Meetings could be arranged with an ease never before possible, both within and without the College. The Staff Association formed an Education Group for the further consideration of educational policy, including teaching programmes and methods. The Fundamentals of Science Group continued to meet in an attempt to formulate a College approach to the teaching of the aspects of science which were their special concern; there were differences of view and different methods were to be tried by different teachers, but there can be little doubt that the whole exercise was of great value and its influence salutary. More attention was also given to 'liberal studies' and a lecturer in English (Mrs. M. Winkler) was appointed who devoted much of her time to this work. The only Department to which she could be attached was Management and Production Engineering, which already had a responsibility for teaching English in some of the engineering classes, a responsibility in which the Head of the Department was specially interested.

Again the White Paper was a source of encouragement to the College in efforts to broaden curricula and widen its educational aims. Therein was a reminder that 'technical education must not be too narrowly vocational'; 'the range of technical education goes far beyond the study of materials and mechanics'; 'such subjects as economics, business management, wage systems and human relations must be given more prominence'; 'in a sense, all technical progress rests upon the common foundation of language, and more attention will have to be given to the teaching of good plain English.' This last point found acceptance among the teaching staff generally, but some of them were less enthusiastic about other features of the 'liberal studies' programme. Was there not an implication of something illiberal about education in science and engineering? And should not 'some of these things' have been taught at school or acquired elsewhere and in other ways? But this questioning was all part of a reorientation of attitudes to learning and teaching, and of the ferment of ideas that was going on—and continued for some years.

There could be no doubt that the Diploma in Technology Courses, supported by various firms, were proving attractive to an increasing number of students who joined firms as student apprentices. The number of college-based students increased too, particularly in the sciences. Some of them came straight from school with at least two A-Level passes in the G.C.E. examination; others were specially selected ordinary national certificate students, the top ten per cent or so of these students being judged capable of following a sandwich course successfully—a confidence which was amply justified. Numbers of full-time students in the College began to rise in 1956-7, as the figures in Table 5.1 show. The figures for 1948-9 are given for comparison (see page 41).

TABLE 5.1

Numbers of Students at Acton Technical College

Session	1948-9	1954-5	1955-6	1956-7
Full-time	385	531	487	568
Part-time	1,270	1,618	1,561	1,651
Evening	2,861	2,493	2,601	2,349
Totals	4,516	4,642	4,649	4,568

The annual Report for 1956-7 also noted that 'over seven hundred students attended post-graduate lectures, which indicates one of the main ways in which the work of the Brunel College of Technology will develop in the future.' Some 34 of these courses were listed; most were held in the evenings but a few, like those in chromatography (a developing interest in the Department of Chemistry), were accommodated with difficulty during the day. Before the Session started in September 1956 there was a three-day conference on electronic digital computers, with a distinguished group of visiting lecturers from the Cambridge University Mathematical Laboratory and from industrial firms. Another burgeoning interest was Nuclear Engineering, in which the County Chief Education Officer showed lively concern,[22] and there were suggestions about a small nuclear reactor being built. The Conference on the Peaceful Uses of Atomic Energy held in Geneva in the summer of 1955 had stimulated a growing involvement in this field.

The White Paper of 1956 painted a broad picture of the technical college scene in England and Wales in the middle nineteen-fifties. There were then about 500 technical or commercial colleges varying from large colleges of technology to small technical institutes, and in addition there were colleges of art, adult education centres and some 9,000[23] evening institutes. The number of students totalled about 2 million, as shown in Table 5.2.

TABLE 5.2

Number of Students in Grant-Aided Establishments of Further Education

(England and Wales in Thousands)

Session	1936-7	1946-7	1954-5 (Provisional)
Full-time	20	45	64
Part-time	89	200	402
Evening only (estimated)	1,094	1,166	1,575
Total	1,203	1,411	2,041

The growth in the last ten years had been extraordinary, particularly bearing in mind the post-war economic disorders and difficulties. The figures would have to be increased even more over the next decade, so the White Paper suggested, for the country faced 'an intense and rising demand for scientific manpower and by no means for men and women with the highest qualifications'. Technicians and craftsmen were needed as well

[22] 'The Middlesex School of Nuclear Physics and Reactor Engineering will ultimately be housed in the Science Block', Middlesex Education Committee, Minutes, Jan. 1956.

[23] These numbers might be compared with those in 1938-9 quoted on page 1.

as technologists. Fortunately 'more boys and girls are staying on at school after the statutory leaving age; more are taking science and more are continuing their education after school; and more are succeeding in the courses on which they have embarked. These are welcome signs that the base of the pyramid is growing stronger. It will also grow larger, since the age-groups from which industry and the technical colleges are now recruiting are the smallest for a hundred years. Soon the figures will climb upwards. Last year the number of 18 year olds in Britain was 640,000; in ten years' time it will be 850,000.'

Already some of these factors were influencing the numbers of science and technology students in the universities, which had reached a peak in 1949-50 and had fallen slightly later.[24] They are now rising again, proclaimed the White Paper; 'In the current session (1955-6) full-time students of science and technology have reached a new peak of 29,013, 124 per cent above the 1938-9 figure. They now represent $34\frac{1}{2}$ per cent of the University student population, as against 26 per cent in 1938-9. The number obtaining first degrees in science and technology is now just over 6,000.' Further increases were to be expected during the quinquennium 1957-62.

On the other hand from advanced courses in technical colleges in England and Wales at that time the annual output was about 9,500—a figure that included roughly 1,000 who gained degrees in science and about 500 who gained degrees in technology. Perhaps about half this total number became technologists, in the sense defined by the White Paper. The Government expressed its intention of putting in hand immediately a five-year programme of development, designed to increase by roughly a half the output of students from advanced courses in technical colleges—from 9,500 to about 15,000. There would also be a proportionate increase of students at the lower levels and it was hoped to double the numbers released for part-time courses during the day. 'This will call for building to be started in the period 1956-61 to the value of about £70 million. When these objectives are secured, the Government will consider what further measures are needed.'

In the euphoric climate of such a five-year plan Brunel College of Technology came into existence. It was just in time.

[24] See page 39.

The White Paper had been greatly influenced by the Report on the 'Recruitment of Scientists and Engineers by the Engineering Industry' published in September 1955 by the Committee on Scientific Man-power, of which Professor S. Zuckerman was Chairman. This Committee had examined some of the consequences of the post-war expansion of university departments of science and technology, aware that some authorities thought the expansion had not gone far enough whereas others feared it might have gone too far. 'Certain sections of the engineering industry seem to take the view that both the expansion of engineering education at the Universities, as well as the encouragement of post-graduate research in engineering at the Universities, conflict with the real interests of industry.' Inquiries showed however that some leading firms were able to recruit only three out of every four graduates for whom they advertised and the Committee came to the conclusion that there was an urgent need to increase the number of graduates further. The importance of quality was again emphasized, as was the need to provide highly specialized post-graduate courses of instruction, 'preferably for men who have had some industrial experience after taking their first degree'—post-experience courses as they came to be called, and in which Acton and other technical colleges were already deeply involved.

The Committee also considered the effect of the expansion in universities on the intellectual level of boys available as student apprentices; had the quality of such boys already deteriorated or was it likely to deteriorate as more and more of the brighter boys were 'creamed off' to the universities? Their answer was fairly confidently no, and in any case there would be a very substantial increase over the next decade in the number of boys reaching the age of eighteen, a consequence of the bulge in the post-war birth rate—a recurring theme.

The conclusion, in so far as one can be drawn from the replies we received, appears to be that industry needs both good student apprentices and good graduates, and that the two are to a large extent complementary, for they are often employed on different work. For the man with a capacity and taste for intellectual work, the universities give the best chance to develop; but for the man with more practical tastes it is felt that the student apprentice schemes have much to offer by way of extra industrial experience at a relatively early age. There is a fairly wide range of talent which could probably benefit equally (though in different ways) from either method of training.

As to the future

the demand by industry for scientists and technologists trained to graduate level is bound to increase at an ever-expanding[25] rate in response to the rapid growth that is taking place in scientific knowledge. Some of the firms we approached appreciate this point fully; at the other end of the scale are those who neither yet want the university trained scientist/engineer, nor indeed have they much call for student apprentices.[26] This will have to change if these firms, and British industry, are to maintain their present competitive positions. The future of our country is vitally dependent on advances in techno-logical knowledge, and these must stem from research work at the universities as well as in industry and government laboratories. In any event, the scale of post-graduate research work in engineering which is contemplated for the expanded university departments as a whole is no greater than is necessary to ensure that these departments will thrive as scientific institutions.

A few months later another report was published by the Committee on Scientific Manpower jointly with the Ministry of Labour and National Service. With a mixture of caution and confidence it concluded:[27]

The statements made by industrialists about their need for scientific manpower should be seen, at least for the next decade, as statements of intention, statements that without scientists and engineers manu-facturers cannot transform the character and also the scale of their operations. At the national level the conclusion that over the next ten to fifteen years we should aim at an annual figure of 'graduations' in pure and applied science of about 20,000, as compared with 10,000 today, is a statement of a minimum goal which needs to be achieved if the economy is to grow at an acceptable rate. If the universities and technical colleges can achieve more, so much the better. We are reluctant to believe that less could be accepted as a target.

The minister accepted the Committee's advice, as the White Paper showed.

[25] The use of this adjective is interesting.
[26] The College's experience with some firms confirmed this.
[27] *Scientific and Engineering Manpower in Great Britain*, HMSO, 1956. Reprinted 1959, 16.

These were views common to many in industry, in universities and in colleges of technology at that time. Some of us had still to learn that man-power planning was far from an exact science; satisfactory estimates of industrial needs proved elusive and forecasts of student numbers were almost as uncertain. The Percy and Barlow Committees had been wide of the mark, and even the University Grants Committee was surprised to find the student population jumping to nearly 90,000[28] in 1956-7. It simply noted in its report[29] that one of the outstanding features of the 1952-7 quinquennium was 'the growth in student-numbers which set in after the effects of the Further Education and Training Scheme had worked themselves out', and confessed 'in our last report we said that the demand for technological courses was less keen than that for courses in pure science. This is no longer the case.' However, elsewhere in the report the UGC noted that

a decline of just under 5,000 in student population between 1949-50 and 1953-54 was the net effect of a decline of about 24,000 in ex-service students holding awards under this scheme (FETS) and an increase of over 19,000 in students in other classes. The main reasons both for the relatively small effect on student numbers of the falling away of the ex-service demand, and for the subsequent increase in numbers, are that the number of pupils remaining at school to the age of 17 and over is nearly twice as great as before the war, and that the ending of the FETS has been largely made good by the great increase in the number of other university awards from public funds.

By the time the report of the next quinquennium (1957-62) came round the UGC was able to comment more positively on the factors that had affected the continued increase in demand for university places. In 1961-2 total numbers reached 113,000, a rise of 40 per cent over the figure for 1953-4; moreover the number of entries had risen by 52 per cent and the number of advanced students by 60 per cent.

The same social factors affected other sectors of higher education including the colleges of advanced technology.

---

[28] See page 39 (Figure 2.1).
[29] *Educational Development, 1952-57*, HMSO, 17.

CHAPTER 6

Brunel College of Technology, 1957-9

THE new College was formally opened on 30 September 1957, by the Minister of Education, Mr Geoffrey Lloyd. He had been Minister for only a few days, having on 17 September succeeded Lord Hailsham who following a Government re-shuffle had been appointed Lord President of the Council. It was the new Minister's first public engagement.

The Minister was received by the Chairman of the Middlesex County Council (County Alderman W. R. M. Chambers, CBE), the Clerk of the County Council, the Chairman of the Middlesex Education Committee and the Chief Education Officer. The Bishop of London was present, as was the Mayor of Acton (Alderman J. A. Sparks, JP, MP) who welcomed the assembly to the Borough. There could be no doubt that the County Council were very proud of the College; though named Brunel it was after all a Middlesex College of Technology, an achievement to be put alongside the major colleges in London established earlier. One day it would no doubt become a College of Advanced Technology.

'Today and for at least a generation ahead,' the Minister said in the course of his opening address, 'the country will have to direct its energies and its ablest men towards the decisive strengthening of the economic sector. The educational reforms could not have been better timed to produce the flow of more highly educated workers essential for the more intricate processes and machines of the atomic and electronic age.' He had high hopes of the four-year sandwich courses which he described as a peculiarly British blend of theoretical study and down-to-earth practical training and an application to industry of the educational system long used in medicine. The name of the great engineer Brunel was commendably appropriate, and he added,

'The achievements of Sir Christopher Hinton and Sir Frank Whittle tell us that Britain still produces great innovating engineers of the highest quality in the world. May our new technological systems help many more to make their mark.' He hoped the new colleges might produce 'leaders of a new kind, highly qualified in the most advanced technologies, yet able to inspire the technicians and workmen around them'.

A small booklet published for the official opening referred to the College's educational aims, described the work of the six departments of the College and pointed the way the College hoped to travel. 'It will be 1960 before the first Diploma in Technology students from the College go out into the world; thereafter they will go in increasing numbers and with, it is hoped, increasing acceptance by industry and society generally.'

The College had a new Governing Body which held its inaugural meeting on 22 May 1957. Only a few months earlier the County Council had drafted an Instrument of Government for the College, had submitted it to the Acton Technical College Governors and to the Acton Divisional Executive for comment, and after making some modifications[1] had adopted an Instrument and Articles of Government much in keeping with current thinking. 'The Governing Body of a Regional College should not exceed about 25 members largely representing the Local Education Authorities of the region together with industry and commerce' read the APTI/ATI report[2] of June 1954. 'The full representation of industry and commerce in a region cannot usually be satisfactorily secured on a Governing Body without unduly increasing its size. It is therefore suggested that Governing Bodies will secure the further assistance of representatives of industry and commerce by setting up Regional College advisory committees.' The Brunel Governing Body was to have a Chairman and 24 members. The Chairman of the Middlesex Education Committee and the Chairman of the Further Education Sub-Committee were the only ex-officio members; six members were to be nominated by the Further Education Sub-Committee; three members by some minor authorities in Middlesex and one by a local education authority other than

---

[1] The Further Education Sub-Committee Panel invited me to their meeting on 20 Feb. 1957, when I was able to present the views of Acton Governors.
[2] See page 69.

Middlesex. The other twelve members were to include five
nominated, one each, by the University of London, the Institution of Mechanical Engineers, the Institution of Electrical
Engineers,[3] the Royal Institute of Chemistry and the Institute
of Physics, and seven nominated to represent industry. The
Chairman was to be appointed on the nomination of the Further
Education Sub-Committee and he 'need not necessarily be
appointed within the foregoing representative Governors'. Sir
Miles Thomas accepted the invitation of the County Council
and became the first Chairman of the Brunel Governing Body;
among his many industrial activities he had been Managing
Director of Morris Motors and Chairman of BOAC, and had
recently been appointed Chairman of Monsanto Chemicals
Ltd. Sir John Paget was elected vice-Chairman by the Governing Body at its meeting in January 1957. The names of the
members of the Governing Body are given in Appendix A.

The Instrument of Government also laid down that 'the Clerk
of the Governing Body shall be the Chief Education Officer or
his representative', and further that 'no member of the teaching
staff or other person employed for the purposes of the College
shall be a Governor thereof'—as with Acton Technical College
the Principal was not a Governor but it is interesting to note the
words 'for the time being' appeared in the first draft of this
clause. The minutes of the inaugural meeting of the Governing
Body record that: 'The Committee decided unanimously to
recommend to the County Council that Dr. J. Topping, M.Sc.,
D.I.C., F.Inst.P., should be appointed the first Principal of
Brunel College of Technology. Dr. Topping was then invited
to join the meeting.'

The Articles of Government were a modification of those that
had applied to Acton Technical College, and continued to apply
to other Technical Colleges in the County; the general intention
was to give the Governing Body more freedom and responsibility, particularly with respect to the appointment of staff. 'The
Governing Body shall be responsible for the appointment of all
teaching staff except only in the case of the Principal, where the
Governing Body shall submit names of three candidates and

[3] Acton Governors had also suggested the Institution of Production Engineers but the
County Council did not wish to increase the numbers and suggested the Institution be
asked to nominate a member of an Advisory Committee.

recommend one of them to the County Council for appointment.' Again 'the numbers and gradings of the heads of department and of the full-time staff shall be determined by the Governing Body after consultation and agreement with the Education Committee.' As to finance 'the Governing Body shall submit to the County Council an annual estimate of income and expenditure required for the purposes of the college for each ensuing financial year in such form and in such time as the County Council may require. The Governing Body shall only incur expenditure within the estimate as approved by the County Council and in particular such expenditure shall not exceed the amount approved by the County Council under each head of the estimate in any year.' The APTI/ATI report had, however, recommended 'direct grants to the Governing Bodies of Regional Colleges based on agreed estimates covering a period of not less than three years,' but this was on the assumption that a Regional Colleges Grants Committee would be established or the Colleges received grants direct from the Ministry— proposals more likely to be applied to Colleges of Advanced Technology than to Regional Colleges.

It was a financial matter that led to the first difficulty between the College Governing Body and the County Education Committee. All went smoothly for the first year; in May 1958 the Governors expressed the opinion that the articles of government 'had proved both satisfactory and adequate' except in one particular and decided to recommend that the articles be amended to give the Governing Body responsibility 'for approving the attendance of teaching staff at conferences and courses . . . and for the granting of any necessary leave of absence with payment of salary . . . (and) reimbursement of travelling and other reasonable out of pocket expenses . . .'. The County Education Committee was initially unable to accept this amendment and it was a year before the matter was resolved, but in April 1959 the Chief Education Officer reported that the County Council had agreed that the articles of government of Middlesex Technical Colleges (not only Brunel[4]) should be amended by the inclusion of an additional paragraph incorporating changes in keeping with the Governors' recommendation, subject to a number of

[4] Though the College had special features it was difficult, if not impossible, to get decisions that applied exclusively to Brunel.

safeguards which were set down in detail. 'The Governors decided to record their appreciation of the action of the County Council.'

The annual estimates were a recurring problem as the Governing Body struggled to find a basis on which their financial requests to the County Council could be framed; Governors familiar with the ways of industry felt particular frustration in conforming with local government regulations. In October 1958, the Clerk provided at the request of the Governors a detailed statement on financial estimates which set out how the County Council's Standing Orders limited the powers delegated to Committees and Sub-Committees, and in consequence those granted to the Brunel Governing Body, and how notwithstanding such delegation certain decisions were reserved to the County Council itself. Committees other than the Education Committee were involved, in particular the Establishment, Finance and General Purposes Committees. There were different procedures for Revenue Estimates and for Capital Estimates and, to the chagrin of some Governors, revenue and capital were defined in a particular and unusual way. Capital estimates were perhaps the more difficult. The Chief Education Officer explained:

As far as the annual estimates of the Governing Body are concerned, however, the bulk of the capital expenditure will at least for the time being arise on new or additional equipment and this is subject to close scrutiny by the Ministry. The Principal is asked to provide by the end of May in each year preliminary details of any new or additional equipment which is likely to be required during the following financial year. After scrutiny and any necessary discussions with the Principal and approval by the Governing Body (usually at the first meeting after the summer vacation) details of the equipment are submitted informally to the Ministry at officer level for approval in principle. The consideration by the Ministry is detailed and involves discussion with the various H.M. Inspectors as to regional development and suitability and cost of the equipment proposed. A period of some 6–8 months usually elapses between the list being submitted to the Ministry and approval in principle being received and substantial alterations are sometimes made. The Governing Body is then advised of the revisions and the formal recommendation to the County Council as required by the Local Government Act is made at this stage on the basis of up-to-date quotations. Subject to consent to the loan being

given by the Ministry of Education the Governing Body may then
authorise the placing of the orders.

To help them with the assessment of the need for new or
additional equipment the Governors decided to enlist the
guidance and assistance of the Advisory Panels, which had been
established to advise the Principal and with a very different
constitution from that of the Advisory Committees which
functioned earlier in accordance with County Council usage. In
particular the Panels included 'representatives of both industry
and the College staff', and six of them, one for each of the main
departments, came into operation towards the end of 1958.
'They contributed significantly to the work of the Departments'
noted the Annual Report for 1958-9 'and helped in the planning of courses, in the selection of projects and with research.'

In due course the Governors agreed to re-constitute the
Finance Sub-Committee, on the lines of a report by a special
group with Sir John Paget as Chairman. The membership was
to include the chairmen of the six Advisory Panels as well as
'a member of the Governing Body who shall have special
responsibility for matters relating to College administration'.
These specialist Governors, as they were called, gained an
insight into the affairs of Departments which enabled them
to speak with authority when particular matters were under
consideration and the Governing Body looked to them for
guidance. 'Specialist members of the Finance Sub-Committee
will be asked particularly to make recommendations to the
Governing Body with regard to items of a capital nature
included in the budget when final sanction to purchase is
requested.' It was an arrangement that worked well and seemed
to give confidence to the Governors that they were exercising the
measure of supervision of financial expenditure that was
expected of them. Indices of expenditure of individual departments were calculated but comparisons continued to worry the
committee; if Physics cost £x per student annually and Social
Sciences £y, what then? A judgement had still to be made as
to how much x might exceed y, and compromises had to be
reached; it was all rather imprecise but the balance of pressures
achieved a rough sort of justice.

Another policy issue which engaged the attention of the

Governors was research activity in the College, its place in the educational schemes and how it could be financed. A report from the Principal in April 1958, outlined the need to appoint research assistants and research fellows, and raised questions as to the acceptance of a research contract from outside the College. At that time research was almost entirely restricted to the Department of Chemistry where a few staff were actively engaged and there were three full-time and sixteen part-time research students. 'In other Departments some members of staff were working on problems of their own choice; three in the Physics Department, one in the Mathematics Department and one in the Management Department. In the last named Department several members of staff were engaged on investigations within industrial firms.' The Governors recommended the appointment of three research assistants immediately and gave continued attention to other ways in which research could be fostered.

It was hoped that finance would be available from industry, the Department of Scientific and Industrial Research and various Foundations. A break-through was not easy; in April 1958 for instance two applications were made to DSIR for grants in support of special researches in the Department of Management and Production Engineering. The applications were unsuccessful but the Human Sciences Committee of DSIR sent two of its members to the College on 20 November 1958 and subsequently the Secretary wrote as follows:

Professors Drever and Gluckman reported to the Human Sciences Committee how impressed they were with what they saw during the visit to the College, and that they regarded Brunel College as a favourable contender amongst the technical colleges for support from the Human Sciences Committee. I have been asked to tell you of these views, which were accepted by the Committee, and to say that we hope that the fact that your earlier applications for grants were turned down will not discourage you from making a further proposal.

The Governors asked the Principal to prepare another paper on research policy, which was presented and considered in April 1959. The Board of Studies had also commented on the paper, which offered a comprehensive review of research in technical colleges generally, referred to the vitalising effect research might have on teaching, and pointed the way ahead, including the development of Research Centres in the College and the extension of sponsored research in association with industrial firms.

The Governors considered that it was essential to ensure a proper balance between the research programme and the teaching responsibilities of the College, and accordingly agreed that the Advisory Panels should be closely concerned with the selection of research projects. With regard to the source of projects, it was felt that the successful connections which the College had already established with Industry in the research field should be extended and further that small firms should be made more aware of the benefits which could be derived from research in technical colleges.

The Principal was asked to prepare a further report both amplifying the details with regard to arrangements for sponsored research and dealing with consultant work which members of the teaching staff might undertake.

These two points were further considered in July, 1959.

The Governors discussed the report at some length and agreed generally with the arrangements suggested. There was, however, some comment on the proposal quoted from the report of the Willis Jackson committee that teaching staff undertaking research and consultation work should be permitted to retain honoraria and fees. A number of the Governors felt colleges should receive a share as a matter of principle. It was finally agreed to keep consultant work in the College under review and to examine further its scope and implications as and when this proved necessary.

The Governors welcomed the reference in the Principal's report to research into teaching methods and asked Dr. Topping to report in due course on the points he had in mind in this field.

Perhaps the most important research development was the application to the Nuffield Foundation for support of a Centre for Psychological and Social Research, a scheme for which Robert Harcourt was initially responsible. The proposals put to the Governing Body in October 1958 envisaged the establishment of a Research Centre within the Department of Management and Production Engineering which included in its staff 'persons with high qualifications and considerable experience, both experimental and clinical, in the conduct of psychological and social research'. Notably Dr Marie Jahoda had joined the

Department a few months earlier; other psychologists on the staff were R. Harcourt, R. Borger and L. F. Thomas. The Department had a number of projects in progress or at the planning stage which to start with were to form the core of the Centre's activities, but the one that engaged my own personal interest was named 'Technical Education and attitudes to work' and seemed to offer an opportunity to examine some of the questions relating to the integration of the academic and industrial phases of sandwich courses which were becoming more and more urgent, and I used what influence I could so to direct the enquiry.

Earlier in January 1958 I had had a talk with L. Farrer-Brown, the Director of the Nuffield Foundation, at the College, but it was not until 15 July 1958 that I sent him a draft prepared by Harcourt of 'some proposals for the establishment of a small centre for psychological and social research into problems of education and training'. In reply he suggested that as he would be away for two months in Africa we might see one of his colleagues, who was able to come to the College on 2 September 1958 and he talked with me, Robert Harcourt and Dr Jahoda. As a result a revised application was drafted, discussed with Sir John Paget and with his approval sent to the Foundation on 22 September. The Foundation acted more speedily than I anticipated; on 30 September Farrer-Brown wrote to say that the day after he got back from Africa there was a Trustees' meeting, and he was able to bring our application forward. The Trustees had reacted sympathetically; he suggested I might go to see him which I did on 3 October, to discover, to my great pleasure, that a grant was likely. I wrote to Dr Gurr on 8 October:

> The Trustees will make their decision towards the end of the month and so I am rather concerned that in spite of the short notice the Governors should consider this at their meeting tomorrow. I have, of course, kept Sir John Paget informed of our tentative application to the Foundation and it had his full support. I should now like to ask the Governors to allow me to make a firm application to the Foundation and to agree to the setting up of a centre for psychological and social research here if, as seems likely, the Trustees of the Foundation agree to make a grant of £15,000.

In recommending the scheme to the Governors I suggested

that 'research which might be fruitful in extending our knowledge of college–industry collaboration in education merits
much more support than the College is at present able itself
to provide'. The Governing Body decided that the proposals
should be submitted to the County Council for consideration
and that 'in the meantime the Principal should continue discussions with the Nuffield Foundation'. In the event the County
Council approved the application,[5] the critical decisions in
support being made by the Further Education Sub-Committee
at a meeting on 28 October to which I was, at Dr Gurr's
suggestion, invited to attend and asked to explain the proposal
—an exceptional happening. The Foundation's response, in a
letter dated 29 October 1958, was to offer the College a grant of
£15,000 over a period of three years, a sum which supplemented
by the County Council enabled the College to appoint and
maintain a small research team. Dr Marie Jahoda was asked to
direct the investigation and the Research Centre came into
being in April 1959. Some months later the County Council
provided accommodation for the Centre in a house at 30, Mill
Hill Road, very near to the College, a facility which proved of
greater value than many realized.

This recital of the main stages in the negotiations perhaps
understates the difficulties encountered, but their successful
outcome is another example of how the seemingly cumbrous
procedures of the County Council could respond generously to
an unusual application from a College pioneering in new fields.
The application was indeed too novel for some of the academic
staff, and even for some Heads of Departments; a few staff felt
they had not been sufficiently consulted, and others were
suspicious of anything emanating from the psychologists in the
department mainly concerned. To dispel their misunderstand-
ings concerning the nature of the project and of the research
methods to be employed, I called a meeting in the College on
10 December 1958, which Dr Jahoda[6] and I addressed; thirty-
six members of staff attended. The outcome was as satisfactory
as could be expected, and Dr Jahoda was able to write later:[7]

[5] Meeting of Middlesex County Council, 31 Dec. 1958.
[6] Dr Jahoda also attended a special meeting of the Board of Studies on 25 Nov. 1958
called to discuss the project. This was lively.
[7] *The Education of Technologists*, Tavistock Publications, 1963, xii.

'My colleagues in the science and engineering departments collaborated fully. . . . This collaboration is all the more appreciated because quite a few of them had, at the outset, to suspend some disbelief in the potential contribution of the human sciences to an understanding of their task.' Perhaps only Dr Jahoda could have achieved such success. It has to be added however that outside the College there were no doubts about the achievement of Brunel in gaining the support and recognition of the Nuffield Foundation for such an investigation; it contributed greatly to the growing reputation of the College.

Whilst the Governors were wrestling with their main preoccupations important developments were taking place in the College that effectively moulded its future. In the brochure used at the official opening of the College, the County Council had expressed some of their hopes for the future:

> The Brunel College of Technology when completed will consist of several blocks of buildings housing departments of science, chemistry, mechanical and civil engineering and electrical engineering, in addition to administrative and communal accommodation. The College will contain 30 laboratories, more than half of which will be allocated to advanced work, post-graduate research and specialised technological studies, and there will be 20 lecture-rooms and two large lecture theatres. The ultimate cost of the College is expected to be in the region of £2 million.

The first part (and as it turned out the only part) of the project to be completed, the Science Block, cost nearly £0.5 million, including fixtures and services but exclusive of furniture and equipment. The original estimate of almost £0.7 million had been severely cut by omitting the top storey, by cancelling the automatic stoking plant and by various other economies.[8] Simply rectangular in design, the building consisted of four storeys of double-banked rooms, with a central entrance hall, staircase and lifts,[9] and was deemed capable of housing some 1,200 students and teaching staff. It was a steel-framed structure, 'cased in concrete, with timber cladding and steel insert windows, and with a certain amount of brickwork to ground floor'. Outwardly attractive it proved a pleasant building to work in. At one end at right-angles to the main

---

[8] Minutes of Middlesex Education Committee, June 1953.
[9] Only one lift.

structure a large lecture theatre had been added, known as the physics lecture theatre but intended to serve the needs of the whole college and to be suitable for functions such as conferences of professional bodies. It seated 260. There was some controversy about its inclusion in the project and in particular about its size, but it proved a godsend for the developing College.

The Chemistry and Biology department occupied one-half of the building; on the ground floor applied chemistry, mainly plastics and metallurgy but including an interesting industrial chemistry laboratory, was concentrated; on the first and second floors were laboratories for physical, organic and inorganic chemistry, as well as a laboratory for radio-chemistry with another alongside devoted to nuclear physics, a vestige of optimistic schemes for nuclear engineering. There were also some small research laboratories, staff rooms, and a tiered lecture room, known as the Chemistry Lecture Theatre, extending from the first floor to the second floor which seated about 90. The third floor (the fourth storey) accommodated biology; there were several laboratories including one devoted to microbiology and another to biochemistry. A greenhouse had been erected on the top of the building, initially the only structure at that level except for a caretaker's flat at the other end. However, the brochure promised 'a kitchen, dining rooms for students and staff and a common room are shortly to be built on the roof'.

The other half of the building had been planned to provide for the Physics Department and the Management work in the College. On the ground floor applied physics balanced applied chemistry at the other end; there was an excellently planned and equipped high vacuum technology laboratory, a workshop with some machine tools which symbolized the importance attached to workshop training as part of the curriculum for physicists, and a few small laboratories for X-ray technology and other applied physics specialisms. The first floor had classrooms, some of which had to be partitioned and used as offices, and three laboratories of which two were assigned to the new Department of Electronics. The second floor had however three other large physics laboratories, and some small rooms used for teaching and research. The Department of Management and Production Engineering occupied rooms on the third floor, including a Conference Room which served the whole College. With great foresight the Head of the Department (Robert Harcourt) insisted that it should be well furnished, with chairs and tables appropriate to its functions and incidentally more tasteful (and costly) than those on the usual County Council lists. On this floor there were also two works-study rooms, a class-room, a workshop, a 'psychology' laboratory and a room which *faute de mieux* was turned into a metrology laboratory; it was neither temperature-humidity controlled nor vibration-free.

After the cramped conditions in the High Street buildings the Science Block seemed a splendid place to move into; spacious, light and colourful it immediately influenced the attitudes of staff and students alike. There were inevitably difficulties, some arising from the creation of new Departments and others from the setting-up of two Colleges and the use of two sets of buildings about half a mile apart. The Departments of Electrical and Mechanical Engineering were still housed in the Acton Technical College building. These were problems destined to stay with the College for many years; later the two sites were ten miles distant, at Acton and at Uxbridge.

A Department of Mathematics had been established by dividing the Department of Physics and Mathematics; similarly a Department of Electronics in addition to a Department of Electrical Engineering had been started, but there were no special facilities for either of these new Departments and somehow provision had to be made using whatever accommodation was available. Heads of Departments had to share rooms and the staff workrooms became very overcrowded.

These new Departments were deemed necessary on several grounds; firstly it was hoped to improve the teaching of mathematics throughout the College (the service function of the Department) and to change the emphasis of the courses towards statistics, numerical analysis and computing, and secondly, to develop courses leading to the Diploma in Technology in Mathematics and so make a contribution to the education and training of industrial mathematicians. As to electronics, I was dissatisfied, as were others at that time, with the teaching of the subject to physicists and engineers, and hoped that a new approach might be fostered by a separate Department of

Electronics with a mixture of electrical engineers and physicists on its staff. I was aware too of the ways in which electronic devices (even gadgetry) were invading other sciences more and more, and surmised that the service teaching function of such a Department would grow in importance with the years. Dr John Crank, a mathematician with many years' experience in industry, was appointed Head of the Department of Mathematics and took up his post on 1 September 1957. The Head of the new Department of Electronics was Dr R. T. A. Howell, who also came to the College from industry and started on 1 January 1958. The new Head of the Department of Mechanical Engineering, Dr J. Houghton, also joined the College on 1 January 1958, followed by Dr C. A. Hogarth as Head of Physics on 1 April 1958, and Dr P. D. Aylett as Head of Electrical Engineering on 1 May 1958—a considerable strengthening of the leadership in the College.

When the College opened in September 1957, some temporary arrangements had to be made. W. F. Giddings continued as Head of the Department of Electrical Engineering besides serving as Deputy Principal of Acton Technical College; C. Davies, Senior Lecturer in Physics, and F. J. Williams, Senior Lecturer in Mechanical Engineering, were asked to serve as acting-Heads of Departments until the newly appointed Heads were able to take up their posts. R. Kitchener, Senior Lecturer in Electrical Engineering, was also given some special responsibility in that Department as Giddings became more and more involved in the affairs of Acton Technical College, of which he was appointed Principal as from 1 September 1958.

The first session was one of improvisation and consolidation.

Educationally the main preoccupation of the College was the development of the sandwich courses leading to the Diploma in Technology [ran the Annual Report for 1957–58]. The course in applied biology was started, and those in applied chemistry, applied physics, electrical engineering and mechanical engineering were continued, and now seem to be well-established. The mathematics course which did not attract enough students this session will start next year [as it did]. Two other courses, in metallurgy and production technology, were submitted during the year to the National Council for Technological Awards and both were approved, so there is every likelihood that next session all the sandwich courses, covering the whole range of engineering and applied science in which the College is interested, will be in operation.

The first submission of the course in Metallurgy had been rejected by the NCTA and the course in Production Technology had an even more difficult passage. In spite of all the time devoted to the latter by the Departmental Development Panel,[10] which included a number of industrial members, the NCTA Subject Panel referred the course back to the College twice and on the second occasion took the unusual step of asking for specimen examination papers for some of the subjects in the course—an index of its outstanding novelty. The course in Metallurgy was deemed 'a very heavy one for four years and might with advantage be spread over five years', a fault common to many courses in the early years of the National Council for Technological Awards. There was, in fact, criticism from within the College that some courses were overloaded and others lacked novelty.

The Staff Association had set up in June 1957 an Education Group which issued a first report the following November, concerned with 'the early phases' of the Diploma in Technology courses. The criticism was direct: 'it is surprising to find the Hives Council approving courses that do not differ radically from degree courses or from courses specifically designed to meet the requirements of certain Professional Institutions'. The College was at fault and examples were cited: 'the staff are open to censure for not having taken advantage of the opportunity available to them when designing a completely new course' was one comment on the Mechanical Engineering course. It was acknowledged however that there were special features[11] in some courses that could with advantage be incorporated in others. The criticisms concerning teaching method and course development were constructive and salutary:

the group is of the opinion that the function of each Diploma in Technology course and the general lines along which the function is to be fulfilled should be explicitly stated, and existing syllabuses and teaching methods revised with these considerations in view. Revision of syllabuses is a short term project, but development of different teaching methods a long one. The educational development necessary

[10] C. Sofer and G. Hutton, 82. See also page 103.   [11] See above.

to make Dip. Tech. courses qualitatively superior to other courses constitutes the most important research problem confronting Colleges such as Brunel, and must be treated as such if Industry is not eventually to reject these courses with the judgment no-change and nothing new.

The Group recommended the formation of an Educational Development Panel 'one of whose functions would be to consider the best ways and means of investigating problems arising from the Dip. Tech. courses'. It was set up immediately, the members being G. D. Smith (Mathematics), F. J. Williams and G. Halcrow (Mechanical Engineering), and L. F. Thomas (Production Engineering and Management); I gladly accepted the invitation to act as Chairman.

The Panel met regularly in the early months of 1958 and one of its first decisions was to try to involve every member of staff in the educational problems that had become apparent and were being tackled by several relatively small groups of staff which had sprung up independently through a number of initiatives. Meetings and discussions on a variety of topics were arranged, and most Wednesday afternoons were filled with one meeting or another, evidence of the College's deep involvement in sandwich course theory and practice. A typical notice read as follows:

Brunel Staff Association Education Development Panel

Wednesday Staff Meetings

2-3.30 p.m.

in Conference Room.

26 March.   1) Liberal Studies 2.
The aims and purpose of English, Fundamentals of Science and Social Studies in Dip. Tech. courses. Discussion and proposals for further action.

23 April.   2) Industrial Training Periods 2.
The purpose and design of the Industrial Training Conference to be held on 21st May.

7 May.   3) Examinations in Dip. Tech. courses.
Dr. Houghton and Mrs. Winkler will open a general discussion on the purpose and method of assessing students' attainments with reference to examinations, prepared work and projects.

There had been earlier meetings on Liberal Studies and Industrial Training, and it was in response to some of the questions raised at the latter meeting that I drafted a paper, 'Some comments on the Diploma in Technology courses', in an attempt to 'make clear what we hope the standard of the Diploma in Technology will be and to indicate some of the differences between Diploma in Technology courses and Degree Courses'. The Industrial Training Conference was, in fact, held on 4 June 1958 and over 50 industrial representatives from some 37 firms or research establishments were present, as well as about 40 members of the academic staff of the College. Sir John Paget of D. Napier and Son, Ltd., Acton, and Vice-Chairman of the Governing Body of the College was Chairman of the Conference and opened the proceedings. Three main topics were discussed; firstly, 'the ways in which Diploma in Technology holders will ultimately be employed. What does industry require from Diploma in Technology courses, given the same human material, which it does not get from degree courses', opened by I. Leff of Glacier Metal Co. and G. W. Warren of GEC Laboratories, Wembley. Secondly, 'the planning of a progressive course of industrial training over the full four year period, with special reference to the integration of the College and works periods', which was opened by I. K. Ferguson of C.A.V., Acton, and thirdly, 'Tutors—their place and function' opened by Dr J. H. Skellon. It was a valuable occasion, not that quick or ready-made solutions were provided but it lent ample support to the belief that sandwich courses are a mode of education and training sustained by college and industry in collaboration. Integration, in the sense of a one-to-one correspondence between the industrial training period and the earlier academic work in the College, might be impossible or even undesirable, but the closest co-operation between the two partners in the enterprise was essential and needed to be developed.

The Annual Report for 1957–8 commented:

The Staff, particularly through the Education Group of the Staff Association, have given much thought to such matters as the industrial training of sandwich course students, to the work of College tutors, to liberal studies and to the reform of laboratory courses in the College schemes. In June, 1958, the Staff were responsible for the holding at the College of a Conference on Diploma in Technology courses which was attended by some 160 teachers drawn from most of the large technical colleges in the country. It was an outstanding success.

The conference had the co-operation of the Association of Teachers in Technical Institutions. A report[12] summarizing the papers and the discussions which was published later, provided an interesting commentary on the problems that were exercising teachers involved in Diploma in Technology courses at that time. These ranged over the whole educational activity associated with the courses, not only their aims and organization, but practical work, projects and teaching methods, the place of liberal studies, industrial training and its integration with the college courses, and examinations and assessment both in the colleges and in the firms. The report is a fascinating historical record of the growing thinking about Diploma in Technology courses. That the conference was held at Brunel College reflected the lively involvement of the staff in this thinking and their concern that the courses should develop in new and educationally sound ways. It was by common consent a direct consequence of the activity of the Educational Development Panel in the College. Moreover it marked appropriately the end of the College's first year.

At this time the number of students was just under two thousand, less than half of the total number of students before the separation into two colleges. There were however some 350 full-time students, including 139 who attended sandwich courses leading to the Diploma in Technology. The following year (1958–9) the number of Diploma in Technology students nearly doubled, and two new courses, in mathematics and metallurgy, were started, making seven such courses in all. Another interesting feature was the number of part-time students, more than 600 and many of them graduates, who attended the short postgraduate courses on special topics, mainly concerned with recent advances in science and technology. There was only a handful of research students, but as noted earlier research in the College received an impetus in several directions, notably through the support from the Nuffield Foundation. Other projects attracted grants from the Salters' Institute and from the Department of Scientific and Industrial Research.

[12] Diploma in Technology, Teachers Conference, 20 June 1958. Brunel College. (Conference Secretary, Eric E. Robinson.)

The Instrument and Articles of Government of the College made no reference to and made no provision for an Academic Board or Board of Studies. This was not unusual at the time; few if any of even the larger Colleges of Technology had an Academic Board. As at Acton Technical College (page 51) the Principal continued to have the responsibility of formulating educational policy; naturally he consulted Heads of Departments and he had the guidance of the Departmental Advisory Committees and later the Advisory Panels. Consultations with Heads went on continuously and, developing a practice started at Acton Technical College earlier, there were also formal meetings of what came to be known as the Heads of Departments Committee, at which the Principal was able to discuss administrative matters with Heads of Departments and share with them the preparation of other proposals. Meetings were held about once a month. In addition the Principal set up a Board of Studies composed of Heads of Departments, a Senior Lecturer from each Department, an additional Senior Lecturer from the Chemistry Department, and four other members. The Board met seven times during the session 1957–8 and twice a term the following session. Minutes of meetings of the Board of Studies were made available in the Library, and summaries of the work of the Heads of Departments Committees appeared in the College News Letter, the first number of which was published in December 1958. It was an attempt to ensure that 'happenings in one Department were made known in another', and that developments in educational policy and plans for the future, particularly concerning buildings, were publicized. Communications within a quickly-growing community became more and more important, and increasingly difficult to achieve in adequate measure. Alongside this need and mixed with it was the growing desire, particularly among the more politically-minded members of staff, for participation (though that word had not come into common parlance) in College government and academic decision-making. The setting-up of a Board of Studies failed to satisfy some members of staff, and in consequence some of the early meetings were difficult, but it did succeed in gaining the support and devotion of others, and provided a useful half-way house (perhaps a necessary one) across the uncharted terrain that had to be traversed before an Academic Board was formally established.

If all the educational activity was very demanding so was the building programme, of which even Phase I had not been fully completed, and Phases II and III were still in prospect. Additions to the Science Block were started in May 1958, and for over a year there was some disruption of the academic work of the College whilst another storey was added to the building. The original plans for the top floor had to be changed to take account of the College's new purposes and different needs;[13] it was found possible within the space available to provide a students' common-room and refectory, kitchens, an animal room and other special rooms for biology (desiderata suggested by the National Council for Technological Awards) and two small class-rooms. These were in some measure make-shift arrangements dictated by the limited space and the constructional complexities,[14] which it must be recognized the County Architects faced with a nice blend of imagination and resignation.

The new facilities came into use in September 1959. 'The work of the Students' Union was greatly helped and the whole life of the College quickened by the new common rooms and refectories which became available at the beginning of the year' ran the Annual Report for 1959–60; 'never were such amenities more appreciated.' For the first two years of the College's existence the students had had to use the 'canteen' at Acton Technical College and so had the staff, although some staff were glad to take lunch in the students' restaurant of the Hotel and Catering School which until facilities became available in Ealing Technical College continued to use buildings and kitchens on the Woodlands site. Moreover, another Woodlands building, the gymnasium of the former secondary school, was temporarily transformed to provide additional canteen facilities for the College.

Other improvisations had to be effected. The College library, for instance, had to be shared between the two locations. 'During the summer vacation, 1957, the stock of books, journals and pamphlets at Acton Technical College was divided, and those for use by students taking advanced courses were transferred to Brunel College', and a temporary 'library' was established in

---

[13] See page 100.
[14] These included the loading limits of the top floor, which precluded the stacking of even a small number of sacks of potatoes in the kitchen area!

a class-room on the second floor. 'Advanced engineering books are still kept at Acton Technical College library, which has its own staff. During the session duplicate records of these books were prepared so that readers could use the catalogue in either library'.[15] These arrangements worked better than some of us initially feared and were only the first in a succession of changes[16] made to provide some semblance of a library. Ideas about using the library 'as an educational instrument'[17] had to be put aside until provision was ampler.

The students formed the Brunel and Acton Colleges Students' Association in the hope that one student organization would serve the purposes of the students of both colleges, but as early as March 1958 a separate Brunel Students' Union was established. However, clubs such as rugger, soccer, cricket and badminton continued to function jointly because of the limited facilities and the relatively small numbers of students. Brunel Union was quickly involved in national students' affairs and one of its leaders, J. F. Corbett, was elected vice-President of the National Union of Students.

There was a constant to-ing and fro-ing of Brunel students and staff between Acton Technical College and the Brunel building; somewhat naturally the latter came to be regarded as *the* College and there developed a feeling of separation into two camps, one better provided than the other. The engineers seemed to enjoy referring to themselves as 'poor relations', an attitude which continued until, some years later, they moved out to Uxbridge into relative affluence.

[15] *Annual Report, 1957–58*, 18.
[16] See page 134.
[17] *Aslib Proceedings*, Vol. 10, No. 1, 1957.

CHAPTER 7

Other Building Plans
(Phases II and III)

THE Governing Body called for regular reports on the building programme, discussion of which became a feature of all the early meetings. After the Science Building two other stages, Phases II and III, had been envisaged and there was general concern that these should be completed speedily. In October 1957, the Clerk explained that part of the Phase II programme had been included in the top-storey contract and would be known in future as the second instalment; the remainder would with Phase III be in the 1958–9 Building Programme and constitute the third instalment. 'It will house the electrical engineering department and mechanical engineering department, including chemical and civil engineering sections, and will include workshops, drawing and design offices, general teaching rooms, lecture, demonstration and tutorial rooms, staff study rooms etc. This phase will also include the library and reading rooms as well as rooms for administrative purposes. 1/16″ Scale drawings have been prepared and are in process of being approved'—so ran the Clerk's report.

When completed the Engineering Building would allow the engineering departments to move from Acton Technical College, giving relief to that College and a new sense of unity to Brunel, besides allowing both Colleges to fulfil the educational programmes they had in mind. A photograph of the model prepared by the County Architect is shown in Plate 3; it adorned the cover of the first number of a new journal with the title *Technical Education* which appeared in February 1959. The buildings with black roofs are those opened in September 1957, and include the Science Building (A) and the physics lecture-theatre (B). A projected six-storey Engineering Building (C) is shown parallel to the Science Building with a link (D) between them. Behind the Engineering Building is a Workshop Block (E). The other building alongside is an Assembly Hall (F).

The Clerk of the Governing Body further reported that the sketch plans had been sent to the Ministry of Education and to the Town Planning Authority for approval. Allowing 21 months for the preparation of working drawings, engineering drawings, bills of quantities and a suitable tendering period, and a further $2\frac{1}{2}$ years for the actual execution of the contract it was suggested that the earliest date for the completion of the project was April 1962—a long way ahead indeed. Even worse, the workshops would be further delayed as they could not be started until the Woodlands Building (the Annexe) was demolished and that in turn depended on transferring the Hotel and Catering School to new accommodation at Ealing Technical College about which no firm decision had at that time been made by the Minister, although anticipating approval the County Architect had prepared sketch plans.

How the needs of an expanding college were to be satisfied over the next three to five years gave rise to some concern. 'For the natural expansion of the Diploma in Technology courses, and assuming all other work is restricted to its present dimensions' I reported to the Governors in April 1959

we shall need at least another ten classrooms (by 1962), six of them next session and the others subsequently. I have suggested that some of our present classrooms might be partitioned, (and) that the Woodlands Gymnasium, which is at present used as a temporary dining-room and will be vacated at the end of this session when the top floor of the Science Block is complete, could be used as a College Library and Reading-room until Phase II (the third instalment) is finished. We are using one of the classrooms as a library and it is exceedingly cramped. A move to the Gymnasium would free this room for its original purpose, and give us much needed space for the library and a room where students could read.

The Governors readily agreed and 'asked that the terms negotiated for the exchange of land to enable the assembly hall to be built should be such as to ensure that the College could use the gymnasium until permanent library accommodation

became available'—in the new Engineering Building! Yet there
were snags; 'although the preliminary plans for the assembly
hall have been approved by the Ministry of Education' the
Clerk reported in July 1959 'some difficulty has arisen with
regard to the necessary acquisition of land. The Minister of
Housing and Local Government does not feel inclined, on the
information before him, to give permission for this development
because it involves the demolition of fifteen houses which would
normally have many years of useful life. The Minister is, however, prepared to consider further representations and these are
being made by the County Council without delay.' The County
Architect was asked nevertheless to proceed with the preparation of detailed drawings. The difficulties were later resolved
and the Gymnasium came into use as a library in September
1959; there was provision for about fifty-four readers, as well as
office and storage space. Strangely enough, though it was only
about 100 metres from the main entrance of the College it
seemed shut away behind the Woodlands Building with a sense
of remoteness, and much to our disappointment was not as well
used as we had hoped. Another move[1] made later transformed
its use and significance in the life of the College.

   With all this involvement in building provision it is not
surprising that the article on 'Technical College Buildings—
their planning, design and equipment' which I was asked to
write for the first number of *Technical Education* (page 132)
opened as follows:

   The planning of a new college is in many ways fascinating, but it
is no easy task. It may be that it is not one of the additional responsibilities that should be laid on the shoulders of a busy principal, who is
necessarily involved in directing the educational programmes of his
college, in stimulating educational ideas and new teaching schemes
amongst his staff, and in taking his rightful place in all the exciting
developments in technological education today. It should, however,
be stressed that there is certainly a need for someone, be it the principal
or a specially appointed planning officer, to act as an essential link
between the architects and the specialists in the departments of the
college—someone able to interpret the needs of the college to the
architects. It is just as well if he is familiar with the Ministry of
Education standards as set out in Building Bulletin No. 5, and with any
special regulations of the local authority.

[1] Page 152.

I was perhaps beginning to feel the burden of several years' arduous work on buildings. Dr Skellon[2] had carried the load of responsibility for Phase I, and indeed continued to help with later phases. I had only a little to do with some of the last-minute changes to the Science Building, but was more intimately concerned with the top-storey additions to that building and with the third instalment as a whole. The College did not have a planning or buildings committee, except in so far as the Governing Body assumed some of the general responsibilities. The building of the college was a County Council concern and the Chief Education Officer and the County Architect with their staff were deeply involved. Dr C. Whitworth, the assistant education officer for further education, and G. A. Holden, of the Architect's Department, shouldered the day-to-day administration of the planning. The County Council made the formal submissions to the Ministry of Education, the College having no direct contacts with the Ministry, but the Principal had many, almost continuous, discussions with H.M. Inspectors about the contents of the schedules of accommodation—the size, number and variety of rooms and laboratories, and the equipment required. In turn the Principal was advised by Heads of Departments and senior staff about the needs and requirements of particular sections of the College and likely developments in the future. The amount of detailed work on equipment and services undertaken by members of staff was considerable. As was to be expected additional requests and proposals for changes continued to be made beyond prescribed dates, much to the disturbance of those preparing drawings or 'finalising' submissions. What was remarkable was not the frustration that everyone experienced at one time or another, but that reasonable orderliness prevailed.

A schedule of accommodation, dated August 1956 and headed Final Schedule, the outcome of much discussion about the provision needed in the engineering building and workshop block, was submitted to the Ministry of Education in January 1958. The County Architect was able to write on 14 March 1958, 'I have conferred informally with the Ministry of Education's Architect who assures me that the project in its new form would appear to be acceptable to him. The Ministry's

[2] Page 99.

maximum permissible nett and gross costs, as stated in their letter of 11 Feb 1958, are applicable to this revised scheme—subject only to any abnormal costs.'

In April 1958 came the news that the Ministry of Education had informed the Chief Education Officer that the estimate for the main engineering and workshop blocks was about £135,000 above the net cost limit of £424,293 which they were prepared to approve and that the ratio of ancillary space[3] to teaching space was too high. The Architect had been asked to prepare a fresh set of draft plans, and a further round of discussions with H.M. Inspectors had to be embarked upon. A new schedule was in due course agreed after a meeting at the College on 4 June 1958 at which Officers of the County Council and several H.M. Inspectors were present. A cost figure of £462,000 was provisionally accepted.

By July 1958 amended plans and schedules had been submitted to the Ministry of Education for approval, but it was clear to everyone, and accepted with resignation, that although the main engineering building might be completed by the end of 1962, the whole project including the workshops could not be finished before 1964. The new Catering School premises at Ealing might be built and occupied by September 1962.

Hopefully the preparatory work went on, the Architect continued with the working drawings as speedily as possible, and among other matters the County Council successfully negotiated an exchange of land with Acton Borough Council to make possible the building of an Assembly Hall (page 134). Moreover by April 1959 the Ministry had re-instated an Assembly Hall in the schedule of accommodation and agreed to include it in the third instalment of the building programme. The latest variation on the completion date was 'the end of 1964'.

For a further year many people—officers of the County Council, the Governors, H.M. Inspectors and staff of the College—continued to devote much time and thought trying to ensure that the construction of the Engineering Building was started. The following extracts from reports to the Governing Body record developments.

[3] Bulletin No. 5 of the Ministry of Education laid down: 'Add an area of circulation space and ancillary accommodation on the basis of a flat rate allowance of one-third of the total area of agreed teaching, administration and communal provision.'

October 1959

Satisfactory progress is being maintained with regard to the preparation of working drawings for both the main engineering block and the assembly hall which form part of the third instalment.

There are no special points to report regarding the erection of the workshop and heavy laboratory block. . . . Work in connection with the Ealing premises is progressing and the bills of quantities are now in course of preparation.

January 1960

Working drawings with regard to the main engineering block and assembly hall are progressing satisfactorily and it is anticipated that the quantity surveyors will be approached at the end of January in connection with the preparation of bills of quantities.

Progress is being maintained with regard to the erection of the catering school at Ealing and tenders are due to be received on 13 January 1960. Work should therefore begin very soon, the contract period being twenty-seven months.

April 1960

(i) Main Engineering Block and Assembly Hall.
It is anticipated that tenders will be received by August 1960 enabling work to be started by November 1960.

(ii) Workshop and Heavy Laboratory Block.
With regard to the erection of the new Catering School at Ealing Technical College which will enable the existing buildings on the Brunel site to be vacated and demolished preparatory to the erection of the Workshop and Heavy Laboratory block, the contract has been completed and is awaiting exchange with the contractor. Work should start on the Ealing site during April 1960.

It was in April 1960 that the County Council authorized, subject to the approval of the Ministry of Education, 'the third phase of the development at Brunel College of Technology at an estimated cost of £405,000'. This was to include the erection of two buildings: (i) a central six-storey block linked to the science block, and (ii) a smaller block containing the hall and its ancillary accommodation.[4]

There had been a new development in January 1960 concerning other building plans which reflected the County Council's interest in providing some hostel accommodation for the College. The Ministry of Education had published an

[4] See Middlesex County Council Minutes, Apr. 1960.

important circular (No. 320) on Hostels in March 1957. The
Governors were informed that 'included in the County Council's
1961/62 building programme which is at present being considered by the Ministry of Education is a project for a college
hostel to be located at Uxbridge Common'. This was the first
indication that land at Uxbridge might be available for the
College, even for an outpost. Much as I welcomed the possibility
of some residential accommodation I was not very enthusiastic
about having a hostel ten or more miles away. However 'after
some discussion with regard to possible alternatives for the site
the Governors agreed to recommend the provision of permanent
hostel accommodation in Uxbridge together with playing
fields'. There was a more general welcome for the accompanying proposal that 'in the meantime as a temporary measure
residential facilities at Brondesbury might be shared equally by
students from Brunel and graduates who are following a one-
year teacher training course at Maria Grey College. The
suggestion is that the two student bodies should form one
residential community and that a warden should be appointed
who would be a member of the academic staff of Brunel
College.' At the next meeting in April 1960 the Governors
carried this proposal a step further by asking the County
Council to agree that the post of Warden at the Brondesbury
Hostel be advertised, but the Governors had second thoughts[5]
about the Uxbridge hostel and 'discussed the desirability of
seeking a site nearer the college without, however, modifying the
plan to provide playing fields at Uxbridge.' Three members of
the Governing Body were asked to make 'urgent enquiries'
about land in the Hammersmith area. These proved fruitless,
but more time became available than was expected, as the
Ministry were not able to include the proposal in the 1961-2
building programme; 'they have, however, provisionally
accepted its inclusion in the Authority's programme for 1962-
63. A draft schedule of accommodation has been prepared in
consultation with the Principal and is at present being considered by H.M. Inspectors. It is anticipated that the final draft
will be available and approved by the Ministry by mid-May.'[6]

[5] The Board of Studies was also opposed and passed a motion: 'This Board is aware
that there is an urgent need for hostel accommodation, but thinks it unwise to proceed at
present to build a hostel on the Uxbridge site', 31 Mar. 1960.
[6] Report of the Clerk, Apr. 1960.

The debate went on however, and six months later (25 October 1960) when the Clerk of the Governing Body confirmed that the Ministry of Education had accepted 'a proposal to erect a College Hostel for 100 students' as part of the 1962–3 building programme a lengthy discussion

centred on whether the Governors should take advantage of the available site at Uxbridge, in spite of its distance from the College, or whether they should defer any decision for a further period, in the hope of finding a nearer site. It was appreciated that delay at this stage would cause the hostel project to be removed from the building programme, and the reinstatement of the hostel project in the building programme in the very near future was understood to be problematical. The Governors agreed that the College Playing Fields should be in the Uxbridge/Hillingdon area, but felt that it was essential that some nearer site be found for the permanent hostel. The Governors thought that if possible the hostel should be situated either on the college site or within walking distance. . . .

As to the temporary hostel at Brondesbury, this opened in September 1960, with eighteen Maria Grey College women graduate students and twenty-three students from Brunel College of whom three were women. A further ten Brunel men students joined in January 1961, and under the direction of Dr A. J. Lacey, lecturer in biology at Brunel who had been appointed Warden, the hostel had a very successful first year. It was an interesting experiment that worked reasonably well and provided experience that served the College well later.

These and other attempts to find accommodation of one kind or another in various locations only emphasized the growing misgivings that the four-acre site on which the new buildings were to be concentrated was fundamentally inadequate. The planning of the Hall had been an exercise in compression. A gymnasium in the original schedule had been postponed 'to a future instalment' because of 'site restrictions'. The Acton Borough Council was pressing to take over the old gymnasium for its own purposes. One or two houses in Mill Hill Road had been acquired for College use, but it was manifest that the housing shortage in the Borough was still so serious that other houses would not become available around the periphery of the site to allow the College to expand. Playing fields and hostels would have to be inconveniently remote.

Nevertheless planning discussions continued throughout the summer term of 1960. There was a conference on 13 July 1960, 'between the College, Local Education Authority[7] and H.M.I. Mr Sutton' at which a final revision of the schedule of accommodation for the workshop block was made. One late decision was not to proceed with the proposed Chemical Engineering Unit. I wrote to Sir John Paget, Chairman[8] of the Governing Body, on 11 July 1960 as follows:

I should explain there is hardly any Chemical Engineering in the College at the moment; only a small H.N.C. course and there is little demand from industry. It does seem foolish, therefore, to provide accommodation for Chemical Engineering, and at the same time restrict the work of the Mechanical and Electrical Engineering Departments. I have become increasingly aware of the rather limited provision we were making for these two Departments, and I think it essential they should be given this additional accommodation. The proposal would allow us to provide some additional space for Metallurgy, as has been strongly recommended by the specialist H.M. Inspector.

The Chief Education Officer wrote to me on 9 September 1960:

HM Inspectors have now finally agreed the revised schedule of accommodation for the Workshop and the Laboratory Block and the Ministry's formal approval is awaited. As indicated in earlier correspondence, variations and additions to approved Schedules which involve excess expenditure or time delay will not normally be approved. I attach for your information six copies of the revised Schedule of Accommodation which is being referred to the County Architect in order that he may prepare a sketch plan for the project. A meeting with HM Inspectors will be arranged as soon as the sketch plan is available.

There is little point in giving details of the final version of the Schedule of Accommodation. It has of course interest as a comment on the prevailing ideas about technical college provision, even for senior colleges. There was the usual array of class-rooms, lecture-rooms, drawing offices, design offices and

[7] Dr G. S. Brosan had taken Dr Whitworth's place as Senior Assistant Education Officer (Technical Education).

[8] He had been appointed Chairman on 6 July 1960 to succeed Sir Miles Thomas who had resigned.

laboratories; a rather large number of class-rooms had been included to balance the shortage of class-rooms in the Science Building which had a relatively large complement of laboratories. A major innovation however was some fourteen small tutorial rooms, each about 14 sq.m. in area, intended as places where members of staff would meet students individually or in small groups—an essential addition if new teaching methods associated with tutorials were to be introduced. These were not individual staff-rooms, but were to be used by members of staff at programmed times. Indeed only Heads of Departments were assigned rooms of their own; other academic staff were accommodated in staff work-rooms in small groups—a far from satisfactory arrangement. About such rooms Building Bulletin No. 5 stated: 'The way in which these rooms are provided will depend on the level and nature of the work done in the college. The important thing is to ensure that staff can use these rooms without inconvenience to one another, which may often mean having a number of small rooms rather than the few larger rooms which might be preferable on other grounds'—and even that was a considerable advance on earlier thinking. In the new Engineering Building there would have been ten staff work-rooms each about 37 sq.m. in area.

The Library was planned to house 15,000 volumes and with a Reading Room providing seating for at least 50; the total area was about 420 sq.m. but 'accommodation adjoining Library and Reading Room should be designed to allow for growth of such facilities'.

The Assembly Hall, which had to satisfy a multitude of needs including examinations, films and plays and special functions, was to seat about 650 and to include a small balcony, projection rooms and dressing-rooms.

Everything at last seemed to be set fair for contracts to be signed and excavations to commence; indeed the Governors were informed on 25 October 1960 that tenders had been received for the Main Engineering Block and Assembly Hall 'and the lowest, from Prestige and Company for £471,000 was approved by the Chairman of the Council in August. Approval from the Ministry of Education is awaited and work will begin when it is received.'

Work did not in fact begin, for it was a very different kind of approval that in due course came from the Ministry, embodying a major change of policy. Difficult but far-reaching decisions[9] were made not to proceed with further building at Acton, the third instalment was to be cancelled, and in its place there would be built 'a completely new College at Uxbridge where there would be ample space for the College buildings, for halls of residence and for playing fields, all part of one campus.'[10]

And as an integral and dominant part of the new policy the College was to be recognized as a College of Advanced Technology. If several years' work had to be abandoned, the future seemed bright.

[9] Chapter 10.
[10] Brunel College of Technology, *Annual Report*, 1960–1, 9.

CHAPTER 8

Brunel College of Technology
1959-61

THE third year in the life of the College (1959-60) was marked
by continued development in all phases of its work. The
Diploma in Technology course in Production Technology
started in September 1959, making eight such courses in all, and
the number of students in these courses rose to 333, some 220 of
them being industry-based. By this time the total number of
students in England and Wales attending sandwich courses
leading to the Diploma in Technology was 3,412. Brunel had
twice as many Diploma in Technology students as any other
regional college, and its numbers exceeded those in some of the
Colleges of Advanced Technology.[1]

There was also an expansion in the number of students
attending part-time day courses, as well as in the numbers in
evening courses of post-diploma and post-graduate standard.
The total college enrolment reached 2,421, a rise of about 450 on
the year before, but the following year (1960-1) there was a fall
to 2,196, mainly because some of the post-graduate courses
though well-supported did not attract the very large numbers
that marked the start.

The pattern of the College's programmes having been
established it was possible to devote more time and thought to
the content of courses, some of which were revised, and to
teaching methods and general academic arrangements. If other
Diploma in Technology courses were to be introduced they
would be in fields new to the College, such as teacher education,
a development in which I particularly wished Brunel to be
involved. There were also new ideas about liberal or general

---
[1] Comparative enrolments are given in Appendix B.

studies, and as recounted earlier a growing involvement in research.

The Nuffield Research Group which began its work in April 1959 presented its first Progress Report[2] in October. J. Parsons had been appointed Research Associate as from 1 September 1959, and a Research Project Advisory Committee had been established which included all Heads of Department and a member of the academic staff of each Department nominated by the Head. The Principal was Chairman. The Staff Asssociation was invited to nominate a member but declined, taking the view that there was 'no objection to members of the Staff Association, nominated by Heads of Department, serving on this committee but they cannot, in any circumstances, be regarded as Staff Association representatives'. The use of the word 'representative' was always fraught with difficulties. *Progress Report No. 1* reviewed the first few months' work of the Group, the purpose of which had been 'to identify some of the factors whose presence or absence appear to enter into the educational impact of the first industrial period'. About a dozen intensive interviews had been conducted with second year students, and a few less systematic discussions with groups of students and individuals had taken place. There had been a directed exploration of the problems and preliminary decisions made about the form the enquiry should take—the research plan, as it was called. Measurements were to be taken at three points in time: at the beginning of the first college period; at the end of the first college period, and at the end of the first industrial period. 'It lies in the logic of such a study of process,' the report added, 'that the variables will serve different formal purposes at different points in time. In this respect a study of process differs both from a merely correlational study and from a fully controlled experimental study'—no doubt the authors had some sceptical technologists in mind! This first report, produced so soon after the start of the enquiry, fulfilled admirably its main purpose of informing all immediately concerned of what was being attempted and how. Copies of the report were distributed to the Governing Body and at the suggestion of the Advisory Committee to members of the Board of Studies.

The second stage of the enquiry turned from the students'

views of the first industrial period to those of the tutors, and *Progress Report No. 2*[3] which appeared in June 1960 surveyed tutors' ideas and opinions elicited through a series of interviews which members of the Nuffield Team conducted with members of the staff; '45 out of 50 tutors agreed to discuss their views of the industrial training period with a member of the Research Centre'. To enshrine in one report 'the outspoken and diverse opinions', some I suspect subject to rapid change, of so many members of the College staff was a major achievement. Three main topics were discussed: the shared responsibility of college and industry for the education and training, the different types of training organization (five were described and their relative merits discussed), and the 'equivalence' of the diploma in technology to a university honours degree. Dr Jahoda was aware that the report was incomplete, obsolete (even then) and controversial, but its reception inside and outside the College justified her hope that it was, at least, a challenge and a help in the task of developing even more appropriate practices and policies. The report was discussed at a staff meeting in July and it was agreed to distribute copies to firms sending students to the College. The Governing Body commended it and proposed an even wider distribution to include all colleges having Diploma in Technology courses. The reactions of interested parties were of importance to the research team—an investigatory technique which I had to learn to appreciate, so different as it was from procedures in natural science.

To continue the assessment of the consequences of the first industrial period the third group to be interviewed was a number of supervisors and training officers in the firms associated with the College. The mode of selection of a sample had to be decided and was discussed by the Advisory Committee in September 1960, when it was also agreed that some members of the teaching staff might help with the lengthy interviewing involved. In fact 30 firms took part, and the shortest interview lasted over an hour and the longest over five hours. The research team had also to maintain the interviewing of students in accordance with the three point plan referred to earlier. There were changes in the team too; J. Parsons resigned as Research

---

[3] *Progress Report No. 2*, June 1960, 'The first industrial period; tutors' views and experiences'.

Associate in December 1960, on being appointed to the academic staff of the college, and he was succeeded by Miss Athol Hughes, who was joint author of *Progress Report No. 3*,[4] issued in March 1961.

Acknowledging the difficulties which beset the task of making the industrial period a genuine component of the educational process, the report discussed the content and organization of the industrial training periods in a number of firms, including the problem of assessment in industrial training. It went on to examine the firms' views of collaboration with the college and in particular their experiences with college tutors—at a time when ideas about the role of tutors, inside and outside the college, were changing quickly, and when some firms were beginning to experiment with company tutors (sometimes known as industrial tutors).[5] The report concluded by questioning where the responsibility for the industrial training lay; should it be 'a shared responsibility on a planned basis through advance negotiations on the organisation and content of the industrial periods'? The College had no doubt as to the desirability of this arrangement, but the interviews with firms 'made it very clear that not all firms see this alternative as the best'. Some firms wished to be fully responsible for the industrial period; others favoured a shared responsibility on an *ad hoc* basis, 'when difficulties are discussed and resolved on the spot by a College tutor and industrial personnel'. There was doubtless much collaborative work still to be done.

The Report was widely distributed, and discussed at a conference held at the College in June 1961, attended by training officers from firms and members of the staff. By the time the Report reached the Governing Body in November 1961, however, its importance was dwarfed by an item on the agenda that referred to the future of the College as a College of Advanced Technology.

By then the project had reached its final year. Originally scheduled to end in April 1962, it was extended to August 1962, by permission of the County Council, on the understanding that the total expenditure would not exceed the initially estimated

[4] *Progress Report No. 3*, March 1961, 'Industrial training periods. Views and experiences in a sample of firms'.
[5] See page 89.

sum of £17,000. It was an unusual if not unique experiment, well-devised and conducted, on which Dr Jahoda received many well-deserved commendations. Her book[6] with the title *The Education of Technologists*, giving a full account of the project, received wide acclaim and has become almost a classic.

Dr Jahoda explained that the investigation began as a study of the development of students' attitudes (my hope was that it might tell us something about the effect on students of the alternation of study and training which characterizes sandwich courses), but branched out into a study of an educational institution. She wrote,

> The pilot study changed somewhat the focus of subsequent more systematic work. It became clear that, notwithstanding the importance of students' attitudes and of any changes in them, the college and the Diploma in Technology were too young as institutions to justify such a relatively specialised focus of research, and that it was more important to make the main distinguishing feature of this new form of higher education—that is, the industrial period and the problem of integrating it with the academic work of the students—the main theme of the three-year project.

The research group collected a good deal of information about students' attitudes to what was taught, showed up some weaknesses in industrial training and in the tutorial system, and made explicit some of the ideas the College had only vaguely formulated about its educational aims. Inevitably some of the College procedures had to be re-thought and various changes had to be made, particularly with respect to the role of tutors and the modes of assessment of work in and out of college. It also turned the thoughts of some of us to teaching methods and strategies of learning.[7]

Other research activities in the College were expected to receive a fillip when the National Council for Technological Awards decided to create a higher award[8] and to give it the title Membership of the College of Technologists (MCT). The Board of Studies responded by setting up a sub-committee which proposed (January 1959) a sequence of internal procedures that should be adopted in dealing with applications for the new

---

[6] Marie Jahoda, Tavistock Publications, 1963. See page 219.
[7] Later work by Dr L. F. Thomas.
[8] An award higher than the Diploma in Technology. NCTA (HA) 1, Oct. 1958.

award. There were in fact very few registrations, only four by March 1961 (one a member of staff), and although it was agreed to set up an Advanced Awards Sub-Committee this never functioned.[9] Nationally too developments were slow; by the end of 1960 NCTA had received a total of 29 applications and 20 of them had been registered. Two years later the number of registrations had risen to 54, and the first two awards had been made.

The College Board of Studies turned its attention to other matters, in particular to liberal studies, and in June 1959 asked a group to consider the provision for the teaching of this component of all the Diploma in Technology courses. The members were Eric E. Robinson (Convener), Dr Marie Jahoda, Mrs M. Winkler, D. J. Isaac, D. G. Mitchell, Dr P. D. Aylett and the Principal (Chairman). It was a strong sub-committee which presented an interim report to the Board in October 1959, followed by further papers in December 1959 and January 1960. A more complete review, headed Report of the General Studies Committee (a new title agreed by the Board earlier), was considered in March 1960, and the recommendations accepted. The interest created in the College was widespread; two Wednesday afternoon meetings of the Staff had been devoted to the subject, and the committee had had a discussion with a group of students who had also been considering the issues. The proposals included a scheme of general studies for the first two years of the courses, based on the rejection of simply adding topics to existing courses and favouring an 'integral approach' comprising three elements called Fundamentals of Science, Fundamentals of Language and Social Studies, which important in their own right were also to provide bases for subsequent work. 'If the first phase courses are successful they will enable the student to benefit fully from various courses and facilities, including formal lecture courses, which would be provided in the third and fourth years.' A new committee was to be asked to help develop the second phase. Special responsibilities for organizing the general studies programmes had been given to Mrs M. C. Winkler (English and Social Studies) and D. J. Isaac (Fundamentals of Science) who in October 1959 were promoted to senior lectureships; the Principal remained in

[9] Board of Studies Minutes, 31 Mar. 1960.

7. Administration Building

8. Communal Building, as later modified. Renamed Refectory Building

9. Lecture Centre from the south-west

general charge. A fairly full account of the proposals appeared in the weekly journal *Technology* in April 1961 under the title 'Liberal Studies reviewed'.

Another problem to which the Board of Studies gave continued attention was the possibility of offering 'end-on' courses, an arrangement which involved dividing the students into two groups and phasing their programmes so that when one group was in college the other was in industry. The obvious advantage for firms was that their manning arrangements could be continuous as they would be able to have students with them throughout the year. For colleges there were a number of disadvantages which one college, Northampton College of Advanced Technology (later City University), managed to live with. For Brunel, however, there were a number of serious difficulties that arose in part from the special character of its student body and the College's concentration on sandwich courses. Unlike Northampton College of Advanced Technology it had no traditional three-year full-time courses.

The Board of Studies had set up a sub-committee on paired courses in March 1958, and later accepted the three main conclusions of the sub-committee, namely, that 'under present conditions it would be extremely difficult to operate end-on courses in this College, that the staggering of courses at different colleges would be the best way of meeting the demand from certain firms for end-on courses, and that the possibility of staggering Diploma in Technology courses should be explored with appropriate colleges in the London area'. It did not prove possible to achieve such a co-operative arrangement; Northampton College of Advanced Technology developed its own end-on schemes; Battersea College of Advanced Technology decided on 'thick-sandwich' courses which included one full year of industrial training and so end-on problems did not arise, and no other college seemed to have a programme of sandwich courses with which dovetailing on a worthwhile scale was possible. It would have meant that a firm would send one group of its apprentices to college A for one part of the year and another group to college B for the other part of the year, theoretically possible no doubt but neither firms nor colleges were then ready to face all the work involved; the demands were too heavy at so early a stage when both partners had still much to learn about industrial training.

Discussions continued desultorily as one or other firm, sending students to the College for the first time, raised questions about the possibility of an end-on scheme. There was a further revival of interest in April 1960, occasioned by a letter from Dr Gurr to the Principal:

In informal conversation with the Ministry of Education it was suggested that the Diploma Course at Brunel should be run 'double-banked' in a similar fashion to those at some Colleges of Advanced Technology. This would mean, of course, a virtual doubling of the staff engaged on courses but would have some advantages in respect of economy of equipment. Before taking the matter any further, I should very much like to know the reaction of your Board of Studies to this suggestion.

The Board of Studies set up aother sub-committee which in due course recommended[10] that 'pending the completion of the new building, it is inadvisable to initiate "double-banked" courses in any department of the college', but went on to suggest that 'the long-term future of sandwich courses in the college with particular reference to end-on courses' should be considered. At a meeting on 7 December 1960 with Dr G. S. Brosan, Senior Assistant Education Officer, present, the Board considered the sub-committee's further report on long-term policy which included a recommendation that 'the College should not make plans to double any of its courses by the introduction of "end-on" courses'. Some relaxation of 'the present rigid 6-month system' should however be considered so as to increase the length of some of the college periods. 'As far as this college is concerned much new development is possible in the Dip. Tech. schemes' the Report went on to stress, 'and we expect the courses to be undergoing continuous, and perhaps radical, change for some years to come. We are anxious to avoid the crystallization, or ossification, of the courses which would accompany the introduction of the end-on system.' In the event the College did not introduce end-on schemes, but for a variety of reasons changed the pattern of the courses in a number of ways; the main change was to reduce the training periods to three by

[10] Board of Studies, 20 June 1960.

eliminating that at the end of the fourth year and extending the fourth college period to a whole academic year. This pattern continued unchanged for many years and still obtains. The fourth-year change was based on experience; firstly, a practice grew up whereby some firms placed the students for the fourth industrial training period in the job they were to do as 'graduates' and so increasingly this period ceased to be part of the course, and secondly the College found that a full academic year was needed between the Part I and Part II examinations held at the end of the third and fourth academic periods.

Outside the College too there was considerable interest in end-on schemes, and early in 1961 the National Advisory Council on Education for Industry and Commerce set up a sub-committee under the Chairmanship of E. L. (later Sir Lionel) Russell, Chief Education Officer, Birmingham, to examine the organization of sandwich courses, and 'in particular the end-on arrangement of courses with a view to using college accommodation, equipment and staff to the best advantage'. The sub-committee was sensitive to the difficulties of colleges such as Brunel, as I found when I was invited to give evidence, and although the report[11] encouraged the introduction of end-on courses where certain conditions were satisfied, it noted that 'there is as yet no widespread demand for the introduction of end-on courses except from certain large companies in the electrical manufacturing industry' and added the caution 'the end-on arrangement inevitably reduces the degree of flexibility available to a college for devising and experimenting with new patterns, and it would in our view be undesirable that any college should, at any rate for the time being, adopt the arrangement for such a high proportion of its sandwich work that it removed its freedom to experiment with other sandwich patterns and to benefit from a study of the results achieved by such experiments'—much in keeping with the Brunel view.

At the meeting of the Board on 7 December Dr Brosan was concerned not only about end-on courses but about hostel provision. In particular he wished to ensure that the Board of Studies appreciated the consequences, as he and the Chief Education Officer saw them, of the College not accepting the County Council's proposal that a permanent hostel should be

[11] NACEIC Report, Nov. 1962, p. 19.

built at Uxbridge. The Board had recorded its opposition at a meeting[12] in March 1960. Dr Brosan stressed that 'a pre-requisite for recognition of a college as a College of Advanced Technology was that firm plans for a Hall of Residence should be in existence',[13] but this changed opinions little. The Principal expressed the view that 'the temporary hostel provision at Brondesbury together with the possibility of the Kew Bridge site would be sufficient to satisfy any Ministry requirements for recognition', and there the problem was left. Urgency was taken out of the decisions by other developments; by the time the Board met again, in February 1961, the Governors[14] had agreed to inform the County Council of their acceptance of proposals that the Engineering Building be not proceeded with and that an enlarged college be built on another site, where presumably space for hostels would be available.

It was immediately clear that for some years ahead, whilst the new college was being planned and constructed, severe accommodation problems would have to be faced. The Governors recommended[15] that pre-fabricated class-rooms, up to the value of £6,000, be erected on the grass verge in front of the College by 1 January 1962. In addition the Woodlands Annexe would, except for some laboratories occupied by Acton Technical College, become available for College use when the Acton Catering School left the site in September 1962. On the other hand, the exchange of land which had been agreed with the Acton Borough Council meant that the old gymnasium, where the College Library was housed,[16] would pass out of college control and other accommodation for the library would have to be provided. The Library Committee of the Board of Studies, which had been set up in March 1958 with Dr J. Crank as Chairman, helped to direct College thinking about the library and the services it should offer as and when better facilities became available.

In fact in January 1962 the library was moved again, this time into a prefabricated building just outside the main entrance to the College which, though not ideally suited to library purposes,

[12] See page 138.
[13] Board of Studies, 7 Dec. 1960. See also Ministry of Education, Circular 320.
[14] See page 142.   [15] Governing Body Minutes, 22 Mar. 1961.
[16] See page 134.

proved invaluable. Its influence was immediate; even in its first year there was a considerable increase in the number of students applying for borrowers' tickets and in the loan figures. Near the library two other huts were erected providing six temporary class-rooms, each with a floor-area of 400 square feet, which relieved the pressure on other accommodation and allowed the College to provide more suitably for the expanding student population. Other prefabricated huts had to be erected later, filling every available corner of the site and making car-parking an increasing irritation.

Looking back it is clearer even than it was at the time how formative the period 1957–61 was in the life of the College; manifestly these were critical years. The account of the early work of the Governing Body and of the Board of Studies has given a glimpse of how the machinery of government and control was tested and fashioned. The College grew, not only in numbers of students and staff, but as an academic community with a life and identity of its own, something more than a mere collection of separate and independent departments. The appointment of new staff was a continuing responsibility at a time when it was necessary not only to maintain a devotion to good teaching and an enthusiasm for the sandwich mode of education, but to improve the levels of research and to introduce new areas of learning and expertise. One quickly recognized that the selection of staff was perhaps the most important of a number of new tasks that faced the Principal. Only too frequently had academics nurtured in other universities to be brought face to face with a new educational philosophy and with different methods of teaching and learning; for them a period of induction, even training, was often necessary.

The number of academic staff increased from 78 in 1957 to 102 in 1961, and new departments were created, though restrictions of accommodation inhibited growth at several points. I was cautious about the proliferation of departments, for I was opposed to the fragmentation of knowledge and the narrowness of teaching and research which separate small departments implied or tended to perpetuate. However, other factors, some strengthened by the possibility of designation as a college of advanced technology and including an urgent need to change old attitudes and to bring in new staff, had a fissiparous effect. I came to accept that new departments had to be established and ways found of ensuring that groups of departments with near affinities worked closely together. Ideas about schools that were introduced later were beginning to take shape.

There seemed little doubt in any quarter that the large Department of Chemistry and Biology, of which Dr J. H. Skellon was Head, should be sub-divided. A new Department of Biology was in fact created and the first Head, Dr J. D. Gillett, OBE, took up his appointment in September 1962; he had earlier given distinguished service in Uganda, at the Virus Research Institute in Entebbe, where he had been Assistant-Director. Other sub-divisions were envisaged but the setting up of Departments of Metallurgy and Polymer Science, or of a School of Materials Science, had to await a more propitious time. Meanwhile three Diploma in Technology courses—in applied chemistry, metallurgy and applied biology—within one department were a considerable responsibility for the staff, who were increasingly involved as tutors, as supervisors of students' final-year projects, and with visits to industrial firms. Nevertheless research expanded; industry financed some research fellowships and two honorary research fellows joined the Department —Dr A. T. James from the National Institute for Medical Research and Dr R. Spence, who was then Deputy Director of the Atomic Energy Research Establishment. 'In addition to research, postgraduate courses theoretical and practical were held in paper chromatography, gas chromatography, polarography, electroanalytical techniques, recent advances in lipid chemistry, radio-chemical analysis, and were attended by graduates from all parts of the country as well as a group from overseas.'[17] Also over five hundred part-time day students attended other courses, leading to Higher National and Endorsed Certificates and to a variety of specialist examinations in plastics, metallurgy and biology. The whole demanded much of the Head.

Similar changes in another wide area comprising management, psychology and production engineering, all of which were the responsibility of a single department with Robert Harcourt as Head, were becoming more and more pressing, and a number of re-arrangements were canvassed. Should the department be

[17] *Annual Report, 1960–61*, 15.

divided and if so how? The Social and Psychological Research Centre had brought into active association psychologists and social scientists, and given strength to the idea of a new department of Psychology and Social Science. The majority of the staff were psychologists and naturally wished to give an emphasis to psychology; my own view was to favour developments covering the social sciences generally. Much depended on the progress of the Nuffield Research Project and the activities that flowed from it. Robert Harcourt wrote in the *Annual Report* for 1960–1:

During the year, the Research Centre was much concerned with the future place of the sciences of behaviour within the College. These sciences form the basis of many technologies in industrial and other large-scale organisations, and though less developed than the natural sciences, have their hard core of concepts, methods and findings which justify their being taught and developed at the College in their own right. It is, therefore, hoped that it will be possible to establish later a Department concerned with Psychology and Social Science; plans are being made for the teaching and research functions of such a Department.

Meanwhile production engineering needed a new impetus; L. H. Hancock who had given devoted service from distant Acton Technical College days was the only production engineer in the department, and there were mounting interests in production engineering in the Department of Mechanical Engineering. The whole college effort in this field required co-ordination and rectification. The growing recognition of the importance of production engineering in industry prompted the question as to whether the Diploma in Technology course in production technology, the acknowledged originality of which derived in part from the composite character of the Department responsible for it, was the appropriate contribution Brunel should be making to the nation's special needs. Was a new department of production engineering necessary? If so, what ought its relationships with the other two departments of engineering to be?

The Annual Report of the Department for 1960–1 recorded that recruitment for the Diploma in Technology course in Production Technology had been poor and that the first-year course scheduled to start in September 1960 had been cancelled. 'During the year, however, the Department visited or corresponded with a large and scattered sample of schools and companies, and twenty-four candidates for this course were provisionally enrolled; of these eleven were finally accepted and began the course in September 1961. Three candidates are College-based and opportunities for works-training have been offered for each of them.' I established an Advisory Panel which comprised A. L. Stuchbery (the Metal Box Company), R. C. J. Whittaker (the Glacier Metal Company), F. W. Cooper (Institution of Production Engineers), D. B. Foster (Consultant) and Harcourt, Maxwell and Hancock from the College; I served as Chairman. The Panel 'met frequently and actively and made recommendations concerning the range of work on production which a department might undertake within a College of Advanced Technology and outlined some of the courses which might be offered'.[18] Later a new department of Production Technology was set up, and R. W. New was appointed the first Head; he joined the College in November 1962.

The planning of the third instalment of the building programme, described in Chapter 7, had concentrated thinking on the future of engineering in the college. Moreover, there had been some significant changes within the engineering departments. In March 1961 Dr G. C. Shipp[19] was appointed Head of the Department of Mechanical Engineering, in succession to Dr J. Houghton who moved to Middlesbrough as Principal of the Constantine Technical College (later to become the Teesside Polytechnic). Somewhat earlier Dr P. D. Aylett had resigned as Head of the Department of Electrical Engineering, having decided to return to industry, and I had felt constrained to recommend that the two departments of Electrical Engineering and Electronics should be combined, reluctant though I was to go back on earlier decisions[20] which established them separately. 'Dr Aylett's resignation provides an opportunity to re-consider the relationship of these two departments,' my report (20 January 1960) to the Governors ran;

It has become increasingly clear that it is difficult to define the frontier between them and the allocation of responsibility for certain

18 *Annual Report, 1960–61*, 22.   19 He later became Vice-Principal.
20 See page 124.

sections of the work, e.g. telecommunications, had become artificial. Moreover the electrical industry in the region from which the College draws most of its students is such that the majority of students wish to specialise in light engineering, rather than in heavy engineering, so that if the Electronics Department were allowed to develop it might seriously reduce the number of students in the other Department. I have therefore come to the conclusion that there would be a real gain in efficiency, and organisational and personal difficulties would be avoided, if the two departments were amalgamated as one. The work of the two departments would not be curtailed in any way, but could develop more easily under the direction of one Head.

I recommended, and it was agreed, that Dr R. T. A. Howell be appointed as Head of the joint Department of Electrical Engineering and Electronics as from 1 May 1960. Also R. D. Kitchener was given special responsibility for the courses in heavy electrical engineering and promoted to a principal lectureship.

In addition to the four departments referred to above (Chemistry and Biology, Management and Production Engineering, Electrical Engineering and Electronics, Mechanical Engineering) there were at the end of the 1960–1 session two other departments, namely, Mathematics and Physics. Both had grown in stature over the past four years. In 1960–1 there were developments in mathematics that were indicative of the pattern of activities ahead; 'the sandwich course leading to the Diploma in Technology in Mathematics[21] was more firmly established with the coming of 14 new students in the first year'; a part-time course in Numerical Analysis and Statistics intended primarily for those engaged in computation and statistics in Government establishments and industry, continued to attract a good number of students (and had the co-operation of other colleges in different parts of the country); ten special evening courses, most of postgraduate standard, were attended by 137 students; and the County Council and the Ministry of Education agreed to the acquisition of an Elliott 803 digital computer by the Department, and it was installed in October 1961. Dr Crank wrote,

we are grateful for this tangible recognition of the status of the Department and of the untiring efforts of the Staff to teach the sort of

[21] *Annual Report, 1960–61*, 23.

mathematics which we believe industry to be looking for. The new installation will greatly facilitate the development of both teaching and research and also, we hope, further strengthen our bonds with industry. Meanwhile, good progress was made in the building up of a general mathematical laboratory. The analogue computer built by Mr. Ritchie and Mr. Young in the Department became operational during the year.

The Physics Department had sent out its first group of Diploma in Technology students in December 1959, and eleven more gained the Diploma in December 1960, three with first-class honours. Thirteen Higher National Certificate successes were recorded, and there was a growing programme of post-graduate lectures. 'Research work on vacuum physics, ultra-sonic propagation in solids, and crystal growing continued and some students' project work opened up new fields such as the eddy-current examination of metals, noise in buildings, and properties of thin films.'

The distribution of students in the College was as shown in Table 8.1.

TABLE 8.1
Number of Students in Each Department, 1960–1

Department	Full-time including Research	Sandwich Courses	Short full-time	Part-time	Total
Chemistry*	4	112	66	533	715
Electrical Engineering and Electronics	2	100	—	320	422
Management and Production	—	9	39	120	168
Mathematics	—	22	—	177	199
Mechanical Engineering	—	94	113	185	392
Physics	—	63	—	164	227
General degree	—	—	—	73	73
Totals	6	400	218	1,572	2,196

* Including Biology and Metallurgy.

Administrative arrangements and provision did not keep pace with the increased responsibilities that had devolved on the College. G. S. Horner, appointed Registrar in June 1957, was

459

faced with the task of building up a central office and co-ordinating much of the work that hitherto had been done in and through departmental offices with little or no central direction. He was responsible, aided by a Deputy Registrar, T. P. Chambers, for all the spending of the College, including specialist departments and the refectories. A growing number of technicians, cooks, caretakers and cleaners all came within his purview and he had a general responsibility for the appointment and service of all such staff. Although he did not act as Clerk of the Governing Body, he had a multitude of contacts with the Middlesex County Council, and served as secretary of the Board of Studies and serviced its committees. He was not adequately paid; in July 1959 the Governors recommended that his salary scale be raised from APT III to APT V, but only after protracted negotiations and the application of considerable pressure by the Governors did the County Council agree to APT IV (as from 1 October 1959). Not surprisingly Horner soon found a more attractive post elsewhere; in August 1960 he moved to Bristol, where provision and attitudes were more liberal, and became Registrar of the Bristol College of Technology at the very moment it was designated a College of Advanced Technology. Later when that College became the University of Bath he was appointed its first Secretary. E. R. Chandler succeeded Horner as Academic Registrar of Brunel College in September 1960.

CHAPTER 9

Some Educational Ideas

EARLIER chapters (particularly Chapter 5) record how the College from 1955 onwards was involved in trying to devise new Diploma in Technology courses and to modify its educational schemes and teaching methods to achieve the aims it had in view. These aims changed little from those originally stated in the first brochure[1] on sandwich courses but they were deepened and strengthened as experience grew. The Nuffield Study was part of that process, and Dr Jahoda in her book *The Education of Technologists* used the findings of the research team to review and clarify some of the issues. The College had by then travelled far; it had not solved all the many problems but it could claim that at least it was beginning to ask the right questions and to make headway towards formulating acceptable answers, particularly about such fundamental concepts in education as relevance and breadth.[2]

National developments ran on similar lines; the first report of the National Council for Technological Awards (NCTA) which covered the period December 1955 to July 1957 referred to some educational features that marked (or should have marked) Diploma in Technology courses. They had been adumbrated in the Council's original memorandum (of May 1956), and included liberal studies and the integration of academic and practical training, as well as an emphasis on the place of a project in the educational schemes and the need for a reasonable amount of time for private study. The memorandum NCTA.1 stated,

Since the courses are intended for those aiming at becoming professional technologists they should include a thorough education in

[1] See page 80 et seq.   [2] See page 127.

the fundamentals of science and technology and their application to development and design. To help fit the students for future responsibilities the courses must include liberal studies and some instruction in the principles of industrial organisation.

And again, 'At a suitable stage in the course, students should be able to participate in a substantial project and facilities should be available for this purpose.' The Council's second report (August 1957 to March 1959) showed their continuing concern about industrial training and liberal studies, while the third report (April 1959 to August 1960) devoted a section to a discussion of projects and cited some of the more outstanding which students had undertaken.

When I wrote the foreword to Dr Jahoda's book my own early enthusiasms had been tempered by experience in and out of the College, and in other colleges into which I had gained an insight as a member of numerous visiting parties from NCTA. For me 'relatedness' had become a dominant theme;[3] I found it more acceptable than the term 'integration' which over-stated what could be attempted, still less achieved. The same change could be found in the first of the industrial training requirements of the Council[4] which read, 'it is of fundamental importance that the academic study and the industrial training which together comprise a course leading to the Diploma in Technology should be as closely *related to each other as is practicable*'.

I was surprised to find that 'relatedness' was a relatively new idea in technical education.[5] I wrote,[6]

it is worthy of note that the separation of theory from practice which started so long ago, and the naive belief that the student 'will apply it in practice' when placed in an industrial situation, still persist, and mar some of our thinking about technical education and render some of our teaching less effective than it should be.

This is not to deny that the courses in many colleges are strongly vocational 'in motive and character', but rather to emphasize the need for a closer relationship between the students' experiences in the colleges and in the firms. The report (1959) of the Central Advisory

---

[3] See page 78.

[4] 'Memorandum on the industrial training of students following courses recognised as leading to the Diploma in Technology', NCTA (IT), 1, May 1960. The Industrial Training Panel was set up about a year earlier with Sir Walter Puckey as Chairman. I was a member.

[5] See page 5.   [6] Jahoda, *Education of Technologists*, Foreword.

Council for Education (England), widely known as the Crowther Report, underlines that many young people in industry today 'are climbing two ladders simultaneously'. It adds:

'One is the apprenticeship ladder, in which the training is practical and (usually, though not invariably) untested by any authority other than the employer . . . Four-fifths of a boy's time is normally spent on this ladder . . . what he does on it is no concern of the educational system. There are, however, disadvantages in too strict a separation between education and industrial training which ought to be closely related' (pp. 334-5).

This last sentence is a magisterial understatement.

When in 1955 Acton Technical College deliberately turned to sandwich courses as the mode of education which the College should foster and develop, it quickly became involved in tackling a number of problems which come under the heading of 'integration' or 'relatedness'. 'Whatever might be the educational validity of sandwich course schemes' I wrote 'and some of us had a strong intuitive feeling that they were soundly based, we soon came to recognise that their success might well depend on the degree of relatedness between the two parts of the courses. Later experience reinforced the suspicion that this was at once the most difficult and the most important element in this form of education.'

Dr Jahoda discussed 'relatedness' in terms of the degree of openness in the educational system; 'It is reasonable to expect that technical education, perhaps more than other forms of education, will benefit from "open" system thinking.' But to what extent should the boundary of the system include industry, and how should the educational and training functions be shared? The Brunel view[7] was that the central task of the College was 'to educate technologists, academically to the level of an honours degree, and to make such arrangements with industry that practical training is related to the students' educational progress. On the other hand, while this combination of academic education and industrial training is deliberately designed for students who plan to make their careers in industry, it must not be designed to serve the more limited goals of a particular industry or company only.'

Though it is sometimes said that sandwich courses merely

[7] Jahoda, 196.

train for industry, even for one industry, it would be nearer the truth to say they educate *through* industry. Deliberately the College used the words 'education and training' inseparably, and in its brochure on sandwich courses quoted a comment by Sir Philip Morris to the effect that 'we customarily talk of a classical education and a scientific training, and we have got into the way of assuming that there is little training in the former and still less education in the latter'.

To use the terms synonymously only confused; they were sometimes qualified as 'academic education' and 'industrial training' to specify that the location was the college and industry respectively. Such usage was not without its difficulties but worked reasonably well. If elsewhere the name 'Training College' was changed to 'College of Education', the education and training of teachers remained the aim.

Dr Jahoda concluded[8] that

in our terminology, the system Diploma in Technology should not include industry, but it should be constructed in such a way that the boundaries are as open to industry as possible in terms of:

consultation on all levels from national policy formation to individual persons in each firm;

inviting industrial participation in examinations;

establishing industrial advisory panels for each department;

organizing advanced courses for industrial personnel;

conducting research on industrial problems;

accepting opportunities offered by industry for college staff to work in a company for limited periods.

Under such conditions of close co-operation, all arrangements in the diploma courses would nevertheless ultimately be subject to final decision within the educational system only.

This summarized effectively the development in the College's outlook and practice.

One of the outstanding advances was related to the tutor system.[9] 'Throughout the course each student has the pastoral guidance of a member of the staff who acts as his tutor not only in the College but whilst the student is in the firm, and keeps closely in touch with him and his industrial supervisors.' This

[8] Jahoda, 206.
[9] 'Some Comments on the Diploma in Technology Courses', by the Principal, Feb. 1958, 5.

was a novel development in the College and in technical education generally; it was not easily achieved; to forge good personal relationships did not come easily to some staff or to some students but on the whole the experiment was successful and affected the teaching for good.[10] Tutors visited students two or three times during each industrial training period, met the education officers in the firm and saw something of the techno-logical work in progress. Whatever good effects these visits had on the quality of the training, and they were not insignificant, no one doubted the importance or the value for the tutor of a renewed acquaintance with current industrial processes. How-ever, the outstanding responsibility for the training lay with the firm; a tutor's visits could correct deficiencies and effect changes, but to ensure that a well-devised scheme of training achieved the aims which the College and the firm had initially agreed some-thing more was needed; further steps had to be taken. It was out of the College's deliberations with one firm[11] that the idea of appointing industrial tutors arose; there was common recogni-tion that day-to-day supervision by a technologist with whom the student worked in the firm was essential and that such a person should formally be given a supervisory responsibility and appointed 'industrial tutor', an arrangement that other firms adopted in due course. Good relationships between industrial and academic tutors were crucial, and helped to strengthen the bond between the College and the firm. At a conference on industrial training held at the College one industrialist sug-gested 'that the next step was for industrial tutors to visit the students in their college period'; certainly there was a recogni-tion that industrial tutors needed to be familiar with the content of the academic courses students were following. To this end the College's booklet on industrial training summarised the cur-riculum in each year of the course and suggested the broad lines of the associated training.

It is hoped that the firm will appoint an industrial tutor to the student. The industrial tutor should be in such a professional position that he can be a model to the student's ambition. He will cooperate in arranging the training schemes and meet the student for short periods at regular intervals, say weekly or fortnightly for consultations and be available at fairly short notice if necessary; he might arrange short

[10] See page 92.   [11] See page 89.

projects or assignments for the student. Personal contact with a professional person is of particular value to students in the earlier part of their course, when they may feel that the work on which they are engaged has little to do with the technology at which they are aiming. While the duties of an industrial tutor might seem a heavy burden to impose on busy men, it has not been difficult in some firms to find suitable technologists, genuinely interested in education, prepared to give their time in this way.[12]

The College was indeed fortunate to have such support.

The tutorial difficulties were not all in the firms; the College itself had to devise appropriate arrangements, and notes for the guidance of academic tutors had to be written. 'It would seem that as a College we are not as clear about our aims as we ought to be,' I wrote in February 1958;[13] 'tutors are not adequately aware of the role they have to fill, students find the tutor-student relationship novel and some are at a loss to know what to do, and industrial firms are probably less clear than we are as to the place and function of tutors in our schemes.'

There was much discussion and some innovation; tutorial-days were held when all students, once during each industrial period, returned to the College, met their tutors and lecturers, and exchanged experience in general conference. A number of other practices were established and formally set down for the guidance of staff; it was intended that they would also help the student realize that the firm and the College were committed to the same educational aims. (The Nuffield Research Group reported students' comments in answer to the question 'How much relation, if any, was there between what you did in industry and what you did in College?' The answers showed as Dr Jahoda picturesquely wrote 'a much more relaxed attitude about the problem of integration than exists among educators.' But all together almost half the students (45 per cent) were aware of some connection.)

The College's general procedures were of course refined and modified from time to time as experience broadened; for instance tutorial-days lost their initial significance and were gradually abandoned by some departments; however, they

---

[12] *Industrial Training for degrees in technology*, Brunel, Jan. 1970, 8.
[13] 'Some Notes on the tutor system for the guidance of staff', by the Principal, Feb. 1958, 4.

retained importance for first-year students even when second and third year students found them unnecessary.

In the booklet on industrial training the College later distilled the essence of its practices in the form of a number of general principles 'offered as a guide in the formulation of training schemes'; they included:[14]

The student should work in company with, or under the direct supervision of other engineers, scientists or mathematicians.

The student should at some stage be given opportunity to learn something of the whole range of work undertaken by the Company, to appreciate the importance of his field of work in the Company's activities, and to gain insight into its mode of operation and into some of the economic and managerial problems involved.

Some assessment of the student's industrial training should be attempted; this could be by means of an oral examination, or an essay. The company is invited to report to the College at the end of each industrial period.

The need for good industrial training that made itself felt at this time was one of the factors that led to the Industrial Training Act of 1964 and the proliferation of Industrial Training Boards thereafter.

THE PROJECT

Another link between the College and the firms (including other extra-mural institutions that provided the practical training) was the project[15] which each student undertook, normally in his final year; usually it was closely related to his experience in the firm, was sometimes suggested by the student himself, and occasionally arose from research work being done in the College. But in all cases the project had, for the student at least, a research element in it and was intended to provide him with the discipline and excitement of working on the boundaries of knowledge. Only too often did university students have to wait until the postgraduate stage and consequently some missed this experience altogether. The project was designed to fill the gap and did so admirably.

This is not to claim that projects were a completely new departure; in technical education perhaps, but they had been

---

[14] Industrial Training, Brunel, 1970, 5.   [15] See page 82.

used earlier in a number of universities with success (and given up in others). In some university physics departments for instance a project had replaced the final practical examination. The Hale Committee on University Teaching Methods[16] said little about projects except to comment on the great variety of forms of practical work ranging from the set experiment 'to the open-ended research project in the later years differing only in scope and duration from the work of a postgraduate research student'. What was specially distinctive of many of the projects in sandwich courses was that they were real problems arising from a real situation in a firm the student knew at first hand.

The interest these problems provoked was exceptional. Students became so engrossed that they often spent undue time on their projects and had to be restrained. Staff too became deeply involved; they gave guidance to students of course but sometimes their contribution was considerable and not easily isolated from that of the student. Marking of projects was for this and other reasons far from easy, and even when this was satisfactorily achieved to combine the grading of the project with marks gained in the written examination papers remained a problem and relative weightings varied from department to department. The educational value of the project was however not in doubt; by common consent it was one of the most fruitful elements of sandwich course arrangements, as beneficial to the student as it was stimulating to his tutor.

One useful by-product was that a project sometimes expanded into a research topic which staff and/or student pursued further. Projects also led to a deeper questioning of the place of 'problem-solving' in educational processes and in particular the *raison d'être* of college practical work was seriously examined and considerable revisions made. I have to confess that I had hoped that greater changes would have resulted from the students' spending nearly half their time in industry, but it proved impossible to devise a multiplicity of college laboratory programmes that complemented each student's industrial experience. There were of course a number of basic techniques that could best be learnt or acquired in the college laboratories and for this certain items of equipment were essential, but the nature and extent of the other specialist equipment that was necessary were questions

[16] See page 176.

that did not seem to get the full exploration they merited. Departmental Advisory Panels turned to them from time to time but too often the discussion ranged round some particular piece of equipment, usually costly, rather than the general principles guiding what should be acquired and why. No informed visitor to the laboratories could have deduced from the range of equipment that sandwich courses were the main preoccupation of the College.

Distinguishing features were however apparent elsewhere, not least in the contents of the courses and their general framework.

BREADTH AND DEPTH

The Diploma in Technology courses in science and engineering were specially designed for those who intended to become technologists. Such titles as applied biology, applied chemistry, applied physics and mathematics with technological applications (applied mathematics was ruled out by the traditional use of that term) were intended to denote the special emphases of the courses both in content and in teaching method, and that they had relevance to the particular contributions scientists and technologists could be expected to make to society. Designed for specialists they were however broad-based and included studies that complemented the particular specialism. Course content though important was not the only consideration; proper regard had to be given to the avoidance of over-crowded syllabuses, to the teaching methods employed and, as mentioned earlier, to the nature of laboratory work and the general use of the students' experience in industry. Some of the courses showed major departures from the university norm, not surprisingly perhaps as they were devised with the help of technologists and others in industry. University courses changed too and there were mutually interacting influences.

I wrote in an article[17] with the title 'Liberal Studies Reviewed':

There must be many ways of attempting to provide a liberal education. There are peculiar pedagogic problems for students of science and engineering; there are different ones for those whose main

[17] *Technology*, Apr. 1961.

studies are in modern languages, or history or classics. There can, however, be no excuse for not allowing the specialist subjects to provide the fullest measure of 'liberalization' of which, in the hands of good teachers, they are capable. We cannot be satisfied, for instance, if mathematics and science are taught in a narrow way. It would be alarming if we omitted or neglected just those aspects of these subjects in which the liberal element might mainly reside.

It is natural, then, in approaching the problem of providing a broader education for scientists and engineers to emphasize the need for some reform of the teaching of scientific and technological subjects. There is much that can and ought to be done in this respect, but I do not think reform, by itself, would achieve all that is needed. It is necessary but not sufficient. There are other methods we might employ, other subjects we can and must use.

Considerations of breadth led the College (see page 82) to include some liberal studies—later called general studies (page 148) and later still complementary studies (page 292)—additions to the curriculum, of themselves not necessarily 'liberalizing', but intended to help the College to provide a broader education. It was soon realized that adding subjects to a curriculum was beset with problems; there was in fact a real danger in asking specialists on the staff to teach what were called 'liberal studies', for it could encourage other teachers to feel they had no responsibility for contributing to the 'liberalizing process' through their own teaching. The notion that all teachers have a measure of responsibility for providing a liberal education is an obvious one, but the College found the process of accepting this helpful and illuminating.

The first additions were English, Social Studies and a course called, for want of a better name, Fundamentals of Science (page 82). The first two might well have been called Fundamentals of Language and Fundamentals of Society. The ideas behind them were simple. The College considered it important, and found it necessary, to help the students to express themselves in speech and writing. Secondly, students live in a world of people as well as things, and it was considered essential that they should have some introduction to the study of people and society and to the social sciences, and so be helped to sense the complexity of many social phenomena.

It was readily admitted 'that there are plenty of other

desirable additions, if time were not so limited. But with general studies, as well as with the main subjects, there is a great danger of overloading students by overcrowding the syllabuses and of inviting failure by attempting too much. We have constantly to remember that breadth in education is not provided by mere extent of subject matter.' In particular, general studies were not likely to achieve 'liberality' through the provision of more and more courses in other subjects, good as each may be.

'Our principal challenge is to try and provide a good education through a deep enough study over a limited range, assured that if we have done our job properly students will be able to tackle new fields of study later with confidence and success. If they cannot tackle new work unaided they have not been educated, they have merely been taught.'

TEACHING METHODS

To achieve a balance of breadth and depth was one thing; to experiment with new teaching methods was another. 'As all our first year courses in English are conducted as discussion groups the first need is one of induction—to the new methods', wrote the lecturer in English, and 'both training and practice in discussion are needed and difficult to initiate.'

The early experiments with the teaching of social studies included first- and second-year lecture courses of one hour a week on industrial history, social psychology, the psychology of perception, learning and skill, and industrial psychology. One lecturer commented: 'My lectures suffer from informality and an unscientific approach to my material, but I make no apologies for this because I think I have been successful on the whole in my threefold aim: to arouse the students' curiosity, to prod them into an awareness of how interesting life is, and people in particular, and to encourage in them a sense of being involved in the world.' He added: 'The engineers expected to be involved in human problems in industry and the O.N.C. lads had experience of the shop floor. The physicists, in spite of one six months industrial period, did not identify themselves with industry as much as with science. Industry was almost a second best; certainly they did not see themselves as future managers. They would have preferred more formal, information-packed lectures than the stimulation type of teaching I was doing.'

The physicists however (and others) found John Isaac's treatment of Fundamentals of Science (page 82) very stimulating indeed. I recall the delightful experience of listening to three physics students effectively convincing some sceptical members of staff of the Department of Mechanical Engineering that 'there was something in this fundamentals of science idea after all'. Dr Jahoda commented:[18]

> Among the three subjects taught to first-year students under the heading of general studies, Fundamentals of Science has a special place. Not only is it mentioned spontaneously by all students slightly more often than the other two subjects (39 free comments versus 33 and 33), but those who do mention it speak about it as an important intellectual event and, with the exception of one student, entirely in positive terms.

The Fundamentals of Science courses were not intended simply as introductions to the history and philosophy of science. They arose from a concern about some deficiencies in university science courses, such as the lack of explicit teaching of scientific method and the absence of any serious consideration of how science has developed in history and how it has influenced, and been influenced by, society. Students seemed to have little understanding of the nature of 'explanation', of the sort of answers that are acceptable in science, and of the use of concepts and models in all scientific work.

Isaac maintained that courses in the history and philosophy of science were likely to fail unless they were preceded by some discussion of the place of concepts in science. 'Students enter Diploma in Technology courses', he wrote, 'with an attitude to science which retards their learning even in their main subjects. To them science is down to earth—it has to do with facts, not ideas. For many students, at this stage, concepts in science have a physical existence.'

One of the main achievements of the courses, as conducted by Isaac and his associates, was that students were led

> to recognise that science provides an imaginative interpretation of the physical world rather than a realistic description. This is important in itself, but it has also removed hindrances to their appreciation of other branches of knowledge; social science and psychology, for instance,

[18] Jahoda, 90.

have become respectable and, partially at least, acceptable; they are no longer simply 'all talk'. Such a change of attitude has not been effected easily but only by an inspired use of group discussion, which is unusual if not unique in technical college teaching.[19]

About the same time as Isaac was developing his methods at Brunel Mrs M. L. Johnson Abercrombie was involved in an exciting teaching project with medical students at University College, London which she described in her important book *The Anatomy of Judgment*. Like Isaac she used not the formal lecture or tutorial teaching to small groups but free group discussion with about twelve students in each class.

It will be clear that freedom and spontaneity of discussion is essential to this type of course [she wrote][20] and that this entails the danger that it may appear chaotic and meaningless. It often seems that discussion goes off the point, but it must be remembered that what is a red herring to one person is relevant to another. . . . It often happened that a student spontaneously announced that the relevance of certain passages which bored or puzzled him at the time had become clear in retrospect, or on listening to recordings. It is the teacher's job to make clear the relation of such significant red herrings to the main topic.

Mrs Abercrombie and Professor H. Levy,[21] of Imperial College, London, were two of the outside speakers who came to join in discussions with the staff of the College on Wednesday afternoons.

After the early years of experimentation there was general recognition that 'liberal studies' needed a new structure, and in June 1959 the Academic Board asked a group of its members (page 148) to examine the provision anew. They came to the conclusion that certain introductory classes were necessary, if the students were to profit from formal lecture-courses outside their main specialisms, and so recommended a two-phase programme. The first phase was to extend over the first two years of each Diploma course and to comprise the three elements English, Social Relations and Fundamentals of Science, and the aim would be to change some of the students' attitudes to knowledge and to learning, to help the students to express

[19] J. Topping, *Liberal Studies Reviewed*.
[20] *The Anatomy of Judgment*, Hutchinson, London, 1960, Chapter 5.
[21] A distinguished lecturer, ahead of his time on many aspects of teaching science.

themselves better in speech and in writing, as well as to appreciate the social forces to which they were subject and to which they contributed. The classes were to be conducted as discussions with small groups of eight to twelve students.

In the second phase, covering the third and fourth years, the classes were to be more formal, conducted as lecture-discussions in bigger groups, and planned so that several, from which the student could choose, were going on at the same time. It was expected that courses in the second phase would grow naturally from those in the first; courses in the history of science, in scientific method and in philosophy would follow the fundamentals of science courses; the English course would lead to courses in literature and the arts, including music and painting; interest in foreign languages would grow and the first-phase discussions on social relations would stimulate interest in the social sciences and psychology.

As to examinations associated with liberal studies there were some who dismissed them as an illiberal process. My view was that the case for examinations was as soundly based as that for examinations in other subjects, and it was important that liberal studies should not lose status in the eyes of the student and be regarded as a mere appendage to the curriculum 'because we do not examine in them'. I readily acknowledged, however, that the appropriate modes of examination were not necessarily those commonly used with other subjects, and that the possibilities of oral examinations should be explored to the full. In English a pattern was developed whereby in their second term at the College students chose a theme and wrote a paper on it. 'This is orally examined by the English lecturer and a member of the student's own department, who together interview each student. Their responsibility for the choice of theme and the method of examination', wrote the lecturer in English, 'have been most valuable in convincing students of the difficulties of handling and exploring ideas.' As a mode of examination it proved acceptable to staff and students and subtly influenced attitudes towards examinations and assessment. I had hoped it might be extended, as in continental countries, to technological subjects.

General studies, aided no doubt by their novelty, gave rise in these various ways to a number of innovations, but the heavy hand of tradition retarded major changes in the teaching of the scientific and technological subjects. The project and the laboratory classes, as mentioned earlier, offered the main areas for new developments but the lecture system was retained and changed little. However, the students' practical training outside the college made it possible to teach through an appeal to the world of industry as well as the natural world of physical science or the built environment of the architect and engineer, and so enabled the teacher to combine theory and practice more effectively. There are some students whose learning processes do not seem to depend greatly on first-hand experience or on visual and practical aids, but many more are stimulated thereby, have their imagination excited and their learning quickened. For these students the alternation of academic study and practical experience provided by sandwich courses is fruitful and conducive to the further development of their powers. Added to this must be the satisfaction in the acquisition of certain practical skills, the sense of independence and growing maturity of the students arising from their industrial experience and their mixing with men of backgrounds, skills and outlooks different from their own; these are all elements in the sandwich mode of education and training which are not to be under-estimated.

CHANGES IN UNIVERSITIES

Universities were quite independently subjecting their own educational schemes and practices to critical examination, and it is a sad comment on the barriers between 'the two systems' that few in technological education were aware of this. Nor were there many in universities interested in the changes in technological education. The reports of the UGC for the period 1947–62 record their concern about the dangers of departmentalism and over-specialization, about failure-rates and the education of generalists as well as specialists. Moreover in 1958 the British Association for the Advancement of Science set up an enquiry 'into the problem of achieving breadth in the education at school and university of scientists, engineers and other technologists', and the report of the study group was published in 1961 under the title *The Complete Scientist*.[22] A special survey

[22] *The Complete Scientist*, Oxford University Press, 1961. Chairman and Director of Study Group; Sir Patrick Linstead, FRS.

had to be made of the practice of a group of universities in
making provision for the study of non-scientific subjects; it was
found that 'after spending 15 or 16 hours a week in the sixth
form at school on lessons and laboratory work in their chosen
subjects most students went on, at their university, to spend
much more than this in lectures and classes, laboratory work or
tutorials. A variable proportion gave some attention to non-
scientific subjects, mostly in their first year and seldom for more
than two hours a week.' Reforms were needed, including some
pruning of first-year syllabuses and a parallel overhaul of teaching methods, with more tutorials and the appointment of tutors
or directors of studies. But such reforms 'welcome as they would
be, could not be expected to reduce the total time-load by any
significant amount. They would thus fall short of achieving the
main objective: the securing of more time, whether for the study
of non-scientific subjects or for leisure.' Because of the likely
increased pressure on university places four-year courses for all
students or postgraduate courses for some, the study group
sombrely concluded, 'must largely remain castles in the air at
least until the end of the decade 1965-75'; for the next fifteen
years[23] little if any modification of university courses in science
and technology to allow more time for non-scientific elements
could be expected. It was therefore vital that everything possible
should be done to enable schools to give more emphasis to non-
scientific subjects; the amount of time devoted to these in the
sixth forms should be doubled, and Advanced level GCE examination syllabuses should be redesigned to give more weight to
underlying principles and less to the memorizing of facts.

The lukewarmness of the Report about what might be done in
universities was disappointing, especially to those who favoured
the introduction of broader courses. One great exponent of
liberalization was Sir Eric (later Lord) Ashby[24] who in his book
Technology and the Academics challenged the assumption that
specialisation and a liberal education are antithetic.

The habit of comprehending a technology in its completeness: this is
the essence of technological humanism, and this is what we should

[23] It was expected that the pressure on university places in the faculties of science and
technology would continue until at least 1975.
[24] *Technology and the Academics*, Macmillan, 1959. Sir Eric Ashby was also a member of
the study group responsible for *The Complete Scientist*.

expect education in higher technology to achieve. I believe it could be achieved by making specialist studies (whatever they are: metallurgy or dentistry or Norse philology) the core around which are grouped liberal studies which are relevant to these specialist studies. But they must be relevant; the path to culture should be through a man's specialism, not by by-passing it.

And he went on to suggest the changes in curriculum that would be necessary, adding that these could not be successful unless 'accompanied by subtle adaptations in academic thought'— both on the part of professors of technology and professors of arts subjects.

In March 1961 the University Grants Committee asked a group of academics, with Sir Edward Hale as Chairman, 'to make a comprehensive study of undergraduate teaching methods and practices current in the universities and colleges of Great Britain in the fields of arts and pure and applied science'. Their final Report,[25] published in the summer of 1964, provided a sound commentary on and valuable appraisal of the various teaching methods in use; its effects were salutary, not least because it demonstrated that the aims and functions of universities are not limited to the pursuit of research. Its impact was perhaps softened by the dominating influence at that time of the Robbins Report on Higher Education which had been published a few months earlier (November 1963). Both reports commented on the content of first degree courses; the Robbins Committee suggested that the remedy for the overloading of courses was twofold:[26]

we are hopeful that an extension of post-graduate studies, which we recommend later, may produce some relief. If those who prepare syllabuses are assured that a higher proportion of the academically minded will have an opportunity to take even a short post-graduate course of further instruction and training, they may feel able to include a smaller content of specialised knowledge in the requirements for the first degree. But beyond this, a thorough revision of syllabuses is also necessary.

And 'by this we do not mean merely marginal reassessment of detail but a radical review of courses as a whole, and of the scope

[25] *University Teaching Methods*, HMSO, 1964.
[26] *Higher Education*, HMSO, 1963, 90.

of subjects, to make sure that with the passage of time their content has not become too great for a three-year course'.

Much earlier, in the report for the 1947–52 quinquennium, the UGC had commented on the dangers of departmentalism and over-specialisation.[27] And in the report for 1952–7 turned again to the educational problems that faced universities, and particularly to the increased need for universities to concern themselves with general education.[28] 'We do not hold the view that the need for the universities to pay more attention to the general education of the student applies only to scientists.' Quite generally there should be breadth as well as depth;

we shall no doubt be told that if the universities are to take seriously the general education of the university student time will be needed; that if the length of the university courses is not to be increased this time can only be obtained at the expense of the various specialised courses, and that this will result in a lowering of standards. We are not convinced that, at any rate in some courses, a reduction of the time occupied by formal teaching need involve a lowering of standard.

They added: 'we should not regard a reduction in the amount of information absorbed by a student during his first degree course as necessarily disastrous, since if the time saved were well spent he would come out better prepared for life in other, and as we think more important, ways.' And they proceeded to discuss how time released for general education might be used.

Five years later in the Report for 1957–62 the Committee was more optimistic.[29]

We found almost everywhere the fundamental thinking that we had felt to be so necessary. The content of courses and curricula is being examined; the dividing lines between faculties and departments are being breached; new fields of study are being developed; increasing attention is being paid to teaching methods. Everywhere we found evidence that the universities were regarding the years ahead not merely as a period of physical expansion but also as an opportunity to re-examine their aims and purposes.

Much of the re-examination was associated with the creation of new universities (page 195).

[27] *University Development, 1947–52*, HMSO.
[28] *University Development, 1952–57*, HMSO, 39.
[29] *University Development, 1957–62*, HMSO, 86.

CHANGES IN TECHNICAL COLLEGES

There were stirrings too in technical colleges where considerable developments followed the publication in 1955 by the National Institute of Adult Education of the report *Liberal Education in a Technical Age*. A major step forward was the appearance in May 1957 of the Ministry of Education Circular 323 bearing the title *Liberal Education in Technical Colleges* which had the avowed purpose of stressing 'the importance of introducing a liberal element into technical education', and set out a number of ways of so doing. One of these ways was: 'increased use of the college library, of seminars, discussion groups, directed study periods and project assignments; and in general the fostering of a tutorial relationship between teaching staff and students'—all innovations for technical colleges; their inclusion in the circular reflected the influence of Diploma in Technology courses that were developing in the senior colleges. More space, improved facilities and better libraries would have to be provided.

Circular 322 (April 1957) of the Ministry of Education acknowledged that libraries in technical colleges, even in the major institutions, were very poor. The paucity of the provision had certainly to be remedied if education in the colleges were to be broadened. A report of the Library Association had remarked that 'of the 555 Colleges in the United Kingdom dealing with technical education only about 160 have 300 or more books in a room called a library'. Reform was needed on several fronts, not only better provision, but libraries had to be regarded as important and as essential as laboratories and workshops, and become closely integrated into the life and work of the colleges. Above all the college library should be an instrument deliberately used by the teachers as one of their regular teaching tools to help students to read, to search and to discover. That students should have ample time to use the library was another reason why timetables should be lightened.

Once we have arranged that students have time to spend in the library and we have got them there, it is important they should know their way about. They can discover this by searching around, by browsing; and one does not wish to minimise how excellent this is. But really they need a formal introduction to the library. A talk from the Librarian about the contents of the library, the arrangements, the classification and similar matters can be invaluable. I like to think that lecturers will, early in the session, bring each group of new students to the library to be introduced and to hear the Librarian talk about his domain. Besides being good for the students, it is often salutary for the Staff. It can avoid much waste of time; it helps students to feel quickly at home in the library; they get to know the Librarian and are able freely to ask for advice and guidance. Clearly the Librarian has to be no mere purchaser and dispenser of books. He has an important contribution to make to the teaching in the College; indeed he is a member of the teaching staff in a very special and important sense.[30]

Besides better libraries and more imaginative liberal studies social facilities would have to be greatly improved. Circular No. 320 (1 March 1957) on Hostels in Technical Colleges asserted 'it is desirable that at least the students taking the most advanced full-time or sandwich courses should be able, during some stage of their college career, to spend a period in residence'. Not only at Colleges of Advanced Technology, but 'the Minister will be prepared to consider proposals for providing hostels at other colleges'. With three such circulars, on Hostels, Libraries and Liberal Education, the year 1957 could claim to be the annus mirabilis of technical education. The Crowther Report[31] of 1959 added momentum to the stream of change, more particularly for those in the 15 to 18 age range. 'The education provided in the colleges today is far too narrowly concentrated on the immediate vocational target. Some of it is perilously close to the line that separates education from mere instruction. Even where this is not so, the syllabuses are so heavy (inevitably so) and the time so short that the students are unable to lift their eyes from the immediate objectives even to glance at the surrounding intellectual country.' The Committee pleaded for more block release and more sandwich courses as well as extended part-time day release. The White Paper 'Better Opportunities in Technical Education' followed in January 1961, and eighteen months later the Ministry of Education published a report with the title 'General Studies in Technical Colleges'. In five years there had been something approaching a revolution.

[30] J. Topping, 'The Technical College Library as an Educational Instrument', ASLIB Conference, October 1957.
[31] *Crowther Report*, 15 to 18, 369. See page 87.

CHAPTER 10

College of Advanced Technology

EARLY in 1961 the Chief Education Officer intimated to the Governors of the College that the whole pattern of further education in Middlesex was being reviewed with the Ministry of Education and that the immediate future of the College was likely to be affected. Dr Gurr later[1] revealed that the Ministry of Education[2] had been considering the recognition of Brunel as a College of Advanced Technology, and added, 'whereas a few months ago the optimum size for a College of Advanced Technology was to accommodate approximately 1000 students, the optimum size now was felt to be accommodation for approximately 2000'. The land available at Acton was too limited to envisage an expansion of the College on such a scale, and 'the best policy would be to stop further building at the Woodlands site and concentrate on the provision of an entirely new building as soon as possible.'

The Report of the Ministry of Education[3] for 1961 records the developments in the following terms: 'Towards the end of 1960 discussions were held between the Department and the Middlesex local education authority about the designation of a tenth college of advanced technology, the Brunel College of Technology at Acton. The Minister informed the authority that in his view the standard of work in the college and the quality of its staff made it well suited for designation. It was apparent, however, that on its existing site the college could not look forward to the development which would be appropriate to a college of advanced technology. The authority therefore undertook to secure for the college an alternative site where new

---

[1] Meeting of Governors, 1 Feb. 1961.
[2] See letter from Ministry of Education to Middlesex LEA, 30 Jan. 1961.
[3] *Education in 1961*, HMSO, 38.

10. Lecture Centre from the south-east

11. Mathematics Building

teaching accommodation for a student body of the order of 2,000 and halls of residence for an appropriate proportion of this number could be provided.' The Report added, 'Though comparatively small, with some 400 students enrolled in full-time and sandwich courses, the Brunel College has already made a distinguished contribution to the development of advanced technological education. It offers a wide range of courses for the Diploma in Technology, and 374 students were reading for this award there in 1960–1 (compared with 3,641 in the nine existing colleges of advanced technology).'

By March 1961 discussions had gone so far that the Chief Education Officer was able to report that the County Education Committee had considered the Ministry's proposals and had 'recommended to the County Council that the County should build a new College of Advanced Technology, and that in effect this would be a replacement for the existing Brunel College of Technology (though the name would be transferred)'. The proposal was subject to a suitable site being available elsewhere; meanwhile all major building on the Woodlands site would cease. Though the plans for the Engineering Building could be utilised as seemed appropriate, a completely new college would be planned. 'Bold and imaginative' was the comment of one Governor on the proposals.

The Governing Body did not meet again until 2 November 1961, the Middlesex triennial elections having intervened; much else had happened too. On 22 June 1961 the Minister (Sir David Eccles) had announced[4] that he was proposing to the local education authorities that the control of the colleges of advanced technology maintained by them should be transferred to independent governing bodies who would receive direct grant from the Department. As *Education in 1961* commented: 'The Minister specifically included the Brunel College of Technology within these proposals since, although it was not a college of advanced technology at the time they were made, its designation was imminent.' In fact, the day after his announcement in the House of Commons (23 June) the Minister included in his address to the Conference of the Association of Education Committees a statement confirming the designation of Brunel.

Dr Gurr informed the Governors in November 1961 that the

---

[4] *Hansard*, Commons, Vol. 642, 1960–1. 162.

County Council had accepted in principle the proposal that Brunel should become a direct-grant institution, and added,

> At a meeting with the Minister the suggestion was put to him that the future of Brunel as planned by the local education authority was in effect to be a campus of colleges at Uxbridge forming what might well be termed a Technical University. While the Minister appeared to think well of the suggestion which is in line with the full autonomy for which local education authorities are asking for Colleges of Advanced Technology (Direct Grant status being treated as an intermediate step), it does not appear likely that there will be any development in this direction in the immediate future.

The Middlesex plan for 'a campus of colleges at Uxbridge', of which Brunel would be one along with a College of Business Studies and Management and a College of Art and Industrial Design, was a concept cherished by Dr Gurr and he could only have abandoned it very reluctantly. The choice of Uxbridge was dictated by the availability of land; earlier the County Council had acquired land there and other acquisitions were possible. Uxbridge Common was one site where a College hostel and playing fields might have been established earlier (page 138).

The Minister's proposals modified in the light of wide-ranging discussions were communicated to the local education authorities and to the Colleges in a letter from the Ministry of Education dated 3 October 1961.

> I am directed by the Minister of Education to refer to his proposals, announced in the House of Commons on 22 June 1961, concerning the transfer of responsibility for Colleges of Advanced Technology from local education authorities to independent governing bodies financed by direct grant from the Ministry.
>
> The Minister has it in mind, if the Authorities concerned agree in principle with his proposal, to proceed as soon as possible with the establishment of new governing bodies for each of the colleges of advanced technology in advance of the transfer of responsibility. It would then be possible for negotiations to take place between each new governing body and the authority concerned on the various legal and administrative problems involved in the transfer of sites, buildings, equipment, etc.
>
> It is proposed that the constitution of each new governing body should be determined by a Trust Deed to be executed by one or more members of the new governing body. It would appear appropriate

that in most respects the deeds for colleges should be similar and accordingly, following informal discussions with representatives of the local education authorities concerned, the existing governing bodies and the Principals of the colleges, the Minister has prepared a model Trust Deed and Scheme of Government which would in his opinion be suitable for the purpose. A copy of this document is attached.

The discussions referred to had resulted in at least two significant changes in the constitution to which the letter specifically drew attention: 'It will be noted that the model Scheme of Government contains no provision for the appointment by the Minister of an assessor to the governing body', and 'with regard to the appointment of a Chairman, the model scheme provides for him either to be appointed by the Minister or to be elected by the members of the Governing Body. The Minister is prepared to agree to either alernative.'

The date originally proposed for the change-over was 1 January 1962, but to allow time to clear some of the legal, financial and other difficulties a postponement to 1 April 1962 was agreed.

The Brunel Governing Body decided (2 November 1961) to nominate Sir John Paget 'for appointment by the Minister of Education as First Chairman of the Governing Body of Brunel College of Technology under the new arrangements proposed by the Ministry of Education for the government of the College'. Secondly, the Governors appointed a sub-committee to consider the proposed Trust Deed and Scheme of Government 'with power to act on behalf of the Governing Body, and to interview the architects who were prepared to undertake the planning of the new buildings'. Thirdly, after some discussion as to where the new college might be built, it was agreed to record the opinion 'that the proposed site at Uxbridge should be utilised for the building of the new College'.

The Sub-Committee acted quickly; by the end of November some proposed amendments in the Trust Deed were ready for submission to the County Council, and the Authority in turn submitted an amended version to the Ministry. Some further negotiations followed.

Progress was also made with the acquisition of the Uxbridge site. In June 1961, the Chairman of the Education Committee had reported to the County Council that the County Valuer had been instructed to negotiate for four 'parcels' of land, one for the extension of a secondary school and the other three intended for the Brunel development; their areas were 66, 20 and 52 acres respectively. Negotiations went smoothly, and Dr Gurr informed the Governing Body on 1 February 1962 that 'it would be possible to proceed immediately with plans for the utilisation of approximately 81 acres, but there were various difficulties associated with the remainder of the site.' The Minister did not wait for the completion of the purchase and transfer of the whole area; he decided formally to designate Brunel a College of Advanced Technology. A letter from the Ministry dated 16 January 1962 recounted earlier discussions and decisions, and added that

the Minister has noted that arrangements are being made, with his cooperation, to acquire a large site to which the College will be transferred in course of time when new buildings have been provided. The prior condition of designation laid down in the official letter of 30th January, 1961, has therefore been met and the Minister has no doubt that the various other conditions set out in the Appendix to Circular 305, particularly in regard to the number and quality of the teaching staff and the development of research work, are, or will be, satisfied.

The letter concluded: 'since the Minister confidently expects and assumes that all the necessary arrangements will be made to enable responsibility for the College to be transferred to the new Governing Body from 1st April next, I am to state, subject to any observations the Authority or Governing Body may have, that the College is hereby designated a College of Advanced Technology with effect from 1st April 1962.'

And so Brunel became the tenth College of Advanced Technology, which confirmed, so someone flippantly said, 'the Government's conversion to the decimal system'. The College was elated even though it had known for a year, and the students marked the first of April by blazoning 'under entirely new management' across the roof of one of the huts outside the College. It was a tight squeeze for had not the Minister said 'that he would not be designating any further colleges after Brunel or proposing any further change in their status until after the Committee on Higher Education[5] had reported'?—perhaps the

---

[5] Set up with Lord Robbins as Chairman on 8 Feb. 1961.

first of many statements that came to be labelled 'waiting for Robbins'. This increased rather than diminished the gratification the College felt and stirred everyone. 'The College is gratified by such a recognition of its work,' read the *Annual Report* for 1960–61;

it would like to take this opportunity of thanking all who have helped its development in these early years and particularly those in many industrial firms who supported its educational aims at a time when such support was critical for its success. With continued support, of which the College feels assured, it will hope to carry to fruition the many schemes and developments it has started.

Some outside the College were perhaps surprised, but there was wide agreement that the designation had been well-earned. Burgess and Pratt[6] commented: 'the oddest case of all was Brunel which did not exist in 1956, but whose principal and staff so successfully set about doing precisely the kind of work the CATs were created for that designation could not be denied them in 1962'. The County Education Committee in February 1962 minuted[7] 'the Ministry of Education has decided that Brunel College of Technology shall be designated a College of Advanced Technology with effect from 1st April, 1962. This is a most welcome culmination to the efforts of your Committee in providing for advanced work at Brunel and is in part a recognition of the very considerable contribution made by Middlesex in the development of advanced technology.' Members of the Education Committee must have had mixed feelings; delighted that their policy of establishing a College of Advanced Technology which they had single-mindedly pursued had been fulfilled, but sad that they were to 'lose' their College. However, in the event they were magnanimous and generous to a degree. From 1 April 1962, all responsibility, including financial responsibility, for the College was to rest with the new Governing Body. During the interim period while the necessary organisation to deal with the full administration of the College was being set up, the County Council was asked 'to agree to continue to deal with the day-to-day liabilities of the College, subject to appropriate financial arrangements and safeguards

[6] *Policy and Practice: the Colleges of Advanced Technology*, The Penguin Press, 1970, 40.
[7] Education Committee Minutes, Feb. 1962. MCC Reports.

during this period'. Later[8] the Clerk reported to the Governors that a first draft of an agreement respecting the transfer of the assets of the College from the County Council to the new Governing Body had been prepared and a copy sent to the First Chairman Designate. Further, the final draft of the Trust Deed and Scheme of Government had been approved by the Ministry and steps were being taken to arrange a preliminary meeting of the nominated Governors. This took place on 27 March 1962, and Sir John Paget was appointed the first Chairman of the new Governing Body. Unfortunately he was unable to continue for very long owing to his taking up a new appointment in Somerset, and Mr W. B. D. Brown succeeded him as Chairman in June 1962.

The Trust Deed and Scheme of Government was widely acceptable. There were a number of innovations, of which[9] 'one of the most noteworthy is the inclusion in the new governing bodies of a significant proportion of governors appointed from the teaching staff of each college'. Of the Brunel Governors five[10] were appointed from the staff by the Academic Board; the other Governors included two members appointed by the Ministry of Education, four by the Middlesex County Council, and one by each of the following bodies: the Regional Advisory Council, the Royal Institute of Chemistry, the Institution of Electrical Engineers, the Institution of Mechanical Engineers, the Institute of Physics and the Physical Society, the Institution of Production Engineers, the University of London, the Trades Union Congress and the Federation of British Industries. The Principal was also a member, and the Governing Body had power to appoint six other persons—twenty-eight members in all, including the Chairman. The Minister also appointed A. D. Collop, one of Her Majesty's Staff Inspectors, as an assessor 'to attend meetings of the Governors'. He was not a member of the Governing Body.[11]

In the paper on 'General Procedures to be followed by Colleges of Advanced Technology' published on 4 July 1962 the Ministry pointed out that

[8] Report of the Clerk of the Governing Body, 21 Mar. 1962.
[9] *Education in 1961*, HMSO, 39.
[10] The initial proposal of four was changed to five at the suggestion of the Ministry.
[11] See page 183.

Under Regulation 17(b) of the Further Education (Grant) Regulations 1959 the Minister may require, as a condition of the payment of grant, that an assessor appointed by him shall attend meetings of the Governing Body. For an initial period the Minister proposes to appoint assessors who will normally be members of Her Majesty's Inspectorate. No provision to this effect has been included in any of the new Trust Deeds of the colleges, and the arrangement is thus subject to review. To begin with, however, when Governing Bodies have much to discuss concerning the development of the Colleges and the administrative procedures appropriate to their new status, the Minister considers that it would be of advantage both to them and to him if a person were present at governing body meetings who could provide information as need arises on the Minister's views.

The pattern was common to all the colleges: 'most of the governing bodies have between 25 and 30 members and include in varying proportions representatives of industry and commerce, of professional and scientific institutions, of local authorities and universities, as well as the academic members appointed by the boards. The chairman and vice-chairman of the governing body are in every case elected by the members themselves.'[12]
The composition of the Brunel Governing Body was in fact not very different, except for the inclusion of some academic staff members, from that of the body set up in 1957, but significantly wider powers were given to the new Governing Body. No longer was it a sub-committee of a sub-committee of a committee of the County Council. The College's recurrent and capital costs were to be met not by the County Council but by a direct grant from the Ministry of Education, and the Governors became the employers of the staff of the College. This transfer of responsibilities to the College entailed a re-organization of its administrative staff; the Governors at their first meeting[13] resolved to appoint a Secretary to the College as soon as practicable, appointed the Academic Registrar, E. R. Chandler, as acting Clerk of the Governing Body and confirmed the very recent appointment of J. M. Crook as College Accountant. Until the College's own administrative machinery was established the County Council agreed 'to continue the use of the services of the County Treasurer for the payment of wages and

---

12 *Education in 1962*, HMSO, 42.
13 Following the meeting of the nominated Governors on 27 Mar. 1962.

salaries and the settlement of invoices, and of the Chief Supplies
Officer for the supply of apparatus, materials, printing and
transport'. As the new employers the Governors offered all
teaching and non-teaching staff employed at the College on
1 April 1962 appointment to the service of the Governing Body
'on terms and conditions to be determined but no less favourable
than their existing conditions of service with the Middlesex
County Council'. And to cover those members of staff who
might not wish to accept transfer of appointment immediately
the Governors further resolved 'that in the event of any such
appointment taking effect from a date later than 1 April 1962
the County Council be asked to secure the secondment of
persons concerned to the service of the Governors during the
intervening period in accordance with the terms of the agreement to be entered into with the County Council'. Dr Gurr
confirmed this in a personal letter to each member of the staff
dated 22 February 1962. And in order to ensure the smooth
running of the College the Governors further agreed that new
staff be appointed to the service of the Governors 'on terms and
conditions of service to be determined, but not less favourable
than those used by the County Council for its own employees'.

These and other essential preliminaries completed, the
Governing Body was ready to face its main tasks which, as many
realized, were formidable. Sir David Eccles, the Minister of
Education, in sending his best wishes to the new Governing
Body, the Principal and the Staff, added 'an exciting future lies
ahead for the College and one which will clearly mean much
hard work for us all'. How exciting and how hard had still to be
discovered.

One of the first decisions of the new Governing Body was
to 'express thanks to the County Council for all it had done to
make possible the creation and development of the Brunel
College of Technology. It also recorded its appreciation of the
invaluable assistance it had received from Dr. C. E. Gurr, as
Clerk of the Governing Body and as Chief Education Officer.'[14]
Dr Gurr was one of the four members nominated by the Middlesex County Council to serve on the new Governing Body. The
others were Mrs Muriel Forbes, Miss J. L. Scott and Alderman J. W. A. Billam to all of whom the College was especially

[14] Annual Report of the College, 1961–2, 9.

indebted; they had contributed much to the formulation of
County policy with respect to the College and continued to give
it strong support as a College of Advanced Technology.

An urgent task was the appointment of architects for the new
buildings at Uxbridge. Earlier the sub-committee on the Trust
Deed and New Buildings had recommended the appointment of
Professor S. R. Sparkes as Architectural Consultant and this the
new Governing Body immediately confirmed. He had been
deeply involved in the massive re-building and expansion of
Imperial College from 1953 onwards, and he proved a valuable
member of the planning team. On 1 February 1962 the earlier
Governing Body had agreed that 'the preparation of plans for
the 81-acre site should be proceeded with on the understanding
that the new Governing Body would take over negotiations for
the purchase of this site if the negotiations being undertaken by
the County Council, on the Governors' behalf, were not completed by 1 April 1962'. Some months earlier I had been
requested[15] to ask some seven architects and a few other firms,
selected with the help of Alan Thompson of the Ministry of
Education, if they would be interested in accepting a commission for the building of a new college, and interviews were
ultimately arranged in March. For me if not for the whole group
involved (Sir John Paget, W. B. D. Brown, Professor Sparkes
and the Principal) it was a memorable affair. We recommended
the appointment of Richard Sheppard[16] (Richard Sheppard,
Robson and Partners), and the Governing Body agreed to ask
him to prepare in the first place a Master Plan[17] for the new
College and to submit it not later than 31 August, 1962.

The Governors had to give immediate attention to financial
matters; the estimates for 1962-3, which had been prepared
earlier, were with small amendments agreed by the Ministry of
Education in March, and those for 1963-4 had to be ready by
October, 1962. A Finance Committee chaired by Sir Joseph
Latham, a co-opted member of the Governing Body and earlier
Deputy-Chairman of the National Coal Board, was set up and
financial procedures agreed. The other members of the committee were the Chairman, the vice-Chairman, D. P. Sayers,

[15] Report to Governing Body, 2 Nov. 1961.
[16] See chapter 11.
[17] Minutes of Governing Body, 26 Apr. 1962.

A. L. Stuchbery and the Principal. It is of interest that the Ministry's letter of 14 March 1962 commented on income from tuition fees:

the universities are charging increased fees of £60 for Arts courses, £75 for science and technology courses, and £75 for post-graduate courses, as from next Autumn. The fees which have been charged in the C.A.T.s have been less than half of these figures, and you will no doubt agree that this disparity, which is due to historical circumstances, has no real justification. It may not be advisable to raise C.A.T. fees to a level nearer to university fees all in one go, but we should like to see governing bodies submitting proposals for a staged programme of increases, with a fairly substantial increase—say £10–£15 this autumn. I am writing in the same terms to all the colleges.

The Governors agreed in fact to defer an increase in tuition fees until the 1963–4 Session, but to raise the Students' Union fee to £5.5.0 (£5.25) from September 1962.

The tuition fees were later raised from £25 to £50 per annum for Diploma in Technology students and £60 for other full-time students with effect from 1 September, 1963.

Another important feature of the Trust Deed was the establishment of an academic board, with functions analogous to those of a university senate. It consisted of the Principal and Vice-Principal, the Heads of Departments and a number of elected members of staff, with the Principal as Chairman. The Governors agreed that the number of elected members of staff should be six. 'Such boards are not of course new in establishments of further education,' commented *Education in 1962*, 'but in the new trust deeds their constitution and functions were explicitly recognised.' The Brunel Trust Deed stated.

Without prejudice to the rights and duties of the Principal of the College, the Academic Board of the College shall exercise the following functions in accord with any rules from time to time made by the Governors:

    (a) The regulation of the teaching work of the College.
    (b) The regulation of the admission of students to the College.
    (c) The regulation of the examinations conducted by the College.
    (d) The award of diplomas, certificates and other distinctions.
    (e) The promotion and regulation of research.
    (f) The making to the Governors of such reports as they think fit on

any academic matter or on any matter which may be referred
to them by the Governors.

(g) Any other functions relating to the academic work of the
College.

The Academic Board met for the first time on 20 March 1962
to nominate five of their number to serve on the Governing
Body, and again on 22 March to consider a draft of the
Constitution of the Academic Board which was submitted to
and approved by the Governing Body on 26 April. Only a few
slight amendments were proposed and later agreed. The
Academic Registrar, E. R. Chandler, served as secretary of the
Board, and the first formal meeting was held on 11 April 1962.

The transition from the Board of Studies was smooth and
simple; the early strains had gone, the new constitution satisfied
the elected members and the new Board quickly settled to its
responsibilities. Some of these were new; in particular, appointments of academic staff, which earlier had been made by
committees of the Governing Body with the Principal present
and taking an important part in the decisions.

The Trust Deed stipulated that in future the Vice-Principal
and Heads of Departments were to be appointed by the
Governors in consultation with the Principal, but 'other
members of the academic staff of the College, within such limits
as the Minister of Education may from time to time approve,
shall be appointed by the Principal in consultation with the
Academic Board'. In June 1962 the Academic Board agreed
that a Standing Appointments Committee for each department
should be set up annually: 'This committee shall consist of the
Principal, the vice-Principal, the Head of the Department, and
two nominees of the Academic Board, one a Head of Department, the other an elected member not a member of the department concerned.' It was further agreed that the Committee
should have power to co-opt from the staff or from outside the
college for a particular appointment. 'The Principal shall
proceed with the appointment in consultation with the other
members of the Standing-Committee,' and 'Appointments shall
be reported to the next meeting of the Academic Board.' One or
two features of the procedures are worthy of note; it was agreed
that 'for all appointments there should be coopted to the
Committee any member of staff who was responsible for the

work of the teacher appointed,' and even more important that no appointment would be made without the agreement of the Principal, the Head of Department and the coopted supervisory teacher. It was an arrangement that worked excellently; never could a member of staff in a supervisory position claim, should difficulties later arise, that he had not agreed to the appointment. Its other positive virtues were that it established relationships between the supervisor and the new member of staff from the very beginning, and gave weight to the importance of these relationships. By the end of the 1962-3 session some 17 appointments had been made, and these committees continued to function satisfactorily. It is significant that a decade later their structure remained unchanged.

In April 1962 the new Governing Body reviewed the gradings of Departments and agreed to the creation of a Department of General Studies, 'to further this important work in the College, and incidentally to relieve the Principal who has had the general responsibility for the courses and arrangements in the past few years'. There followed in June 1962, the adoption of a proposal to establish a new Department of Psychology and Social Science, which had been discussed at great length by the staff[18] concerned and had been approved by the Ministry of Education. Dr Marie Jahoda was appointed Head with effect from 1 September 1962, on completion of the Nuffield study. Robert Harcourt took charge of a relatively small Department of Management, and there were high hopes that these arrangements would allow the new Department to carry to fruition the ambitious schemes the Head had in mind. The timing seemed propitious for with the publication of Circular 1/60 by the Ministry of Education in April 1960, which proposed a new type of diploma course in management studies, management education nationally entered a new phase. 'The Ministry is convinced,' ran the Circular, 'that there is both an educational and a pressing economic need for a major advance. This can be achieved by the development of postgraduate courses and research on management comparable with the activity on technological subjects which the Colleges of Advanced Technology and major technical colleges are now increasingly providing.'

[18] See page 155.

Three Heads of new departments were appointed in June and July; Dr J. D. Gillett as head of the Biology Department, R. W. New as head of the Department of Production Technology and Dr J. Burnett as head of the Department of General Studies. They took up their appointments the following session. The number of departments had risen to ten and no further development seemed possible until new buildings became available. At least the way had been prepared to permit the College to make its contribution to higher technological education as a College of Advanced Technology.

To promote the research activities of the College the Governors agreed to a recommendation that posts of Reader be established, and in April 1962 the first two Readers were appointed: Dr D. F. C. Morris in the Department of Chemistry and C. C. Ritchie in the Department of Mathematics. Dr Morris's contributions to radio-chemistry and Ritchie's to computing in the College were regarded as so outstanding as to justify promotions from senior lectureships.

The number of Diploma in Technology students grew from 374 in 1960–1 to 451 in 1961–2, and the total number of students rose from 2,196 to 2,429; there was a significant increase in the number of evening students, from 921 to 1,103. The latter trend seemed likely to be affected by the decision to run down the Higher National Certificate courses over the next few years as provision was made for them in Middlesex technical colleges. On the other hand some expansion in the number of part-time students attending postgraduate courses was foreseen as the College developed its policy of making a much wider provision of courses for graduates.

On the development of the Colleges of Advanced Technology as a whole *Education in 1962*[19] commented: 'Seldom in the history of higher education has so new a departure been so swiftly accomplished. If the ethos of the colleges of advanced technology has still to be fully developed in the give-and-take of governance and the lecture-room, this is as it should be in a country whose disposition has always been to learn why it does things in the act of doing them.'

In the academic year 1961–2 the ten colleges had 9,731 full-time, 7,057 part-time-day and 10,242 evening students. Of the

[19] *Education in 1962*, HMSO, 7.

full-time students 1,869 were reading for degrees (mainly of the University of London), 4,756 for the Diploma in Technology, and 281 were taking post-graduate courses of study or research. There were also 400 part-time-day and evening students at post-graduate level.

CHAPTER 11

Planning the Move to Uxbridge

BRUNEL College was the first college of advanced technology to be planned as a whole. Most of the other colleges were in old buildings in large cities on inevitably restricted sites. The exception was Loughborough which had a large campus and good residential accommodation, and had grown over a long period under the forceful direction of the principal, Herbert Schofield. So there was little in the past to guide the architects. New universities were however at that time being built or planned, usually outside the cities with which they were associated. The establishment of the University of Sussex was approved in 1958, and six more universities—East Anglia, York, Kent, Essex, Warwick and Lancaster—followed soon after. The principles that were being applied and the new ideas that were being developed influenced everyone involved in the building of new academic institutions. It is interesting that these universities usually had in mind a student population of around 3,000, possibly rising to 5,000, while a campus area of about 300 acres became the norm. Warwick had grander ideas of 15,000 students or more. 'Most of these universities are expected to be largely non-residential in the early years' wrote the Robbins Committee in 1963, 'but some of them are experimenting with new methods of providing students with a satisfactory framework of social life and promoting those close and informal relations between teachers and students that are a characteristic feature of this country's tradition.'[1] And architects too were experimenting with new styles, concepts and materials.

Richard Sheppard's master-plan[2] for Brunel, commissioned in April 1962 (page 189) was ready by the end of August. A

[1] *Higher Education*, Report of the Robbins Committee, 24.
[2] Plan for the development of the College, Richard Sheppard, Robson and Partners.

number of groups and individuals had contributed to the initial
thinking about the form the new college should take. The Board
of Studies in June 1961 formed a Planning Advisory Committee
of which Dr Skellon became Chairman, and Heads of Departments and some academic staff were members; it explored the
views of staff and students and confined itself mainly to drawing
up a schedule of accommodation that was discussed in detail
with Her Majesty's Inspectors. The Ministry of Education wrote
on 9 March 1962, approving a revised schedule and indicating
the next steps to be taken. There was to be a phased programme
and details of the first instalment were required urgently.

When Richard Sheppard had his first meeting with the
Governors at the end of April consideration was given to a
suggestion that a sociological survey of the Uxbridge area
should be undertaken. Discussions with Dr Jahoda and with
E. L. Trist, of the Tavistock Institute, followed which were
constructive, but in a report to the Governors in June I wrote: 'it
would seem that the College should look elsewhere for assistance
in this matter, particularly if as agreed the architects are to
produce the master-plan by the end of August 1962. It may be
that town planning specialists could best produce the guidance
needed.' In the event it was decided to appoint John Morton as
a consultant to the Governors in addition to Professor S. R.
Sparkes. Morton was a member of the firm of Townmakers,
Ltd., and had impressed the sub-committee that interviewed
the prospective architects with the fertility of his ideas and his
broad vision. He joined the Planning Group formed in September 1962 by the Governing Body to advise 'on the implementation of the plan for the development of the College'. The other
members were Professor Sparkes and S. A. Urry, who was
seconded from his teaching post in the Mechanical Engineering
Department of the College to be full-time Planning Assistant to
the Principal; he became Secretary of the Group. Richard
Sheppard and another member of his firm, John Heywood,
were also usually present at meetings of the Group and I took
part in many of them. The Chairman, Wilfred Brown, was also
deeply involved. Dr G. C. Shipp, Head of the Mechanical
Engineering Department, who was appointed vice-Principal of
the College in 1963 took an increasing part in the work of the
Group subsequently.

The Planning Group reported to the Governors through the New College Committee, established in June 1962, with the following composition: Chairman and Vice-Chairman of the Governing Body, Alderman Knaggs, Professor McGee, Dr Wilson and the Principal of the College; it was charged 'to consider and report back on all matters relating to the New Buildings for the College at Uxbridge'. The Chairman and Principal were given power to invite persons other than Governors to attend meetings of this Committee as occasion demanded or seemed appropriate.

The first major decision to be made, even before Richard Sheppard's Plan was available, was to provide playing fields as speedily as possible on the 20 acres to the east of Kingston Lane, Site 3 as it came to be known. A proposal to provide 'two rugger pitches, two soccer pitches, two hockey pitches, a cricket square, two pavilions (one with dressing and washing facilities, the other essentially a hut on the cricket field) and some tennis courts' was put to the Governors in June 1962, and they agreed to ask the Ministry of Education to approve an estimate of £30,000 for this work. Difficulties proliferated about the use of this piece of land; a main road (the Iver Link Road) might later be built across the middle of it, there was essential drainage work that was likely to delay the availability of pitches and tennis courts until the winter of 1964–5, and there were uncertainties even about the date on which the land would come into the possession of the Governors. There were also legal complexities, some still unresolved at the end of June when the College Solicitor reported that he had been unable to discover the beneficiaries of some of the restrictive covenants on the land. However, by December the Ministry of Education had accepted a revised estimate of £25,000, and the Planning Group was able to report that the fields were to be sown in the Spring, and it was hoped they would be available for limited use by October 1963.

The other main area available to the College, known as Site 2, covered about 65 acres, and was on the other side of Kingston Lane from Site 3; the River Pinn ran through roughly parallel to Kingston Lane and divided it into two nearly equal areas. The boundary opposite to Kingston Lane was the branch railway line from Uxbridge to West Drayton, interestingly enough built by Brunel himself. The southerly boundary was a private bridle-way, along which the transport authorities planned to run the Iver Link Road, a new main road by-passing the centre of Uxbridge and joining Hillingdon with Iver. The remaining boundary to the north was irregular with St. John's Hospital, an active branch of Hillingdon Hospital, at one corner; there was a narrow strip of land reaching out to the Uxbridge Road, and some houses and the Greenway School along the rest of the boundary; to any planner it cried out for rectification. The main college buildings were to be erected on this rather unattractive area; it was fairly flat but fell gently from Kingston Lane to the Pinn; a horticultural firm, Lowe and Shawyer, had once flourished there, and the remains of greenhouses and heating plant stretched as far as the eye could see with weeds and saplings trying hard to obliterate the ugly mess. Birds and rabbits were returning too. Richard Sheppard described it at an architectural seminar held some time later in very uncomplimentary terms. All the courage and faith and vision one could command were needed to imagine an academic institution arising thereon. There were occasions, however, when it had a strange fascination, particularly on sunny days with the larks singing and Uxbridge remote, and the only visible activity the distant movement of one or two gardeners in the greenhouses to the south, on Site 4, where order prevailed.

The Iver Link Road, the railway, the Pinn and the general setting of Sites 2 and 3 were recurring themes in the Master Plan. As to the buildings themselves, proposals were confined to Site 2 (Figure 11.1) and limited by the schedule approved by the Ministry, but other sites would be needed. An area of 35 acres to the west of the railway line and referred to as Site 1 'should be purchased if possible. It is separated from Site 2 by the Railway. This line is likely to be closed and its future use uncertain, but it could either be bridged, or filled, and thus bring the Site into close relationship with Site 2. Moreover, if the railway closed, the frontage of Site 1 to the Cowley Road and its relationship to Uxbridge would be extremely valuable to Brunel.'[3]

There was a further recommendation that the College should purchase if possible an area to the south, known as Site 4, 'although divided from Site 2 by the Iver Link Road and access from it denied.' It was remarked that 'it is at present owned by

[3] Master Plan, 13.

Lowe and Shawyer and, as far as we know, no application for development has been made. It would be a valuable reserve for

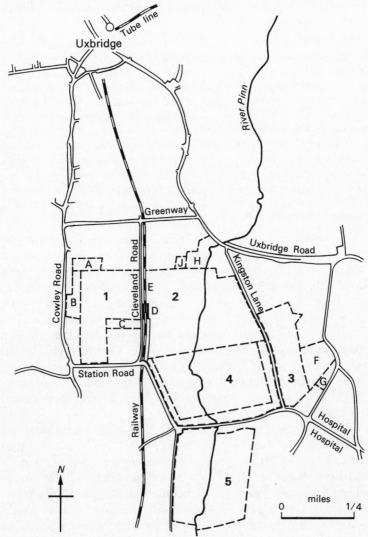

FIG. 11.1. The University Sites.

Brunel in the future, but could be left in its present use for many years.'[4]

[4] Master Plan, 14.

The remaining piece of land, Site 5, was included in the
original proposal of the County Council, the third of the three
parcels of land which they hoped to purchase. Richard Sheppard commented:[4]

> Site 5 is an interesting one with good trees standing and with more
> landscape appeal. It is being acquired from Messrs. Wimpey by
> Middlesex County Council to allow Brunel an option on it for future
> playing fields. At present it is restricted to agricultural use. We cannot
> predict how Sites 4 and 5 should be developed, and it must be admitted
> that the Iver Link Road will be a formidable barrier. We have been
> unable to obtain any information on the date of the construction of this
> road, or on its future level in relation to the adjoining land. We cannot,
> therefore, comment on the possibility of going under or over it. A study
> of the existing levels, taking into account the likelihood of a round-
> about at the junction with Kingston Lane, suggests that the new road
> will be well above the ground on either side, and the two areas could be
> connected under it to Site 2.

The probability of the Link Road being built worried the
Architects and the Planning Group for a very long time, but it
was not constructed; whether the idea will be revived some time
in the future remains to be seen.[5] The College later attempted to
purchase Site 4 but failed.[6] Site 5, after some initial difficulties,
came into its possession but lay undeveloped, because of lack of
finance, for many years; local children appreciated it as an open
space and horse-owners as offering free if illicit grazing. It was
1965 before a part of it could be developed as additional playing
fields for the students, a very modest remnant of the many
imaginative and optimistic schemes that had been canvassed
over the years.

The Architects were in no doubt that all five sites were 'no
more than adequate for future needs', and boldly asserted that
'the success of Brunel could be endangered unless there is
sufficient land to allow for its development'. They made
suggestions too about the development of nearby land and
buildings; the County Council should be asked if they would
consider moving the Greenway Secondary Modern School to
a neighbouring site; St. John's Hospital might in the distant

---

[4] Master Plan, 14.

[5] The possibility of the Iver Link Road being constructed became much more remote
when the inner relief road in Uxbridge was opened.

[6] See chapter 14.

future be closed; the closing of the railway line could provide a better link 'between the town and the Iver Link Road than any other route; a road along this line, and at the present level of the track, would be an advantage to the community and to Brunel.' Emphasis was laid on the proposed redevelopment of Uxbridge; 'an extensive shopping precinct is to be built centrally with access limited to pedestrians, and extensive car parks adjoining and related to a new inner ring road. The scheme was prepared some time ago and the developers, Messrs Hillier, Parker, May and Rowden, whom we have seen, agree that the establishment of Brunel could make a considerable difference to their proposals.' This led to suggestions about the redevelopment of the whole area between the town centre and the Brunel buildings, ideas which were followed up later but they were perhaps too visionary and came to nought.

Another novel possibility that had intrigued some of us, and was later pursued without tangible results, was mentioned in the Report. 'The pattern of education of Brunel calls for a close and continuous association in laboratory and workshop with institutions and companies,' wrote Richard Sheppard; 'it would be desirable if, at the outset, consideration could be given to the means by which developments and associations of this sort could be encouraged. Not least would be the ability to offer sites or even laboratory facilities to such institutions.'

Immediate decisions had, however, to be made about the planning, construction and design of the teaching and residential buildings and spaces on Site 2, mainly about general principles that might guide the Architects in their detailed planning and design. The development plan showed a possible distribution of academic and communal buildings, of residential units and some proposed housing—for academic and non-academic staff. 'It would be even more desirable if their homes were closely integrated with Brunel.' A perimeter road was planned with access roads off it as necessary to the various buildings, and a pedestrian way was to run west to east across the site through the communal centre. The River Pinn was to be re-directed; in the lay-out of the College buildings, the stream and its course could be made to form a natural centre to the complex of buildings. 'We propose that the stream shall be widened to form a small lake to act as a storage reservoir with a weir at the outfall end. The Thames Conservancy Board have no objection to this'—alas, they had and the River Pinn had to continue undisturbed on its age-long way. Still, trees could be planted; 'we propose that this central area should be developed as soon as possible and substantial tree planting programmes put under way. This area should be laid out with lawns and large deciduous trees, planted singly in order to produce an urban park-like character.' And other areas should be similarly treated.

The Architects envisaged a building programme with four phases, each costing about £1.5 million, and it was hoped that the first could be finished by June 1967. This was to include accommodation for the Mechanical and Production Engineering Departments, as well as the metallurgical workshops and laboratories, and provision for management, social science and general studies. Some part of the communal buildings would have to be erected at the same time; 'a proportion of all communal buildings and social facilities should be available from the time academic studies commence; also dining facilities for up to 600 students'. Residential accommodation for 300 students 'to accommodate 55% of the student population moving from Acton' would be needed too. The central boiler house was planned to be completed by the autumn of 1966. There were similar details about the other phases, each of which would take about a year to complete—to June 1970, but there is little point in even outlining them for they were changed considerably subsequently both in content and timing.

Richard Sheppard's report was considered by the Governors on 18 September 1962, and the twenty recommendations summarized at the end were discussed in detail and accepted, some in principle and subject to further investigation. The Governors had agreed earlier in April that if the Master Plan were accepted, Richard Sheppard would be appointed 'as coordinating architect for the whole building programme, on the understanding that Messrs. Richard Sheppard, Robson and Partners will undertake some of the work and that other firms and architects will be brought in'. So from September he assumed the main responsibility, and at the next meeting of the Governors his firm was formally appointed supervising architects; also Miss Sheila Haywood was appointed Consultant

Landscape Architect and a decision was made to 'consider and appoint contributing architects'. A little later, on the recommendation of the New College Committee, Messrs Stillman and Eastwick-Field were appointed associate architects 'in connection with Phase One of the new buildings', and so began John Stillman's association with the College, continuing that of his father who as Middlesex County Architect planned the Brunel Science Building at Acton.

The work of the Architects, the New Buildings Committee and the Planning Group was henceforward concentrated on Phase One, and the story of its progress and the development of the building programme will be recounted later (chapter 14).

It might, however, be added that in July 1964 the Architectural Association in association with the Royal Institute of British Architects arranged a seminar on university planning at the University of Sussex, and brought together a number of Vice-Chancellors, Principals and Architects who were concerned with the planning of some of the new universities. Richard Sheppard and I were invited to talk about Brunel. The seminar was an important event, for never before had university planners come together to discuss their work; incidentally they were helped to lose the feeling of working in and on a single institution and to gain a sense of taking part in a widespread social activity. I found it a stimulating occasion; if it was an overstatement to write, as the Architectural Review did at the time, that 'the great new university movement in Britain [is] somewhat similar to, and perhaps as exciting as, the cathedral building movement of the early twelfth century,' there was no doubt about the excitement. The contributions of those taking part in the seminar were later (1967) published, along with accounts of other new university projects. This full report[7] contained the schemes of all new universities planned in this country between 1959 and 1967, and enshrined much of the academic and architectural thinking associated with the development.

[7] *University Planning and Design*, Architectural Association Paper Number 3, Lund Humphries. 1967.

CHAPTER 12

The Years 1962–4

THE years 1962–4 were significant in the history of the College in that they covered its short existence as a college of advanced technology. Nominally at least it continued as such until 1966, but the two years from 1964 onwards saw the College engaged in preparations for the transition to university status. In November 1963, the Committee under the Chairmanship of Lord Robbins published its eagerly awaited report on Higher Education, an event of outstanding significance for education in Britain and particularly for the Colleges of Advanced Technology. They were, so the Committee recommended, to be designated as technological universities with power to award both first and higher degrees. Almost immediately the Government's intentions were made clear and thereafter the colleges of advanced technology became more and more involved in university discussions. For Brunel, a newcomer among the colleges, it meant that two major changes followed in quick succession and dominated in turn the two periods 1962–4 and 1964–6.

Early in 1962 Governors and staff alike became absorbed in establishing the College in its new role as a College of Advanced Technology; there were new policies to be decided and instruments of change to be developed. Necessarily the administrative arrangements of the College had to be strengthened, indeed re-modelled. E. R. Chandler, the Academic Registrar,[1] faced a rapidly growing volume of work; in April 1962 he became Clerk of the Governing Body as well as Secretary of the Academic Board, and both of these bodies had new features and functions. Many responsibilities, particularly those relating to finance and buildings, previously undertaken by or referred to the Middlesex County Council now fell to him. Under entirely

[1] See page 159.

new management, as the students phrased it, had wider ramifications than many in the College realised. A College Accountant, J. M. Crook, had been appointed in March 1962, to supervise the financial work, most of which was new to the College, and he acted as Secretary of the Finance Committee. The appointment of a Building Superintendent followed in November 1962, when L. A. Grant joined the College with a special responsibility for the Acton buildings, including maintenance, day-to-day accommodation arrangements and the erection of new temporary buildings; he was also called upon to assist in a number of ways with the Uxbridge developments. The College employed at that time about 20 administrative and clerical staff, some 60 laboratory staff and over 50 domestic, caretaking and refectory staff.

It was manifest that at the most senior level other administrative staff were needed, and the Governors agreed to establish a new post[2] of Secretary of the College, and to re-shape the responsibilities of the Academic Registrar to be more in keeping with the title of the post. The Secretary would be the chief administrative officer 'responsible to the Principal for the organization and control of the administrative staff and arrangements in the College, and for other functions associated with the Governing Body and the work of the sub-committees'. The Academic Registrar on his part would in future be responsible for all academic matters including registration, records and examinations, and all the activities of the Academic Board of which he would be Secretary. It was a division of responsibilities that worked well, and an arrangement that was followed in other colleges.

The post of Secretary was advertised, and B. H. Winstanley was appointed; he joined the College in January 1963. Earlier he had served in the Overseas Civil Service in Tanganyika and with the Tanganyika Permanent Commission to the U.N. in New York. Chandler was happy to continue as Academic Registrar; it was work he enjoyed and did very well. Together Winstanley and Chandler fashioned the administrative structure that served the College well over the next few years of rapid change and development. It was a period of almost continuous innovation, when new situations constantly arose and many decisions had to be made 'for the first time'.

[2] See page 187.

I was further relieved from the mounting responsibilities by the appointment of a vice-Principal. Unlike many other colleges of technology Brunel had not had a vice-Principal earlier. I must confess I had not been enamoured of such an appointment, partly because I had never seen the role satisfactorily defined or vice-Principals used in a way that adequately recognized their worth. However, to guide a developing college was demanding enough, to be intimately involved in the planning of another at Uxbridge was impossible unaided. There seemed no way out other than by creating a new full-time post, and I readily agreed. Dr G. C. Shipp was appointed, took up the post in September 1963 and continued as Head of the Department of Mechanical Engineering until his successor, G. Jackson, could join the College which he did in September, 1964. Previously he had been Assistant Director of the Department of Aeronautics at the Imperial College of Science and Technology.

The first meetings of the new Governing Body and of the Academic Board have been referred to earlier (chapter 10). The Academic Board was soon deeply involved in decisions about academic policy; in September 1962 it took up a reference from the Governing Body 'to report on, and make recommendations concerning, the Advisory Committee structure that would be appropriate to the College'. It also discussed in detail a policy report submitted by the Principal in consequence of which a number of working parties were established; one on the Tutor System, another on the teaching of materials (science) throughout the College, and others, on a departmental basis, 'to consider the nature of laboratory work and equipment'—a continuing cause of concern. That was not all; a report from two members of the Board on a joint meeting of Boards of Studies of Colleges of Advanced Technology held at Loughborough in July, and in particular on views expressed there on the award of higher degrees, led the Academic Board to ask a group of its members 'to consider the regulations and arrangements required when the College awards its own degrees'; Robbins was in the air.

At the same meeting the Academic Board gave detailed consideration to the report[3] of the visiting party from the National Council for Technological Awards that had spent two days in the College in May considering six of the Diploma in

[3] Letter from NCTA, dated 28 Aug. 1962.

Technology courses. These were given renewed recognition for a period of five years; the main criticisms were directed as we expected at the limited accommodation; 'the Council are concerned about the present inadequacy of staff work room accommodation particularly in the engineering departments. They appreciate that the College intends to make provision in the proposed new building at Uxbridge but they feel that the College should arrange for some temporary amelioration of the present conditions prior to the move to Uxbridge.' And further 'the Council do not consider that the present temporary library provides adequate space either for books and periodicals or for private study; it is their view that the library should be extended, if necessary by the erection of further temporary buildings.' Consequently the Council (NCTA) accepted reluctantly the College's arrangements to admit two streams of students to the Electrical and Mechanical Engineering Courses in the academic year 1962-3 (one entry in September and another in January), and emphasized that 'this does not represent any weakening in their views about the accommodation for the two courses and they expect the College to give the highest priority to the provision of improved accommodation'.

It was not simply the increase in student numbers; the creation of new Departments and the appointment of additional members of staff added to the difficulties. As Burgess and Pratt[4] commented: 'Brunel College operated as a C.A.T. in a building finished in 1956; Heads of Departments had rooms provided for them, though as the College grew some had to share. None of the other staff had anything more than departmental Staff common rooms, which were always grossly over-crowded.'

Some additional temporary buildings[5] were started in the autumn of 1962; they included five class-rooms, a mathematics laboratory, an automatic control laboratory and an extension to the reading-room provision in the Library, all pre-fabricated huts tightly packed on the limited area between the Science Building and the Woodlands Building. They were ready early in 1963. Also a small piece of land was acquired on the other side of the Science Building between it and Gunnersbury Lane, where an old factory was demolished and the space prepared for car-parking. Changes were effected too in the use of the Woodlands

Building; Acton Technical College gave up the use of a few
rooms in exchange for rooms in their main building, and the
detached building, formerly used by the Catering School and
known as Room 1, was taken over by the Department of Production Technology as a Production Processes Laboratory in
the autumn term of 1963-4 and an impressive array of new
equipment installed. An even more significant addition to the
facilities was the Crown Building in Mill Hill Terrace, only a
short distance from the College. Once a cinema, and later used
by the English Electric Company (Napiers) as design offices, the
College was able to rent it and some 10,000 square feet of accommodation was laid out as laboratories, workshops and tutorial
rooms, and came into use by the Mechanical Engineering
Department in September 1963. This acquisition more than
doubled the Department's total laboratory and workshop area.
'The equipping of the Crown Building was completed,' ran the
Annual Report for 1963-4, 'providing a new workshop which
allowed the old workshop to be devoted to machine tool studies,
a greatly enlarged instrumentation and control laboratory, stress
analysis laboratories and a combined elementary mechanics/
project area.' It cheered the Department considerably. In these
and other ways, including the division of some rooms in the
Science Building, the College extended its accommodation.
Space was found for yet another pre-fabricated hut, with three
class-rooms for general college purposes, which came into use
in January 1964; two other huts were later squeezed into the
only space available, one a language laboratory and the other
used by the Department of Psychology and Social Science. By
then the distribution of buildings and huts was as shown in
Figure 12.1. Little if any more expansion was possible, and
hopes were concentrated on the speedy completion of some of
the new buildings at Uxbridge.

The Academic Board's recommendations concerning Advisory Committees reached the Governing Body in December
1962, and were accepted with a few amendments. It was agreed
that the main need was for groups of industrialists and
academics to advise Heads of Departments concerning courses
and syllabuses and other allied matters, including equipment
and research. Such groups were not to be committees of the
Governing Body and so would be known as Advisory Panels; it

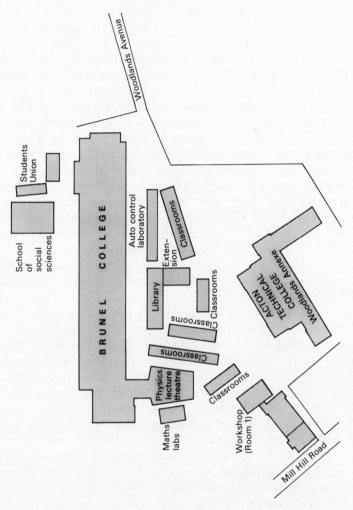

Fig. 12.1. Plan of Brunel College showing huts and Woodlands Annexe.

was envisaged that the Heads of Departments would report on meetings of the Panels to the Academic Board from time to time, and that matters requiring the attention of the Governing Body would be brought to the Governors by the Principal. The Panels were to be constituted to include the Specialist Governor concerned who was to be Chairman, the Principal, the Head of Department, at least two members of the academic staff, and at least three specialists from outside the College invited by the Head of Department in consultation with the Principal and the Specialist Governor. Nine such Panels were set up early in 1963, began to function immediately and were greatly appreciated by the Departments. The College was fortunate to have as Specialist Governors men of distinction in the world outside the College; they were H. J. Bunker, a well known industrial mycologist and later (1967-8) elected President of the Institute of Biology; R. C. Chirnside, an industrial chemist, for many years at the GEC Research Laboratories (later the Hirst Research Centre) at Wembley and nominated to the Governing Body by the Royal Institute of Chemistry; D. P. Sayers, Chief Commercial Officer with the Central Electricity Generating Board and nominated by the Institution of Electrical Engineers; A. W. Manser, Chief Mechanical Engineer (Railways) at the Chiswick Works of London Transport and nominated by the Institution of Mechanical Engineers; E. R. Davies, for many years Director of Research at the Kodak Laboratories, Harrow, and nominated by the Institute of Physics; A. L. Stuchbery, Chief Production Engineer of the Metal Box Company and President of the Institution of Production Engineers in 1969-71, and Dr A. T. M. Wilson who was well-known for his work at the Tavistock Institute, was later Personnel Adviser with Unilevers and became a Professor at the London Business School. Dr C. E. Gurr, Chief Education Officer of the Middlesex County Council and a mathematician, was Specialist Governor for the Mathematics Department. To these names should be added those of the many industrialists who served on the Panels, gave willingly of their time and afforded invaluable help to the Departments and the College.

The Governors had many preoccupations, not least the move to Uxbridge. Others derived from their becoming the employers of the staff of the College, or at least of some of them for in April

1962 nearly half of the academic staff elected to remain in the employment of the County Council and were seconded to the College (page 188). The Chairman of the Governing Body, W. B. D. Brown, was concerned that any contract of employment of the teaching staff of the College should embody certain principles concerning the appointment of staff, their promotion and the assessment of their work; these he explained in a paper presented to the Governors in October 1962 when I was asked to re-draft 'the proposals' in the light of the discussion and to submit them to the Academic Board for comment, which I did in November. The appointment procedures raised no problems, for as explained earlier, the Governing Body agreed to the setting-up of appointments committees on lines accepted by the Academic Board (page 191). Assessment, however, was a sensitive area, the issues being at least as difficult as those presented by the continuous assessment of students. In a paper to the Academic Board I asked for comments on some possible assessment procedures. But it is significant that the Minute of the meeting simply reads: 'The Board discussed some matters raised in a paper on Conditions of Service for Teaching Staff referred to them by the Governing Body.' At the next meeting of the Governing Body in December 1962 I asked that the College be left to work out acceptable schemes and this was agreed in the knowledge that discussions were going on elsewhere concerning the conditions of service of teaching staff in all the colleges of advanced technology. In fact the Committee of Principals of Colleges of Advanced Technology had set up a Sub-Committee[6] in May 1962 that led to a general exchange of information about conditions of service; the sub-committee was also involved in discussions with the Ministry and the Teachers' Organizations concerning staff salaries.

At Brunel negotiations with the AUT, the ATTI and the Staff Association dragged on for a long time chiefly round the issue of assessment. In October 1963 the Governors were informed that Draft Conditions of Service for Teaching Staff had been issued to the bodies concerned and discussions were continuing. By the next meeting in December a second draft had been received from the staff, and I was asked to proceed to discuss the two

---

[6] I was a member of the sub-committee; I was invited to join the Committee of Principals in November 1961 just before the College was formally recognized.

drafts with the Associations; further 'in view of the urgency it was agreed that a special meeting of the Governing Body be called at a date to be arranged'. Dr Shipp and I met the Staff Associations on at least three occasions and I had two further meetings with the Staff. After a meeting on 8 January 1964 the Staff Association wrote: 'the repeated rejection of assessment sections in successive draft documents emphasises that the Staff is vigorously opposed to the inclusion of assessment in a conditions of service document. Whilst this Committee understands that one of your reasons for including this formal assessment is that it would ultimately benefit the Staff, we hope that, in view of the almost universal feeling against it, you will consent to its withdrawal.' Some headway was made at the later meetings, and on 13 February the Staff Association passed a resolution agreeing that 'the Tenth Draft Document on Conditions of Service issued by the Principal to all members of the teaching staff on 7 February 1964 be accepted with the exception of words and phrases underlined and with the exception of the last sentence in the second schedule, Section B, Paragraph 3 and subject to solicitor's advice'. They also re-affirmed their 'objection to the inclusion of an assessment clause in a conditions of service document and that the Principal be asked to convey their objection to the Governing Body'. They conceded, however, in a later letter (20 February 1964) that 'assessment is necessary for the efficiency of the College and in the interests of staff promotions', and suggested that a working party consisting of representatives of the Academic Board and the Academic Staff be set up 'to investigate all aspects of the principles upon which assessment can be equitably based'. That was as far as we could get; a full report was put to the Governors at their next meeting on 9 March 1964 and the draft conditions of service were agreed *with the references to assessment deleted*; also a section of the second schedule was changed to read: 'Decisions concerning probationary teachers, the promotion of teachers and the termination of appointment of teachers shall be made in accordance with policies established by the Governing Body from time to time.'

What effect this long debate had on assessment practice is difficult to disentangle, but there can be no doubt that it deepened the awareness of everyone in the College concerning the significance and importance of the issues. On the other hand it strained, or at least did not improve, relations between the Governing Body and the Staff at the very time that work was beginning on the Draft Charter and Statutes, which provoked even stronger differences.

Many believed that decisions on the conditions of service were precipitated by complications that arose about the salaries of those members of the Staff who were in the employ of the Governors and those who were still in the service of the Middlesex County Council. What was known as the CAT Interim Award[7] on salaries was applied, with effect from 1 April 1963, to all members of the Staff whether seconded or otherwise, but in December 1963 the Chief Education Officer[8] of the County Council pointed out that seconded members of the staff must as a statutory requirement be paid in accordance with the 1963 Burnham Award for teachers in further education, announced in July 1963, and back-dated to 1 April 1963. The confusion was all the greater as the National Incomes Commission's recommendations concerning the salaries of teachers in colleges of advanced technology had not then been formulated, but it was not unlikely that the new scales would be preferable to those of the 1963 Burnham Award. The report of the National Incomes Commission was in fact presented to Parliament in March 1964 and new salary scales for teaching staff in universities and colleges of advanced technology were accepted by the Government and came into operation with effect from 1 April 1964. (See chapter 15.)

However, the County Council decided on 1 January 1964 that secondment of staff should be terminated not later than 31 August 1964 and that any of the teaching staff concerned who had 'not accepted transfer to the service of the Governors by 31 May 1964 should be transferred to a maintained college on 1 September at the grading and salary appropriate to that obtaining on the date of their original secondment'. The Ministry of Education also pointed out that 'if further difficulties over staff paid on different scales are to be avoided, it is highly desirable that seconded staff be prevailed upon to enter the Governors' service by 1 April rather than the target date fixed

[7] Letter from Ministry of Education, 25 June 1963.
[8] Letter from Dr Gurr, 8 Jan. 1964.

by the Authority for ending the secondment arrangements'. In the event, of the 53 seconded members of staff, 51 transferred to the service of the Governors on 1 April 1964, one on 1 May 1964, and the remaining one elected to stay with Middlesex and moved to another college. And so ended the period of second-ment of so many of the staff; that it lasted two years is difficult to understand, but the instability of the quickly changing fortunes of the College must have contributed. For some of the Staff the changes of 1957, when Brunel College was created, had been traumatic and were vividly remembered. Five years later came the new challenges of the College of Advanced Technology with its sharper demands and greater uncertainties, especially those of more advanced work and research, followed in 1964 by the promise of university status with its even more searching demands and need for personal adjustment and versatility. These were countered in some measure by the satisfactions of achievement, but everyone was so involved that very few recognized or acknowledged the pressures upon them.

As to salaries, for one year from 1 April 1963 different scales had to be applied to the two groups of staff, but from 1 April 1964 all the staff were paid according to the scales for teachers in Universities and Colleges of Advanced Technology. Transfer to the new scales and to a new grading structure was not straight-forward in every case; in general lecturers and senior lecturers went on to the university lecturer scale while principal lecturers moved to that for university senior lecturers, but a few problems of assimilation arose at all the Colleges. A special national committee was established with Mr B. Nelson, Pro-Chancellor of the University of Liverpool as Chairman, to hear appeals from members of academic staff and I was asked to serve on the Committee. Dr J. S. Tait of Northampton College of Advanced Technology took my place when Brunel appeals were heard; there were only three of these and two of them were regarded as outside the terms of reference of the Committee, while the decision on the third was to leave the grading unchanged. However, the Governing Body accepted a suggestion that one of the appellants (an assistant lecturer) should be appointed a lecturer as from 1 September 1964.

One consequence of the adoption of the new scales was an increase of 15 to 20 per cent in the salaries of the staff. Burgess and Pratt pointed out 'that salaries in the CATs rose very rapidly indeed between 1956 and 1966. The average mean salary in 1956 was £1,080. In 1966 it had increased by 127 per cent to £2,450. This was a rate of increase faster than for any other major income group in the country.'[9]

The Academic Board's concern with policy and development continued with undiminished intensity. The working party on the Tutor System made recommendations[10] that were issued as a standard policy document to the staff and considerably influenced the quality of the tutorial supervision that the students received. The Board discussed student failure and the assessment of examination results, important problems in which the Governors maintained a lively interest, and notes on 'wastage rates' accompanied the Principal's reports to the Governors on examination successes, a procedure that strengthened my conviction that lists of failures, as well as successes, at school and college prize distributions might be salutary for educators. In a paper on Student Performance presented to the Governors in March 1963 I reviewed the progress of students in the Diploma in Technology courses completed by 31 December, 1962; out of a total entry of 246 students 164 had obtained diplomas, a pass-rate of about 67 per cent. I had no wish to explain away the high wastage-rate, but I did point out that the pass-rate for the whole country according to the National Council for Technological Awards was as low as 63 per cent, and that as there had been a noticeable rise in the quality of the students entering the Brunel courses some improvement could be expected. However, a considerable problem remained. I quoted the figures for universities which had been brought to the notice of the Robbins Committee: 'the proportion of students who leave the universities of England and Wales, Oxford and Cambridge excepted, without obtaining a degree or diploma is of the order of 15 per cent. For Oxford and Cambridge the figure is about 4 per cent.' But these average figures did not reveal the great variation in the wastage rates of different faculties and different departments; in many of the technology departments rates of 18 per cent to 22 per cent pertained, and some departments had rates of 30 per cent. Even more important the wastage-rate of 15 per cent had to be further qualified; included in the successes (85 per cent of the whole) were a large number of students who gained an ordinary degree (some 25 per cent of the whole), which meant that only about 60 per cent of university students gained an honours degree. I concluded: 'there is no satisfaction for Colleges of Technology or Universities in these figures. I can only express the concern of this college that we should improve our selection procedures in every way we can, and we should continue to feel a responsibility towards the students who fail and help them to proceed to other courses more appropriate to their abilities.' I felt strongly there was a need to introduce courses designed specially for those who would find an honours degree course too demanding. I prevailed upon the Academic Board to set up a Working Party in June 1963 'to consider and make recommendations on general courses at both honours and at a lower standard'; it produced an interim report in February 1964 when the Board agreed in principle that general courses at both honours and at a lower level should be conducted on a faculty basis, and expressed the hope that general courses at a lower level might be introduced in 1965-6 (if accommodation permitted). It was an issue that continued to worry some of us and for which no satisfactory solution was found.

The concern extended outside the College; in September 1963 I reported to the Academic Board that 'at the request of the Committee of Principals of Colleges of Advanced Technology, the College had undertaken to conduct an enquiry into student failure in both Diploma in Technology and other courses in all the Colleges of Advanced Technology. Dr. Jahoda had devised a scheme for the enquiry, which was to be submitted to the Ministry of Education. If the scheme were approved, it was possible that funds for a small research team would be provided by the Ministry.'

The investigation was not in fact undertaken, but the Ministry did carry through its own survey on behalf of the Robbins Committee.[11] This related to full-time (and sandwich) students taking courses for first degrees or Diplomas in Technology in Colleges of Advanced Technology or Regional Colleges. In November 1961, at the end of the period covered by the inquiry, such students formed 90 per cent of all those studying

[11] *Higher Education*, Appendix 2(A), Section 4.

full-time for these qualifications and 33 per cent of all full-time
students in further education in England and Wales. The data
used showed that 'of degree students, 62.4 per cent left without
the special qualification they sought, compared with 36.8 per
cent of students for the Diploma in Technology'. Special reasons
could be adduced to account for the very high degree students'
figure which was based 'on information provided by the University of London on the progress by 1962 of all home and overseas students resident in the United Kingdom who registered for
external first degrees of the University in 1954/5'.

The UGC also conducted a number of inquiries into the
'success or failure' of certain groups of students, in particular
those admitted in October 1952, 1955 and 1957. The report for
1957–62 recorded[12] 'that 82.8 per cent of the undergraduates
admitted in October 1957 had succeeded in obtaining their first
degrees, 3.0 per cent had been re-admitted and 14.2 per cent
had fallen by the wayside.[13] Of the 82.8 per cent successes, 76.9
per cent were successful in the normal period required for the
course and 5.9 per cent achieved success in more than the
normal period. Of the 14.2 per cent who left without success,
11.8 per cent left for academic reasons.' The report went on to
discuss the different wastage rates in different faculties and
commented in particular on the relatively high rate in the
Applied Sciences; 'moreover there is a wide variation between
institutions in the incidence of this failure rate; while the
proportion of the 1957 entrants was 20.8 per cent the range
stretched from 5.1 per cent to 36.1 per cent.' Further investigation within universities of this 'apparently high rate of failure'
would, the UGC suggested, be welcomed.

The Robbins Committee[14] took a similar view. 'It should be
an essential part of the responsibility of any university department towards its students to investigate this problem carefully,
both in regard to the general level of wastage over a period of
years and in regard to the individual students who fail in any
given year to complete a course successfully. Such full and continuous inquiry, as part of the university's proper concern for the
progress of all students, can scarcely fail to yield clues as to the

[12] *University Development 1957–62*, HMSO, 30.
[13] A strange euphemism.
[14] Robbins Report, 191.

kind of action that would reduce waste substantially in faculties where it is at present high.' It has to be added that the clues necessary to afford a general reduction in the middle range were not readily discernible.

There was similar concern expressed by NCTA about failure rates in the Diploma in Technology courses. Figures were quoted in the Reports for 1962-3 and 1963-4; the latter showed that the failure rate for entrants to courses in 1959-60 was 31 per cent. Some evidence had been gathered about the subsequent careers of students who failed and left their courses; 100 of a group of 134 students for whom information was available continued their education on courses leading to other qualifications such as Higher National Certificate or Diploma.

It was not possible to survey examination successes and failures without subjecting the examination procedures themselves to critical scrutiny—'an examination of examinations'. The Academic Board received in June 1964, a report of its Study Group on Examinations and made available to members of staff 'Notes for Guidance of Internal Examiners'. This was followed up by asking another Working Party on Examination Techniques to look into the modes of examination, including oral examinations, used by the College, long before students in universities and elsewhere clamoured for changes. If all this helped to make some of the internal examiners more enlightened, it did not rid examiners' meetings of the difficulties of conflicting judgments, or stop some markers of papers from maintaining that a mark of 38 was 38, no more and no less.

Among new developments that the Academic Board considered was the Brunel Diploma in Psychology course which started in September 1963. The new Department devoted much time during its first year to the intensive preparation of this course, a four-year sandwich course in Psychology leading to a Diploma of the College. It was envisaged that it would in due time become a degree course, and so there was little point in asking the National Council for Technological Awards to consider it, which was unlikely anyhow; the precaution was taken however of seeking the approval of the British Psychological Society, which decided[15] that students who successfully completed the course would 'be entitled to Graduate Membership of

[15] Annual Report, 1963, 33.

the Society'. In selecting the students the Department experimented with several new approaches: 'students took an advanced intelligence test and were interviewed separately by two members of staff, who rated each candidate on three scales'. Out of 160 applicants, 18 were chosen: 'the number and quality of the applicants is a reflection on the shortage of university places in the country. Most of the students come from grammar schools, on the average with three A levels. Current limitations of classroom and laboratory space made it necessary to reject many suitable candidates.' Dr Jahoda later reported:[16] 'the first year of the sandwich course in Psychology and Social Science proved to be an absorbing learning experience for staff as well as students; its success was in no small measure due to the enthusiasm of the staff for developing their teaching techniques and to their readiness to permit colleagues to sit in on their lectures and seminars so as to create a common pool of knowledge concerning methods of instruction. The students experimented with programmed text-books and prolonged periods of independent study outside the classroom.'

The Department embarked too on new researches; the Ministry of Education sponsored a four-year project entitled 'A Search for Optimal Conditions of Learning', a natural sequence to the Nuffield Study.[17] The latter was made available more widely on the publication in 1963 of Dr Jahoda's book *On the Education of Technologists* (chapter 8) an event that enhanced the high reputation of the Head and gave the Department a good start.

The slimmed Department of Management aimed to establish a programme of post-graduate courses, about which Robert Harcourt wrote in the Annual Report:[18] 'the post-graduate course in the Study of General Management, a sandwich course which has been approved for some time by the Ministry, was considered and with especially welcome assistance from the Ministry approved by the National Joint Committee. It leads to the Diploma in Management Studies.' He continued:

the course itself has aroused some interest in a country notorious for giving the least time and attention of any in Europe to post-graduate management education. The extensive discussions the Head of

[16] Annual Report, 1963–4, 22.   [17] See chapter 8.
[18] Annual Report, 1963, 22.

Department has undertaken with companies have constituted something of a market survey of graduate recruitment and schemes of training. During the year companies have been confronted by a proliferation of plans of various types of course leading mainly to the Diploma in Management Studies, proposals and counter-proposals for the establishment of a 'Harvard' and extensive press correspondence. Among this the OECD report 'Issues in Management Education' published in January [1963] offered a well documented view of management education as an integral part of the European education scene and within it a not inconsiderable contribution from Brunel is imbedded. Yet only a few of the Diploma courses seem able to appeal as post-graduate courses in their own right or to be capable of containing the advanced studies and individual research that could make them so. It is also clear that companies are concerned that their potential managers should have an increased awareness not only of the organisational issues affecting production and development, but of marketing too.

The Ministry of Education reported that by October 1963 some 2975 students had enrolled in 90 courses leading to the new Diploma in Management Studies, and that the number of centres in England and Wales offering the diploma had risen to 42 with the approval of courses at three more colleges of advanced technology (making seven in all). Of the 90 courses only ten were full-time or sandwich.

The Brunel course, organized for the first time as a one-year full time sandwich course, started in October 1963 with twelve students. It had strong support from a number of firms and the Glacier Institute of Management collaborated closely in parts of the teaching. 'The course was recognised by the DSIR for the award of Advanced Course Studentships, which should enable more graduates directly from university to use the sandwich nature of its postgraduate study as an un-committed introduction to the world of business. The design of the course allows it to be converted into a first higher degree course when the College is able to award its own degrees.'[19]

Liaison with the Glacier Institute of Management was strengthened, and investigatory work concerned with specific findings of the Glacier Project was undertaken. For example, the Board of a local manufacturing company gave permission for the Department to collect extensive data on employee payment

[19] Annual Report, 1963-4, 17.

and 'level of work' as an aid to the analysis of criteria used within the company for the identification of managerial capacity. Robert Harcourt commented: 'this will offer an opportunity for the careful examination of some of the hypotheses and procedures used by Dr. Elliott Jaques in his investigation of industrial work. Data have also been collected from a contrasting small company with international connections and situated in the north of England, and a further invitation received from an interested oil company.'

Dr Elliott Jaques, who had been appointed an Associate Senior Lecturer in the Department in 1960, gave support to another development in the College, an investigation by D. J. Isaac on 'Levels of Capacity' which grew out of the teaching of Fundamentals of Science, the special contribution Isaac continued to make to General Studies.[20] This was additional to, and developed alongside, the programmes of the Department of General Studies. Also Isaac had initiated earlier, with the help of Eric Robinson, some courses of training for teachers in Middlesex Technical Colleges based on the methods used in the Fundamentals of Science courses. To foster such novel and important work a Division of Educational Method was set up in September 1963, with Isaac in charge, and I had every hope that a Department of Education would follow fairly soon.

Earlier in February 1963 the Academic Board looked again at the teaching of General Studies and appointed a working party under the chairmanship of Dr J. Burnett, the Head of the new Department, who had just joined the College. Its recommendations were accepted by the Board in June 1963, and were carried into effect the following session. The basic structure of the General Studies scheme was not altered, but some useful changes of detail were made. The most important innovations were the introduction of a course on the Visual Arts into the second year, and the doubling of the time allocated to elective courses[21] in the third and fourth years. Both of these changes proved popular:

the second year course in Fundamentals of Design evidently captured the interest of students and produced some outstanding project work, while the increased allocation of time to elective courses in the third and fourth years enabled students to make a deeper and more satisfying

[20] See page 148.   [21] See page 148.

study of their chosen subjects. The new elective courses which were introduced during the session,[22] Economics and German, proved to be popular choices, and it is clear there is considerable demand among students for modern languages, both for conversational and technical purposes.

This was not to suggest that students' problems associated with their own language had been solved or could be dismissed. Much thought was given by the Working Party and the staff of the Department to improving standards in written and oral expression.

The main difficulty is that linguistic ability varies so widely that formal classes in English Language have little value after the first year. It has therefore been decided to institute a system of individual language tutorials for those students in need of remedial work, which may continue into the second and third years if necessary. Individual errors can be corrected more easily and with less embarrassment in a private tutorial, a fact that has been amply demonstrated by the English oral examinations which have been held for some years.[23]

The Department contributed much to the general life of the College by organizing a number of extra-curricular activities jointly with the Students' Union, including the Humanities Lectures given each Thursday lunch-time by guest speakers. Also a member of the staff, E. S. G. Evans, helped in the formation of a students' Dramatic Society, known as the Brunel Players, and directed some of the productions. During 1963-4 'the Brunel Orchestra and the Brunel Choir both began in a modest way and were able to give creditable public performances.' Dr Burnett felt strongly that 'at a time when an active Students' Union is still emerging, members of staff can contribute guidance and continuity to activities which might otherwise have to be re-created each session'. I was fearful that too much help might inhibit rather than promote growth of the Students' Union as an effective body, but I recognized gratefully the contribution of the Department to activities that were generally welcomed. The impetus it provided meant much at the time and was appreciated by the students.

The Students' Union was in fact making its influence felt both in the College and in the student world outside, at for instance

[22] Annual Report, 1963-4, 23.   [23] Annual Report, 1963, 35.

NUS and WUS conferences and with the Unions of other Colleges of Advanced Technology. The Secretary of the Union, writing in the College Annual Report for 1963, noted the steady growth of the Union since the College became a CAT and commented:

The Union is taking a great interest in the plans for the new College at Uxbridge and is looking forward to participating in this exciting project. Committees have been set up to investigate the organisational changes that will be required at Uxbridge for the greater number of students. We particularly welcomed the fact that work started this year on the temporary playing fields on the new site. The sportsmen amongst us are delighted that from the Autumn term onwards they will truly be able to play 'at home'. The administration made full use of the Union hut situated at the rear of the main building.

This hut had been refloored and put in reasonable condition and some office furniture installed; it served as the Union's headquarters. Social activities flourished; 'the dances and social evenings organised within or near the College were all very successful and we feel that we have maintained our excellent reputation for holding "swinging jazz hops" at Brunel. Clubs and Societies were very active. To the ranks of the Clubs and societies were added a Film Unit, Sailing Club and Dramatic Society.' The Sailing Club had to sail as far away as Bosham near Chichester. An outstanding event each year was the Presidential Dinner which outgrew the facilities available in the College and was held in a London hotel. In February 1964 Richard Sheppard, the College Architect, was the guest of honour.

To turn to other academic matters, the new Departments signalled their independence with a flourish of activity; Biology had more applications for admission to the Diploma in Technology course than ever before, nearly three hundred for 1963-4 although only eighteen places could be offered. Until that year, when four industry-based students were enrolled, all of the students joining the Biology courses were college-based which presented the Department with a formidable task of finding industrial training places. Established departments too had similar problems, especially Applied Chemistry, Applied Physics and Mathematics, in all of which the proportion of

college-based students was high. The actual figures are shown in
Table 12.1. The Departments of Electrical Engineering and
Mechanical Engineering were fortunate in that nearly all their
students were industry-based. On the other hand Production
Technology which had small numbers to deal with had to place
some of its students as far afield as Glasgow and St. Austell.

TABLE 12.1

Distribution of Diploma in Technology Students (1962–3)

Course	First Year	Second Year	Third Year	Fourth Year	Total
Applied Biology	18 (0)	16 (0)	12 (0)	11 (0)	57 (0)
Applied Chemistry	24 (7)	16 (8)	16 (9)	14 (8)	70 (32)
Applied Physics	15 (6)	16 (12)	20 (14)	11 (9)	62 (41)
Electrical Engineering	46 (43)	23 (23)	20 (20)	21 (21)	110 (107)
Mathematics	26 (5)	13 (6)	12 (4)	3 (1)	54 (16)
Mechanical Engineering	35 (29)	34 (31)	18 (17)	20 (20)	107 (97)
Metallurgy	20 (9)	16 (10)	9 (7)	6 (1)	51 (27)
Production Technology	12 (6)	10 (6)	—	7 (7)	29 (19)
Total	196 (105)	144 (96)	107 (71)	93 (67)	540 (339)

The numbers in brackets refer to Industry-based students.

If finding an adequate number of training places was difficult
enough, ensuring that the quality and nature of the training
were appropriate demanded more and more attention. In
November 1962 the College published a booklet (page 166) with
the title *Industrial Training for the Diploma in Technology* which
suggested a set of principles on which such training might be
based and gave illustrations of the kind of industrial activity
the students might take part in during successive years of the
courses. It was a pioneering effort which was well received by
many in industry and in education, and contributed to a fuller
understanding of some of the deeper issues, particularly that of
trying to relate more closely the college and industrial phases
of the courses. Assessment of training was, except in a few firms,
still rudimentary, but Dr Jahoda's Nuffield Study and the work
of the Industrial Training Panel of the National Council for
Technological Awards, of which the Principal was a member,
stimulated the College to further effort. Attempts were made,
with a group of mechanical engineering students, to conduct
oral examinations in which college and industrial assessors

co-operated, an experiment which was further developed later (see page 302).

Though the College was surrounded by a large concentration of industrial firms in the Southall–Acton–Wembley area little was known of the potential of industrial training places in firms other than those which had supported the College for many years. Moreover, as the College was to move to Uxbridge it was important to know what additional support might be available further to the west, particularly in Slough and Watford, where large pockets of industry had more recently developed; a survey of the region was clearly desirable. An Industrial Survey Committee was later established and D. J. Burningham was appointed to the staff of the College in December 1963 with a special responsibility for the main part of the preliminary work.

The Diploma in Technology courses almost monopolized the time and energy of the staff; nevertheless there were significant developments in post-graduate work. Research grew in most departments, helped by financial support from firms and other organisations. International Nickel Company (Mond) Ltd. and Unilever Ltd. were among the firms which supported the research activities of the Department of Chemistry, and the Ministry of Aviation placed a contract in the Department of Electrical Engineering and Electronics; the Atomic Energy Research Establishment gave financial aid to the Department of Physics. Publications by the staff began to appear with greater frequency, but it was still difficult to attract research students; our own diplomates preferred the higher degrees of a university to the award the College could offer. However, a student in plastics technology, Kevin Westman, was awarded the MCT (Membership of the College of Technologists) in October 1964, being the first student of the College to gain that distinction.[24] His firm, BX Plastics Ltd., had been most co-operative, and two of their staff, Dr F. C. Lloyd and Dr J. A. Hetherington, had supervised the work along with G. J. L. Griffin, a member of staff of the College. Alongside this it might be mentioned that Ronald Brown who gained a Diploma in Technology in Applied Chemistry with first-class honours in 1960, at the same time as Westman, moved to Imperial College as a research student and

[24] Nationally seven awards were made in 1964, bringing the total membership of the College of Technologists to 12.

was there awarded the degree of Ph.D. There were other similar
successes.

Departments organized a variety of post-graduate courses,
some as short full-time courses, others as series of weekly lectures.
To discover how the needs of graduates in industry could best be
met, the College experimented with courses of different types
and duration; there was little doubt that courses of study beyond
the first degree or diploma were becoming increasingly necessary and should be a more important feature of the work of the
College. In 1963–4 the number of short full-time course students
was 452, and there were also 1,283 part-time students, while
the number of those in diploma in technology courses rose to
585 with another 30 in sandwich courses in psychology and
management.

The Governors maintained a close interest in the academic
growth of the College, and in March 1963 asked the Principal to
prepare, in conjunction with the Academic Board, a paper on
the future academic policy of the College. This was ready in
April, was given the title 'The New Brunel' and presented to the
Governors in May and considered by them at a special meeting
called in July 1963. There was no certainty at the time that
Brunel would become a university; in fact the paper opened
with the words: 'Brunel is a College of Advanced Technology;
it will become a technological institute of university rank. It
will, however, be different in some important respects from a
university, and indeed from a "technical university" such as the
Imperial College of Science and Technology in this country or a
Technische Hochschule on the continent.' The paper reflected
the immediate concerns of Departments and of the Academic
Board, and deliberately did not look too far ahead. It noted the
College Departments so far established, and added,

There is a Metallurgy division within the Department of Chemistry,
and this must be given departmental status fairly soon. A Department
of Education may grow out of some of the College's present activities,
and a Department of Biochemistry may develop from the work at
present undertaken in the Department of Biology. Departments of
Chemical Engineering and Nuclear Technology are likely to be added
in due course. There will be other developments particularly concerned with new technologies and in fields of theory and practice
which cannot be contained within the traditional departmental

boundaries, for example, control engineering, metal physics, computing with all its wide ramifications, and constructional or architectural engineering.

The paper went on to discuss sandwich courses, industrial training, methods of teaching, postgraduate activities and the liberalization of education. A very optimistic view was expressed about residential provision—'it is intended that the College shall become mainly residential'. Emphasis was placed on the increasingly important place of the Students' Union in the life of the College and the need for varied facilities—playing fields of course, but a sports barn too and provision for health services and counselling. It proceeded to discuss the buildings that were to be erected at Uxbridge and the ideas that were guiding the Planning Group in their deliberations with the Architects, including the importance of the links with Uxbridge: 'a community of three thousand or more cannot be established at Uxbridge without considerable consequences to the existing society around it.' The paper was hastily prepared, perhaps too domestic in emphasis and restricted in its sights. The Governors, and particularly Wilfred Brown, recognized that for a wider public another paper with a wider sweep and greater vision was needed; that it never saw the light of day is to be regretted but it would quickly have needed revision for within a few months the whole future of the College was transformed by the publication of the Robbins Report.

One consequence of the New Brunel paper was that the Governors (October 1963) seized with the need for more industrial training places agreed that a preliminary survey of industry in the vicinity of Uxbridge should be undertaken forthwith, and authorized the creation of a special post. D. J. Burningham, as noted earlier (page 225), was appointed; he worked in close association with Dr G. C. Shipp and presented a report to the Academic Board in June 1964. From the point of view of the availability of industrial training places the findings were disappointing, for most of the firms were small, some very small, and unable to offer the facilities Brunel students required. However, the survey was valuable in other ways, particularly as an exercise in public relations; it engendered much goodwill towards the College as a newcomer in Uxbridge, and gave the College an insight into an important part of the society into which it was moving. In an appendix to Burningham's report I suggested[25] that the College's arrangements for placing students, which depended so much on the work of staff in the various Departments of the College, should be rationalized and centralized and that a new Department of Industrial Training should be created. Although its immediate task would be the finding of suitable training places in more and more firms, I suggested that such a Department might include later an Appointments Board for students requiring help at the end of their course, and that it might also be concerned with the assessment of industrial training, sponsored research and other matters associated with the relations of the College and industry. A Department was later (October 1964) established, the first of its kind, with S. A. Urry as the first Head.

The Academic Board turned its attention more and more to the many questions that were likely to arise on the designation of the College as a technological university. A working party scrutinized the structure and content of the courses, mostly based on the Diploma in Technology schemes, that would later be proposed as first degree courses in the new university, and a Post-graduate Courses Committee was asked to consider and report on proposals for courses of study for higher degrees; the whole range of academic development of the College came under review.

This process was accelerated by the appointment of an Academic Advisory Committee. The Chairman of the University Grants Committee, Sir John Wolfenden, wrote to the Principal on 19 November, 1963 as follows: 'At the meeting[26] at the Northampton College of Advanced Technology on the 14th, I promised to write to you and the other Principals about the establishment of Academic Advisory Committees to assist the Colleges of Advanced Technology in taking the necessary steps to obtain university status in accordance with the Government's statement of 24th October (Cmnd. 2165) about the Robbins Report.' The letter recalled the procedure that had been followed in the case of the Royal College of Science and

---

[25] Minutes of Academic Board, 15 June 1964.

[26] Mr Brown and the Principal were present. There were a number of such meetings at which Chairmen and Principals of the Colleges of Advanced Technology had discussions with the Chairman of the UGC.

Technology, Glasgow, when it had been agreed that an Advisory Committee would be of very real benefit to the College and would ensure the confidence of the existing University institutions in the full maintenance of academic standards. The University Grants Committee therefore wished 'to propose to the Colleges of Advanced Technology that they should now take steps, in consultation with the Committee, to establish similar Academic Advisory Committees. I should like to make it clear that these Committees would be appointed by the Colleges and would be advisory to them. It would be for the Colleges themselves to consider the reports of the Committees and to decide whether to adopt them or to put forward alternative proposals for consideration by the University Grants Committee.' Further 'the University Grants Committee consider that the membership of the Academic Advisory Committee should be kept small, a Chairman and perhaps 5 or 6 other members, mainly academic but including representation from industry. The membership should include the Principal of the College concerned. Other members would be selected in agreement between the Colleges and the University Grants Committee.' The College was asked to put forward two or three names.

The Governors discussed the letter at their meeting on 2 December 1963, and to make clear the Committee's relationship to the Governors proposed some small amendments in the terms of reference which then read: 'To consider and advise the Governing Body of the College how best to implement the recommendation of the Robbins Committee, accepted by the Government in their statement of 29th October 1963, that the College should have University status; and to advise the Governing Body generally on the future development of the College and on academic matters related thereto.' Sir Walter Worboys very kindly agreed to be Chairman, and the other members were Professor J. T. Allanson (University of Birmingham), Professor E. R. Andrew (University of Nottingham), Noel Annan (then Provost of King's College, Cambridge), A. N. Knox (Unilever, Ltd.), Professor A. J. Sutton Pippard, FRS (formerly Imperial College of Science and Technology), Dr G. Templeman (University of Kent) and the Principal. The Committee met for the first time on 8 May 1964 and discussed a paper (AAC/1) prepared by the Principal on the College's history, development and plans for expansion, which was more complete and in some ways more satisfactory than the New Brunel statement. It was of course written for an outside group unfamiliar with the College; incidentally it provides an interesting record of the College in early 1964. In surveying academic policy it summarized the work of the Academic Board and the particular concerns that had recently engaged its attention, which have been described earlier in this chapter. Not surprisingly the Academic Advisory Committee approached the sandwich course philosophy warily but in the end they gave sympathetic support. Their initial reactions to other parts of the paper were cautious, notably to what I had written about student failure and wastage, but these and other matters were discussed at greater depth as the work of the Committee proceeded. The Charter and Statutes of the university had first to be tackled and to these we turn in chapter 13.

The summer of 1964 marked the departure of Dr J. H. Skellon who had been head of the Department of Chemistry and Biology for many years and had contributed outstandingly to the development of the College and of his own Department, the work of which extended beyond the normal boundaries of chemistry into biology, metallurgy and plastics. Indeed he was responsible for laying the foundations of three new departments (see chapter 16), and at the same time he extended significantly the activities of the Department of Chemistry by including a growing volume of postgraduate and research work. His achievements at Acton Technical College and in particular his notable contribution to the planning, servicing and equipping of the Science Building at Acton have been referred to earlier (chapter 5). The year 1964 was indeed the end of an epoch.

CHAPTER 13

The Charter of the University

To make a start on the drafting of a Charter for the University the Governors were provided in December 1963 with short extracts from the Charters of two new universities, Sussex and Strathclyde, which illustrated the three-tier form of government common to many universities—Court, Council and Senate. The Governors asked that a first draft of the Charter be drawn up by the Chairman and the Principal, with the assistance of the Vice-Principal and the Secretary of the College. I sought the views of the Academic Board and suggested to the Governors at the next meeting in March 1964 that the Academic Board be requested to submit their views concerning the constitution and functions of the Senate and other associated matters, and this was agreed. I also drew attention to the discussion of the internal government of universities in chapter XV of the Robbins Report.

There was ready acceptance that the name Brunel should be retained and that the University be known as Brunel University, and not given a place name like other British universities. Heriot-Watt College in Edinburgh made a similar decision. In any case 'University of Uxbridge' was ruled out if only because of the use of Oxbridge as a common title for the two ancient universities. But if there was a single view about the name there were many about some of the important elements of the Charter, and particularly about the powers of the Council and Senate and the role of the Vice-Chancellor. The Governors quite early (December 1963) recommended 'that careful thought be given when drafting the Charter to ensure that the powers of the Vice-Chancellor were adequate'. Discussions went on over a long period, and many drafts of the Charter, nineteen in all, had to be made before reconciliation of the various views could be achieved. It was the summer of 1965 before a submission could be made to the Privy Council.

The first draft that reached the Academic Advisory Committee at their second meeting on 2 June 1964 embodied the views of the Governing Body and the recommendations of the Academic Board. The Board had held three special meetings in March and April; at the first of these the purpose of Faculties was the main issue and it was agreed to hold discussions with teaching staff. Dr Skellon was appointed to convene a joint meeting of the Biology, Chemistry, Mathematics and Physics staff, Dr Howell the Electrical, Mechanical and Production Engineering staff, and Dr Jahoda the staff of the Management, Psychology and General Studies departments, to consider whether the Senate should function through Faculty Boards or Standing Committees and also to seek views on the representation of staff (professorial and non-professorial) on the Senate. Reports made to the next meeting of the Board showed a variety of views on both these topics which were discussed at length and compromises reached. At the third meeting parts of a Draft Charter dealing with the Senate were considered further and amendments proposed, and an amended document was accepted at the next meeting on 27 April for submission to the Governing Body.

Draft Charter B as it was styled was carefully considered by the Governors at their meeting on 1 June 1964. There were provisions for Court, Council and Senate; the Court 'would be small and as at present proposed would consist of the Council, the Senate, plus representative members from outside bodies, e.g. local authorities and industry. It would meet once a year to receive reports on the work of the University and would have the right to discuss any matter relating to the University.' The Council and Senate 'would be equivalent to the present Governing Body and Academic Board. The Council would have the executive power and the Senate would deal with academic matters under the Chairmanship of the Principal.' The recommendations of the Academic Board regarding the Senate were noted, and the Governors 'endorsed the proposal that the Senate should be responsible for the academic work of the University subject to the provisions of the Charter and Statutes and to the general control and approval of the Principal'—the latter clause proved rather controversial. It was agreed to constitute a Statutes Committee (W. B. D. Brown, E. R. Davies,

L. J. Sapper[1] and Dr J. Topping) with the first task of re-drafting
the Charter in the light of the discussion at the meeting and of
preparing a draft of the Statutes to accompany the Charter.

All this I reported to the Advisory Committee at its meeting
the next day (2 June 1964), when Draft Charter B was examined
clause by clause and a number of changes proposed. In particular it was agreed that the sections on the Senate merited
further detailed discussion and I was requested 'to prepare a
paper on the subject of the powers of the Vice-Chancellor and
Principal and his relationship with the Senate'. Reference to
Charters of other universities showed that the powers, duties
and responsibilities of the Vice-Chancellor were expressed in
very general terms; there seemed, I suggested, 'to be reluctance
to clarify the role of the Vice-Chancellor and to express this in
the Charter and Statutes'. I could have added that the Robbins
Committee had written: 'His is a role which, probably fortunately, is seldom spelt out in written constitutions.' In one
Charter the Vice-Chancellor had a 'general responsibility to the
Council for maintaining and promoting the efficiency and good
order of the University'; in another he 'shall subject to such rules
as may be framed by the Council ... be generally responsible ...';
and in a third he 'shall have general responsibility to the Council
and the Senate'. The Governors of the College had expressed
their view that 'lack of definition of the role of Vice-Chancellor
in Universities has often led to the real executive authority for
the University being placed in the hands of the Senate', a view
that along with others reflecting the principles enshrined in the
Trust Deed of the College was expressed in the first draft of the
Statutes prepared by the Statutes Committee. My paper on the
Vice-Chancellor and Principal and the first draft of the Statutes
were presented to the Academic Advisory Committee at the
meeting on 10 July 1964, along with a further draft of the
Charter (referred to as C) which included most but not all of the
amendments proposed by the Advisory Committee earlier.

The record of the meeting runs 'During discussion it became
apparent that the Academic Advisory Committee did not consider that precise definition of the Council : Senate relationship

---

[1] Mr Sapper had joined the Governing Body as the nominee of the Trades Union
Congress, and later became the General Secretary of the Association of University
Teachers.

and the duties and responsibilities of the Vice-Chancellor was
necessary. The Committee believed that the traditional method
of University Government with its apparent lack of definition
allowed for greater flexibility. The Vice-Chancellor acted as
the vital link between the Council and the Senate. His duties
and responsibilities were best left undefined to allow him the
maximum freedom. He was the acknowledged leader of the
academic staff of the University and much depended on his
character and personality. The Committee did not think he
could adequately perform his difficult task were he required
to work within a management framework'—an orthodox
academic view which contrasted sharply with that of some of
the Governors with industrial management experience and
especially those who saw that lack of definition, contrary to
conventional wisdom, was likely to restrict freedom rather than
promote it; it was necessary to know where one had freedom
before one could exercise it.

The Advisory Committee suggested a number of amendments to clauses in the Draft Charter and in particular to one
that read: 'There shall be a Senate of the University which shall,
subject to the provisions of this our Charter and the Statutes and
to the control of the Council and the approval of the Principal be
responsible for the academic work of the University . . .'; the
word 'control' was changed to 'powers' and the phrase 'and the
approval of the Principal' was deleted—changes that were later
agreed, but only after the Statutes Committee had put forward
another version which was not accepted.

The draft Statutes too were amended in a number of ways; for
instance a clause that read 'Professors, Heads of Departments
and the University Librarian shall be appointed by an Appointments Committee of the Council constituted in such a manner as
may be prescribed by resolution of the Council' was changed
to read 'The appointment of Professors, Heads of Departments
and the University Librarian shall be made by the Council
on the recommendation of Committees constituted in such a
manner as may be prescribed by the Council after consultation
with the Senate.' The succeeding clause on the appointment
of other academic staff was revised too, and more than one
attempt had to be made to find wording that expressed the
practice adopted by the College earlier (see page 191) which

the Committee accepted. In many another place the words 'in consultation with the Senate' were introduced. Occasionally changes were stylistic but more often they expressed a difference in viewpoint from that of the Statutes Committee.

To act as a go-between was never easy, but the burden was lightened by Sir Walter Worboys' friendly understanding. It became increasingly clear however that a meeting between the Academic Advisory Committee and the Statutes Committee was necessary if some of the differences were to be speedily resolved. A meeting was arranged on 28 July 1964, following another meeting of the Academic Advisory Committee at which I tried to explain the outstanding difficulties concerning certain clauses of the Charter and the Statutes. These were traversed again at the joint meeting and some headway was made but I was left with the hope that after a summer break the way forward would be clearer.

At the end of July Sir John Wolfenden wrote to the Principal concerning when and how the Academic Advisory Committee might report. 'I do not envisage that the reports need necessarily be of great length or cover a great deal of detail,' he commented, 'but the broad academic and financial implication of the proposed development plans of the Colleges must be of great concern to the U.G.C., and we would be glad to see the Advisory Committee's proposals—and perhaps be invited to comment upon them—before the final views of the Governing Body are formulated and formally communicated to the U.G.C.' On 28 September when the Advisory Committee met again the Secretary (B. H. Winstanley) and I were asked to draw up a first draft of the report, and it was agreed that the report should first be submitted to the Governing Body and thence to the University Grants Committee.

At this meeting I was able to report that the Statutes Committee had met on 22 September 1964 and had discussed the Academic Advisory Committee's comments on the draft Charter and Statutes made at the meetings on 10 and 28 July 1964, and that 'the amendments proposed by the Statutes Committee substantially met the points raised and as soon as the Charter and Statutes had been re-drafted they would be re-submitted to the Academic Advisory Committee'—on 26 October 1964, it was hoped.

Meanwhile the Committee turned to other matters. A list of Heads of Departments recommended for appointment as Professors was completed; it comprised Dr J. Crank, Dr C. A. Hogarth, Dr J. D. Gillett, Dr M. Jahoda, G. Jackson and Dr R. T. A. Howell, appropriate support from outside experts having been obtained for all of them.

The Committee decided to examine in more detail the general academic policy of the College, which it had surveyed at its first meeting. In September it proceeded to consider the post-graduate work of the College having before it the draft report of the Academic Board's Working Party on Regulations concerning courses for higher degrees. I had reiterated that 'the power to grant higher degrees is of more immediate significance to the College than the power to grant first degrees.' And although the College could not possibly accept students for a Master's degree in the session 1964–5 it was hoped that students preparing for a Ph.D. degree could be accepted immediately on the understanding they could not be presented for the degree before June 1967, by which time the College was likely to have received its Charter. A number of amendments to the degree regulations were proposed and the Principal was requested 'to prepare a paper on the conception and content of the Master's degree and the part it would play in the future educational policy of the College'. Among other comments the Committee welcomed that part of the Ph.D. regulations which allowed for the submission of work done outside the university under proper supervision—a continuation of a procedure already followed for the award of MCT (Master of the College of Technologists).

Undergraduate courses also came under more detailed review. In a paper (AAC/14) presented to the Committee I had explained that the Academic Board had agreed that there should be no change in the distinctive features of the courses, namely, they should continue to be four years in length and conducted on the 'thin' sandwich principle of six months in college followed by six months in industry, but in future the fourth year of all the courses would be organized as a complete year in college.

The sandwich principle was enshrined in the Charter as follows: 'The objects of the University shall be to advance learning and knowledge by teaching and research. The University

shall be particularly concerned to provide that form of education which allows students to spend periods of intra mural
learning associated with periods of extra mural work so that
upon graduation they are possessed not only of a range of
academic learning but know also of the relevance of that
learning to the affairs of Our Realm.' It should perhaps be
added that the word 'relevance' was used and readily accepted
before it achieved notoriety in discussions of the purposes of
university education.

Paper AAC/14 also referred to lower level courses about
which the Committee continued to show caution; it was pointed
out that 'Universities favoured a diagnostic year; in some cases
all students were admitted to honours courses and transferred
after the first year as necessary to ordinary degree courses; in
other Universities the first year was neither an honours nor an
ordinary course, but a course common to both types of students.
The institution of a specially designed lower level course might
lead to some difficulties where students admitted to such courses
proved to be of higher academic ability than was first thought.'
However, the Committee supported 'in some measure the
suggestion that if the general standards of honours degrees were
to be maintained and all new places filled in the future
expansion of Universities, it would be necessary to institute
lower level courses and alter the qualifications for admission to
such courses'. It was also noted that 'the future policy of CNAA
with regard to the type of degree which would be awarded by
this body would have some bearing on the lower level courses
which might be instituted.' The Council for National Academic
Awards (CNAA) was established in September 1964 and given
powers, unlike its predecessor the National Council for Technological Awards (NCTA), to award degrees (as well as other
distinctions) to students who had pursued courses of study
approved by the Council[2] at educational establishments other
than universities. From the beginning until the regulations were
revised in 1971 the Council awarded honours degrees and
ordinary degrees, courses for the latter being separately planned
and distinct from those leading to an honours degree. After 1971
the adjective 'ordinary' was not used.

[2] I was a member of the Council from 1964 to 1970, and Chairman of its Board of
Studies for Science and Technology.

My paper (AAC/14) also pointed out that the College did not wish to widen the range of studies offered to students 'far beyond the boundaries of its present courses', but there were three developments it would like to foster—in Social Science, in Education and Teacher Training, and in Architectural and Constructional Engineering. The last of these, it was acknowledged, could not be pursued immediately, although discussions with architects and others would continue.

In Social Science, however, there were unexpected moves. Dr Jahoda intimated in May 1964 that she had accepted a professorship at the University of Sussex and would be leaving the College in the summer of 1965. 'In considering the appointment of a successor,' I explained to the Academic Advisory Committee,

the Governors have taken the opportunity of reviewing the area of work in social science which the College should undertake. It is likely that they will wish to establish a School of Social Science, which will be responsible for an undergraduate course in Psychology, Sociology and Economics for students hoping to go into public or industrial administration of various kinds. Additionally the present course in psychology may be continued in its present form or may be modified or discontinued. Other courses in Sociology and Economics might be introduced. The School would also be responsible for the service teaching in Social Science in all the other Departments of the College and take over in this respect the work of the present General Studies Department which would be discontinued. The School would also be responsible for a range of post-graduate studies which would include the course leading to the Diploma in Management Studies at present organised by the Department of Management. The research activities of the School would be mainly in Sociology and Psychology.

Here was a whole complex of ideas and possible changes which had still to be clarified and refined, but they were given general approval by the Academic Advisory Committee.

The Committee also supported the setting up of a School of Education which 'would organise (a) a four-year undergraduate course directed to the training of teachers of science and engineering, and (b) a postgraduate course leading to a Diploma in Education. It would have mainly in mind the training of teachers in Technical Colleges and in Secondary Schools.'

All these matters were included in the First Report of the Committee which was accepted in its final form in January 1965 and reached the Governing Body on 8 March 1965. But before this the Committee had continued its discussion of the Charter and Statutes. On 26 October 1964 the draft Charter (AAC/19) was accepted with a few small changes, and the draft Statutes amended in a number of ways; there was for instance a long discussion on the constitutions of Senates—'two basic concepts were considered; the first being a Senate on which all Professors were members as of right, the second being a Senate on which some limitation was imposed on the membership of Professors.' The Committee was concerned that the College should consider again the type of Senate that was best suited to the conditions in the new University, and agreed 'to support whichever type of constitution the College, after full consideration, wished to see adopted'.

I was able to report at the next meeting of the Committee on 30 November, 1964 that the Academic Board and the Governing Body,[3] after full discussion of the Committee's suggestions, had decided to retain a small Senate. The constitution proposed did not include *all* Professors but made some provision for the representation of those who were not Deans of Faculties or Heads of Schools or Departments by including eight members elected from among their number by the Professors (other than Deans and Heads of Schools and Departments) and the Readers, full-time Senior Lecturers and Lecturers of the University; the number eight was to be increased as the university expanded to ensure that the number of members in this category always constituted one third of the total membership of Senate. At a later stage the eight members were specified as two professors and six from among the Readers, Senior Lecturers and Lecturers. There were also to be five co-opted members drawn from the academic staff of the university.

Other changes to the Statutes had been agreed by the Governing Body and these the Advisory Committee noted. One new clause referred to the continuance of an Academic Advisory Committee on the granting of the Charter, a decision on which had been delayed until it was known that such an arrangement would apply to all the Colleges of Advanced Technology. The view of the University Grants Committee was that

[3] See Minutes of Governing Body, 23 Nov. 1964.

it would be desirable to include, in the Charters of those Colleges which were planning to become separate universities, provision for an Academic Advisory Committee to operate for an initial period after the creation of the new university institution. We felt that such provision would be of benefit to the universities concerned, not as a form of tutelage or probation, but as strengthening the universities' own academic position and guaranteeing their standards to the university world at large; similar provision had been made in the Charters of the new university foundations.[4]

The main preparatory work was thus completed, and on 4 January 1965 I informed the Academic Advisory Committee that as agreed 'a copy of the printed draft Charter and Statutes had been submitted by the Principal to Sir John Wolfenden and by the Secretary to the Officers of the Privy Council'. I also reported that the Staff Association of the College had indicated their objections to certain parts of the Charter and Statutes, particularly those relating to the powers of Council and Senate. At the same meeting the Committee discussed in detail the draft of its own first Report and empowered its Chairman 'to approve the final draft for submission to Governors'. The section on the Charter and Statutes read:

We have been concerned throughout our deliberations that the College should establish a sound framework of government when it achieves University status and have therefore directed considerable attention to the draft Charter and Statutes. We have had discussions with the Chairman and representatives of the Governing Body and have submitted numerous recommendations to the Governors for the improvement of the initial draft. We are pleased that all our recommendations have either been accepted by the Governors or compromises have been reached acceptable to both sides. We are of the opinion that the Draft Charter and Statutes will provide the sound framework necessary for the vigorous development of Brunel as a Technological University.

Copies of a Draft Charter and Statutes had been made available to the Staff early in October 1964. I later met representatives of the Staff 'Association, the AUT and ATTI, after which they submitted their proposed amendments, and the Governors considered these at a special meeting on

[4] *University Development, 1962–67*, 62.

23 November 1964. The Academic Board had also considered the Draft at a meeting on 11 November and made a few suggestions.

At the meeting of the Governors on 23 November 1964 a motion 'that the form of University Government proposed by the Statutes Committee be adopted in preference to that contained in the Staff Document' was carried with three members of the academic staff dissenting. The Governors went on to make a number of small changes in the wording of the draft and finally agreed that 'the Charter and Statutes, amended in the light of the alterations approved, should be printed in order to submit the draft to the Officers of the University Grants Committee in the first instance, and thence to the Officers of the Privy Council.' The latter made certain alterations confined to legal drafting which were incorporated in later drafts.

At the next meeting on 7 December 1964 the Governors had before them a resolution passed at a meeting of the Staff Association which read: 'The Brunel Staff Association regrets that it was neither involved nor consulted in the drafting of the proposed Charter for Brunel University, and that its main objections regarding the relative powers of Council and Senate have been disregarded by the present Governors'—a contention which the Governors rejected.

A meeting between the Statutes Committee and representatives of the Staff Association was however arranged on 28 January 1965 but failed to achieve agreement; 'it confirmed that the differences between Governors and academic staff are fundamental,' wrote the Honorary Secretary of the Staff Association.[5] He went on, 'The Governors want the Council to be the final authority on *all* matters—not only in the sense of having a broad financial sanction but of being able, if necessary, to decide academic issues directly, even if this means overriding the Senate.' By contrast 'the Staff Association see the Senate as supreme in academic matters and responsible for making academic policy. The Council retain a financial veto where a Senate decision involves large expenditure of money, otherwise its endorsement of academic decisions by Senate should either be unnecessary or purely formal.' He also wrote on 19 February

[5] Letter to members of staff, 11 Feb. 1965.

1965 to the Chairman of the Academic Advisory Committee to 'emphasize the nature and extent of the disagreement between the Governors and the Academic Staff', and concluded, 'Insofar as the Academic Advisory Committee may wish to commend the present draft Charter and Statutes to the U.G.C. we hope that it will regard the non-involvement of the academic staff in its preparation, and their fundamental opposition to it, as being of some relevance.'

Sir Walter Worboys in his reply explained that the Committee had been particularly concerned with the clauses of the Charter affecting the relationship between the Council and the Senate and emphasized the Committee's belief that 'the Charter and Statutes in their present form will provide a good constitutional base from which Brunel University can grow and prosper.' The Honorary Secretary's letter and the list of amendments submitted by the Staff Association were presented to the Advisory Committee at its next meeting on 11 March 1965 and discussed at length. The Committee was aware that Sir John Wolfenden had written to the Principal on 8 March indicating that the UGC had serious reservations on some aspects of the Draft Charter and Statutes but these would not be known until after the meeting of the UGC on 8 April. On the main issue the Committee tried to find acceptable compromises but turned down proposed amendments of some other clauses. It was decided that the Chairman should suggest to Lord Brown[6] a meeting between the Staff Association, the Academic Advisory Committee and the Statutes Committee.

Such a meeting was not agreed; what in fact happened was a meeting of the Academic Advisory Committee and the Statutes Committee on 31 March, followed by a Special Meeting of the Advisory Committee on 9 April at which the Committee met representatives of the Staff Association.

The meeting on 31 March was difficult; I seem to remember it was after that meeting that Winstanley, who had an African story for every situation, relieved my gloom by saying, 'Sir, it is said in Africa that when two elephants fight only the grass is trampled on.' We were both sensitive to the need to keep the grass in good order.

[6] Mr W. B. D. Brown's new title; a Life Peerage was conferred on him in December, 1964. He also became a member of the Government's Advisory Council on Technology.

The Governing Body held a special meeting later the same day and the minutes record:

The Statutes Committee/Academic Advisory Committee meeting had not proceeded as expected. The Academic Advisory Committee had refused to discuss their detailed proposals on the grounds that they had been made in the expectation of a meeting either tripartite between the Academic Advisory Committee/Statutes Committee/ Staff Association or bipartite between the Academic Advisory Committee and the Staff Association. The Statutes Committee held the view that it was not the role of the Academic Advisory Committee to intervene in the internal affairs of the College. Lord Brown had read out their terms of reference which clearly stated that they were advisory to the Governors and he had deprecated the action of Sir John Wolfenden in writing to the Chairman of the Academic Advisory Committee which allowed Sir Walter Worboys direct access to the Chairman of the UGC.

The minute went on: 'The Academic Advisory Committee had indicated that they accepted the advisory nature of their role but nevertheless considered it vital that a meeting should be held between them and the Staff Association. They had requested Lord Brown to seek the approval of Governors to such a meeting.'

Governors were in some difficulty as acceptance would entail one sub-committee of Governors, the Academic Advisory Committee, usurping the role of another, the Statutes Committee. In addition the position of the Principal might be one of some difficulty if the Academic Advisory Committee dealt direct with the Staff Association. Governors agreed that the agreement of the Principal to the meeting should be a necessary condition. The Principal informed Governors that in the special circumstances which existed he would have no objection to such a meeting taking place.

My ready agreement was motivated by a desire to avoid a confrontation of any kind, and did not imply that I accepted the point of view of some of the more vocal members of the Staff Association. In any case it seemed the only way out of the impasse.

The Governors finally agreed that 'in view of the special circumstances and the reassurance of the Principal that the proposal was acceptable to him, the Academic Advisory Committee should hold a meeting with the Staff Association representatives', and that the Committee 'should present in writing to Governors any amendments which were supported by the Committee.'

Members of the Advisory Committee came to the meeting on 9 April fully aware that it was essential 'to bring about a rapprochement between the Governors and the Staff Association'. Noel Annan had prepared certain amendments, including a suggestion that there might be 'lay representation on the Senate of four members of Council'; this I opposed for it was the powers of the Senate and not its composition that was the main source of trouble.

The representatives of the Staff Association expressed their fears 'that the present draft relegated the Senate to a minor role in the government of the University which would restrict its activities to those of advising the Council.' They admitted however 'that in some respects it was not different from other University Charters but the Staff Association could not divorce the content of the Draft Charter and Statutes from the Chairman of Governors' publicly expressed views on a hierarchical system of university government.' Apparently remarks the Chairman had made in an address at a Diploma in Technology conferment ceremony in the College on 27 March 1963 still rankled in the minds of some staff. The representatives agreed they were conscious that the Association's proposal for the Senate to be 'supreme governing body of the University in all academic matters . . .' reflected the extreme position the Association had chosen 'in attempting to correct the imbalance between Council and Senate'. The Committee in reply said it was prepared to recommend substantial amendments to the draft aimed at preserving the powers of the Senate in matters that were wholly academic, but did not accept that the remuneration and conditions of service of academic staff could be so regarded.

The Committee's amendments were submitted to the Statutes Committee on 26 April and to the Governors on 28 April 1965, when a final re-draft of the Charter and Statutes was agreed— final except for the wording of two Statutes which were to be discussed at a meeting between the Statutes Committee and the Staff Association representatives on 14 May. Members of the Academic Advisory Committee were informed of the developments.

12. Biology and Chemistry Building

13. Physics Building

At the meeting a great measure of agreement was achieved; the Honorary Secretary of the Staff Association later wrote to Lord Brown stating that 'the full Committee have now met and it was agreed that at a meeting next Thursday we could recommend to the academic staff the full acceptance of the documents amended last Friday, with the exception of 19.4.' This Statute referred to removal from office 'for good cause'. A full meeting of the Staff followed on 20 May when the Draft Charter and Statutes were accepted, but with proposed amendments to Statutes 18.5 and 19.4. The former was a new point and raised no difficulty; the latter however had to be left unresolved. The Staff Association wished to have some wording added 'which would quite explicitly give a member of the permanent staff tenure of office, except for the Good Cause Section.' The Governors could not agree; 'to do so would be exceeding their public duty'.

Lord Brown wrote to the Honorary Secretary:

It is of course a pity that we are not able to put on record complete agreement between the Governing Body and the Staff Association vis a vis the Charter and Statutes. Nevertheless our disagreement is about a quite clear-cut point and I think that the differing doubts of the parties concerned are perfectly understandable from their different points of view. The presentation of a petition to the Privy Council by the Staff, if they so wish, therefore resolves itself into a request for the degree of protection of employment envisaged. It is not a complex emotional issue and should be readily resolved by that body by taking a simple decision.

And there discussions ended.

At last the re-draft could be submitted to the University Grants Committee; copies were sent on 21 May 1965 in time for its meeting in June. By August 1965 the draft Charter and Statutes had reached the Privy Council, and 'the humble Petition of the Governors of Brunel College of Advanced Technology' had been referred to a Committee of the Lords of Her Majesty's Most Honourable Privy Council. The Governors were informed of submissions and objections received and were invited to comment.

Nearly a year elapsed before the Committee of the Privy Council reported that a Charter might be granted. There came an announcement that at the Court at Buckingham Palace on the 9th day of June 1966

Her Majesty having taken into consideration the said Report, and the Draft Charter accompanying it, was pleased, by and with the advice of Her Privy Council, to approve thereof, and to order, as it is hereby ordered, that the Right Honourable Roy Jenkins, one of Her Majesty's Principal Secretaries of State, do cause a warrant to be prepared for Her Majesty's Royal Signature, for passing under the Great Seal a Charter in conformity with the said draft, which is hereby annexed.

A few weeks later the Charter with Her Majesty's Royal Signature arrived at the College, and was greeted with general rejoicing.

The year of waiting had passed slowly; the Academic Advisory Committee had met on 13 January 1966 and noted that 'petitions from the Association of University Teachers and the Staff Association had been forwarded to the College by the Privy Council and replies had been sent by the Governors. No new matter of principle had arisen in the petitions.' In fact apart from proposals for minor alterations the main objection of both Associations was to Clause 19. The Committee did not meet again until 12 July 1966 and then 'expressed pleasure at the grant of the Charter as from 6 July 1966', and noted the amendments made to the Charter and Statutes by the Privy Council. The wording of the contested clause 19.4 (re-numbered 20.4) had been left unchanged.

The outcome owed much to the patient chairmanship of Sir Walter Worboys and his skilful guidance at difficult times. There was common consent that if the Charter enabled the University to get through its first ten years successfully the Committee would be well satisfied. Universities were without doubt entering a period of significant change, but few observers anticipated the nature or the intensity of the student troubles that exploded in the late nineteen-sixties in Britain and Europe.

At Brunel there was little pressure for student participation in university government, certainly little from officers of the Students' Union with whom I had discussions throughout. The National Union of Students, however, took a much stronger line and made submissions to the Privy Council. The University Grants Committee reported:[7]

[7] *University Development, 1962–67*, 62.

The Privy Council, after considering representations made to it by the National Union of Students and receiving advice from us, decided to put to the bodies sponsoring new Charters the desirability of including the following provisions.

1. The Senate and the Council of the new universities should be expressly empowered to establish joint committees of themselves and representatives of the student body.
2. Provision should be made whereby a procedure would be laid down for a right on the part of a student suspended or expelled to be formally heard by the Senate or by a body appointed by the Senate before the decision became final.
3. Provision should be made for an association representing the student body.

The Report went on:

The provision for joint committees of the Council or Senate and the student body reflected a general feeling that systematic arrangements should be made for consultation between university authorities and students on matters of proper concern to the students. It gave formal expression to a practice which had already developed widely, though often on an informal basis, among the existing universities. Apart from this aspect, the new Charters did not in general introduce innovations in the matter of student participation in university government. Proposals for such participation, such as those put forward by the National Union of Students for student representation on Council and Senate, seemed to us to raise a number of serious difficulties.

The comment concluded: 'It seemed doubtful whether in practice provision for such student representation would be as effective a means of bringing student opinion to bear as provision for matters involving student interests to be discussed by joint Council/Student and Senate/Student Committees.'

This last view appealed to me and I pressed it in later discussions with Governors and students. Participation should grow 'from the grass-roots'—in departments and schools, rather than trail downwards from above. At the initiative of the Privy Council, provision was made in the final form of the Statutes for such joint committees to be set up. The Powers of the Council were extended 'to establish Joint Committees of the Council and representatives of the Students' Union and to prescribe the method of appointment of such representatives and the functions of such Committees.'

Similarly, the powers, duties and functions of the Senate were amended to include the following:

To establish Joint Committees of the Senate and representatives of the Students' Union and to prescribe the method of appointment of such representatives and the functions of such committees.

To regulate the discipline of the students of the University and to determine in what manner disciplinary powers shall be exercised.

After consideration of a report from the Vice-Chancellor and Principal, and subject to the provisions of Statute 23, to expel any student who, having been suspended or excluded by the Vice-Chancellor and Principal, appears to the Senate to have been guilty of grave misconduct.

And Statute 23 set out the processes by which a student who had been suspended or excluded could appeal and such an appeal could be heard.

It remained to be seen how these and other provisions in the Charter and Statutes would function. For some students Joint Committees were at best inadequate and there developed increasing pressure for direct student involvement in the work of Senate and Council. Changes were made later.[8]

A final word: the first schedule accompanying the Charter gave the names of the first officers of the University. The first Chancellor was the Earl of Halsbury, who had kindly accepted an invitation from the Governing Body, and the first Pro-Chancellor was Lord Brown.

[8] See page 371.

CHAPTER 14

Buildings at Uxbridge—Phase One

THE first report of the Planning Group was presented to the New College Committee at the end of November, 1962. The Group had already met five times, and in addition there had been meetings with members of the academic staff and with officials of the Ministries of Education, Transport, and Housing and Local Government.

Early completion of some of the buildings was a first priority, and ways were sought to speed up the procedures. The Development Plan indicated that the first phase could be completed by July 1967, but the Architect later informed the Planning Group that this could be achieved by July 1966 if exceptional means were taken, namely, the appointment of a nominated contractor at an early stage, the use of a two-stage contract, and the provision of an agreed College brief by 30 April 1963. The first of these was the main obstacle and was never overcome; its discussion took endless time.

A.T. Memorandum No. 2 issued in September 1962 by the Ministry of Education set out the 'Building Procedure for Major Projects at Colleges of Advanced Technology'. In particular, the contractual procedure was precisely formulated: 'since major projects at Colleges of Advanced Technology will often be of a specialised type, the Ministry expects that Colleges will usually find it appropriate to adopt selective rather than open tendering. This procedure entails the preparation of a list of contractors chosen according to their known ability to do the work in question.' It went on: 'the Ministry's prior approval should be obtained if Colleges wish (a) to negotiate a tender with a nominated contractor, or (b) to accept a tender other than the lowest.'

In February 1963 Richard Sheppard reported on his visit to

the Ministry seeking approval for a nominated contractor procedure. The Ministry's idea of such an arrangement 'was a contractor who, having received from the Architects the detailed drawings *and* the priced bill of quantities, had quoted for the construction of the new buildings by giving a *total* price for the completed work. The only saving of time gained by such a procedure would be the normal period given for the delivery of tenders.' The New College Committee, on the other hand, hoped to reduce the time of completion of the buildings by at least one year 'by nominating a contractor who, without detailed examination of the bill of quantities, would enter into an agreement to perform the work at agreed costs per cubic foot or similar basis but without quoting a total figure for the completed work'. Mr Brown, Professor Sparkes and the Principal were asked to negotiate with the Ministry but it was of no avail; the officers remained adamant.

The Planning Group and the New College Committee had many other issues to decide; their discussions ranged over all the proposals adumbrated in the Development Plan and even more widely. They were concerned about the playing fields, about the acquisition of the various pieces of land mentioned in the Plan, about housing policy for students and staff, public relations and the integration of the College with Uxbridge. They had suggestions to make too about the college buildings and the purposes they were to serve; in particular there were long discussions about the advantages of concentrating all the lecture-rooms in one central building for general use instead of distributing them throughout the College with some assigned to each Department. Members of the Group paid a visit in November 1962 to the University of Manchester Institute of Science and Technology (UMIST) then in the middle of an extensive building programme, part of which included a grouping of lecture rooms, some larger than the Brunel planners had in mind but of great interest nevertheless. One of them, I recall, was large enough to house an orchestra and an audience of several hundred. It was out of these deliberations that the concept of the Brunel lecture centre took shape. Initially the building was to have housed Management, Psychology and General Studies as well as the bulk of the College lecture-rooms, but other counsels prevailed. First designed as a high building, it was transformed into one with only three floors and, for cheapness, no lifts except a small one to move equipment to the large lecture theatres, six of which were incorporated into one end of the building giving it a very distinctive form.

The work of the Architects and the Planning Group had not progressed very far when a request came (in September 1962) from the Ministry of Education for advance notice of building projects which the Governors foresaw as likely to start in 1964–5 and 1965–6. The best guess, or expression of hope, that could be made then was as in Table 14.1. The list served as a basis of discussion with the Ministry of Education and many of the buildings in the projected 1964–5 starts were later agreed and included in Phase One, but the others and those listed under 1965–6 had to wait until 1966–7 or even later.

TABLE 14.1

	Start on Site	Complete
Year 1964–5		
Mechanical, Production Engineering Depts } Other Studies Depts, Metallurgy. }	April 64	June 66
Part Communal Building	June 64	June 66
Hall of Residence (300 students) } Boiler House }	September 64	June 66
Electrical, Mathematics, Physics Depts	December 64	June 67
Year 1965–6		
Part Communal Building	December 65	June 67
Second Hall of Residence (400 students)	September 65	June 67
Chemistry, Biology Depts	June 65	March 68

In December 1962 the Solicitor to the College reported that the contract had been completed for the purchase of Sites 2 and 3; he also suggested that instead of the Governors taking an option on the purchase of Site 5 the County Council might be willing to sell forthwith. The Governors thereupon instructed the Solicitor to obtain a firm offer from the County Council as soon as practicable. Negotiations concerning the acquisition of Sites 1 and 4 were also started, and in February 1963 Richard Sheppard was instructed by the New College Committee to proceed with an application for planning permission in respect of Sites 1 and 5, while the Surveyor to the College (Mr Hill of Messrs Matthews and Goodman) was asked to continue his enquiries with regard to Site 4. The owners of Site 4 so it turned out were unwilling to sell, and ideas about its acquisition and of a link between Sites 2 and 5 through Site 4 were ultimately abandoned. However, arrangements for the purchase of Site 1 went well; Alan Thompson of the Ministry of Education wrote on 25 June 1963, 'if planning permission is granted on the basis of the development proposed by the College (and on no other basis) the Ministry would be prepared to finance the acquisition of the site subject of course to the agreement of the District Valuer on the price'. Planning permission for Site 1 was granted subject to a number of conditions, but the application to use Site 5 for playing fields was turned down 'on agricultural land use grounds'. In spite of this the Governors decided in July 1963 to buy Site 5 from the Middlesex County Council at the agreed figure of £10,000 'as the prospective value of the site to the College far outweighed the temporary difficulties arising from a refusal by the Local Planning Authority to grant planning permission for its use as playing fields', a decision that entailed negotiating a loan from the Midland Bank and meeting any loan charges from College resources—which had still to be assembled! There was some confidence however that an appeal against the planning decision would in due course be successful, in which case the Ministry of Education would, the College was assured, provide funds to meet the cost of the purchase.[1] The outcome was a happy one for the Governors; in June 1964 I reported that 'planning permission for the use of Site 5 *as playing fields* has been obtained and the Department of Education and Science[2] has provided the purchase money'. I added, 'the bank overdraft facilities authorised by the Governors have now been cleared and the bank interest, amounting to £37-5-6 has been paid from the Principal's Fund'—a rather frail College resource, but having the virtue that it did not come from public funds. It has to be added however that the Ministry questioned the procedure of purchase that the College had adopted.

There was progress too with Site 3. The Ministry of Education approved the proposals for the lay-out of playing fields[3] and the erection of pavilions at costs of £18,150 and £6,900

<hr />

[1] Letter from the Ministry of Education, 6 June 1963.
[2] The new department was created in April 1964. See chapter 15.
[3] See chapter 11.

respectively, and an order was placed with Messrs J. S. Bishop[4] & Co. Ltd in February 1963 for the first part of the work which included twelve hard tennis courts. Alterations to the plans for the main pavilion, made on the recommendation of the Ministry, raised the estimate to £8,200, and the tender finally accepted was for £11,971 12s. 6d. By October/November 1963 the playing fields were available for 'limited use' and the main pavilion completed. They were of course a long way from Acton and as long as the College remained there the facilities were not fully used, but they were increasingly appreciated by the students. Their acquisition was celebrated by students and staff at a formal opening on 20 May 1964. (B. H. Winstanley and I had the pleasure of beating our student opponents at tennis; I hardly need add that B. H. W. was a strong player.)

A groundsman's house was added later, but the Ministry did not agree to the erection of a number of other service staff houses which the New College Committee had in mind. Permission much later to purchase a house in Cleveland Road for the Chief Caretaker was the only concession.

Earlier, on 28 May 1963, the College Architects, Richard Sheppard and John Stillman, had been able to present to the Governing Body their preliminary sketch designs for the new college, about a year after Richard Sheppard began to prepare his development plan. He pointed out that certain changes had been made in the original plan 'inasmuch as the initial plan had suggested the siting of the new College on an east–west axis on which would be placed the central core of the college, to the north of which would be sited residential accommodation and to the south the academic buildings of the College.' He explained the advantages of using a radial and not a linear basis, with the refectory facilities in one central building and the lecture centre nearby; he had tried to ensure that the College community was not more than a short walking distance from the centre. Richard Sheppard also outlined the buildings that were to comprise Phase One, but changes were made later in the light of the advice of the Planning Group. Essential elements were a hall of residence, the Engineering Complex and the central boiler-house, part of a communal building with common rooms, refectories and kitchens, part of a central lecture building and

---

[4] Bishop's tender was for £15,967 13s. 11½d.—what delightful accuracy!

an administration building. Provision for Social Science and General Studies was desirable too, and whatever else could be provided out of the total sum of £2.7 million of which £0.5 million would have to be spent on site-works.

At the next meeting of the New College Committee on 19 June 1963 I questioned whether the Architect's outline plan for the College was likely to take up too much land on Site 2 and whether 'it might not be advisable at this stage to consider building to six-storey level, particularly for halls of residence, in order to leave room for expansion should the number of students in the College reach a figure of 5000 or more'.

The Architects took the view that 3,500 was the maximum number of students that could be accommodated on Site 2 with residential provision for 2,000 students; they added, 'the construction of six-storey buildings would create problems in circulation space, the communal areas and in ancillary areas such as car parks'. Also it was possible 'that the Planning Authority might consider that the population on Site 2, even as at present planned, was too concentrated'. The Committee accepted 3,500 as a maximum figure, noted that the Architects had allowed for a 30 per cent expansion in the academic buildings with a possible 50 per cent expansion in the Engineering Complex, and that any further expansion would probably take place on Site 1 'if and when acquired by the College'.

As to the Engineering Buildings it was explained that the proposed siting of staff offices and drawing offices away from the laboratories and workshops, which had been questioned at the Governors' meeting, had the support of the staff of the departments concerned and the Architects were authorized to proceed with the preparation of detailed drawings.

Messrs Zisman, Bowyer and Partners, who had been appointed as Engineering Consultants to the College, presented a report on space heating and electric power generation. They suggested that an oil-fired plant would be more suitable for heating, but

separate consideration of electric power supplies indicated that generation by the College itself of its own electric power was more economical than extracting power from the National Grid because of the ability of the College to utilise waste heat from the generating plant. It was noted, however, that the capital cost of a power installation would be of the order of £140,000 in excess of that of connecting to the National Grid. It was further noted that this sum could be amortised over 10 years by savings of approximately £14,000 per year on lower running costs. . . .

The Committee then discussed the proposition[5] that in the interests of the National economy consideration should be given to the installation at Brunel of a heating and power generation system which would use pulverised fuel and mechanical stokers. It was realised that this would involve about £140,000 extra investment. It was agreed, however, that there would be benefit to the College if its students could have first-hand experience of a pulverised fuel installation, and benefit to the national economy if at least one College of Technology was to provide an advanced unit of this kind to demonstrate both to students and to industry the viability of using indigenous fuels. . . .

It was finally decided that the Chairman should write to the Chairman of the National Coal Board, Lord Robens, and if the Coal Board were actively interested in promoting such a scheme then the matter should be fully investigated, and subject to the results of this investigation being favourable a recommendation should be made to the Ministry of Education accordingly.

The reaction of the National Coal Board was generous but to accept their offer would in the opinion of the Architects and Consultant Engineers have caused delay in the preparation of the plans for the Central Boiler House; there were also some technical difficulties and so it was decided to install an oil-fired heating system as recommended by the Consultants, who were asked, however, to prepare a further report[6] on the site generation of electricity.

The New College Committee's concern about delays was heightened by the report (8 October 1963) of Messrs Stillman and Eastwick-Field that work could not be started on the Engineering Complex by May 1964, as the Planning Group had proposed, because of delays caused by uncertainties arising from the siting of the engineering buildings and the type and size of the Central Boiler House. The imminent acquisition of Site 1 by the College had led Richard Sheppard, with the agreement of the Planning Group, to modify the distribution of some of the buildings in the overall plan, having in mind the long-term future of the College. This was clearly a wise decision, but it followed that work could not be started on the Engineering

---

[5] Strongly supported by Wilfred Brown.
[6] Proposal for Power Generation combined with Heating, Nov. 1963.

Complex earlier than late 1964. Completion could be expected two years later. The Committee called for 'the closest study of all methods to restore the original completion date of the first phase', but one unexpected development after another conspired to push completion further into the future.

Site 1 came into the possession of the College in October 1963, the Ministry of Education on the District Valuer's report having approved the purchase price of £235,000. Moreover the conditions attached by the Authority to the planning permission for this area were not regarded as too restrictive, and a number of other decisions cleared the way forward; in particular the Ministry agreed to cost limits totalling £1,958,213 for some of the buildings and services included in Phase One. In November 1963 we wrote to the Ministry pointing out that the Planning Group had recommended that Sites 1 and 2 should be linked as soon as possible. 'To strengthen the idea of the unity of the sites, and for other reasons, it is proposed that the social science block which is in the first phase should be constructed on Site 1. If this is done essential services must be provided on Site 1 from Site 2.' The immediate requirement was for a footbridge about 8 feet wide which would span the railway and carry the essential services (hot water and electricity) within its framework. The Architects, in their outline drawings, had shown a footbridge for pedestrians and two other bridges for use by vehicles, but financial provision for these bridges had not been included in the Phase One cost limits, and the College sought approval. The upshot was that the Ministry agreed in principle to the provision of a footbridge, but postponed a decision on the road bridges as they would 'not be needed for some time to come and their provision might be affected by any proposals which the College might have to acquire the railway land itself'.[7] British Rail had decided to close the railway line.

A less controversial addition to the programme was the CLEAPSE building. The Ministry of Education had written in June 1962, to follow up proposals made at a meeting which Dr Gurr and I attended; the conference of chairmen of the education committees of London and the Home Counties had agreed in principle to the formation of a consortium for science equipment, which became known as CLEAPSE. Such a body, whose

[7] Letter from Ministry of Education, 21 Jan. 1964.

full title was Consortium of Local Education Authorities for the Provision of Science Equipment, would need a small development group of teachers, scientists and designers who would assist in the compilation of a basic equipment catalogue for schools, test equipment and develop apparatus 'in fields where no suitable apparatus is available at a satisfactory price'. The Ministry[8] was prepared to locate the group at Brunel and to provide accordingly, an offer which the Governors willingly accepted. It seemed to me that to have such an activity on the campus would support very acceptably the work I hoped a Department of Education in the College would undertake. A schedule of accommodation was in due course agreed, about 6,750 square feet for offices and laboratories costing around £35,000. The unit became an integral part of Phase One.

Another possible addition that was canvassed but did not materialize concerned the National College of Rubber Technology which had been associated since its inception with the Northern Polytechnic but was looking for a new home. The Robbins Committee had concluded that 'on the future of the six National Colleges no simple pronouncement is possible' and had recommended that the future of each of the colleges should be considered on its merits. Wilfred Brown and I had discussions with the Chairman and vice-Chairman of the National College of Rubber Technology at their invitation and it seemed possible at one time that the College could be linked with Brunel, but our recommendation of a post-graduate school closely connected with industry did not prove acceptable then. Interestingly enough a working party set up by the National College to consider its future reported in November 1964 and recommended that the College should become a post-graduate centre of polymer technology affiliated to Loughborough College of Technology (later Loughborough University of Technology) and the College moved there, leaving its courses of undergraduate standard at the Northern Polytechnic in London.

By the beginning of 1965 the New College Committee's ideas about housing for the staff were beginning to take more definite shape although a number of problems were still unresolved, particularly the type of Housing Association that might be set

8 Letter from Ministry of Education, 3 Apr. 1963.

up. John Morton proposed an association consisting of three groups, namely, representatives of Brunel, representatives of Uxbridge and representatives from an existing housing association. He took the view that a mixed association would enable the College to make a contribution to the social as well as the educational life of Uxbridge and that a community including local residents would provide a better social environment for the Staff. For such a venture land other than that owned by the College would probably have to be acquired. Some members of the Committee were opposed to links with other external housing groups and stressed the advantages of a Brunel Housing Association, in the complete control of the College, able to build houses for use by newly recruited academic staff; transitional housing as it was called 'might well prove a deciding factor in obtaining the highest quality of staff available'. Other possibilities were examined and re-examined; one difficulty that was never surmounted was the likelihood of a Housing Association in the course of time passing out of the control of the University. Another was the ownership of the land on which the houses were built. Could the University sell its land to the Association, which had to own the land to qualify for Government grant?

The debate went on; it became clear that any housing for the staff erected on the College campus would have to be built by the College from College funds, and that any Housing Association or Society would have to acquire land outside the campus (preferably close by) and with Brunel representatives controlling the Association or Society. In spite of all the efforts of John Morton the latter did not prove possible. The Committee, however, pressed on for a while with the idea of transitional housing, and in June 1964 asked the Architect to submit a planning application for the maximum number of houses that could be built on the tongue of land at the northern extremity of Site 2 contiguous to the Uxbridge Road, but this foundered basically because the Ministry could not provide funds, and there were planning permission difficulties too.

The Uxbridge Borough Council were helpful in these attempts to provide houses for the staff of the College, even though they had housing problems of their own, but planning permission for housing on the land owned by the College was bedevilled by the Authorities' refusals of earlier applications by the previous owners, Wimpeys. Local residents who lived near the College boundaries were sensitive too.

From the outset the Governors had pursued a policy of fostering good relations with the Borough Council and of ensuring that the people of Uxbridge were adequately informed about the College's purposes and likely development. In January 1963 the Mayor and Town Clerk and about twenty members of the Council came to Acton and had a discussion with Governors about the College's plans for the future; it was the inauguration of a series of joint meetings which were arranged about twice a year and proved very useful. The Planning Group devoted a good deal of time to 'public relations' and helped the College to realize the importance of maintaining a constant flow of information about its work and aims. The Principal, vice-Principal and Heads of Departments spoke at schools and public meetings, and to groups like the local History Society and Rotary Clubs; a mere trickle at first which grew later into a stream with some force and direction. There were proposals at one time about appointing a Public Relations Officer but our own amateur efforts had to suffice.

When the Borough of Uxbridge was absorbed into the larger London Borough of Hillingdon in April 1965 the College maintained its policy, and meetings were held with representatives of the new Borough from time to time. The New College Committee still hoped that joint planning schemes, particularly concerning the area between the College buildings and the centre of Uxbridge and referred to earlier as Uxbridge-Brunel, would be possible, but such a project needed resources which the College did not have and Hillingdon was too new, with its own problems of uniting three different local government areas and creating new civic arrangements and loyalties, to be able to accept in reasonable time a town planning venture with such wide and costly implications. College and Borough had to be satisfied with much simpler modes of co-operation. Moreover, more straightforward problems such as road access to the College's main sites, the exchange of small areas of land, and the use of the railway-line areas which the Borough acquired, were complex enough.

To get Phase One started, and completed by September 1966, dominated the College's problems. An outline planning application, submitted in August 1963, was approved in December 1963 and the preparation of detailed working drawings was begun. In January 1964 Richard Sheppard informed the New College Committee of the satisfactory progress of the work on the Hall of Residence 'on which tender was likely in April 1964, contract in May, a start on the site in June for completion in September/October 1965'. The Central Lecture Block and the Administration Block

had both been held up by adjustment to the schedules of accommodation by the College.[9] He welcomed the Ministry's acceptance of the construction of six lecture theatres in Phase One and was awaiting details from the College as to the size of rooms to be fitted into the 19,000 sq. ft. for lecture class-rooms now approved by the Ministry for Phase One. Discussions would also be held with the College on the administration block in view of the Ministry's suggestion that temporary refectory accommodation should be provided in the first phase, within the revised total for the block.

And John Stillman's preparatory work for the Engineering Complex was going well too; he reported 'that the necessary application forms to the Ministry had been completed by him, which together with two sets of drawings would be submitted by the College to seek approval for final cost limits including extra costs'.

Both Architects pressed once more for urgent decisions by the Ministry on negotiated contract procedure and on-site generation of electricity—problems that were still with us, and I was asked to approach the Ministry again. But the Committee agreed that 'even if the Ministry decided against negotiated contract procedure or against the proposal for site generation of electricity, the Architects should be instructed to proceed immediately with the remaining alternatives'—which indeed they had to do.

The Architects' later reports in May 1964 showed that satisfactory progress was being maintained; the Ministry had approved the construction of the southern half of the perimeter road, drawings were being prepared to enable detailed planning application for Phase One to be made by the end of the month, and three national contractors had indicated their interest in the

[9] There was a continuing tension, not unfriendly, between the Architects and the College as to the causes of delay.

work. It was hoped to go out to tender for some of the buildings in September 1964, by which time a model illustrating the whole of the Phase One development would have been constructed (Plate 4). Shops were also to be included in the first phase subject to the availability of finance, and the Midland Bank was to be approached. Car-parks, for which little expenditure was likely to be sanctioned by the Ministry, would somehow have to be provided.

With so much of the general plan of the new College completed the demands on the Planning Group and the New College Committee began to change. Much of the 'planning' still to be done related to details of individual buildings and services, and to the commissioning of equipment which the Engineering Consultants could not be expected to undertake. The Planning Group was therefore re-constituted,[10] its members being the Principal, the Vice-Principal, the Planning Assistant (S. A. Urry) and Richard Sheppard; also a member of the academic staff, John Eden of the Mechanical Engineering Department, was seconded to assist with the selection and purchase of specialist equipment of all kinds. He became Planning Assistant (Equipment). The appointments of Professor Sparkes and John Morton as architectural consultants, both of whom had made invaluable contributions, were not continued, but the services of Professor Sparkes were retained on a more limited basis.

This did not mean all the problems had been solved and all the issues decided. Alongside Site 1 was the Uxbridge Football Club ground; the future of the Club was uncertain and rumours had been circulating for some time about what was to happen to the ground. Could the College take it over? Or would the Directors wish to get planning permission for housing on it before selling at an enhanced price? Or was the Club desirous of developing the site by providing squash courts and similar facilities? A few of us met some of the Directors and explored a number of possibilities; might the Club sell the ground to the College but be allowed to rent it on a long lease? And how was the College going to develop playing facilities on Site 5? Was a joint enterprise with the Football Club or other Uxbridge interests feasible? It was a friendly exercise but little came of it;

[10] New College Committee, 24 Feb. 1964.

the New College Committee however went so far as to instruct the College Surveyor to negotiate a purchase price for the football ground with the owners and offer a long-term lease of ten to fifteen years' duration but 'no commitment should be made on behalf of the College for the joint development of Site 5'.

The Surveyor was also asked (September 1964) to attempt to negotiate the purchase of Site 4 for £125,000, 'subject to the agreement of the Department of Education and Science to the purchase and the District Valuer's approval of the price' but the approach was unsuccessful although at one stage the owners indicated they would be interested in an offer of £150,000. There was never any indication that DES would provide the money.

Phase Two began to assume a greater urgency, if only to make it possible to give contractors tendering for Phase One reasonably accurate information about the next stages in the development. Even more the whole pattern of building ahead had to be shaped, and to avoid the stop and start discontinuities of a succession of separate phases the Planning Group was asked to draw up an ordered sequence of buildings for the future.

The list they presented to the New College Committee in September 1964 was as in Table 14.2.

It also included a fifth hall of residence and a second communal block, and looking even further ahead referred to buildings for materials science, constructional engineering, chemical engineering and nuclear engineering, and postgraduate residences.

The list is interesting as an index of College policy at the time and of the College's outlook about the future; what was achieved was very different. The first two items, for instance, were not built and the Third Hall of Residence only got into a later programme because finance became available through the Appeal which the University launched. On the other hand the Shops and Bank were moved forward to Phase One, made possible by the generosity of the Midland Bank, with a gift of £25,000 to the building funds.

The Committee's consideration of the future programme was timely for the Chairman of the University Grants Committee wrote on 3 and 4 September 1964, indicating that of the £83 million allocated to universities for building starts in

1966-9 the sum of £33 million had been apportioned to 1966-7, and the College was requested to submit not later than 15 October 1964 a list of buildings regarded as being highest in priority. Out of £33 million the College had little confidence that it would be granted the sum of money it needed, and its share turned out to be £620,000, the beginning of the less liberal treatment it was accorded as a university.

TABLE 14.2

Starts	Buildings	Approximate Cost	
		£	
April 1966	Service Staff and Provisional Housing	225,000	
	Vice-Chancellor's Residence	20,000	
	Second Hall of Residence	225,000	
	Electrical Engineering	300,000	
	Mathematics	130,000	
	Physics	250,000	
	Students' Union	150,000	
	Third Hall of Residence	225,000	
	Shops and Bank	20,000	
			1,545,000
April 1967	Chemistry	330,000	
	Biology	200,000	
	Central Lecture Block (Second Part)	100,000	
	Playing Fields	60,000	
	Sports Barn	30,000	
			720,000
April 1968	Fourth Hall of Residence	225,000	
	Hall	80,000	
	Theatre	30,000	
	Library	200,000	
	Department of Education	100,000	
			635,000

The New College Committee had more immediate decisions to make. Tenders had been received for the building of part of the perimeter road including a bridge over the River Pinn, and the lowest, totalling £72,342 17s. 5d. from W. J. Glossop & Co., was accepted subject to the approval of the Department. I had urged earlier that there were good reasons why this road should be constructed as soon as possible and should not wait for a start on the Phase One buildings. The Architects were not very enamoured of such a procedure but they ultimately agreed. And

so it came about that the road was the first part of the new
University to be built. It entered Site 2 from Kingston Lane far
enough away from a possible roundabout, and after two right-
angled bends, left and right respectively, ran parallel to the
likely route of the Iver Link Road, which still conditioned much
of the planning, and across the Pinn to the western boundary of
the site. Contractors arrived in October 1964, and the work
began. If there were technical reasons for not starting the road
first, they were insignificant compared with the psychological
boost the College got from the visible signs that the new University was being built—four long years after the expansion at
Acton had been stopped. It seemed a more significant event
than the completion of the playing fields on Site 3 a year earlier,
important though that was.

The Planning Group had good reason to feel well pleased
with the results of its two years' work; it had by common consent
contributed outstandingly to the planning of the College, a
contribution that owed much to S. A. Urry as Planning
Assistant and Secretary. In October 1964 the Group lost his
valued services on his appointment as Head of the new Department of Industrial Training in the College. Much of his work
was taken over by Dr G. C. Shipp who became responsible for
all the liaison work with the Architects and the University
Grants Committee, and continued to have the assistance of John
Eden as Planning Assistant (Equipment). These changes reinforced those made earlier in February 1964. The Group met
less frequently but continued to report to the New College
Committee. Two Clerks of Works and a Site Engineer were
appointed and they took up their duties in February and March
1965.

Tenders for the Phase One buildings were received in
November 1964 and that of Messrs George Wimpey & Co. was
accepted. There had been protracted discussions about which
buildings should be included in Phase One, about their size and
content and whether they should be built in part only; together
they had to form a workable whole and there was a firm restriction on total cost, namely £2.7 million. After the receipt of
tenders negotiations continued between the Architects, Quantity Surveyors and the Ministry, and agreement was reached on
the following costs.

	£
Administration Building	117,863
Central Lecture Building (part)	312,846
Communal Building	227,164
Hall of Residence	247,062
Engineering Complex (including Science	
Equipment Consortium)	1,111,567
Central Boiler House	129,362
Additionals (external work etc.)	560,971

It was understood that as these totalled £2,706,835 some further small adjustments had to be made.

A letter of intent was sent to Wimpey's on 8 January 1965 but a last-minute difficulty arose that delayed the signing of the contract. National economic troubles had led the Government to introduce a Control of Office and Industrial Development Bill which placed a moratorium on all buildings with office space greater than 2,500 square feet, and so the inclusion of the Administration Building in the Phase One contract came into question. To proceed a special permit was required from the Board of Trade and application could not be made until the Bill became law. It was March before the difficulties were resolved, a very unfortunate delay of three months and the first of a number of adversities that afflicted the project. To make a start possible the Administration Building had to be excluded from the contract. As late as May 1965 the New College Committee noted that the Bill 'had been delayed in the House of Lords and the issue of an office development permit was not yet possible', and it was mid-summer before the Administration Building was restored as part of the contract.

However, in May the Architects were able to report that the rest of Phase One was proceeding reasonably well; moreover the south perimeter road contract had been completed satisfactorily in March and the road handed over to Wimpeys.

So far so good, but there was regret that a number of buildings including the Social Science Block and the Vice-Chancellor's residence had had to be omitted from Phase One. Earlier the College had expected that in addition to the £2.7 million, which had been associated with 1964-5 starts, a further sum would be made available for 1965-6 starts, but this did not happen. I had written to Alan Thompson at the Ministry of Education in

November 1963, asking if funds could be made available for other Halls of Residence and for bridges over the railway line so as to link Sites 1 and 2 (see page 256), and although his reply[11] was not very encouraging he had gone so far as to say: 'What we could do provisionally is to provide for the start of a second hall of residence in the 1965/66 building programme. This hall might be a duplicate of the one included in the first instalment and might indeed follow on immediately after the completion of the first.'

The College hoped that its allocation for 1966–7 building starts would take account of its outstanding needs, but as mentioned earlier the UGC granted a meagre £620,000.

The Governors[12] 'expressed very serious concern at the paucity of the allocation which radically altered the policy previously accepted by the Department of Education and Science for the rapid development of Brunel at Uxbridge', and the Chairman and Principal were asked to represent their views to Sir John Wolfenden. This was of little avail, and Lord Brown followed it up in his maiden speech in the House of Lords on 4 February 1965. Not only did he complain of the poor support for Brunel University but suggested that technology was neglected in university provision generally, and went on to criticize the functions of the University Grants Committee itself, which was perhaps a blunder. He got little support from their Lordships, some of whom were moved to reply to his criticisms of universities but Lord Snow of 'two cultures' fame lightly recognized their validity and concluded: 'I am afraid to do anything with institutions of a university nature without causing intolerable friction, on the one side, or loss to society, on the other, is going to take all our wits.' The Governors were left to try their wits on members of the UGC when they visited the College a few months later.

Several ways of using the 1966–7 allocation were discussed by the New College Committee, having in mind the imperative need to minimize the period of division of the College into two parts, one at Acton and the other ten miles away at Uxbridge. The academic reasons were overriding, but to unite the two sections would also have led to considerable saving, not least the annual loan charges of about £75,000 that had to be paid to the Middlesex County Council as long as the College remained at Acton.

[11] Letter dated 21 Jan. 1964.   [12] Meeting of Governing Body, 7 Dec. 1964.

Could one building be so constructed that it could be used by the four departments of Biology, Chemistry, Mathematics and Physics temporarily and later revert to full use by one Department only? Or would two buildings be better, even though only half completed, one to be used by Biology and Chemistry and the other by Mathematics and Physics? Initially the Governors accepted the one-building proposal, but more detailed examination of the consequences and particularly of the cost of site-works led to a decision to build part of the Mathematics Building and to complete the Central Lecture Building, which 'could be used for other purposes e.g. housing the School of Social Sciences, the Students' Union, the Library, all of which required a low level of services'. One desirable consequence was a larger proportion of the allocation would be spent on buildings instead of non-productive site works. A major disadvantage however was that the other three departments would have to stay at Acton for a longer period.

The proposed division of the funds available was

	£
Central Lecture Building (Stage 2)	241,000
Mathematics Building (Stage 1)	271,000
Maintenance Building (Stage 1)	29,000
Site works, plant and mains	63,000
Contingencies	16,000

The New College Committee was also still deeply concerned about the provision of transitional housing and recommended[13] 'that should the UGC have any balance available in 1966–67 building starts allocations due to other institutions being unable to start on time, the College should seek an additional grant for transitional housing of the order of £150,000'. The Architects were asked to investigate the possibilities of developing the southern tip of Site 1 for housing, and the Secretary and others had a series of discussions with Housing Corporation Officers concerning the formation of a Brunel Housing Society. Indeed the New College Committee went so far as to set up a small Steering Committee in the hope that a Housing Society could be started, but it proved exceedingly difficult to reconcile the aims of the Governors with the basic rules of a Housing Society. The

[13] New College Committee, 17 May 1965.

local planning authority in due course gave permission for building on Site 1 though with the restriction that only employees of
the College could be so housed, and the Governors decided in
October 1965 'that a Housing Society should be established at an
early date', but a year later a final decision had not been made.

In fact all the effort on transitional housing and Housing
Societies ended fruitlessly; ironically enough Staff acquired
houses, so it seemed, without too much difficulty, far and near,
and there was no evidence of any driving desire to live on or near
the campus; the further away the better was a view to which not
a few staff subscribed.

Housing schemes could hardly have prospered in the economic
climate of 1965. On 27 July the Chancellor of the Exchequer
announced the economic measures which the Government had
decided to take including the 'postponement by six months of
the starting dates for capital projects (other than those in
development districts and areas of high unemployment) for
which contracts had not been signed'. In the result the amount
of university building work deferred from 1965–6 was just short
of £15 million, and the Brunel building programme was further
delayed.

Yet the New College Committee was in optimistic mood at its
twenty-first meeting on 27 September 1965 and recorded 'its
approval of the satisfactory start which had been made with the
whole of Phase One'. The Governors were to be invited to visit
the site prior to their meeting on 12 October 1965.

The Architects' reports on the progress of the buildings were
good; in Phase 1A all four buildings were on schedule; progress
in Phase 1B had been equally satisfactory; the single laboratories
were four weeks ahead of programme; work on the Engineering
Centre was two to three weeks behind programme, but
Wimpeys expected to make up time by the installation of a
tower crane; the external services duct was 60 per cent completed and the external drainage had now been finished. John
Stillman wanted early authority to proceed with the Maintenance Building in the 1966–7 starts so that essential equipment could be ordered at an early date. There was, alas, one
snag; there had been two strikes by steel fixers which had led to
a token strike of all labour on the site on Friday 24 September—
a foretaste of the labour trouble to come.

On the other hand the Administration Building had been granted an Office Development permit; indeed contracts had been signed for the Administration Building and the Central Lecture Building and work had started on both of them. The following programme of completion dates looked likely to be achieved:

Boiler House and Hall of Residence	June 1966
Engineering Complex	November 1966
Administration Building	November 1966
Communal Building	Mid-January 1967
Central Lecture Building	April 1967

and discussions were being held with the Contractors with a view to bringing forward the completion dates of the Communal and Administration Buildings.

The Committee, which towards the end of 1965 took the name of New Buildings Committee, was able to make some progress too with Site 5 having received a report from the Sports Turf Research Institute, and it was agreed to develop that part of the Site to the east of the River Pinn by laying out four pitches and erecting some fencing along the northern boundary. There was progress also with the Bank and Shops, and the Committee noted 'the possibility of acquiring the railway cutting between Sites 1 and 2 by agreement with the local authority which now proposed to zone the land for housing purposes'. To negotiate an exchange of land with Hillingdon Borough Council was clearly the best, perhaps the only, way of acquiring this important link.

As to 1966–7 starts a beginning had been made on the working drawings for the Mathematics Building and the second part of the Central Lecture Building, but the full impact of the Government's six months postponement of starting dates had still to be felt. It seemed unlikely that any 1966–7 project would be started before October 1966.

At the end of 1965 the Secretary of State announced a revised building programme for universities which took account of the effect of deferment by authorizing a higher level of starts in 1966–7 and 1967–8 than had previously been sanctioned for these two years.[14] At the same time a further year was added, so that the authorized programmes became as in Table 14.3.

[14] *Education in 1965*, HMSO, 89. See also page 263.

Early in 1966 the UGC announced the allocations for 1967–8, and the College was granted £1 million for new starts and £12,000 for minor works. The New Buildings Committee 'noted the amount of the allocation with satisfaction. There was now a reasonable certainty of the whole college being on the Hillingdon site by September 1969'. Planning of accommodation for the science departments could go ahead. At this time Richard Sheppard's appointment as Master Architect was extended to 31 March 1968 and he was also appointed as Architect for the Science Building which was expected to be the main item in the 1967–8 programme. The road pattern would also be completed by building the north perimeter road and another bridge over the River Pinn.

TABLE 14.3

Financial year	Value of building work to be started
1966–67	£40 million
1967–68	£30 million
1968–69	£25 million
1969–70	£25 million

Only a few months later (in May 1966) the UGC made further announcements of building starts for 1968–9 and 1969–70, and allocated to the College sums of £1 million and £0.5 million which were provisionally apportioned as in Table 14.4. To be able to plan with some assurance such a major part of the University was heartening, even though gaps in the provision had still to be filled. Another Hall of Residence was urgently needed, as well as buildings for the School of Social Sciences and the Department of Education.

TABLE 14.4

	1968–9	1969–70
	£m	£m
Communal Building Stage 2	0.24	
Physics and Electrical Engineering	0.45	
Library	0.30	
Students' Union Building	—	0.25
Site works	0.01	0.25

If the New Buildings Committee had their eyes on the future they also had to keep in focus the progress of Phase One, and a continuing preoccupation was the provision of equipment and services for the new buildings, with which Dr Shipp and John Eden were intimately involved. Lists of equipment which had been submitted to and agreed by Assessors appointed by the UGC regularly came to the Committee for approval.

By March 1966 it was delays in the Phase One building programme that were beginning to cause concern. W. E. Chapman, the Manager of Wimpey's Building Division, told the Committee that there was considerable unrest in the building industry in the London Area and it appeared that the Brunel site had been singled out as one of the special centres of unrest. Since August 1965 difficulties on the site had increased; there seemed to have been an infiltration of a militant faction among the work force and although no official strike had been called there had been a continued succession of unofficial stoppages.

The Architects reported that most of the buildings were several weeks behind schedule, it was most unlikely that the contractors would be able to make up lost time and the contract was likely to fall even further behind, as indeed it did. The sad story continued throughout the Spring and early Summer; Wimpeys were obviously in serious trouble.

The New Buildings Committee decided in July 1966 that steps should be taken to discuss the problems with Directors of Wimpeys, and a meeting with Dr Watts, Assistant Managing Director, and W. E. Chapman took place on 13 July. Discussions centred on attempting to reach agreement on realistic completion dates for each of the buildings and such a list was compiled, but not surprisingly Wimpeys' hopes were not realised.

However, the Central Boiler House was handed over in July 1966 a month late; the Hall of Residence for which the contract completion date was June 1966 had only five of its six staircases finished when the students 'came into residence' on 25 September and other buildings were similarly delayed. The beginning of term was hectic and with some 147 students in residence marked the start of the transfer to Uxbridge. For another four or five years the University had to live in two places at once.

CHAPTER 15

Finance

SOME account has been given (chapter 10) of the financial arrangements that were introduced when the College was recognized as a college of advanced technology, and of the careful attention the Governors paid to the preparation of the annual estimates.

'More than 85 per cent of university finance comes from public sources,' the Robbins Committee wrote,

and in our judgment it is in general neither practicable nor justifiable that the spending of university funds should be wholly in the hands of the users. Academic autonomy is more likely to be safeguarded where the public has a guarantee that there is independent lay advice and criticism within the universities. Moreover we believe past experience to show that the universities have benefited greatly from the initiative and wisdom of lay members on their governing bodies.

Brunel College was well served in this respect; Sir Joseph Latham was Chairman of the Finance Committee and after he retired in March 1965 Sir Mark Turner was co-opted to the Governing Body and later (October 1965) became Chairman of the Finance Committee. Other Specialist Governors continued to play an important part in the affairs, financial and academic, of the Departments.

The Finance Committee[1] met three or four times a year and in September/October each year received the audited accounts for the previous year ending on 31 March, and finalized the draft estimates for the year ahead. The Governors' financial obligations were specified in the College's Scheme of Government and in the Further Education (Grant) Regulations, 1959. 'The principal requirement is to submit to the Minister each

[1] See page 189.

year estimates of income and expenditure, and to keep their expenditure within the heads of the estimates, as approved by him. The Minister's policy is to allow the Governors discretion to spend within the main heads of the approved estimates.'[2] Some limited virement between main heads of expenditure was permitted, but the specified limits could not be exceeded without reference to the Minister.

The item in the estimates that continued to be most controversial was the provision of furniture, apparatus and equipment; the minutes of the Finance Committee record that in October 1963 'after a long discussion the Committee considered that the only satisfactory method which could be employed when considering the capital estimates for apparatus and equipment was to recommend a total figure which should not be exceeded by the College, and recommended that the Governing Body approve a total capital expenditure for 1964–5 of £120,000. The draft estimates totalling £172,345 should be submitted to the Ministry in support of the proposal.' The latter figure was the aggregate of sums agreed by the various Departmental Advisory Panels after review by the Specialist Governors and the Principal.

The Committee was still searching[3] for standards by which the estimates of a number of items of expenditure, both revenue and capital, could be judged. They expressed their concern at the lack of criteria and the inadequacy of annual budgeting and strongly recommended that the Governing Body should 'urge the Ministry to introduce triennial budgeting at the earliest possible date', and also 'request the Ministry to assist in assessing the College's estimates by circulating statistics from the other Colleges of Advanced Technology as to the number of students, the number of student-hours, the cost of each main heading of revenue and capital'. It noted that the Brunel figures for apparatus and equipment in the capital estimates for 1964–5 amounted to £250 per full-time student, with an additional £50 per student for small apparatus and equipment (items costing under £100) treated as revenue. These indices were obtained using an expected full-time student number of 700, and ignored the total student population which with short

---

[2] General Procedures, 4 July 1962; Ministry of Education.
[3] See chapter 6 (page 116).

course and part-time students was expected to reach about 2,700, roughly equally divided between undergraduates and post-graduates.

The Committee recognized of course that it was reasonable to anticipate a higher cost per student during the period in which the College was establishing itself, but warned 'that high capital estimates should not be allowed to become a recurrent feature of the budget'. The figure of £172,345 was considerably higher than the amounts allowed by the Ministry in previous years, namely, £70,000 in 1963–4 and £53,000 in 1962–3. A small part of the increase arose from the Ministry's ruling that items of equipment costing between £100 and £200 should be included in the capital estimates and not as earlier in the revenue figure, but the main cause was that most departments had anticipated that developments such as fourth year projects and research necessitated significant increases in the provision of major equipment.

Some of the main items of College expenditure were as shown in Table 15.1. The figures in the first and second columns are actual, but those in the third column are estimates as approved by the Governing Body on 14 October 1963, to which some modifications were made later.

TABLE 15.1

	1962–3	1963–4	1964–5 (Est.)
	£	£	£
Academic services—teaching	373,880	426,280	508,250
Upkeep of Acton premises	136,598	136,868	148,210
Total Revenue Expenditure	569,831	632,077	734,795
Net Revenue Expenditure	506,050	551,654	650,805
Capital Expenditure (Acton)	74,298	76,777	124,500
Capital Expenditure (Uxbridge)	186,004	306,108	384,000
Ministry of Education Grants received	769,305	937,847	—

It might be explained that the costs of academic services shown in the first row of the table were mainly salaries of teachers and academically related staff, such as technicians and departmental secretaries, and included costs of teaching materials and the small items of furniture, apparatus and equipment that were treated as revenue expenditure; they amounted in all to about two-thirds of the total revenue expenditure. Much of the proposed increase in 1964–5 arose from a suggested teaching establishment of 152 compared with 134 in 1963–4.

The Minister could set limits within which the Governors could appoint staff. 'So far as the teaching staff are concerned,' stated the General Procedures,

the Minister's specific prior approval will be required for the number of established posts in the grades of Principal Lecturer and above. The gradings of the various heads of departments is also subject to his approval. Any proposals to increase the authorised establishment at this level or to alter the grading of departmental heads should be submitted to the Minister for approval. The Governors have power to vary the establishment of posts below principal lecturer grade within the financial limits of the approved estimates.

And as to non-teaching staff 'the Minister will not require the prior submission of establishment proposals at any level. The only control will be that exercised through the approval of annual estimates.'

The costs of maintaining the Acton premises were inflated by loan charges of over £77,000 in 1962–3 and over £73,000 in 1963–4, for which the College accepted responsibility from April 1962 in accord with the terms of the agreement[4] with the Middlesex County Council; they were charges on the loans the County Council had negotiated earlier to meet the costs of the College buildings and major equipment. The upkeep costs increased with the erection of more huts and the acquisition of the Crown Building which the Mechanical Engineering Department took over in September 1963.

Capital expenditure at Acton in 1962–3 included £21,743 on the new temporary huts and alterations to buildings, the remainder (£52,555) being for new furniture and equipment. The following year (1963–4) the corresponding sums were £9,930 and £66,847 respectively. In the 1964–5 estimates the equipment item was, as explained above, fixed by the Governors at £120,000 and a sum of £4,500 was added to allow for the erection of one more hut, 'the last pre-fabricated building to be

---

[4] Agreement dated 31 Jan. 1964 between the Middlesex County Council and the Council.

placed on the site'.[5] The Minister agreed to a figure of £110,000, and a further £29,500 was allocated to the College from the special computer fund for the purchase of computer equipment, both digital and analogue.

Other capital expenditure reflected the developments at Uxbridge and in 1962–3 amounted to £180,500 for the purchase of land (Sites 2 and 3) and £5,504 for professional fees. In 1963–4 Site 1 was bought for £235,000, the two pavilions on Site 3 cost £10,175 and the layout of playing fields another £13,575; there were further professional fees of £44,083 and sports equipment cost £3,275. In estimating for 1964–5 provision had to be made for the Phase One contract totalling about £2 million, of which £250,000 was likely to be paid during the year as well as £130,000 in professional fees; the total was lowered to £248,000 later.

Fortunately forecasts did not have to be made of likely changes in salary scales of teachers, as the Ministry provided supplementary grants to cover such awards as they arose.

A year later in September–October 1964 the Finance Committee and the Governors were involved in the same sort of forecasting for 1965–6; there were general increases all round. Total student numbers which reached nearly 2,400 in 1963–4 and included 615 sandwich course students were likely to rise to about 2,700 in 1965–6 with around 900 undergraduates; teaching staff establishment was expected to rise to 171 (from 143) and the number of technicians to 89 (from 82) with an additional 22 from January 1966 if new buildings came into use. The total revenue expenditure was estimated at about £880,000 and capital expenditure at Uxbridge at about £1.28 million. There was again detailed consideration of the capital expenditure on apparatus and equipment and a figure of £110,000, as for the previous year, was agreed.

However a major change was imminent. The Ministry decided following discussions with the University Grants Committee and the colleges concerned that the Colleges of Advanced Technology (and the Heriot Watt College, Edinburgh) should be incorporated in the UGC grant list on 1 April 1965, even though by that date not all the Charters would have been confirmed.

[5] Minutes of Finance Committee, 1 Oct. 1963.

14. Bridge over the Pinn, with Lecture Centre (left) and
Mathematics Building (right)

15. Sports Centre

16. Library

The University Grants Committee wrote in September 1964 proposing a visit to the College on 10 March 1965 as a 'preliminary to the determining of the quinquennial recurrent grant', but they later asked to postpone the visit to 14 June 1965. Such visits were made by the Committee to all the universities during the middle year of the quinquennium; 'the quinquennial visitations are an essential part of our activities', the Committee's report for 1957–62 explained, 'and the information and impressions gained by us have a direct relevance to the report which we make to the Chancellor and to the allocation of the grants to each university'. With the addition of the colleges of technology to the 31 universities that existed at the end of 1964 the work of the Committee was considerably extended. The Committee had been re-constituted and its staff strengthened following the setting-up of the Department of Education and Science in April 1964. To this new Department were transferred all the functions of the Ministry of Education together with certain other responsibilities appertaining to university matters in Great Britain.[6]

In making this decision the Government accepted the Robbins Committee's recommendation that ministerial responsibility for the universities' vote should cease to rest with the Treasury, but did not accept another recommendation that there 'should be a minister of Arts and Science responsible for a University Grants Commission, on the lines of the existing University Grants Committee' as well as for other activities. On 6 February 1964 the Prime Minister announced that there was to be 'a single Minister with total responsibility over the whole educational field who should be Secretary of State for Education and Science', a decision in keeping with the note of reservation to the Robbins Report by Sir Harold Shearman. There were to be two administrative units within the Department, one 'concerned with schools in England and Wales, and the other with civil science and, through the University Grants Committee, with institutions of university status in Great Britain'. The University Grants Committee remained an independent body with direct access to the Secretary of State and the two Ministers of State.

The Government asked the University Grants Committee to plan the expansion in universities and colleges of advanced

[6] *University Development, 1957–1962*, HMSO, 189.

technology envisaged in the Robbins Report; this meant that the number of places in all such institutions could be expected to rise from 130,000 in 1962–3 to 197,000 in 1967–8 and 218,000 in 1973–4.

Before the Robbins Committee reported the Ministry of Education had, of course, discussed the expansion of the colleges of advanced technology. A Ministry memorandum, dated 14 September 1962, gave a reminder that the total authorized number of places for full-time and sandwich course students had been taken as 21,000, and pointed out that

even assuming the best possible rate of progress with the acquisition of sites and the planning of new buildings, it seems unlikely that all the buildings required for the accommodation of 21,000 full-time and sandwich students can be started within a period of less than four years after 1963/64. If all the necessary building work were started by the end of 1967/68 this would mean that the accommodation would be available for use by 1970.

The capital expenditure involved would be not less than £20 million excluding the cost of sites, fees and equipment. Forecasts beyond the 21,000 figure had been made and one in 1960 from the Committee of Principals of Colleges of Advanced Technology had suggested a total of 26,000 by 1970. Also 'the Advisory Council on Scientific Policy, in its report on the long term demand for scientists and technologists, assumed (without thereby implying any commitment on the part of the government) that the colleges of advanced technology might expand to a total of 26,000–27,000 places by the early 1970's'.[7]

In 1962–3 the total number of full-time and sandwich course students in colleges of advanced technology was 10,300 (see page 193). In accordance with the memorandum of September 1962 the Ministry asked colleges to put forward their views on the further developments they would like to see by 1973–4 and to specify the distribution of students both undergraduate and post-graduate among the various disciplines. The Brunel estimate was 2,150 undergraduate and 475 post-graduate students; this was made in December 1962.

A year later attention was concentrated on the Robbins estimate of 197,000 places by 1967–8, of which 19,000 were to be

[7] *Education in 1961*, HMSO, 38.

provided by the colleges of advanced technology. Brunel's share of this was to be 1,500, and indeed the Ministry asked for an assurance that the College would be able to provide for 1,500 students by 1967-8. An analysis showed that about 1,700 students could be accommodated if the academic buildings included in Phase One were available by September 1966, but there was considerable uncertainty as to whether this would be achieved. To help meet the Robbins figures for 1967-8, the crash-programme as it was called, the Ministry agreed to increase the total building programmes of the colleges from £4 million to £4.7 million for each of the years 1964-5 and 1965-6. Thereafter the Colleges were included with the Universities, and for 1966-7 were apportioned by the University Grants Committee a share of the £33 million which the Government had allocated to universities for building starts in that year (see page 263).

As to revenue expenditure the UGC requested the College in March 1965 to prepare estimates for the two remaining years of the quinquennium, 1 August 1965 to 31 July 1967, and (to allow for the change in the financial year) the College received for the period 1 April 1965 to 31 July 1965 a *pro rata* allocation of recurrent funds based on the estimates for 1965-6 earlier submitted to the Department of Education and Science. The new estimates had to be presented in a different form and with a changed basis, using instead of student-hours the number of equivalent full-time students, and whereas the Department of Education and Science formerly allowed only restricted transfer between recurrent heads of expenditure, the UGC allowed a great measure of freedom to the College to transfer amounts from one head to another. In addition, the unspent balance at the end of a financial year could, contrary to DES practice, be carried forward to the following year, except for special restrictions that normally applied to the fifth year of a quinquennium. However, for the Colleges of Advanced Technology these restrictions were temporarily waived and the UGC agreed that 'in effect the two academic years 1965-66 and 1966-67 could be treated as a single continuous period, any savings in 1965-66 being available for carry-forward and expenditure in 1966-67'.[8]

The estimates as presented for 1965-6 and 1966-7 are given

[8] *University Development, 1962-1967*, HMSO, 59.

in Table 15.2, with figures for 1964-5 alongside for comparison. The latter are not actual figures but the estimated out-turn for the period 1 August 1964 to 31 July 1965 had the UGC financial arrangements applied throughout that year. That there are other differences from the figures given earlier (page 274) reflects the differences in the revenue and capital categories under the DES and UGC accounting systems. The expenditure under Head 7 was mainly loan charges on the Acton buildings, and some of the proposed additional expenditure in 1966-7 was associated with the commissioning of new buildings at Uxbridge and in consequence more uncertain than usual. Some additional costs were inevitable; new departments were being established and professors appointed, and more non-teaching staff would be needed as the new buildings at Uxbridge came into use. Provision for administering two separate centres, at Acton and Uxbridge, had also to be made.

TABLE 15.2

Estimates for the Years 1965-6 and 1966-7

	1964-5	1965-6	1966-7
	£	£	£
Head 1. Administration	51,225	77,510	110,640
Head 2. Academic Expenditure	619,020	730,385	862,655
Head 3. Maintenance of premises	67,560	94,495	223,585
Head 4. General Educational Expenditure	10,165	17,645	20,725
Head 5. Student facilities and amenities	8,465	10,130	25,740
Head 6. Miscellaneous Expenditure	30	595	15,410
Head 7. Capital Expenditure met from income	84,990	81,280	78,515
Total Expenditure	841,455	1,012,040	1,337,270
Income	59,990	81,230	88,870
Net Expenditure	781,465	930,810	1,248,400
	no.	no.	no.
Student Numbers	950	1,050	1,200
Student-hours	640,000	770,000	910,000
	£	£	£
Gross Expenditure per student	886	964	1,114

These were approved by the Governors on 1 June 1965 and examined in detail by the Finance Committee on 29 June 1965. In January 1966 the UGC made known the allocations of recurrent grant for the two years, and Brunel was given £864,000 for 1965-6 and £932,000 (later £942,000) for 1966-7. The former figure with a small surplus available from the previous year was bearable, but the latter seemed unbelievably inadequate. The prospects for the College's first year as a university were indeed bleak.

In February 1966 the Finance Committee accepted a revised budget for 1965-6 with the total expenditure reduced to £932,240, and at the next meeting in June 1966 a completely revised budget for 1966-7 was discussed. The total income for the year including the UGC recurrent grant, certain supplementation funds, fees and a few other items was likely to amount to £1,087,230 and the expenditure had to be shaped accordingly, with cuts and changes wherever necessary. The revised budget that was agreed is set out in Table 15.3.

TABLE 15.3
Budget for the Year 1966-7

Expenditure	£
Head 1. Administration	98,515
Head 2. Academic departments	779,025
Head 3. Maintenance of premises	144,335
Head 4. General educational expenditure	14,000
Head 5. Student facilities and amenities	20,885
Head 6. Miscellaneous expenditure	22,670
Head 7. Capital expenditure met from income	81,965
	1,161,395

The deficit of £74,165 was to be met from the anticipated balance of £94,420 from the previous year, leaving some £20,000 for such contingencies as a non-teaching staff pay award and costs of the move to Uxbridge. Increases in staff had been trimmed considerably, and very little money made available for the purchase of equipment; fortunately those Departments moving to Uxbridge during 1966-7 received help from non-recurrent funds provided by the UGC for that purpose.

UGC allocations of non-recurrent funds, for new buildings and the associated new equipment, were no more liberal than those for recurrent expenditure, and the New Buildings Committee struggled with the problems of erecting buildings at Uxbridge as soon as possible (see chapter 14). Authority to incur

expenditure of a non-recurrent nature was delegated by the
Finance Committee to the New Buildings Committee, and
no diversions could be made from non-recurrent to recurrent
expediture.

Both the Finance and the New Buildings Committees felt
handicapped by a shortage of money, and unlike older universities the College had no funds of its own. It was high time
it had, and in November 1965 I suggested that the Governors
should make a public appeal for funds with the main purpose of
building halls of residence, especially as lodgings in and around
Uxbridge were likely to prove very limited. The Finance
Committee made detailed recommendations on these lines and
the Governors agreed 'that subject to satisfactory enquiries
being made from other universities, a professional firm of
Appeal Organisers should be appointed to carry out an initial
survey.'[9]

It quickly became apparent that though the engagement of
a professional firm would provide expert guidance a heavy
burden of responsibility would still fall on Governors, particularly the Appeals Committee, and on the officers of the
College, and without assurances that the College could devote
the time and effort required the Finance Committee were
reluctant to recommend that even a feasibility study be undertaken. Representatives of three firms were however interviewed;
there were further discussions with one of them, Wells Organisations Institutional Ltd, and the outcome was that in June 1966
the Governors agreed that this firm be appointed to carry out
a feasibility study and to report. The firm proposed to undertake
the work in July and September.

It was hardly the easiest of times at which to take on an
additional administrative burden of that magnitude. The
pressures on all of us were considerable. What drove us on was
the certainty that a second hall of residence would not be built
for a very long time unless some college money became
available. We also had the assurance that 'if a university is able
to finance a building by means of donations or benefactions, it is
perfectly free to do so, and the cost is not charged against the
building allocations set by the UGC'.[10]

[9] Meeting of Governing Body, 8 Dec. 1965.
[10] Letter from Sir John Wolfenden to the Principal, 9 July 1965.

The June 1966 meeting of the Governors was the last before the College became a University; the Charter was expected any day. Approval was given to the initial steps taken towards the preparation of the Quinquennial Estimates for 1967–72 which had to be submitted to the UGC in November. Also interim arrangements pending the first meeting of the University Council were surveyed and agreed. 'During the interim period Governors had all the rights, powers, duties and privileges conferred on the Council by the Charter and Statutes until the date of the first meeting of the Council.' The Finance Committee and the New Buildings Committee were to continue to meet as required, and indeed they had many important issues to decide.

The prospects facing the two Committees in the summer of 1966 may be illustrated by setting out the grants the College had been allocated by the UGC. See Table 15.4.

TABLE 15.4

Grants allocated by UGC in £m

Year	1965-6	1966-7	1967-8	1968-9	1969-70
Recurrent	0.864	0.942	—	—	—
Non-recurrent	—	0.62	1.0	1.0	0.5
Minor Works	—	0.02	0.012	0.015	0.015

The recurrent grants could be expected to be supplemented to allow for changes in the salary scales of academic staff, but special supplementary grants would not be made towards the increases in the pay of other staff, although it was usual for such increases to be taken into account 'when there was a review of changes in University costs generally during a quinquennium'.

The actual recurrent grants for 1965–6 and 1966–7 turned out to be £0.889m and £0.987m respectively; those for the years of the quinquennium 1967–72 were announced in November 1967 and are quoted in chapter 17. The story of the vicissitudes of the non-recurrent grants is also told later (chapters 17 and 18).

The pattern of grants, recurrent and non-recurrent, for the Universities as a whole for the period 1963–7 may be gathered from Table 15.5.[11]

[11] *University Development, 1962-1967*, HMSO, 37 and 46.

The original quinquennial settlement was supplemented in the light of increases which had taken place in university costs and of the desired expansion of university numbers—first in 1963 to enable universities to reach the 1966–7 target of 150,000 students and again in 1964, following the Robbins Report, in order to finance the much larger expansion to 197,000 by 1967–8. In 1965, further supplementary grants were made for the last three years of the quinquennium to cover increases in University costs up to July 1964.

Table 15.5

Recurrent Grants to Universities, 1963–4 to 1966–7 in £m

Academic Year	1963–4	1964–5	1965–6	1966–7
Quinquennial settlement at 1 August 1962	60.500	65.500	70.500	76.500
Supplementary Grant 1963	3.500	3.900	4.200	4.500
Supplementary Grant 1964	—	3.500	7.200	9.800
Supplementary Grant 1965	—	0.167	2.700	2.933
Salary revision 1962	1.470			
Salary revision 1963	4.310	5.928	6.390	6.934
Salary revision 1964	2.073	7.000	7.688	8.629
Salary revision 1966 (non-clinical)	—	—	0.986	3.165
Colleges of Advanced Technology, Heriot-Watt College and Strathclyde University (part)		5.310*	16.096	18.515
Other items	0.189	0.381	1.415	2.499
Total Recurrent Grant	72.042	91.686	117.175	133.475
Grant for Local Authority rates	2.993	3.544	4.989	5.579
Total	75.035	95.230	122.164	139.054

* From 1 April 1965 to 31 July 1965 only.

There were several changes in salary scales for academic staff. After the National Incomes Commission issued its report in March 1964 Government announced its acceptance in principle of the findings of the Commission and in particular of the recommendations in respect of salary rates and allowances. The new rates involved increases in non-clinical salary scales ranging from 9 per cent to 19 per cent and came into effect on 1 April 1964 in Universities and Colleges of Advanced Technology (see chapter 12). At the beginning of 1965 the Association of University Teachers put forward a claim for a revision of the 1964 scales. The discussions were protracted as new negotiating machinery had to be devised and agreed, and before agreement was reached the Secretary of State (C. A. R. Crosland) announced an increase in salary rates of 5 per cent from 1 April 1966 to remain in force for at least a year.

As to non-recurrent grants to Universities and the former Colleges of Advanced Technology during the period 1962–7 the amounts expended were as shown in the Table 15.6. The yearly totals were considerably lower than the amounts initially approved; for instance, the total allocation for 1964–5 was originally £84.737m; however, the proportion spent by the former CATs proved a little more generous than the initial allocation which was indeed meagre.

TABLE 15.6

Non-recurrent grants: Expenditure 1962–3 to 1966–7 in £m

Academic Years	Buildings		Furniture & Equipment		Total*	
	Excluding former CATs	Former CATs	Excluding former CATs	Former CATs	Excluding former CATs	Former CATs
1962–3	22.155		8.438		35.641	
1963–4	25.344		10.960		42.464	
1964–5	38.107	1.058	13.615	0.033	60.780	1.183
1965–6	41.502	4.513	19.348	1.517	71.081	6.919
1966–7	37.078	5.258	23.747	2.008	68.645	8.760

* Including other grants for Fees, Sites and Properties.

CHAPTER 16

The Years 1964-6

THE two years before the College became a University were filled with preparatory work of all kinds, some of which has already been described. The drafting of the Charter and Statutes and the activities of the Academic Advisory Committee, the progress of the building programme for which the Architects, the New College Committee[1] and the Planning Group were responsible, and the transfer to the University Grants Committee list and the consequent changes in the financing of the College have been recounted in earlier chapters. In all these matters the Governing Body was intimately involved, and particularly the Chairman, Lord Brown, who had devoted himself unstintingly to the College's affairs. In October 1965 to the deep regret of all who had worked with him he announced his resignation, on having accepted an invitation to join the Government as a Minister of State. Congratulations were mixed with a sense of loss, relieved by the knowledge that he was named in the draft Charter as the first Pro-Chancellor of the University, an office he could accept though still a Minister. The Governors had elected A. L. Stuchbery as vice-Chairman and in March 1966 invited him to be Chairman.

To gather together the main threads of the complex pattern of events that formed the fabric of the College's life to the year 1966, it is necessary to take up again the story of the work of the Academic Board which faced a considerable programme. A number of reports were prepared for the Academic Advisory Committee to which reference has been made earlier, and step by step the academic policy of the college as a university was laid down. Major responsibilities were shouldered by the Courses sub-committee which scrutinized all the undergraduate courses

---

[1] Its name was changed to New Buildings Committee in Oct. 1965.

while the Postgraduate Courses Committee supervised the development of post-graduate activities. Working parties took on special problems as they arose.

Several new departments were created. The discussions on industrial training culminated in the setting-up of a Department of Industrial Training in October 1964 with S. A. Urry in charge and he joined the Academic Board in November. It was at the November meeting that I presented a paper to the Board entitled 'On Departments and Schools', which set out some definitions in an attempt to clarify the use of these words and so facilitate discussion of the issues involved. Although I was attracted by the educational merits of the concept of Schools used at the University of Sussex, I felt compelled to propose that Brunel should retain the Department as an organizational unit and should tackle the problems of breaking down the barriers that inevitably rise between departments (see page 154) by forming Schools of two or more departments in association. I suggested that we should use Department to mean 'an organizational arrangement whereby a group of teachers are associated together who are responsible for teaching and research in one field of knowledge', and that we should use School for 'an organizational arrangement whereby all the teachers in two or more departments are associated in one group'. A School of Physical Sciences for instance might have departments of Physics, Chemistry and Materials Science within it.

This molecular model was hardly revolutionary and certainly much less novel than I would have preferred. Somewhat reluctantly, and not unanimously, the Board accepted the proposals but left a number of organizational questions, which I had raised in the paper, for later decision. It was accepted that each School and each Department not in a School would have a Board of Studies which would report directly to the Academic Board or Senate, and if Departmental Boards of Studies were set up within a School they would report to the Board of Studies of the School.

Acceptance of the basic ideas made progress possible, though Boards of Studies were later differently conceived (see page 300), and the first School to be established was in the social sciences. The consideration given to this development by the Academic Advisory Committee has been mentioned earlier (chapter 13), but even at the risk of repetition some elaboration is necessary. Following the resignation of Dr Marie Jahoda I had discussions with Dr A. T. M. Wilson, the specialist governor for the Department of Psychology and Social Science, and with some others outside the College, concerning the future of the Department, and in my report to the Governors on 5 October 1964 I wrote: 'I am convinced that it would be appropriate for this College, as a Technological University, to establish a School of Social Science with a much wider field of work than that of the present department. One of the main responsibilities of such a School would be an undergraduate course in Psychology, Sociology and Economics for students hoping to go into public or industrial administration of various kinds.' I added that such a PSE course might be regarded as analogous to that in PPE at Oxford. I was less clear about what effect the introduction of such a course would have on other undergraduate programmes in the School but all my predilections were in favour of a broad and generalist education, and like others elsewhere I fought a losing battle against the specialists. My report went on: 'There would be other undergraduate courses. Whether the present course in psychology would be continued unaltered or in modified form would depend on advice from specialists outside the College. On their advice too would depend the introduction of other courses in sociology and economics.' Members of the staff of the Department were alarmed, and submitted a paper to the Academic Board (in November) 'seeking clarification of the future organization of the Department and of its undergraduate course in psychology'.

My report to the Governors included other proposals. As to the School of Social Science I boldly suggested that invitation rather than public advertisement might be the best way of attracting a man of the right calibre and outlook to lead the School, and added that 'from discussions with Dr. Elliott Jaques I have discovered that he is most interested in the educational ideas for which the College is now known, and I should be happy if the Governors felt able to invite him to lead this School and to offer him a Professorship', subject of course to the agreement of the Academic Advisory Committee. The Governors found this proposal unacceptable though they welcomed the formation of the School and decided that the post should be advertised; for a majority of Governors public advertisement was an important matter of principle and this I respected. The method of invitation often used by universities seemed to them to have an air of privilege about it.

The post of Head of the School was advertised, an appointments committee set up which included a member of the Academic Advisory Committee, and Dr Elliott Jaques was selected. He joined the College in April 1965, with the rank of Professor, and was the first professor to give an inaugural lecture which he delivered on 3 May 1965 and published under the title *The Science of Society*.

I had been engaged with Heads of Departments in considering how other Schools might be formed; to get agreement about certain departmental combinations proved more difficult than I expected. This was not so in Engineering where the Heads concerned readily supported the setting-up of a School of Engineering bringing together the three Departments of Electrical Engineering and Electronics, Mechanical Engineering and Production Technology. To find a partner for Physics however proved impossible and that Department had to be left in isolation. Schools of Biology, Chemistry and Mathematics were ultimately established, not through combination but by division. The process of division raised misgivings in my mind, seeming to offend a fundamental idea about Schools by increasing rather than reducing departmental barriers, but in some areas division proved more acceptable than combination. And even the School of Social Sciences later created more Departments within it.

The Heads and some members of staff of the three Engineering Departments met in November 1964 to consider at the request of the Academic Board the merits of joint undergraduate courses, and agreed that the introduction of such courses would be facilitated by the formation of a School of Engineering. A recommendation was accordingly made. The proposed constitution for a School was submitted to the Academic Board in March 1965 and with minor amendments approved. Professor R. T. A. Howell was elected as the first Chairman of the Engineering Board and he did much to ensure the smooth working of the School from the start. The appointment of Chairman and vice-Chairman of the Board was to follow an agreed rota, and the Chairman was to act as Head of

School during his period of office. A permanent Head of the School was appointed some years later (page 368).

To help forward the development of the School of Social Sciences the Governors approved the establishment of a small committee to advise on national and local government needs in the field of public and industrial administration; the committee included Sir Walter Worboys, Noel Annan, W. B. D. Brown, Dr A. T. M. Wilson and Sir Joseph Latham—a strong group to whom I could turn, but developments were such that I made few demands on them.

Professor Jaques presented a preliminary policy statement about the School to the Academic Board on 31 May 1965 and followed this, after discussions with the staff of the School, with a more detailed document which was discussed at the next meeting in July. Its reception was mixed, and members raised a number of general issues about the functioning of Schools and the relationships of Departments within Schools, as well as some particular problems such as the place of Management and General Studies within or without the School. However, there was agreement about the proposed combined honours degree course in psychology, sociology and economics, and the honours degree course in psychology. At the next meeting in October 1965 Professor Jaques explained that it was proposed that the School should be comprised of two departments, a Department of Psychology and a Department of Social Institutions. In general terms the former Department would be concerned with teaching and research about individual behaviour, and the latter Department with all other aspects of the School's work with emphasis on institutions rather than individuals. As to management its natural place was within the Department of Social Institutions, a view that did not command full assent. The Governors had agreed to the appointment of a Head of the Department of Psychology with the rank of professor, and Professor Jaques for the time being at least was to be Head of the Department of Social Institutions, as well as Head of the School. The post of Head of the Department of Psychology was later advertised but no appointment was made, and as a temporary measure it was agreed to appoint Professor D. R. Miller of the University of Michigan, who was intending to spend some time in this country, as a Visiting Professor and he joined the College in May 1966.

In my report to the Governors on 8 December 1965 I wrote: 'I have always had in mind that the setting-up of the School of Social Sciences would affect the work of two other Departments in the College, General Studies and Management, and that appropriate organisational changes would have to be made.' I reminded Governors that I had foreshadowed some of these changes more than a year earlier in October 1964. I went on:

Professor Jaques recently explained to the Academic Board that with our new departmental arrangements he sees no need for a separate Department of Management in the College. Its work should be taken over by the new Department of Social Institutions and our present courses in Management continued therein with all the support the School of Social Sciences can give. With this view I fully concur, and I now propose to the Governors that the Department of Management should be discontinued with effect from the end of this term, and that the staff of this Department be transferred to the Department of Social Institutions within the School of Social Sciences.

The main person affected was Robert Harcourt, the Head of the Department of Management, who was to become a Senior Lecturer in Management without change of salary. It was a most difficult decision to make, but it became unavoidable.

As to the Department of General Studies its work has several strands; one of these the teaching of social relations has been taken over by the School of Social Sciences, and two of the staff, Mr. J. Parsons and Mr. D. Marsland, who are mainly concerned with social relations teaching, have readily accepted transfer to the School of Social Sciences. The Head of the Department of General Studies, Dr. J. Burnett, has also agreed to be transferred to the School of Social Sciences and to accept a Readership in the Department of Social Institutions. I wish to ask the governors to agree to this transfer with effect from the end of this term.

All these proposals were accepted by the Governors, but one problem remained which I pondered for a long time—the few members of the staff of the General Studies Department, some full-time and some part-time, who were responsible for the teaching of English, foreign languages, music, art and design. They could be linked together as a Division with a separate existence but inevitably small and isolated. Their work was important and needed to be recognized as such if General

Studies, with which I had been intimately associated from the very beginning, were to continue and prosper. The support of a Department was desirable, even essential, and particularly a Department with some affinity that was sympathetic to the aims of general studies and would extend a welcome; I wanted to avoid a *faute de mieux* solution. The Department of Education seemed the obvious home, but the new Professor had not yet been appointed and so a decision had to be deferred. However, the staff were grouped as a Division of Languages with a Senior Lecturer in charge, and later (May 1966) the Academic Board accepted a proposal by Dr Burnett that a scheme of Subsidiary Studies (later named Complementary Studies) be introduced to replace the existing General Studies scheme; the Division of Languages was to be responsible for this work.

Earlier, in February 1965, the Academic Board had agreed to the establishment of two other new Departments, namely Education and Metallurgy. Both had been under consideration for a long time, and indeed a Division of Educational Method had been in being since September 1963, and a Division of Metallurgy formalized about the same time.

Dr Shipp and I had discussed the introduction of courses for the education and training of teachers with senior people at the Ministry of Education, and on one occasion I was invited to talk to a group of Ministry staff and H.M. Inspectors about the developments we envisaged. I recall the interest engendered by our proposal to start a sandwich course in education which would include at least one period of industrial training as well as the more usual periods of practice in schools; we had in mind too that our experience with the supervision and assessment of industrial training would enable us to assess 'school practice' more effectively and to develop special relationships with schools emphasizing the importance of school–university co-operation in teacher training. I hoped to attract an outstanding educationalist as Head, and to keep the specialist staff small by asking some of the best teachers in other departments of the College to contribute to the teaching—an arrangement designed not only to ensure high standards but to prevent the isolation of the Department from the rest of the College. Departments of Education could so easily become cinderellas. I also wished to develop educational research appropriate to a technological university, and the Ministry responded splendidly by asking us to consider the establishment at Brunel of a national centre responsible for directing educational research in technical education. Considerable research funds were likely to be available.

These ideas gained the support of the Academic Board and the Governing Body, as well as the Academic Advisory Committee. The post of Head was duly advertised and was offered to Mr John Vaizey but unfortunately he was unable to accept. After further advertisement and interviews W. D. Furneaux was selected and he became the first Professor of Education and Head of the new Department. He joined the College in September 1966.

Courses in Metallurgy on the other hand went back to the time before Brunel College was established and had developed within the Department of Chemistry. A Diploma in Technology course was established in 1959 (chapter 6), and by 1964-5 there were 80 students following the course. The staff of the Division of Metallurgy comprised one Senior Lecturer, seven Lecturers and one Assistant-lecturer; Dr R. J. Maitland had general responsibility for the Division under the direction of the Head of Department. New buildings were included in Phase One of the building programme within the Engineering Complex, and the moment seemed opportune to set up a separate Department; the Governors agreed (March 1965). The first Professor of Metallurgy to be appointed was Dr C. Bodsworth, who joined the College in December 1965 as Head of the new Department.

This was followed by the creation of a closely-related Department of Materials Science and Technology. I had suggested to the Academic Board in July 1965 that such a step should be taken even though the department would have no accommodation of its own immediately and would initially have to use the facilities of other departments. A few staff would be transferred from other departments and additional staff recruited in the normal way. In accepting the proposal the Academic Board agreed to set up a working party to begin the planning of an undergraduate course in Materials Science and Technology and to advise on the service teaching of materials science throughout the College. The latter was a controversial educational matter which divided the Academic Board and little progress was made in spite of the excellence of G. J. L. Griffin's written contributions, but the discussions must have been salutary in many ways. The Department was in due course set up and Dr W. A. Holmes-Walker was appointed Head and Professor as from May 1966. A new undergraduate course was introduced in the autumn term of 1967.

Only an exceptional department, such as the Department of Chemistry had become under Dr Skellon's able direction, could have given rise to two new Departments, Metallurgy and Materials Science, and gone on seemingly undiminished in vigour. Reduced in size it was, but it remained significant in its own right with a considerable volume of research and post-graduate courses. This was all the more remarkable as only three years earlier the Department of Applied Biology had been similarly divided from it. Dr Skellon's successor as Head of the Department of Chemistry was Dr K. S. W. Sing who was made a Professor on joining the College in April 1965.

These and other likely developments were explained in a paper presented to the University Grants Committee on the occasion of their visit to the College on 14 June 1965. No other new Departments seemed likely, but the School of Engineering had been established. Whether the Department of Metallurgy should join this School or become a part of a new School of Materials Science and Technology had not been resolved.

The University Grants Committee's visit followed an estab-lished pattern; members of the visiting party talked to groups of professorial and non-professorial staff, to Students' Union representatives, to Heads of Departments, to the Academic Registrar, Warden and Lodgings Officer, and to members of the Governing Body; from some of these groups they had received memoranda. In a concluding session Sir John Wolfenden talked to the Governors about the visit and the future of the College, and later put in writing the substance of his comments.[2]

There was general commendation for the academic policies that were being pursued and particular mention was made of sandwich courses, the common first year in engineering courses, the merging of ONC and A level entry streams, ordinary degree courses and the proposed developments in teacher education. 'The Committee had seen a good deal of evidence of the careful

[2] Document No. GB/61, meeting of Governing Body, 12 Oct. 1965.

thought which had been given, both by the College authorities and the Staff Association, to the problems involved in translating a CAT at Acton into a university institution at Uxbridge.' There had been some reference to communications within the College, particularly concerning emerging policies, and the Committee commented: 'Some of the staff felt that there should be more opportunity for staff voices to be heard. This whole question was very complex and needed a good deal of thought and working out. The student body seemed very well involved in matters which concerned them, including the academic pattern.'

The other main problems that had been raised in discussion included the move to Uxbridge and the difficulties of operating on separate sites, the relatively greater lodgings problems at Uxbridge although 'the Committee had been impressed by the student welfare and lodgings arrangements', the shortage of library accommodation and facilities, and the lack of Students' Union premises. The Committee advised caution in making student-number projections beyond 1967-8, and added: 'Between 1967-68 and 1973-74 it seemed that on present policy only 21,000 extra students would be required from some 50 university institutions', almost all of which had major expansion in mind. 'It was only to be expected that Brunel too would wish to expand rapidly in size, but qualitative growth was no less important than quantitative growth. In present circumstances it did not seem sensible to contemplate the introduction of a Medical School or Architectural courses in the near future.' The Chairman however assured the Governors that 'although the Committee would be unable to provide the resources they would like to have for the move to Uxbridge when they wanted them, this was not for any discriminatory reasons.'

Finally comment was made on the Charter discussions in which the Governors and the Staff Association had been deeply involved; 'indeed even on the basis of the day's evidence alone, considerable vitality and vigour were being devoted to the working out of College problems. This was in itself entirely healthy, and if the vitality could be focused effectively the Chairman felt confident that everyone could look forward to the achievement by Brunel of an enhanced status, based on its traditional role'—smooth words, but considered and timely.

On the whole the College was pleased and encouraged by the day's work, their first experience of such a visit; it helped to give a sense of unity after all the divisive discussions on the Charter. The College was not likely to expand as quickly as was once thought nor achieve the size suggested in the Robbins Report: 'we should regard a student population of some 3,000 to 5,000 as an appropriate size for the college in their role as technological universities. Most of the colleges already have such a size in mind.' That was obviously a very long time ahead; more immediately the College was not likely to get as big a grant for buildings as it wanted, and it would have to remain at Acton for a longer period than anyone wished to contemplate.

But a measure of optimism prevailed; perhaps funds would become available for a library when the UGC, as the Chairman promised, looked into the provision of libraries in colleges of advanced technology. Even medical education was not abandoned and in October 1965 I reported that Hillingdon Hospital Management Committee had welcomed the formation of a Joint Committee and appointed four members to represent them; L. J. Sapper, Professor Gillett, Dr Shipp and the Principal were to be the Brunel members, and so began a fruitful association with the Hospital, another facet of the College's involvement in the society around it. The Joint Committee presented a submission[3] to the Royal Commission on Medical Education in February 1966, arguing that 'the University is a suitable one to possess a medical faculty; that the hospital deserves to be a teaching hospital; that the geographical relationship of the two would enable them easily to be welded into a functional whole'. The Todd Commission[4] came to the conclusion however that the number of medical schools in London should not be increased and suggested that the existing twelve schools should be amalgamated in pairs to form six institutions, each closely associated with a multi-faculty college of the university. That way forward being closed the Joint Committee turned to other avenues along which co-operation could develop and clearly postgraduate teaching and scientific

[3] The memorandum owed much to Dr A. H. James, Consultant Physician and Clinical Tutor at Hillingdon Hospital.

[4] *Royal Commission on Medical Education*, HMSO, April, 1968.

and engineering research in selected medical fields offered the best opportunities.

Perhaps the College, like many others, had not realized how views concerning university expansion had changed, even in the short time since the Robbins Committee had reported. As explained earlier in chapter 15 the Robbins targets for the number of places in institutions of university status were 197,000 by 1967–8 and 218,000 by 1973–4. Of the 197,000 places 170,000 were to be provided by the existing universities—a considerable increase in their rate of growth. The UGC commented later: 'As we saw it, it was not so much the actual amount of the increase itself in student numbers which was formidable as the time-scale, in relation to the existing plans and policies of the universities for expansion and to the possibilities of planning and building the necessary accommodation in time.'[5]

The Chairman of the UGC wrote to all universities in October 1963 asking each university to let the Committee know 'what contribution it felt able to offer to the additional numbers required by 1967–68'. When these expansion proposals were analysed 'it became clear that in aggregate the universities had offered a total of places by 1967–68 which was substantially higher than that required to meet the Robbins objective for that year'.[6]

It followed that there had to be some scaling down, or spreading out, university by university of the proposals that had been put forward, and a realistic programme devised. Increases in recurrent and non recurrent funds would however be needed and these the Government in due course announced. The economic crisis of 1965 had resulted in some £15 million of university building work (out of a total of about £60 million) being deferred from 1965–6 (see page 268), but in spite of this setback steady progress had been made towards the Robbins short-term target. By 1966–7 the total number of full-time students in universities and other institutions had risen to 184,800 and the count for the autumn term 1967 showed a total of 200,287, so that the Robbins figure had been amply achieved.

The UGC report for 1962–7 went on: 'By the time that we began, towards the end of 1966, to consider the financial

[5] *University Development, 1962–67*, 50.
[6] *University Development, 1962–67*, 52.

provision to be made for the 1967–72 quinquennium, it was clear to us that it had become necessary to re-examine the statistical projections on which the Robbins Committee had worked.'[7] In the event the recurrent grants for 1967–72 assumed that the student population in universities would rise to between 220,000 and 225,000 by 1971–2—about ten per cent above the Robbins estimate of 204,000. The Robbins projections had taken into account the decline in the size of the relevant age-group after the post-war 'bulge' had moved on, but there had been an exceptional increase in the size of sixth forms and in the numbers of qualified applicants for university places, the 'trend' as it was called. Moreover, the Dainton Committee's analysis of the sixth form population of schools suggested that the demand for university places was likely to fall for science courses and to rise for courses in arts and social studies. It seemed clear that 'the total number of school-children from whom students in university faculties of science and technology are traditionally drawn will probably begin to fall after the 1965 university entry, and that this downward trend may continue to the end of the (1967–72) quinquennium.'[8]

In these circumstances projections about Brunel's student-numbers were not easy to make, and a new uncertainty arose in 1965 when the colleges of advanced technology accepted an invitation to join the Universities Central Council on Admissions (UCCA).

Their acceptance was ready enough, but the Colleges were concerned that the arrangements should provide not only for A level entrants but for those who had qualified through the Ordinary National Certificate examinations, and that the Colleges should continue to be able to accept industry-based students sponsored by industrial firms. Both points were met, and the session 1965–6 saw the beginning of student admissions to undergraduate courses through this scheme. The College received 2,755 applications, a formidable number for which interviewing and selection arrangements had to be devised. Over a quarter of them had given Brunel as their first or second choice. The total number of new students admitted was 305 and

[7] *University Development, 1962–67*, 65.
[8] *Enquiry into the Flow of Candidates in Science and Technology into Higher Education* (Dainton Report), HMSO, 15. Feb. 1968.

of these 225 came through the UCCA schemes; the others were industry-based students supported by firms. About one-sixth of the new students had an ONC or HNC qualification. The undergraduate population rose to 875, compared with 745 in 1964-5.

Early in 1965 the Academic Board considered the titles of degrees of the University and decided to adopt the title of Bachelor of Technology (B.Tech.) for the first degree awarded to students who had completed successfully a sandwich course. There were a number of different views; the one that gained support was that there should be one first degree title only and that it should reflect the technological character of the University in much the same way as a B.A. was the one award associated with first degree courses in the older universities. For me it was a decision of significance; the titles of the higher degrees mattered less. However, the Academic Board agreed to adopt for the first higher degrees the titles of Master of Science (M.Sc.) when the degree was obtained by full-time attendance at the College and Master of Technology (M.Tech.) when the course was integrated with work in industry. The Ph.D. title was accepted readily, but whether the highest degree should be titled Doctor of Science (D.Sc.) or Doctor of Technology (D.Tech.) led to differences of view. Were both necessary? Should D.Tech. be a degree awarded *honoris causa* only? A decision was deferred. Other universities had similar difficulties and some introduced a degree named Doctor of the University (D.Univ.)—artificial and unattractive it seemed to some of us.

A little earlier (November 1964) the regulations for Master's degrees including some modifications suggested by the Academic Advisory Committee (see page 236) had been approved by the Academic Board, and in February 1965 the Board formally approved the registration of fourteen candidates for the degree of Ph.D., with some of the registrations back-dated to October 1964. Another seven registrations were added in March. These developments were noted by the Governing Body (March 1965) and the Academic Board's decisions endorsed.

Discussion of the styling of higher degrees however continued in the Postgraduate Courses Committee and in June 1966 the Academic Board agreed to accept the Committee's further recommendations that changed in some measure the earlier proposals; the first higher degree of the University was to be styled Master of Technology, and the third higher degree Doctor of Technology awarded on the basis of published work or on an honorary basis. Thus B.Tech., M.Tech., Ph.D., and D.Tech. became the pattern of degree awards. The proposals about M.Sc. and D.Sc. were dropped.

The setting up of other Schools raised no serious reorganizational problems. Professor Crank and I put a paper to the Academic Board in March 1966 proposing the formation of a School of Mathematical Studies, and it was agreed that such a School be established comprising initially the Department of Mathematics and a new Department of Computer Science. The Head of the new Department would also carry the title of Director of the Computer Unit; the first Head was Dr M. L. V. Pitteway who was appointed Professor and joined the College in April 1967. Professor Crank became Head of the School as well as Head of the Department of Mathematics. The establishment of a School of Biological Sciences was considered by the Academic Board in May 1966, and as a first step Professor Gillett was asked to proceed with the planning of undergraduate courses in Biochemistry and Human Biology. Much clearly depended on the recommendations of the Todd Commission on Medical Education which were not then known.

The Academic Board also looked at its own infra-structure, and asked what type of Board of Studies was needed to support its work and that of Senate later. There were no Faculties, but there were Departments and Schools. Should Boards of Studies be associated with Departments and Schools or with courses? (see page 287). Ultimately it was decided to establish a Board of Studies for each undergraduate course in the College, of which the members would be *all* the staff who contributed to the teaching of the course, independently of the Department to which they belonged. The Head of Department or School responsible for the course would be Chairman. There were therefore as many Course Boards as there were undergraduate courses and each reported either directly to the Academic Board or indirectly through the Board of Studies of a School. The terms of reference of the Boards included advising on the instruction and teaching in the course, the admission of students and the regulation of examinations, with the power to set up *ad hoc*

Examining Boards and to delegate to these Boards decisions on student performance. The Boards were also empowered to make recommendations to the Senate for the award of first degrees. Every member of staff was a member of at least one Course Board, and had the opportunity of meeting other course teachers, of appreciating the structure and content of the course as a whole, and of contributing to changes in it. The hope was that he would be enabled to see the relation of his own contribution to the course as an entity. The Course Boards were to meet normally once a term and they held their first meetings in the autumn term of 1965-6. One of their first tasks was to complete the syllabuses of the new honours degree schemes and to devise schemes of study for Ordinary degrees.

During the summer term of 1966 the Academic Board took another critical look at the provision for industrial training, having in mind the Industrial Survey of a wider area around Uxbridge, within fifteen miles of the College site, which D. J. Burningham had undertaken as a follow-up of his earlier investigation of Uxbridge itself (see page 227). His report was considered by the Governors at a special meeting held on 25 November 1965.

The survey had revealed that there were no large firms in the area which had not already been contacted although there were many sections of large firms sited in this area which were not large enough to provide training places. This left only small and medium-sized firms untouched and in the majority of these firms no research or development projects were being carried out. For example, of the 300 firms on the Slough Estate only ten had research programmes in which graduates were employed. In the small and medium-sized firms the attitude of management was often a barrier. Managers in such firms were generally self-made men often suspicious of paper qualifications.

Interviews had been conducted at Director level in 322 firms; of these 158 had indicated that they were not interested or could not help, while 137 firms expressed interest in providing training places and 27 firms were undecided. It looked as if the training places likely to be available in these firms could not exceed 300, which added to the existing places in firms already supporting the College would amount to some 650 places in all—disappointingly small, especially having in mind that about

400,000 people were employed in the survey area in manufacturing activities related to the degree courses offered by the
College.

There was some hope that the Industrial Training Act of
1964, the setting-up of the various Industrial Training Boards
and the payment of training grants to firms would have
beneficial consequences, both on the quality of the training that
firms provided and on the number of places available. S. A.
Urry reporting on the first year's work of the Department of
Industrial Training commented: 'there was no undue difficulty
in finding suitable training places for all our students. Indeed
the University was unable to accept all the places offered.' But
it was a continuing problem, particularly for Departments with
a high proportion of college-based students. It was becoming
formidable too, for in 1966 about 760 students had training
placements.

Urry was given in November 1964 the help of the Industrial
Training Working Party of which he became Chairman; this
brought together members of staff, one from each Department,
with particular experience of and responsibility for the placing
of students. The Principal and Vice-Principal were members
too. The Working Party provided a forum for the exchange
of information and ideas about training, about the placing
and supervision of students, and particularly about methods of
assessment.

In a paper presented to the Academic Board (27 June 1966)
on the assessment of industrial training, Urry drew attention to
a number of ways in which assessment was being tried, and
Professor Jackson elaborated on an experiment conducted by
the Mechanical Engineering Department during 1964-5; 'he
stressed that, apart from its intrinsic merits, the experiment had
had valuable incidental results in that it had led to a greater
awareness by firms of the importance of industrial training,
and to more effective liaison between firms and the College'. It
was the development of a scheme initiated by Dr Shipp (see
page 225) and based on the writing of an essay by each student
on a topic proposed in most cases by the student himself and
accepted as suitable by his College tutor. The essay provided a
convenient start for a discussion 'conducted at the student's firm
between the student and a panel which typically consists of the

firm's education officer, the student's industrial and college
tutors, and an engineer from the firm who is familiar with the
student's essay topic'. The discussion necessarily ranged over
many aspects of the student's industrial training.

The Academic Board agreed that more experiments should
be carried out, and 'that Departments should be encouraged to
attempt in 1966–67 an assessment of the industrial training of
their third year students (or second year or both), the manner
being left to Departments as they thought desirable'. A considerable College involvement in assessment developed.

Assessment was among the problems discussed at a one-day
conference held at the College in June 1966 and attended by
about 130 people including managing directors and senior
officers in government establishments, as well as representatives
of the CBI and the Training Boards constituted at that time.
Some of the firms represented had long experience of sandwich
course training; others were comparative newcomers in the field.
Two of those who read papers, G. S. Bosworth and J. Hebenton,
were technologists of standing with wide experience of training
in large firms.

Not surprisingly the College's interest in industrial training
assessment was reflected in the concern that was increasingly felt
about internal examinations. The Academic Board received
in March 1966 an interim report from the Working Party
on Examination Techniques established some two years earlier
(see page 218), and accepted some of the recommendations.
Whether the deliberations of the Working Party, stimulating as
they were to its members, seriously influenced the majority of
college examiners is open to doubt, but at least they helped to
reduce the variety of examination practices which individual
departments followed and among other matters to clarify the
assessment of projects and the integration of their grading with
other examination marks.

Perhaps the last act of the Academic Board was to have
another look at 'Schools and Departments'. The Academic
Registrar had prepared a paper which surveyed the concept of
Schools as introduced in some of the new Universities, in
particular Sussex, East Anglia, Warwick and Essex, and raised
questions about the developments at Brunel. These the Board
agreed to discuss at a special gathering, held in the evening of

4 July, at which members were free to explore together the outstanding problems without the restrictions of agenda or minutes. It was a useful exercise, but it did not lead to any substantial change of view about the functioning of Schools or of the relationship of one School to another. More experience was clearly needed.

The end of the 1965–6 session saw the publication of the Brunel Bulletin. Although directed to industrial firms it was designed to improve the University's general publicity. It also served as a useful medium of communication within the University. S. A. Urry was the editor and shaped it in many ways. The first number which appeared in June 1966 was devoted to the University Charter, the organization of undergraduate courses, schools and departments, and partnership with industry—a reflection of the College's special interests and involvements at that time.

There can be little doubt that 1965–6 was a 'year of unprecedented activity'. The Annual Report commented:[9]

In academic affairs, then, our forms of organisation and government were settled, our undergraduate work was extended, and our postgraduate work developed more rapidly than in any similar period in the past. It is gratifying that the momentum continues but so much does interest in our work, and demand for student places, outstrip our present facilities that we inevitably suffer the frustrations arising from going more slowly than we wish. We are hopeful that next year the new buildings will give us a feeling of freedom from restraint.

We needed freedom, of course, but even more renewed vision if we were to achieve the aims we had set before us. A discerning observer, Stuart Maclure, editor of *Education* and later of the *Times Educational Supplement*, wrote six articles in 1965 on 'Britain's new universities', and included Keele, Sussex, York, Strathclyde, East Anglia and Brunel. 'I have included Brunel in this series,' he wrote,[10] 'not only because of its own intrinsic interest, but also because it would be absurd to write about new universities without including a College of Advanced Technology.' He continued, 'But this does not mean that Brunel can be put forward as a "representative C.A.T."—no such institution

[9] Annual Report, 1965–66, Brunel University, 7.
[10] *The Listener*, 2 Dec. 1965.

exists mercifully. In some respects Brunel demonstrates C.A.T. qualities in extreme form. It is radical and uncompromising, and it is this which makes it particularly interesting to an outside observer.'

After noting the College's deep commitment to the sandwich principle and concern about 'the quality of the students' industrial experience and the training which goes with it', he selected two of the more recent developments for special comment, the PSE course and the department of education. Of the latter he wrote, 'I suspect that Brunel will do a great deal of pioneer work in the education of teachers if the right man can be found for the job. The possibilities are endless, and because Brunel is a university which is deeply concerned about teaching as well as research, the education department has the possibility of influencing the institution as a whole, instead of being an appendage.'

Maclure was clear about the road along which the University wished to travel; he was also shrewd enough to appreciate the difficulties ahead.

Men appointed under one dispensation must adapt themselves to another. It is a process which is by no means over. Nor is it possible to say yet whether it will be successfully achieved, or whether the difficulties of transition will adversely affect the university during its first ten or fifteen years. The key to it all, obviously, is staff. There can be little doubt that the university will carry, for some years, some members of staff who might not have been appointed if the university had started from scratch. This is liable to sound slightly insulting, but there is no escaping a basic truth about the promotion of institutions from one academic category to another.

He could also have noted the complementary difficulty of recruiting new staff, who were 'radical and uncompromising' enough to shed the traditional university ways in which they had been reared. Too often their influence was towards conformity; there was a continuing need to educate them in the new philosophy. Maclure commented: 'What remains to be seen now is whether the former C.A.T.s can withstand the pressures to become just like other universities. In some respects they must change and they certainly must conform', but he added: 'Everyone in the universities ought to bestir themselves to foster the individuality of the C.A.T.s and protect them from the erosions of academic snobbery. As for Brunel one thing is clear: Dr Topping and his colleagues with their revolutionary ideas and their modest extremism are as likely as any to resist temptation and pressure alike and bring to fruition their own distinctive contribution.'

I suspect we were not revolutionary enough either to promote significant changes or to resist others; it demanded a measure of single-mindedness given to very few. I had earlier feared that becoming a university would inhibit change, and had hoped that the Robbins Committee would recommend that CATs be left outside the university system, yet independent and autonomous and of university rank. I was not alone in this; the Committee of Principals of Colleges of Advanced Technology in their evidence to the Robbins Committee submitted:[11]

There is almost a national inclination on the part of the new institutions to strive to become part of the established order, distinguished of course but not readily distinguishable from it. Many would, therefore, urge that we should develop into technological universities, styled as such. However, we believe in a diversity of institutions, and we are concerned to establish a route in higher education parallel to that of the traditional universities. We think this would be best served by fully implementing a suggestion of the Percy Committee Report [see page 62] in the light of modern requirements, namely, that the Colleges should become chartered Royal Colleges of Technology with the functions, powers and conditions outlined in our statement [which included] that each College shall be an independent corporate institution, should grant its own awards at all appropriate levels; that conditions of service should be at least comparable with those of the universities, the civil service, and research institutions.

How this predisposition subtly influenced the attitudes of the Colleges towards their newly-acquired university status is difficult, even impossible, to assess. But I recall my own increasing doubts as to whether Brunel could as a university achieve its special aims, even though it might succeed in being different in this way and that. One was aware that all the pressures were relentlessly towards conformity, not least the Committee of Vice-Chancellors and Principals where it must be said the CAT Principals were generously welcomed. To take part in the university system undermined one's sense of independence; new

[11] Higher Education (Robbins) Evidence, Part I, Vol. C. 1963, 785.

loyalties had to be accepted and new procedures followed; there was no other way. The rather tight constraints of accepted university practice and of University Grants Committee policy, however, left a few freedoms; each university had a measure of autonomy (a favourite word in the Committee) and could, if it so chose, follow an educational philosophy specially its own, but to do so demanded eternal vigilance.

Outside the universities there were those, including a few people in education and in industry formerly well-disposed towards the Colleges of Advanced Technology, who saw the acceptance of university rank as a sure sign of the failure of the colleges to undertake their main tasks, and they turned else-where for the fulfilment of their educational hopes—some to the new Polytechnics. The White Paper *A Plan for Polytechnics and other Colleges* was published in May 1966, and by 1970 most of the thirty polytechnics had been designated. To my surprise I found myself a rather solitary supporter of the Polytechnics within the Committee of Vice-Chancellors and Principals, but there was of course a good deal of interest among Vice-Chancellors as to how the Polytechnics were going to develop. Only a few, it seemed to me, had a real appreciation of the place the new Polytechnics were expected to fill, but that could also be written of many outside the Universities. Happily a measure of co-operation between Universities and Polytechnics was later achieved (chapter 22).

CHAPTER 17

Brunel University—the
First Two Years

THE Governing Body of the College met for the last time in October 1966 'acting with the rights, powers, duties and privileges of the Council of the University by virtue of Statute 27.10'. To effect the transfer of the assets and liabilities of the College to the University a Parliamentary Bill had to be promoted and until the Bill was enacted (as it was[1] in July 1967) the assets and liabilities remained vested in the Governors of the College.

Another urgent matter was the Fund Raising Campaign and the report of the Finance Committee on the feasibility study. The Committee was unable for a number of reasons to advise the Governors to accept the proposal 'for a further study lasting six months to be carried out at a cost of £7,500 plus promotional expenses which were likely to cost in the region of £10,000'. In fact the Governors decided to press for more specific evidence as to the feasibility of an Appeal Campaign, and to recommend to the Council of the University that 'the whole question of an appeal campaign' should be further examined. At the same time the New Buildings Committee was asked to investigate ways of raising funds for the erection of Halls of Residence.

The first Hall of Residence had been opened, with some difficulty, at the beginning of term. None of the student common rooms was then available and one of the six staircases was not finished, but somehow 147 students had been accommodated (see chapter 14). Of the other buildings the Central Boiler House had come into use though the building was still not complete; the Lecture Centre (Stage 1) seemed likely to be

---

[1] Brunel University Act 1967 (Council, 4 Oct. 1967).

completed by July 1967 and the Communal Building (Stage 1) by March 1967; the Administration Building would probably be ready for occupation in January 1967 and the Engineering Complex by the end of February; the Engineering Centre was likely to be occupied during the Easter vacation of 1967. Of the buildings in the later programmes the Governors confirmed acceptance of the contract for the Lecture Centre (Stage 2) with a completion date of July 1967; they noted that tenders for the Mathematics Building were to be sought immediately, and that Wimpeys had requested not to be included in the list of firms invited to tender; 'it was hoped to start work by December 1966 with a completion date of August 1968'. Also some difficulties that had arisen about the agreement with the Midland Bank had been resolved so that the building of the Bank and Shops was likely to start soon and they would be ready in February 1967. Such were the prospects for the University at the beginning of the first session, but inevitably the forecasts were optimistic and few of the buildings were completed by the dates given.

Preparations went ahead for the installation of Lord Halsbury as Chancellor of the University and the ceremony took place on 24 November 1966 at Hammersmith Town Hall. There were present the Mayors and Town Clerks of Hillingdon, Ealing, Hammersmith, Brent and Hounslow, the Members of Parliament for neighbouring constituencies, the Vice-Chancellors of many of the universities, representatives from industrial firms and a large assembly of staff, students and local residents. For the University the occasion was memorable, marked by a quiet dignity and simplicity—'with the minimum of fuss' one national newspaper remarked. The degree of Doctor of Technology was conferred on Lord Halsbury and on four other distinguished persons who had contributed in their different ways to the development of Brunel over the past decade. They were Lord Brown the Pro-Chancellor of the University, Lord Kings Norton the Chairman of the Council for National Academic Awards and before that of the National Council for Technological Awards, Sir Anthony Part who as Under-Secretary (later Deputy Secretary) at the Ministry of Education had been deeply involved in the development of the Colleges of Advanced Technology, and Mrs Muriel Forbes for many years a Governor of the College nominated by the Middlesex County Council to which body she had given long and devoted service, being Chairman in 1960–1.

The Installation was followed the next day by two Degree Congregations when the Chancellor conferred degrees on some five hundred students, including former students who had earlier been awarded a Diploma in Technology. Lord Halsbury made the first of his Congregation speeches, and set a standard which he maintained with such effect later that many in the University came to look forward to the occasions with evident pleasure. The culmination of the ceremonies and celebrations was a Service of Dedication and Thanksgiving held at Hillingdon Church on 27 November 1966, when the Bishop of London was the special preacher.

The Council of the University met for the first time on 7 December 1966. The membership included the Chancellor, Pro-Chancellor, Vice-Chancellor and Vice-Principal; there were also six members nominated by neighbouring County Councils and one by the London Borough of Hillingdon, four members nominated by Professional Institutions, one by the Confederation of British Industry, one by the Trades Union Congress and one by the Graduates Association of the University, five members of the Senate nominated by the Senate, two members of the non-professorial staff elected by the Staff, two members of the Academic Advisory Committee appointed by that Committee, and not more than ten persons co-opted by the Council; 37 in all (see Appendix D). There was no direct student representation, but later (in October 1969) the Council agreed to co-opt two student members. Many of the members had served earlier on the Governing Body of the College so continuity was assured. A. L. Stuchbery was elected Chairman of the Council and E. R. Davies vice-Chairman; both of them gave distinguished and devoted service to the University.

Relations with the students and the Students' Union were an immediate concern of the new Council, and at the first meeting it was requested that arrangements be made for members to meet the Students' Union executive. A Joint Council/Students' Union Committee was set up in accordance with Statute 15 (xxviii), and with the following terms of reference: 'to consider the provision of facilities made by the University for the recreation and welfare of the students of the University and to make recommendations thereon to the Council.' The Committee was to consist of the Vice-Chancellor and Principal as Chairman, three members of Council and three members of the Students' Union, and the latter were to be 'nominated in such manner as may be determined by the Students' Union Executive'. A similar Joint Committee was established by the Senate, and both committees met regularly from March 1967 onwards.

The new Council also immediately took up the question of starting a Fund Raising Campaign, but it was a year before a decision was made as a number of possibilities, including a suggested loan from the Hillingdon Borough Council, had to be investigated. Ultimately the Council agreed, on the recommendation of the Finance Committee, to appoint a professional firm of Fund Raising Consultants, C and E Organizers Ltd. with Mr Martin as Organizer, and also to appoint an 'Administrator' on the University Staff to work with Martin. A target of £1 million was suggested although some members regarded such a figure as too low, and it was later raised to £2 million. High among the priorities were buildings: 'three halls of residence, one of which would be of a higher amenity standard to cater for the needs of the post-experience courses run by the University; an Assembly Hall and Theatre, a project which would also be of interest to the local authority; improvement of sports and athletic facilities for students, and the erection of a permanent pavilion and Sports Barn.' Funds for some or all of these were not likely to be made available within reasonable time, if at all, by the UGC.

In May 1967 the Council agreed that the Architects should be instructed to plan two halls of residence; one, it was hoped, would be financed by the UGC and the other by the University. The UGC in fact accepted a proposal that a hall of residence be included in the 1968–9 starts, on the condition that the University agreed to transfer the library building to a later programme. For the other hall the Council examined the possibility of raising a loan of £300,000 from a consortium of insurance companies, and the UGC were asked if they could provide fees and furniture grants 'in respect of residential buildings financed by borrowed money', but were unable to do so at the time; it became abundantly clear that the University's fund-raising campaign should be started and pursued as vigorously as possible.

A special Planning Committee was set up; C and E Organizers were appointed in the first place for a four-month period starting on 1 November 1967 and V. G. Owen, their administrator, was accommodated in the College. The University appointed D. A. Lamb, a retired director who had had useful experience with British Fairs overseas, as Liaison Officer and the two men worked closely together from January 1968 onwards.

By November 1968 the main preparatory work had been completed and the University was ready to launch the Appeal; the appointment of the consultants had been extended to the end of December 1968 and a special appeal brochure had been prepared. A number of firms had been approached and the first two donations of £50,000 each had been announced. The Planning Committee had met for the last time and handed over its responsibilities to the Fund Raising Committee of which the Chancellor had agreed to be Chairman.

Alongside these developments building activity associated with Phase One went on but with continued delays which were as exasperating to the University and the Architects as they were depressing to Wimpeys, who faced with labour troubles and a mounting financial loss decided to leave the site as soon as they could. The Administration Building was handed over on 23 December 1966 with the external site works incomplete but likely to be finished by 31 January 1967. 'Internally, further work was necessary in the Council Chamber and on remedial work throughout the building. The building has been very badly finished and the contractors had now selected a number of good workmen to carry out the remedial work,' so the New Buildings Committee was informed at its first meeting in January 1967. Nevertheless that month some of the administrative staff moved from Acton and occupied whatever rooms were available, with a variety of work going on around them. Winstanley, Chandler and I transferred our offices too, but as all the academic departments were still at Acton there was much journeying between the two sites. For the first six months life in the Administration Building was isolated, dull and unusual; the only other building occupied was the Hall of Residence and coaches might be seen morning and evening taking students to and from Acton. Elsewhere there were unfinished buildings and all the seeming chaos that marks a building site.

The Communal Centre (Stage One) was still not ready; the New Buildings Committee was informed in March that 'the new completion date now given by Wimpey's is 17 April', but it was September 1967 before it came into use. Meanwhile the students in the Hall had lunch at Acton and used the limited provision in the Hall for their other meals. Wimpeys kindly allowed the college administrative staff to use the catering arrangements the company provided in temporary huts for those working on the site.

The other buildings that came into use in September 1967 comprised the Engineering Complex which had been taken over by the University, at least in part, a few months earlier. The Departments of Electrical Engineering and Electronics, Mechanical Engineering, Production Technology and Metallurgy transferred from Acton in time for the beginning of the 1967-8 session. Only about half of the laboratory accommodation was then available for use; the remainder was completed in November 1967. 'Whatever uncertainties there have been about buildings that will be ready for the beginning of the new session,' I wrote in the Newsletter (No. 25), 'there can be no doubt that September, 1967, will mark the real beginning of the University at Hillingdon. From then onwards the University will be established on its new campus with the new buildings in use and with more and more of its activities centred there. Increasingly Brunel will be thought of as at Hillingdon, and Acton will lose the importance it has had for us over the years.'

The remaining Phase One building still unfinished was the Lecture Centre and that proved the most troublesome. 'Although good progress seems to have been made on the Lecture Centre building', I commented in September 1967, 'it is still far behind schedule and no date can yet be given for its completion. We are pressing the contractors hard to have part of it ready in January 1968.' In that we were unsuccessful, for in addition to all the other troubles the contractors found it a difficult building to construct, particularly the six large lecture theatres at the northern end of the building. Planned to be built in two stages, the first of which was started in the summer of 1965 and the second in the autumn of 1966, the delays were such that the second stage caught up with the first and finally in September 1968 the whole building became available, to the great relief of everyone concerned. For a year improvised teaching spaces in whatever buildings were ready had had to be used.

The New Buildings Committee was of course also involved with the planning and commissioning of other buildings, in particular with the 1966–7 and 1967–8 starts as they were called. With the withdrawal of Wimpeys the interest of other and smaller contracting firms was explored and the contract for the Mathematics Building went to Messrs Ford and Walton, who submitted a tender of £320,994. The site was made available to them in January 1967, and the date of completion of the building was agreed as 1 September 1968, which happily was achieved. The other projects in the 1966–7 programme were the Central Lecture Building (Stage 2), to which reference has already been made, and a Maintenance Building. The minor works allocation of £20,000 was to be used to extend the pavilion on the playing fields (Site 3) and to develop four additional pitches on Site 5. (See page 269.)

The whole of the 1967–8 allocation of £1.2 million (originally £1.0 m), was devoted to the Applied Science Building which was to house the two Departments of Biology and Chemistry. Richard Sheppard was appointed Architect, and initially it was hoped to have tenders in by 1 October 1967, contractors on the site by 1 January 1968 and the construction finished in about two years, but in fact the programme had to be modified for a number of reasons (see chapter 18). The total expenditure included a sum of £176,000 for the northern perimeter road and other site developments, a large proportion of the total but inevitable at that stage.

The New Buildings Committee turned its attention to the buildings to be provided from the allocations for 1968–9 and 1969–70, amounting to £1.12 million and £0.56 million respectively; there was still a long list with contending claims for priority. The Physics and Electrical Engineering Building (as it was originally named) had obviously to come next, and was included in the 1968–9 starts along with the Communal Building (Stage 2), a second Hall of Residence (see page 311) and some provision for Nuclear Science in the form of a separate building to the north of the Biology/Chemistry Building. The whole of the 1969–70 allocation would be needed, so the Committee decided, for the Library/Students' Union Building about which discussions with the Architects and the UGC were continued. Later the New Buildings Committee agreed that there should be two buildings, a Library in the central area with room for expansion and a Students' Union building which would be 'better situated near the Halls of Residence on the East Side of the River Pinn'.[2] (See chapter 19.)

John Stillman was appointed Architect for the Physics Building and sketch plans were ready and agreed by October 1967; completion was planned for June 1970. There were a number of complications however arising from academic changes particularly those associated with the creation of Schools; the Physics Building was planned with certain areas into which the Department of Electrical Engineering could move either permanently or until a separate building was available, but there were obvious advantages in housing the Department of Electrical Engineering within the Engineering Complex which would have kept together all the Departments of the School of Engineering. On the other hand the Department of Metallurgy, which was first linked with Engineering and so sited in the Engineering Complex, was later partnered by Polymer Science and Technology to form the School of Materials Science and Technology. Was it feasible to build an extension adjacent to the Department of Metallurgy that would enable both the School of Materials Science and the whole of the School of Engineering to be housed in the Engineering Complex? Other possibilities were canvassed, but costs decided that Electrical Engineering should be housed within the existing Engineering Complex (with extensions later) and Polymer Science and Technology in an extension to the Physics Building. Thus the two departments comprising the School of Materials Science and Technology became geographically separated, a disposition no one wanted. 'One of the difficulties about planning future capital development in universities', a UGC report[3] stated, 'is that, if adequate time is to be allowed for the planning and construction of particular buildings, a period of not less than four years on average must elapse between the inclusion of a building in a programme and its being brought into use.' Academic changes could usually be effected much more quickly, and so seeming

---

[2] New Buildings Committee, 10 Jan. 1968.
[3] *University Development, 1962-67*, HMSO, 153.

inconsistencies arose between academic arrangements and the siting of buildings.

Looking to 1970–1 the New Buildings Committee agreed that the UGC should be asked to provide about £1 million for a School of Social Sciences and Department of Education Building, provision of access to Site One, a Vice-Chancellor's Residence and some development of playing fields. The Fund Raising Programme would, it was hoped, make possible the satisfaction of some or all of the University's other needs, which included Halls of Residence, Assembly Hall and Theatre, Sports Barn, pavilion and playing fields, University Health Centre and a number of extensions to existing buildings—a formidable list.

Academic developments in the University were the special concern of the Senate which held its first meeting on 20 October 1966. The Vice-Chancellor was Chairman and the Vice-Principal, the Head of each School and Department, and the University Librarian were members, as well as two Professors elected from among their own number and six persons elected by the Readers, full-time Senior Lecturers and Lecturers; 22 members in all. The first elected members were R. Borger, J. Dore, L. H. Hancock, R. D. Nimmo, G. M. Saul and B. G. Walker. The election of two Professors was not possible at that time as there was only one Professor who was not a Head of Department, John Vaizey, and he became a member forthwith. He had been appointed Professor of Economics in the School of Social Sciences and joined the University in September 1966. Also C. E. N. Childs joined the Senate in October 1967 immediately after his appointment as University Librarian. One of the first decisions of Senate was to offer the degree of Bachelor of Technology, under the terms of Article 4(4) of the Charter, to nine members of the academic staff (Messrs H. Lister, F. D. Gribble, D. W. Lewin, K. W. Course, J. D. D. Russell, R. W. New, L. H. Hancock, P. J. Hawkins and J. F. R. Ibbetson) who did not hold degrees. A special Congregation was held on 18 November 1967 at which the Vice-Chancellor conferred the degrees.

The number of first-year students admitted to undergraduate courses in September 1966 was over 400, the highest figure so far achieved and included about 100 who were 'industry-sponsored'. The total number of undergraduates reached 950

and in January 1967 rose to 1,050. At this time some of the other
new universities[4] were still small; Sussex had grown quickly and
had 2,764 students but Essex had only 755, while among the
technological universities Aston had 2,293. Keele by design was
restricted in size, and though founded as a university college in
1949 and granted a charter as the University of Keele in 1962, it
had only 1,391 students in 1966.

The main constraint on expansion at Brunel was the living
arrangements for students who were unable to live at home;
in 1966 they comprised nearly one-half of the students. The one
Hall of Residence accommodated about one-sixth of the
students, and the others, over a third, travelled daily to the
University from their homes. The Senate viewed the immediate
future with some concern, and at its first meeting heeded the
warnings of the Academic Registrar[5] and decided that the total
number of undergraduates to be admitted in 1967 should not
exceed the number admitted in 1966. A survey of the lodgings
available in the Uxbridge area was urgently needed. Senate
was reluctant to adopt 'an explicit selection policy of giving
preference to local candidates' and so increase the proportion of
students living at home. Although such a policy found favour in
some university circles, with individuals if not with institutions,
it was never given full support. In terms of the economic
circumstances of the time it seemed to me sensible.

The newly-established Departments and Schools made
promising starts. The School of Engineering, with its three
departments, had 365 undergraduate and 25 post-graduate
students, having introduced two post-graduate courses leading
to the degree of M.Tech., one full-time in Systems Engineering
and the other part-time in Electrical and Electronics Engineering; the latter was specially designed for graduate-apprentices in
industry.

The School of Social Sciences also developed rapidly. The
new honours course in Psychology, Sociology and Economics
(PSE) attracted many applicants and started in September
1966 with an intake of 20 students, and 43 the following year.
The honours course in Psychology was modified, especially the
first year, so that it became possible for students to transfer from

---

4 *U.G.C. Annual Survey, 1965-66*, HMSO, Appendix 3.
5 Senate Paper, Doc. No. Sen./8.

one undergraduate course to the other at the end of the first year. The Diploma Course in Management was replaced by a Master's degree course in General Business Management but retained its sandwich basis. The School received a number of research grants notably one of £28,500 extending over three years from the Ministry of Health for an investigation into the 'Organization and Administration of Hospitals and the Hospital Service', inaugurating the School's deep involvement in hospital administration and the health services. The following year the North-West Metropolitan Regional Hospital Board made a similar grant. Maurice Kogan was made Director of the Hospital Organization Research Unit with effect from 1 October 1967, and there were developments in economics too; early in 1968 a Department of Economics was instituted within the School and Professor John Vaizey was appointed Head.

The School of Mathematical Studies introduced an additional undergraduate course, styled Mathematics with Management Applications, in parallel with the well-established course in Mathematics with Technological Applications. It included some economics, econometrics, financial aspects of business and business relations as well as some operational research. Of the 40 students who entered in September 1966 some 15 opted for the management course, and the following year more than half the new students chose this course. There was also a gratifying response to the part-time postgraduate course in Numerical Analysis leading to the degree of M.Tech.; 25 students enrolled. They were required to attend the University on one day each week for two academic years and at the end of that time to sit a written examination, followed not more than six months later by the submission of a dissertation. It proved a popular arrangement and attracted students from far afield. A similar course in Operational Research was started the following year (1967–8), conducted jointly with the School of Social Sciences and the Operational Research Branch of the National Coal Board. There were developments too in the other areas of the School's interests—in computing and statistics. The 803 computer at Acton was no longer adequate to the School's needs; Professor Crank wrote in the Annual Report (1965–6):

students of almost all departments received a systematic introduction to the Elliott 803 computer and, in line with established policy, they all went through the drill of punching tape, processing it through the computer and correcting their own mistakes. This basic instruction was given as early as possible in the course, sometimes on a block release basis, when, for the whole of one week of a term the normal timetable was replaced by computer instruction. The students were then free to use the computer whenever it was appropriate later in their course, subject to its being available, and particularly for project work in the fourth year. All this made heavy demands on what was, by present-day standards, a small computer.

A second similar machine was provided at Uxbridge in 1967, as a temporizing measure until a powerful computer complex could be installed in the new Mathematics Building the construction of which started early in 1967 and proceeded well. C. C. Ritchie was appointed Deputy Director of the Computer Unit and with Professor Pitteway planned its development. Dr P. Macdonald was given charge of the Division of Statistics and Operational Research.

Another School, named Materials Science and Technology, came into existence in January 1967, and brought together the two Departments of Metallurgy and Polymer Science and Technology (see page 315). The latter department had been created by amalgamating the Plastics Division of the Chemistry Department with the Department of Materials Science and Technology (see page 293) and been given the responsibility for the undergraduate course in Chemical Technology, which was started in 1964, and for a new course in Materials Science and Technology which admitted its first group of students in September 1967. Initially there were four undergraduate courses in the School, for there were two courses in metallurgy—one an honours course and the other leading to an ordinary degree. The creation of the School, it was hoped, would influence for good not only the work of the two departments that comprised it, but also the teaching of materials science throughout the University.

For too long have metals been taught separately from non-metals. In these days when engineers are as deeply concerned with new materials as with traditional metals, when physicists are working with all manner of rheological substances as well as with transistors and the new metals, and when molecular biology is transforming our knowledge of living materials an integrated approach to the teaching of

materials should be an important feature of the courses in a technological university like Brunel.[6]

The Department of Education (page 292) also made a start in
September 1966, and began to prepare a course designed to provide initial training for graduates wishing to teach mathematics
and science in secondary schools. The course, of one year's
duration, led to the University's Post-graduate Certificate in
Education and opened in September 1967 with an enrolment of
22. While this was being developed the planning of four-year
undergraduate courses in education proceeded. The Department of Education and Science gave timely support to the
research activities of the new department; in August 1965 the
College had received from DES a grant of £6,500 a year for two
years in support of an investigation into the possibility of
designing self-instructional material suitable for use by students
wishing to prepare for the Higher National Certificate in
Electrical and Electronic Engineering, and J. B. Thomas[7] was
appointed as a Senior Research Fellow responsible for directing
the work, which was extended in both scope and duration, with
the aid of a supplementary grant of £7,200, to include a wider
investigation of the use of programmed materials at HNC level.
Even more significantly DES provided a major research
opportunity in the field of Further Education (page 293) by
making available to Professor Furneaux and his staff a grant of
£75,000 over a period of five years, which enabled a special
Research Group to be set up. It gave the new Department a
flying start.

The three science departments—Biology, Chemistry and
Physics—with well-established undergraduate courses widened
their postgraduate and research activities. Members of staff
extended considerably their involvement in original work,
helped by a flow of research grants from the Science Research
Council, Government Departments and a number of industrial
firms. In Biology Dr R. J. Terry, appointed Reader in Applied
Biology in 1967, added a new field to the Department's research
interests. The Tropical Medicine Research Board supported his
work in immunology and also helped Professor Gillett and Dr
M. D. R. Jones to continue their work on circadian rhythms in

[6] *Brunel Bulletin*, No. 3, Oct. 1967, 4.
[7] *Brunel Bulletin*, No. 2, Dec. 1966, 4.

mosquitos. Various new lines of research in biochemistry were started.

Of the group of 16 full-time post-graduate workers in the Chemistry Department in 1966 nine were directly supported by industry and six by the Science Research Council. Professor Sing's special interests were in surface chemistry and work in this field developed considerably; the International Symposium on Surface Phenomena of Metals was held at the University in September 1967. Work of longer standing, in for instance chromatography and radio-chemistry, continued, and a short post-graduate course in the Practice of Gas Chromatography became an annual event.

The Physics Department initiated two M.Tech. courses, one in semi-conductor physics and the other in vacuum physics and technology, and research activities were extended in both these fields. Professor Hogarth's main interests were in semi-conductor physics, but other members of staff contributed to a number of investigations covering a wide range, one helped by funds from the United Kingdom Atomic Energy Establishment.

The University's higher degree regulations enabled some former students working in industry to register for higher degrees and more full-time research students were attracted. For instance a former student of the Physics Department who originally obtained a Dip.Tech. in 1959 gained his Ph.D. in 1968 for work carried out in the Kodak Research Laboratories under joint supervision, and 'three of the students who graduated in July 1968 stayed on as research students, two with SRC awards and one with industrial support'. There were similar developments in Biology and Chemistry. A feature of these early years was a significant expansion in research programmes throughout the University.

The growth of the University was reflected in the use and extension of the library which in the Spring of 1966 received a special non-recurrent grant of £43,000 from the UGC. The number of volumes was increased from 18,000 to 32,000 and the number of periodicals reached about 1,000. All parts of the library were much improved, and in particular the collection of basic works of reference and the abstracts collection were greatly strengthened, and a start made on building up a social sciences section. C. E. N. Childs took up his appointment as

University Librarian in July 1967, and R. W. P. Wyatt became Deputy Librarian. Planning started on the permanent library building which had been included in the 1969–70 programme. Meanwhile the library was very short of space, but like other departments it profited a little from the occupation of the Phase One buildings at Uxbridge as they became available; in the Autumn term of 1967 it was possible to open a 'branch library' in the Exhibition Hall of the Engineering Centre with space for about 20,000 volumes and about 75 readers. Further temporary provision had to await the completion of the Lecture Centre.

A number of financial changes and decisions, particularly respecting UGC policy, profoundly influenced the growth of the University at this time. They concerned not only non-recurrent grants for buildings and equipment, but recurrent grants for general maintenance and development.

The Finance Committee was told in July 1967 that out of a total of £850,000 of UGC approved furniture and equipment for new buildings (Phase One), orders amounting to £400,000 had been placed, but the UGC had indicated that 'no more than £300,000 would be available for the period 1 April 1967 to 31 March 1968'. Fortunately the UGC agreed later to increase the grant to £400,000, but this was still grossly inadequate, and the flow of equipment into the Engineering Complex which was just coming into use was seriously disturbed. Heavy equipment on long delivery dates had of course been ordered and was supplied, but other items available at short notice from stock had not, so that much of the routine equipment was missing when the laboratories opened.[8] More seriously it looked as if the Engineering Departments were likely to remain under-equipped for some years.

The UGC decision was linked with a new system of equipment grants which they had planned to introduce for the quinquennium starting 1 August, 1967.

The essence of the proposed new system was that in future equipment grants should not be linked to the initial commissioning of new buildings, and that universities should not be expected to provide for the equipment needs of existing buildings from recurrent grant. Instead it was proposed to provide each university with an annual sum of money related in the main to the number of students in the

[8] Annual Report, 1967, 19.

university, weighted to allow for differences in the balance of subjects
and in the proportion of undergraduate and postgraduate students.
These grants were to be fixed for a period of five years in advance, with
provision for supplementary grants to take care of major new developments or other cases where the need for expenditure on equipment
preceded the build-up of the student body in a particular subject.[9]

It did not prove possible to introduce the new arrangements
in time for the first year of the quinquennium, but a memorandum explaining the new system was circulated to universities in
September 1967, and by November each university had been
informed of its basic allocations for the remaining years. Brunel
was to receive the following: 1968–9, £252,000; 1969–70,
£241,000; 1970–1, £142,000; 1971–2, £144,000. The first of
these was effectively for the period 1 April 1968 to 31 July 1969
as the Government, to help some 'hard cases' arising from the
new grant system, had made available for all universities 'an
additional sum of £4.9 million for the period 1 April–31 July
1968, to be added to the sum of £16.5 million for the academic
year 1968/69'. In addition to these non-recurrent grants, for the
purchase of equipment for teaching and research, other sums
were available for furniture through particular grants associated
with a building project or through the recurrent grant, but a
sense of stringency prevailed.

The UGC also made known in November 1967 that the
recurrent grants allocated to the University for the quinquennium were: 1967–8, £1,276,000; 1968–9, £1,335,000; 1969–70,
£1,346,200; 1970–1, £1,445,000; 1971–2, £1,547,800.

The grant of £1.276 million for 1967–8 was about ten per cent
higher than the provisional allocation made earlier in the year
and was particularly welcome as it made possible the restoration
of certain items of expenditure; 'no expenditure had been
possible on equipment nor on increases in technicians or
administrative and clerical staff in Schools and Departments'.[10]

The annual increases in grant had to absorb all additional
costs during the quinquennium, not only for existing commitments but for all new developments planned by the University.
The smaller increase in 1969–70 anticipated the saving that
would occur if the Acton buildings were vacated in 1969, but

[9] *University Development, 1962–67*, 168 et seq.
[10] Finance Committee, 4 Dec. 1967.

the UGC gave an undertaking to make available an appropriate sum if the buildings at Uxbridge were not ready in time. In fact the actual grant[11] for 1969–70 was £1,548,789 and for the two subsequent years £1,860,484 and £2,307,965 respectively. These increases followed the pattern common to all universities and arose from supplementary grants for academic salary revisions and for other cost increases occasioned by price movements. The original grant of £172.5 million to all universities in 1971–2 was increased to £254.4 million, and this included £7.4 million in respect of inflation occurring in that year made retrospectively in the context of the settlement for 1972–7.

The Memorandum of Guidance[12] issued in November 1967 by the UGC to all universities made specific, for the first time, the level of financial provision the Committee had in mind in respect of certain areas of work and indicated where they expected developments to take place. They also gave to each university an indication of the student-numbers on which the allocation for the year 1971–2 had been based; for Brunel the numbers were as in Table 17.1 and much smaller than the University had in mind. The UGC however made clear that their figures were not laid down as directives, still less as 'ceilings'; they did however dictate the level of financial provision. The University took the warning that its rate of expansion would be seriously reduced.

TABLE 17.1

	Undergraduate Students	Post-graduate Students
Science-based subjects	1,180	80
Other subjects	310	80

In the autumn term of 1967 however another 410 new undergraduates entered the University, including over 200 in the School of Engineering, so that the total number of undergraduates reached nearly 1,200, an increase of about 150 on the previous year. It looked as if in two years' time the UGC's projected end-of-quinquennium figures would be reached, as indeed they were.

[11] *University Development, 1967–72*, Appendix 5.
[12] *University Development, 1962–67*, Appendix 12.

Nevertheless there were signs that numbers would fall below those projected by the University; for instance it was not possible to start the proposed undergraduate courses in education to which enrolments in the final year of the quinquennium would, it was hoped, have reached 280—a major over-estimate, but a measure of the enthusiasm for such a development. In a letter from the UGC dated 13 November 1967 about the quinquennial allocations note was made that the Committee had taken particular account of the University's proposals for 'the development of the one-year postgraduate course of teacher training which started this year; and the introduction of a four-year undergraduate sandwich course in Education and another subject, but on a more modest scale than proposed'. Indeed the Committee stated in its report for 1962–7 that to avoid too wide a dispersal of resources 'the provision of further training courses, specially designed for scientists and technologists, is being concentrated in three designated institutions, Bath, Brunel and the Chelsea College of Science and Technology. The Committee welcome experiments in combining "Education" with other specialist subjects in a first-degree course, with the caution that there are technical complications about the acceptability of such courses under existing regulations.' The complications were real enough but the major factor that militated against such an important innovation was the fall in admissions to science and engineering courses generally.

The University's forecasts of student numbers in its under-graduate courses other than education for the years 1967–72 totalled 1170, 1410, 1670, 1870 and 2050 respectively, but the actual enrolments were about 5 per cent down (1336) at the beginning of the second year and over 20 per cent down (1614) in the final year. This figure of 1614 was nevertheless about 8 per cent in excess of the UGC's projection of 1490. Reasonably accurate forecasting was impossible in a situation where the pattern of student demand for undergraduate courses was changing drastically. Although the UGC had 'not felt able to make provision for major developments in Social Studies' at Brunel the number of undergraduate students following such courses rose rapidly, in keeping with changes in universities generally, and even exceeded during the second half of the quinquennium the University's own estimates. In 1967–8 only about 10 per cent of the undergraduates were following courses in the social sciences; by 1971–2 the proportion had risen to 22 per cent, as Table 17.2 shows. The science and technology departments managed, in spite of the national swing against science and technology, to achieve a slight increase in their numbers, while the School of Mathematical Studies more than doubled its total student roll, the undergraduate course in Mathematics with Management Applications and that in Computing proving attractive to students.

TABLE 17.2

Numbers of Undergraduates

	1967–8	1971–2
Social Sciences	124	359
All other courses	1066	1255
Total	1190	1614

As to postgraduate numbers the UGC's figures for Brunel were very conservative. Their memorandum of general guidance explained:

Many Universities will find that in their allocation letters the number of postgraduate students for which the Committee have provided is smaller than the Universities had wished. There are several reasons for this: (a) the Committee thinks that the flow from the schools into undergraduate places should be a real priority; (b) the numerical proportion of the first degree output that embarks on postgraduate work already substantially exceeds the Robbins estimate; (c) there is uneasiness that the rise in the proportion of graduates who stay in the universities for postgraduate studies, rather than moving into teaching or the outside world is greater than the country can afford at present; (d) with the slackening in the rate of growth of student numbers there will be less need in most disciplines for recruitment to University staff, via a higher degree, than has been the case during the past few years.

They were general arguments that applied with less validity to a new university like Brunel, which had well-established undergraduate courses but needed to expand its post-graduate work. This it did in the main by making use of its special links with industrial firms and by developing courses and research facilities for graduates who could only attend the university part-time (see page 318). In the first year of the quinquennium there was a virtual doubling of the number of students registered for higher degrees—from 145 in December 1966 to 279 in December 1967. Many of them attended part-time M.Tech. courses which clearly met local needs. In addition over 400 students attended the short post-graduate courses the University provided. During the session (1966–7) 13 students were awarded the degree of M.Tech. and 3 the degree of Ph.D. By the end of the quinquennium there was a four-fold expansion in the number of post-graduate students to over 1200, including 400 involved in research either full-time or part-time (see Table 22.1).

A new Academic Advisory Committee (see chapter 13) was established in December 1966 to serve, in the first instance, for five years. Later it was reappointed for a further two years from December 1971. The Charter made provision for such a committee 'which shall be responsible for keeping under review the standard of education provided in the University and of the higher Degrees awarded by the University and have such other powers as may be conferred upon it by Statute'. It was laid down that the Committee should consist of 'Seven persons of high academic standing, appointed by the Lord President of Her Majesty's Most Honourable Privy Council, provided that at least one of the said persons shall be actively associated with industry'; the Vice-Chancellor and Principal was also to be a member. Of the old committee Professor J. T. Allanson,[13] Professor E. R. Andrew, Lord Annan and Dr G. Templeman were invited to serve again, and the new members were Professor C. H. Gray of King's College Hospital Medical School, Professor B. C. L. Weedon of Queen Mary College, London and Sir John Paget, an industrialist and former Chairman of the Governing Body of Brunel College. Sir Walter Worboys was unfortunately unable to continue, and he was succeeded as Chairman by Dr Templeman who became a member of the Council. The University was pleased to recognize Sir Walter Worboys's services as Chairman of the first Academic Advisory Committee by conferring on him, in July 1967, the degree of D.Tech. *honoris causa*. Sir John Paget was the other member of the Committee appointed to serve on the Council.

[13] Professor Allanson resigned early in 1969 and the Lord President of the Council appointed Dr S. G. Hooker, FRS, in his place.

The new Committee held its first meeting on 17 April 1967 and embarked on a detailed consideration of Senate Regulations. Other academic matters, such as the creation of new departments or schools, the appointment of external examiners, student failure rates and relations with other colleges, came under review from time to time and recommendations were made to Senate. With respect to that body the Committee had the useful functions of a Second Chamber. As to Council two members of the Committee had a first-hand involvement in its affairs, and reports were made in accordance with Statute 17.6 (iii), namely to 'certify annually to the Council that it has satisfied itself about the . . . organisation and conduct of University examinations including the conditions of appointment and service of external examiners'. Unlike its predecessor the Committee had little of a controversial nature to deal with; it met twice a year, and invited some Heads of Schools and Departments in turn to discuss developments in the academic activities of their particular section of the University.

In May 1967 the vice-Principal, Dr G. C. Shipp, resigned on being appointed Director of the Hotel and Catering Industry Training Board, a post he took up in the summer of 1967. He had had major responsibilities since October 1964 for the general planning of the University's building programme and for negotiations with the UGC and the Architects; moreover with John Eden he had planned and supervised the purchase and installation of equipment of all kinds, particularly in the Engineering Complex and the Communal and Lecture Centres. His contribution to the shaping of the campus was considerable.

It had been clear for some time that the University would have to appoint a Buildings Officer, and R. S. Adlington was so appointed as from 1 April 1967. L. A. Grant continued as Buildings Superintendent in charge of maintenance (see page 205). Adlington took over many of the responsibilities Dr Shipp had carried, but additional help was needed with the general planning of other new buildings and in particular with the new Library. I invited S. A. Urry who earlier had been associated with the Planning Group (see chapter 14) to act as my planning assistant, whilst retaining the Headship of the Department of Industrial Training, for at least one year from 1 June 1967.

These appointments made it possible to change the role of vice-Principal into one that could be assumed by a leading member of the academic staff for a prescribed period, restricted so that even over a decade a number of Heads of Schools or Departments would be able to be associated closely with the work of the Vice-Chancellor; the spreading of such experience would it was hoped have fruitful consequences for the University as a whole. 'I have in mind that a Head of Department would serve for two years in the first instance', I suggested to Council in May 1967, 'and might be re-appointed for a similar period but would normally be succeeded by another Head of Department. This follows the pattern of appointment of Pro-vice-Chancellors in many universities.' Some members of the first Academic Advisory Committee would have welcomed such an arrangement from the start of the University, but there had been general recognition it was not possible then. Council accepted my proposal and Professor J. Crank, Head of the School of Mathematical Studies, was later appointed vice-Principal as from 1 September 1967 and served until 1969. During that period he was a member of Council. The new arrangements worked reasonably well, but it became clear that the role of vice-Principal needed sharper definition than it had been given. Pragmatically we let the role grow; rather should we have guided it along agreed lines but we were diverted by the pressure of other matters, seemingly more urgent.

The Charter made provision for a General Assembly to consist of the Vice-Chancellor and Principal, the vice-Principal, the full-time members of the Academic Staff, the holders of such other posts as might be designated by the Senate and such other Members of the University as might be nominated by the Senate. The General Assembly was empowered to 'discuss and declare an opinion on any matter whatsoever relating to the University including any matters referred to it by the Senate and if it so decides submit resolutions to the Senate'. The Vice-Chancellor was Chairman, and the first meeting of the Assembly was held in June 1967. The second meeting followed almost a year later in June 1968. In some ways the Assembly formalized the meetings I had had with the academic staff, going back over a decade, at which academic policy and building plans had been discussed. Clearly it could be expected to develop into something more than an instrument of communication and have a valuable participatory function.

The Court of the University also held its first meeting in June 1967. 'The Court shall hold an Annual Meeting each year at which shall be presented the audited financial statements of the University for the previous year, and a report by the Vice-Chancellor and Principal on the working of the University during the year.' The Court could discuss 'any matters relating to the University and convey its opinion thereon to the Council', and it appointed the Chancellor and the Pro-Chancellor on the nomination of the Council. By co-options to the Court, up to fifty in number, the University recognized the interest and gained the support of distinguished persons in science and technology, in national and local government, and in society generally. The Court's role in the government of the University needed to be explored and developed—a difficult assignment respecting a body that met only once a year and with a membership many of whom had little opportunity of contacts with the University or its work. However, the meeting did provide the Vice-Chancellor with an opportunity of reviewing the year's work and of high-lighting the major developments; although a publicity exercise in some measure it had the virtue of self-examination and helped the University to ponder where it was going.

By June 1967 the Hall of Residence had been functioning for about a year; 'its first year has not been easy because of the isolation of the students from the rest of the University and the inevitable consequences of living surrounded by builders and the evidence of building. But from many points of view it has been a successful beginning of communal life in the University.'[14] In September 1967 there were to be considerable changes, for several hundred students would be working in the new buildings—mainly engineering students in the Engineering Complex, and with the first part of the Communal Building ready there would be opportunities for students and staff to meet socially outside the lecture room and the laboratory. 'Split-site' working it would be, with all its disadvantages and problems, but there was much that was encouraging too.

As one surveys these buildings one cannot avoid the feeling, [I told the Court] that a university campus of some strength and great

[14] Annual Report, 1965–66, 4.

attraction is taking shape, and a new institution is being born. I continue to marvel that even those of us who have lived with plans and models for the past five years, and have worked amongst the messy evidences of building for some months, cannot escape the thrill and excitement which the buildings even in their present unfinished state can engender. In another five years they should be still more exciting.

Although a Warden's house was built alongside the Hall of Residence a Warden was never appointed. The affairs of the Hall were in the hands of a Hall Committee elected by the students, an arrangement that worked reasonably well with the help and guidance of Dr A. J. Lacey, who as non-resident Senior Tutor devoted much time and energy to the development of the Hall as a community. His experience as Warden of the Brondesbury Hall in Acton days (page 139) served him well. The Warden's house gave me a place on the campus where I lived for a number of years near, perhaps too near, to the students, but it provided me with an insight into the growing university which would not have been possible in any other way.

Life on the new campus demanded facilities that the University had not previously provided, even in rudimentary form. A health service for students and staff was inaugurated; it was first discussed by the Council and the Joint Council/Students' Union Committee and interim arrangements agreed. At the start of the 1967–8 session Dr E. V. Lambert became the University Medical Officer, and a very understanding adviser he turned out to be. His contribution to the developing life of the students in the Hall and the University was considerable. A part-time nurse was appointed, and three rooms in the Hall of Residence were modified to serve as a Medical Centre. E. A. Barr, a dental surgeon in Uxbridge, provided dental services for students and staff on Wednesday afternoons and at other times by arrangement, and discussions were initiated with the Regional Hospital Board to obtain the services of a Psychiatrist, as counsellor and consultant.

Counselling was later strengthened, following discussions in the Senate/Students' Union Committee, by the appointment of four members of staff as Student Counsellors; they were S. R. Cooper (Electrical Engineering), H. S. Deighton (Social Institutions), G. R. Halcrow (Mechanical Engineering) and G. M. Saul (Chemistry). Assigned the difficult task of helping students who needed more time and special advice than tutors normally could be expected to give, they worked closely with tutors and the Medical Officer, and collaborated with the Chaplains appointed to the University by the Churches—a full-time Anglican Chaplain, the Revd Richard Legg, appointed by the Bishop of London; a Roman Catholic Chaplain, Father D. Lawson S.J. and a Free Church Chaplain, the Revd F. H. Kelly, who was a Methodist Minister in Uxbridge.

The year 1968 will be remembered as a period of student demonstrations and unrest in many universities, linked with demands for greater student participation in university government [commented the Annual Report for 1968]. If at Brunel we did not suffer from the kind of disturbance that has appalled many outside the universities, there were of course pressures from our students to modify the membership of the organs of government of the University to make possible student participation on a wider scale. In response to this and following a resolution of the General Assembly in June, Senate set up a Working Party jointly with the Students' Union to consider the fuller participation of students in academic affairs.

The Council/Students' Union and Senate/Students' Union Committees had in fact met regularly and become more effective; the Students' Union had grown in effectiveness too.

Earlier in January 1967 Senate had considered a memorandum from Officers of the Students' Union setting out a proposal to institute a studentship, supported by Union funds, tenable by the President of the Union in his year of office; an arrangement referred to as 'a sabbatical year'. The Senate was generally in sympathy with the proposal but preferred that the President, if still an undergraduate, should not interrupt his studies completely for a year and 'should be required to undertake not less than one-third of his course in his year of office and be subject to regular assessment of work'—a proposal that never appealed to the Union Officers and was soon abandoned. The first 'sabbatical' President was Richard J. Hales, who served for the year 1967–8. A second sabbatical appointment was introduced in 1970 and M. Sturgess became Union Administrator with effect from 1 August. Sabbatical years for other Officers of the Union were introduced later.

The University had in its early years a growing involvement with educational authorities and other groups outside its walls.

The Development Group appointed by CLEAPSE (Consortium of Local Education Authorities for the Provision of Science Equipment) were able to take over in June 1967 the building specially designed and built for them (see chapter 14). Dr J. R. Spooner was the Director of the Group and initially his staff included two scientific officers, and a few technicians and clerical staff. The University became their employer, but the Greater London Council, acting for the Consortium, paid to the University by annual grant the full cost of salaries, wages, superannuation and other incidental items. The responsibility for policy remained with the Consortium and its committees, so the link the Group had with the University was tenuous— a welcome tenant, rather than a member of the household. I visited the workshops from time to time, at Dr Spooner's invitation, and was impressed by the innovative character of the Group's work. I always regretted that there was little positive interaction with the activities and policies of the University, and became increasingly aware of our failure to devise the mechanisms that would have involved the Director and his staff in University affairs. Their influence would certainly have been beneficial. Meanwhile their work went quietly on and prospered.

In a somewhat related field the University initiated discussions with the Borough of Hillingdon respecting the use of television in local schools. A television unit with G. H. Noordhof as Director started work early in 1967. It was envisaged the unit would serve not only the internal purposes of the University but would work closely with the Hillingdon Education Committee which independently had developed schemes for the use of closed circuit television in its schools and had also appointed a Director. Discussions led to arrangements for the joint purchase and use of some items of equipment and for close liaison between the two Directors. As a contribution to the improvement of the teaching of science and mathematics in schools, which the shortage of teachers of these subjects made more urgent and important, a scheme was worked out to transmit special lectures and demonstrations from the University studio through a six-channel network to some twenty schools in the Borough. 'This close collaboration in the field of television between a university and a local education authority is probably unique in the country.'[15] However, with a change of political control of Hillingdon Borough Council came a change of policy; the financial cost to the Borough was deemed unjustifiable and the University was left to go its own way, and a promising experiment came to naught. The Hillingdon Director found a post elsewhere and no further appointment was made. I tried hard to persuade the new leader of the Council that even a modified scheme of co-operation was possible, but without avail; his colleagues would not have it. This underlined once again how dependent a university, particularly a new university, is on the society around it.

The University had its own special concerns, particularly to explore how the new techniques could be integrated with its normal teaching methods, not merely to supplement but perhaps to transform them. The need gained some recognition in university circles generally. Indeed in 1963 a committee on Audio-Visual Aids in Higher Scientific Education was appointed jointly by the UGC, the Department of Education and Science and the Scottish Education Department with Dr Brynmor Jones, the Vice-Chancellor of the University of Hull, as Chairman. Its early enquiries showed that in universities 'the use of newer aids—closed-circuit television, video-tape recorder, language laboratory, 8mm cassette-loaded projector, overhead projector and teaching machines—was very slight. Of these closed-circuit television was used most, in 8 per cent (63) of the departments.' In colleges of advanced technology the use of conventional aids was similar to that in universities 'but appreciably more use was made of the newer aids. For example overhead projectors were used in 11 per cent of departments, language laboratories in 12 per cent and CCTV in 17 per cent'. After the publication of the report of the Committee in 1965 the UGC set up a special Sub-Committee on Audio-Visual Aids (subsequently re-named the Sub-Committee on Educational Technology) to advise 'on developments in this field in the universities'. The response by universities to the ideas and recommendations in the Brynmor Jones Reports showed, as the UGC noted later, 'that a great deal of serious and constructive thought was already being given to the extended use of modern media and to the centralised organisation of these new resources

[15] Annual Report, 1968, 8.

for teaching and learning. For our part, we believe that, given adequate encouragement and guidance, there is every prospect that the use of these media will lead to greater effectiveness in university teaching and, in the longer run, to a reduction in costs.'[16]

The UGC sub-committee visited Brunel in October 1968 and discussed the growth in the University of the use of audio-visual aids and the work of the television centre—the studio had just come into operation; it was a three-camera studio with control room, supported by graphics and photographic sections, the control room being linked with six large theatres in the Lecture Centre so that videotapes could be transmitted. Some lecture courses, notably the physics course for first-year engineering students, had been videotaped and the first experiments in using the recordings had been made. The use of closed-circuit television for simple overflow purposes had been tested, particularly at the Symposium on Computer Graphics in July 1968 which was attended by over 500 people, and the Education Department had used the medium with students in the post-graduate Certificate in Education course, practice lessons being recorded and then played back to the students for criticism. This was extended later to examine teaching methods in the University; also further videotape recordings of lecture courses were made and some interchange of recordings with those of other universities took place.

Another extra-mural teaching interest of the University that developed at this time involved the Schools Council, and in particular Project Technology which was concerned with the teaching of applied science in schools. There had been pioneering work at schools such as Ealing Grammar School, Dauntsey's and Sevenoaks, and the Institution of Mechanical Engineers had published a survey, titled *Engineering among the Schools*, describing the results of an enquiry involving 290 schools.[17]

In September 1966 the Schools Council publicly launched a pilot project, directed by G. B. Harrison of the Loughborough College of Education supported by a small team and with a

[16] *University Development, 1962–67*, 121. See also chapter X, Equipment for Teaching, in the *Report of the Hale Committee on University Teaching Methods*, HMSO, 1964.
[17] See Schools Council Curriculum Bulletin, No. 2, *A School Approach to Technology*, HMSO, 1967.

consultative committee known as the Craft, Applied Science and Technology (CAST) Committee, of which I was invited to be Chairman. The project had the support of five regional groups, one of which was centred at Brunel with Professor G. Jackson, Head of the Department of Mechanical Engineering, as Chairman.[18] Such groups brought together teachers in schools and representatives of the professional engineering institutions, industry, local education authorities and institutions of higher education. Ideas were shared and experiments in schools explored and strengthened. 'Much has been achieved in stimulating and holding an enthusiasm for engineering, and incidentally for science, by enabling and encouraging boys to work on practical school projects of their own. What has been common to all these activities has been an attempt to remove the false and debilitating separation of the pupils from the fascinating world of reality.' The basic aims were much in line with those of the University's own undergraduate projects; the educational values as well as the pedagogic difficulties were the same. It seemed to some of us that the University's association with teachers of applied science in schools and with craft specialists in colleges of education could deepen our own insights, as well as offer valuable support to those who wished to enliven and strengthen science teaching in schools by an appeal to the practical and the creative.

The University's links with industry were further strengthened by the appointment in January 1968 of G. L. Burkitt as Industrial Liaison Officer. The post had been created with the aid of a grant from the Ministry of Technology and carried responsibility for developing contacts with surrounding industries and for publicising the University's resources including its research facilities.

In its second year of operation the Industrial Liaison Centre handled over 400 enquiries from local companies. Some problems were referred to Departments of the University, and others to research associations, government research establishments and to other industrial firms. Conversely, the Centre was able to help in finding solutions to some technical problems arising in the University. In addition, through its activities a number of student training places were obtained.[19]

[18] *Brunel Bulletin*, No. 2, Dec. 1966, 5, and No. 6, Jan. 1970, 8.
[19] Annual Report, 1969, 19.

CHAPTER 18

The University Buildings, 1968

EARLY in 1968 the building programme had progressed so far
that it was possible to think of an official opening of the University. 'With new buildings nearing completion, a general
cleaning-up of builders' debris, and the welcome planting of
trees, the last few weeks have seen a veritable transformation
of the University site,' ran the Newsletter for April 1968.

The removal of the scaffolding from the Lecture Theatre Unit, for
instance, has revealed a most attractive building, enhanced by the
wide paved road along its western side and the terraced square to the
north of it. The latter is clearly going to be one of the most delightful
features of the University campus; it has the Mathematics Building on
its eastern flank, the Communal Building to the west, and the new
Physics Building, which is to be started this year will complete it. One
can imagine it thronged with students in the years ahead.

The opening took place on 4 July 1968 and Lord Beeching
performed the ceremony. He had links with the University, for
earlier he had been a member of the Governing Body of the
Brunel College of Technology; he was an industrial scientist,
well-known to the public for his work as Chairman of the British
Railways Board and in particular for the rationalization of
the railway system which involved the closure of many lines,
including incidentally the branch line from Brunel's Great
Western Railway at West Drayton to the centre of Uxbridge; it
divided Site 1 from Site 2. The Chancellor referred to him as 'an
outstanding combination of technologist, businessman and man
of affairs generally, the kind of person that a technological
university might hope to produce one day'.

The University had no hall to house the gathering; instead a
large marquee was hired, described quaintly as an 'air-house'

for it was an inflated plastic envelope maintained in shape by the continuous use of pumps. There was space for its erection in the central area where the library was later built. It could seat about 1,000 people and the arrangements worked well enough, even if the pumps seemed noisy at critical moments and the special air-lock entrances were difficult for an academic procession to negotiate. For those responsible, however, faith in the associated technology was justified. The University's newest educational technology was invoked as well; the Director of Television Services arranged for the ceremony to be televised in other buildings, and for a record on video-tape to be made of the whole proceedings.

'Although there were trumpet fanfares and processions of dignitaries, the distinguishing characteristics of the occasion were efficiency, speed and an absence of platitudinous oratory that marked off the twenty-five minute ceremony from similar ones elsewhere,' wrote Dr John Burnett.[1]

In opening the proceedings Lord Halsbury, the Chancellor of the University, paid particular tribute to the architects and builders, and to the many people who had been associated with their work. He reminded us that 'Although a Senate may specify and Council may authorise, only an architect can design and only a contractor can build, and neither is professionally capable of talking to the other without the good offices of a quantity surveyor. Without either of them, all you would see here today would be grass fields and dis-embodied ideas.'

Dr Burnett's account continued:

In a short but engaging speech Lord Beeching said that the invita-tion was a very gratifying one for him. 'I have something of a reputa-tion as a closer of things, and you know this is not in fact a reputation that any sensible man would choose. I did not choose it—it was a form of distinction that was thrust upon me—and it does indeed give me much greater pleasure to open things and to see things grow.' Lord Beeching recorded that he had been a member of the Governing Body when Brunel College was first founded and that it was a great pleasure to witness its translation to University status so quickly and well done. ('We are I think a little wanting in things which are well done and quickly and which are wholly satisfying in this country at the present time.') The need for expansion of technological education, in the widest

[1] 'Official opening of Brunel University', *Brunel Bulletin*, Number 5, Apr. 1969.

term, was obvious. Our national well-being and standard of living depended on the activities and efficiency of industry, yet 'there is still a very imperfect understanding and appreciation of the role of industry; there is, in spite of the absurdity of it, a gap in understanding, appreciation and sympathy between quite a section of the population and the big mass of people who are engaged in industry, and I see one of the important roles of Brunel University as being the building of a bridge between these two groups of people.' The establishment of Brunel, as of the other technological universities, was a recognition that technology had now fully entered the field of learning; he wished all success to its future expansion.

'If we were reminded of the past,' Dr Burnett concluded 'the enduring memory of Brunel's opening ceremony is of hope and ambition for the future, some pride in what had already been achieved, but, more importantly, the promise of what is to come.'

One formal little ceremony that preceded the official opening took place on the morning of 4 July when a group of representatives of the West Middlesex Productivity Association presented to the University a silver rose-bowl, 'filled with roses bearing the name independence for 4 July is Independence Day elsewhere'. It was a gesture greatly appreciated by all associated with Brunel.

As part of the general celebrations the University had Open Days on 5 and 6 July when in lovely sunny weather hundreds of visitors saw the campus and the buildings for the first time. The University was *en fête*. A special exhibition which occasioned much interest displayed drawings, photographs and other papers related to the construction and launching of I. K. Brunel's Great Eastern. J. H. Large of the Department of Mechanical Engineering was responsible for its preparation and arrangement in collaboration with the Library.

The air-house was in use again a week later, 12 July, for the first end-of-session Degree Congregation to be held on the new campus. Over 200 students were presented for the degree of B.Tech. and the degree of D.Tech. *honoris causa* was conferred on four distinguished people—Dr Sydney Chapman, Dr S. G. Hooker, Professor A. J. Sutton Pippard and Dr J. H. Skellon. To honour Sydney Chapman, one of the most eminent geophysicists of our time, was for me a special pleasure for he guided my initiation to the ways of research and gave me my first university job.

The morning of 4 July was marked also by a meeting of the Court of the University, the second in its history. In presenting the Annual Report for 1967 I recalled that 'we have spent about £3.5 million on the buildings that can be seen now; we have another £2.5 million promised by the University Grants Committee for the buildings in the programme up to 1969, but for 1970 and 1971 we are likely to get very little indeed'. Although the general mood was one of rejoicing and of thankfulness—'as we look at the buildings today we recognise with gratitude how much has been achieved'—everyone was aware of the difficult economic time through which the country was passing and of the uncertainties ahead.

The buildings that could be seen in July 1968 are shown in the aerial photograph reproduced in Plate 17. On the left is the Administration Building and the Bank and Shops; to the right of these is the first stage of the Communal Building, the second stage of which had not been started. Further to the right is the Lecture Centre with the Mathematics Building just to the north of it. The red-brick building is the first Hall of Residence (later named Clifton), and the other buildings comprise the Engineering Complex. At the bottom left-hand corner is the Boiler House with one tall chimney (two chimneys were included in the Architects' models), and alongside is the Maintenance Building. With the exception of the Lecture Centre and the Mathematics Building, which came into use in September 1968, all the buildings had been in occupation for a year or more.

The Administration Building was a simple three-floored structure, a collection of offices and committee-rooms with little to distinguish it except the Council Room at the northern end to which Richard Sheppard gave considerable attention, not only to its architectural form but to the decoration and furniture. Metal vertical louvres were fitted with good effect to the long windows on the western and eastern sides, and with a little expenditure in excess of the accepted norms some of the starkness was removed and a touch of grace added. The ceiling proved attractive in its unfinished form and was so left. This Room served not only for meetings of Council but for those of the Court and of Senate and for other meetings of all kinds. The

17. Buildings in 1968 (only one-half of the Communal Building finished)

18. General view in 1971

19. General view in 1975

Vice-Chancellor, the Secretary-General and the Academic Registrar had offices in the building, which also housed the Buildings Officer, the Bursar and the Finance Officer and a growing number of administrative and clerical staff. The Finance and Supplies Departments in due course took over the main part of the ground floor. There was an entrance hall that ran the whole width of the building giving access from both sides.

The Communal Building was much more complex; its disposition, size and functions greatly exercised the Planning Group. Clearly it had to be at the very centre of the University with, as was ultimately decided, facilities shared by staff and students and including common-rooms, bars, refectories and kitchens. There was reasonable confidence that there would be 5,000 students by the nineteen-eighties; indeed one of the projections which stretched as far ahead as 1984 suggested that in 1980 there would be 4,650 students and a total population, including academic and other staff, of 6,275. To plan one communal building for such numbers was regarded as out of the question and it was ultimately agreed to proceed on the understanding that two such buildings were likely to be needed, in which case a second one would be built in the centre of Site 1. The Architects were asked to plan the first on the basis that it would be adequate for a student population of about 3,000, and that this figure could be revised later depending on the common-room and other provision in the Students' Union Building which had still to be agreed by the UGC. Accordingly it was decided to include four refectories, each of which was to provide seating for about 250, so that assuming an occupancy-factor of 2.5 some 2,500 students and staff could be catered for at a peak period such as lunch time. In addition there were to be coffee-bars and a staff dining-room, seating about 50. The Catering Manager, Peter Richardson, who joined the College in March 1966 contributed much to the planning, and a consultant was later appointed to advise on the kitchens and equipment.

The Building was designed to front the pedestrian way with two floors only, and had to be built in two stages of almost exactly equal size. On the ground floor of the first stage was a refectory and cloakrooms, with another refectory immediately above, alongside which on the north side were the kitchens; these also serviced the staff dining room at the north-western corner of the first floor. Adjoining this were two small staff common-rooms, with teaching and non-teaching staff segregated to satisfy the wishes of some of the staff concerned, an arrangement that from the start was unsatisfactory and was later changed. Near the first-floor refectory on the south side was a coffee bar—to provide coffee there after lunch increased the occupancy-factor of the refectory; it also served initially as a students' common-room. The facilities were an immediate success and the other half of the building was soon needed; the New Buildings Committee decided to include the second stage in the 1968-9 starts.

The Lecture Centre, as explained earlier (page 250), was planned to provide centrally the major part of the University's lecture rooms. At the northern end, at first-floor level and above, were six large lecture theatres, three seating about 110 students and three about 180, while down the spine of the building were another sixteen rooms, each seating 60; all of them had stepped floors with fixed individual seats and had to be artificially ventilated and lighted. Natural lighting and ventilation, however, were available in the smaller class-rooms that formed the southern end and the western and eastern sides of the building; they afforded teaching spaces for another 1,200 students in all; the floors were horizontal and there were individual desks and chairs with some flexibility as to their distribution. Some rooms on the third floor were taken over to house the television centre and its associated workshops, and later still language laboratories were established there. The southern end of the building at ground floor level had an interesting and novel distribution of open rooms where students could read or meet socially, and it was disappointing that these spaces had to be diverted to other uses—firstly as a temporary library additional to the provision in the Engineering Centre opposite (page 358). At the other end of the building was a spacious concourse, outside the large lecture theatres, which provided another good social space with coffee service facilities; it was attractively furnished and the natural lighting from the roof was good but on one side stretching up to the top of the building was a plain brick wall, painted white and not as well laid in some places as it might have been, which cried out for decoration of some kind. Richard Sheppard was as sensitive to the need as anyone and in due course commissioned Andrew Yates to design some panels which were fixed to the wall; their colourful geometrical patterns were well conceived to match the surrounding concrete forms and to lighten the whole space. The aspect from the gallery which provided entrances to the three upper lecture theatres was transformed.

A plan of the first floor of the Lecture Centre is shown in Figure 18.1. The room at the north-eastern corner was never used for its original purposes—a facility for visiting lecturers and a meeting-place for lecturers from different departments before and after lectures. In the scramble for accommodation it succumbed.

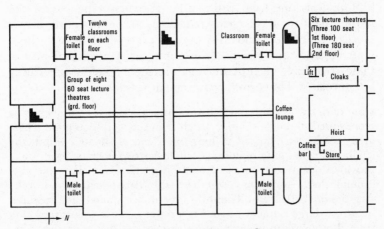

FIG. 18.1. First Floor of Lecture Centre.

A good deal of thought went into the educational technology of the Lecture Centre, from the installation of white-boards throughout to television facilities in the large lecture theatres. Overhead projectors were also provided in all the lecture-rooms. The white-boards were not regarded however as a universal success for though they were a simple and effective aid to the use of projectors, and chalk dust no longer covered everything, coloured felt-tipped pens were a mixed blessing for the staff, whatever good effect colour had on student reception; cleaning the boards (with a wet sponge) was a messy affair and not totally efficient. But the effect on the actual teaching of the new look in the technology must not be under-estimated.

The Engineering Complex, one of the Planning Group's main exercises, was designed to serve the needs of the Departments of Mechanical Engineering, Production Technology and Metallurgy with about 1,000 students, 100 academic staff and 100 technicians. The Department of Electrical Engineering was to be housed elsewhere. Associated with the complex were the Central Boiler Plant and the Maintenance Department. The Architects were Stillman and Eastwick-Field, and John Stillman and David Farrant were closely identified with its design and construction. 'The analysis of the brief indicated that the accommodation could be divided into three basic types of building,' wrote John Stillman.[2] 'The first type covers the requirement for large clear-span areas accommodating heavy pieces of machinery and noisy or dirty processes. Due to the high floor-loadings and the necessity for external vehicular access, these areas have been planned as a series of linked single-storey laboratories.' The second requirement was for

laboratories where the type of work and associated equipment was more suited to the laboratory bench than the workshop floor. These areas have been planned in four tower blocks situated within the chain of single-storey buildings. The lower two floors of each tower provide an entrance to the laboratories above and the adjoining ground floor workshops, together with coat-hanging and toilet facilities for both areas. The third type of accommodation required was for a large number of staff tutorial rooms. It was agreed that instead of distributing these rooms throughout the laboratory complex, where there would have been considerable disturbance from the noise of adjacent working areas, the staff rooms would be grouped in a separate building.

This became known as the Engineering Centre; it housed Heads of Departments and members of the academic staff in individual rooms, and included some design and drawing offices, a number of special classrooms and an exhibition hall where it was hoped old and new machines and equipment could be displayed and

[2] 'The New Engineering Complex', *Brunel Bulletin*, Number 3, Oct. 1967. J. Stillman, Jour.I.Mech.E. 1966.

demonstrated from time to time; unfortunately this hall had to be diverted to other purposes.

Figure 18.2 shows the general disposition of the buildings and (in dotted lines) the extensions that could be built if required. The layout would allow a future expansion of the laboratory areas of up to 50 per cent. 'It was considered that the Tower Blocks and Engineering Centre should be complete in themselves and that any additional accommodation of these types should be situated in separate blocks. At least two new towers could be built to the rear of the existing buildings and, if necessary, additional accommodation could be provided to the east of the Engineering Centre.'

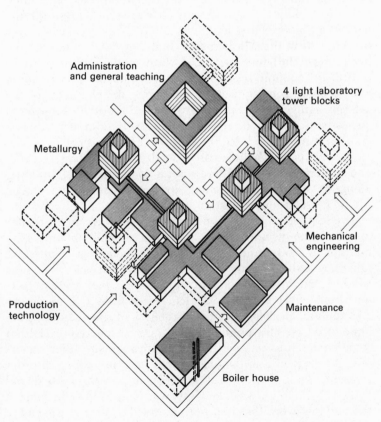

FIG. 18.2. Plan of Engineering Centre.

A decade later the only extension that had been built was a suite of rooms, mainly staff-rooms, for the Departments of Production Engineering and Metallurgy to the west of the Engineering Centre. The expansion in engineering, which the Planning Group had anticipated, did not materialize; indeed, contrary to the initial plans, the complex from the very start was able to accommodate the Department of Electrical Engineering, and later the Division of Building Technology. Later still some of the rooms in the Engineering Centre were taken over by the School of Social Sciences—a strange change that was inconceivable in 1968.

The Mathematics Building came into use in September 1968, though not then completely finished. By that time the north perimeter road was ready, so that the whole road encircling Site 2 was complete; also the entrance area on Kingston Lane had been prepared and footpaths laid to a new footbridge over the Pinn near the Mathematics Building, all in time for the beginning of the new session. The Mathematics Building with its central tower some seven storeys high, and the first building with a passenger lift, seemed to change the character of the campus significantly. The tower provided rooms for some 60 to 70 academic staff, and around it were low buildings of only two floors that accommodated the Computer Unit with all its special requirements, and included other academic staff rooms, research and conference rooms. There was an additional small building alongside with other teaching spaces, making some 40,000 square feet of accommodation in all.

The summer of 1968 was notable in other ways; in particular for the announcement of a virtual stand-still on university building in 1968-9 and 1969-70 in consequence of the measures taken by Government to cope with the national economic troubles. Balance of payment figures were bad and in July, for instance, the visible trade deficit rose from £30 million to £80 million. Earlier, in January 1968, the Prime Minister had announced cuts in public expenditure which required 'that some capital projects in the universities and in other sectors of higher expenditure would be held back in 1968-9 in order to secure savings in educational expenditure in 1968-9 and 1969-70'. Consequently the UGC was obliged to defer some of the building work that had been planned to start at the end of 1967-8 and in 1968-9.

Certain projects that were late in starting in 1967–8 were allowed to fall back into 1968–9, thus reducing the total starts in 1967–8 from the planned figure of £35.1m to £31.9m. In the course of January and February 1968 the Committee made arrangements with particular universities to transfer the start of selected projects from 1968–9 to 1969–70, reducing the 1968–9 starts from £31m to £28.7m. Some projects already in the 1969–70 starts programme had in turn to be deferred, since the authorised total for that year remained unchanged at £29 million.[3]

But this was not the end; in July 1968 the UGC were informed that further savings would be required in the revised level of expenditure in 1968–9 and 1969–70, and early in August the Chairman of the University Grants Committee wrote to all Vice-Chancellors[4] indicating that 'because of further economies in Government spending no further university buildings included in the 1968 programme could be started, unless there were exceptional local circumstances that would justify a contrary decision'.

Fortunately at Brunel the second hall of residence (later named Saltash, after another Brunel bridge) had been brought forward from the 1968 programme to 1967 and contractors (Fassnidge Son and Norris, Ltd) had started work in May 1968 before the ban was imposed. Another project unaffected by the stand-still was the second part of the Communal Building which was also started in May 1968, but the Science (Biology-Chemistry) and Physics Buildings were both delayed (page 314).

The second Hall of residence was positioned near to the first Hall, another red-brick building, but on the other side of the Pinn and the first building in that area. The contract sum was £331,267. Compared with the first Hall it was skimpy with obvious signs of economy everywhere; in particular the kitchens were smaller and the facilities limited, for the UGC norms were less liberal than those that obtained under DES a few years earlier. However, it provided another 220 study-bedrooms which greatly relieved the pressing residential problems. The contractors were seriously delayed by continued bad weather and by September 1969 less than half of the Hall was available,

[3] *University Grants Committee, Annual Survey, Academic Year 1967–68*, HMSO, 17.
[4] In August 1968 nearly all British Vice-Chancellors were in Australia at the Tenth Congress of the Universities of the Commonwealth.

which necessitated some students having to share rooms. Fortunately by the end of October enough of the building had been completed to allow all the students to be housed in individual rooms and the whole of the Hall was ready by Christmas.

The second stage of the Communal Building fared better and was completed in time to be brought into use at the beginning of the autumn term 1969. With two additional refectories, similar in size and function to those in the first stage, and a smaller room offering a snack service the provision seemed more than ample to start with. On the other hand the new student common-rooms and bars, though welcomed by the students, proved inadequate for the many purposes the various union activities demanded. Also the joint use of accommodation by staff and students led to some teething troubles, and a separate Students' Union Building became more and more urgent. Nevertheless, the complete Building, renamed the Refectory Building, was a valued asset which proved an important factor in the developing social life of the University. This owed much to Richardson; not only was he successful as Catering Manager in coping with the many demands of students and staff, but his fame spread outside the University and many societies and groups used the University's facilities for social functions of various kinds. Locally Brunel's name became synonymous with good catering.

As to the other buildings the Science Building alas had more than its fair share of trouble. 'When tenders were received in February 1968,' the Annual Report recorded, 'it was found that the lowest was some £200,000 in excess of the UGC cost limits, a substantial part of this sum being doubtlessly a form of "insurance" against a recurrence of the labour troubles experienced by the contractors, Messrs. George Wimpey & Co. Ltd., during the construction of the first phase of the building programme. All attempts to reduce the lowest tender to a figure within the prescribed cost limits were unsuccessful.' Negotiations dragged on and the building had to be transferred to the 1968 programme. Lengthy discussions with the UGC involving Treasury approval finally 'led to the acceptance of a tender negotiated with a local firm which satisfied all the conditions imposed. At the very moment when this had been achieved the August cuts were announced and building could not proceed.'

The Annual Report for 1968 concluded: 'There is little

point in retailing all the details of an episode of almost overwhelming frustration; it can however be recorded that contract
documents were signed early in 1969, and Messrs. Fassnidge,
Son and Norris are to start the building in April, 1969,' which
indeed they did. The contract sum finally agreed with the UGC
was around £1.1 million.

The 1968 cuts amounted to £10 million nationally and of this
£1.4 million was Brunel's share—an incredibly severe blow
which postponed the move from Acton for a year, from 1970 to
1971. The UGC later gave figures showing that the effect of the
reductions in the building programmes

was to defer[5] more than £15m. of building which universities had been
expecting to start in 1967–68 and the succeeding two years. The
original starts programme was revised as follows:

	Original Programme £m.	Revised Programme £m.
1967–68	35.1	31.9
1968–69	31.0	18.7
1969–70	29.0	29.0
	95.1	79.6

These reductions carried with them consequential reductions in
expenditure on professional fees and on furniture.

Fortunately, the 1969–70 figure remained at £29.0 million
and it was possible for the UGC to agree fairly speedily that the
Science Building could start on 1 April 1969; this was followed a
few months later (July 1969) by a start on the Physics Building
for which the contractors were Messrs William Moss and Son.
The accepted tender was for a sum of nearly £0.75 million. Both
buildings were ready for occupation in the summer of 1971.

Writing in the Brunel Bulletin[6] Richard Sheppard commented on the developments:

There will shortly rise (we hope) the Biology/Chemistry and Physics
buildings. These are planned as separate units but will form part of
a range of teaching buildings extending along the north boundary.
These will eventually link, to the east and west, with other teaching
buildings and so the real and final pattern will, at last, begin to

[5] *University Development, 1962–67*, HMSO, 40.
[6] 'Brunel University—A view in 1969', *Brunel Bulletin*, Number 5, Apr. 1969.

merge—a necklace of 'common use' and servicing buildings arranged loosely along the central concourse and outside these a ring of specialised teaching buildings. An idea of the final effect can be judged now from a view of the Engineering buildings from the central walk. On a wet November day the campus must seem pretty bleak but the architect has to visualise a situation and an environment in ten or twenty years' time. By then the trees, instant and infant alike, will have grown up and the buildings ranged along the principal street will appear as an alternation of court and block. The buildings are usually 'open-ended' where possible and allow for expansions and additions. But they will also front on to green tree-planted spaces and these spaces will be enclosed by future buildings.

We decided that teaching and common-user buildings should be in reinforced concrete since this gave a sufficiently wide range of structural possibilities to meet the immediate and any future requirements. It was also decided that all buildings should be kept down to three or four storeys where possible to avoid lifts which are extremely expensive items. This also meant cheaper buildings generally, since in UK, for some inexplicable reason, three or four storey buildings are always cheaper than high ones. Load-bearing brick construction was chosen for the residential blocks owing to low cost and structural simplicity. Eventually, when more residential buildings are finished, the red brick chosen will form a contrast to the grey concrete. The contrast between the two will emphasize their different function and location.

Richard Sheppard concluded:

It is difficult to predict the future growth rate of the University and a waste of time to produce graphs showing staff and student numbers in 1975 or 1980. Just as the Vice-Chancellor is thankful if he can see the end of the division between Acton and Uxbridge, the architects have learned to look no further forward than buildings actually approved by the University Grants Committee and even then to prepare the University for the almost inevitable delay in completion. In the pipeline, as I have said, are the Biology/Chemistry and Physics buildings which will start in 1969 with the hope of completion in 1971.

By 1970 the new Library and part of the Union should be under way and one would expect the former to finish in the following year. We hope to complete the second residence for 240 in time for the autumn term of 1969 and the second stage of the Refectory soon after.[7] When these buildings are completed the first centre of the new University will have taken shape and then it will be possible to judge what has been done. I hope and believe that it will be liked and that it will form a significant nucleus from which future developments can spring.

[7] See page 348.

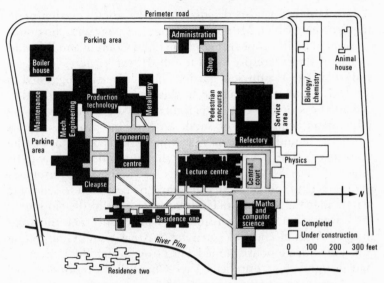

FIG. 18.3. Plan of the University in 1969.

Further developments were conditioned by the purchase of certain areas of land and the sale of others; a crucial decision had to be made as to when and how a link across the railway cutting with Site 1 would be constructed. Richard Sheppard wrote: 'the use of this part of the University land (Site 1) is far away in the future and we have done no more than indicate how it might be developed.' A bridge would be required however across the cutting with a roundabout providing a link with the existing road system. 'Heaven knows,' he added, 'what chaos will ensue outside the site on the surrounding road pattern.'

As far back as November 1963 when the Ministry of Education was approached about a road-bridge (see page 256) a decision had been postponed. Some three years later in February 1967 the University wrote to the UGC proposing the acquisition of part of the railway cutting between Sites 1 and 2. 'The Borough of Hillingdon has agreed terms with British Railways for the purchase of a large section of disused railway line running from Uxbridge to West Drayton. One section, of cutting and parallel roadway, about 3.7 acres in all, has in turn been offered by the Borough to the University' at a price of £65,000. This is marked as D and E in Figure 11.1 (page 199).

The University also decided to make another attempt to acquire Site 4 which Milton Hutchings (see page 262), no doubt stimulated by the appearance of the Land Commission Bill, had indicated they were prepared to sell. It was 31 acres in extent and still in use as a nursery garden. The University suggested to the UGC that 'the purchase of this area would considerably extend the scope of the development of Site 2 and, with the subsequent acquisition of small amounts of property on its southern boundary, greatly enhance the potential of the University's Site 5. A total of more than £154,000 is likely to be required.' To raise the £220,000 involved in these two purchases the University indicated that it would be prepared to sell some of its land to the Borough of Hillingdon for housing development; there were a number of possibilities which concerned the areas marked A, B, H and J (Figure 11.1). Areas F and G adjoining Site 3 included a house named The Grove which the University had in mind to acquire as a Vice-Chancellor's residence, and area C was the Uxbridge Football Club ground (see page 261) and included a house named Honeycroft. The Grove and Honeycroft were items continuously on the agenda of meetings of the New Buildings Committee for the next three years.

The UGC indicated in August 1967 that they were prepared 'to grant-aid the purchase of Site 4 (the nursery garden site) and Site D (the railway cutting) provided that they can be bought at prices approved by the District Valuer and that the whole of the cost can be covered by the sale of the outlying areas A, B, H and J at a figure approved by the District Valuer and not less than the £297,000 which you estimated. The machinery would be for the proceeds of sale to be surrendered to the Exchequer, and for us to grant-aid the purchase of the nursery garden site and the railway cutting.'[8] Indeed in September they agreed to the purchase of the railway cutting even before other transactions were completed, the total outlay being estimated at about £67,000.

Council accordingly decided at its meeting in October 1967 to complete the purchase of the railway land 'between the bridges' and of Site 4 subject to confirmation of the selling price of £150,000, and to sell to Hillingdon Borough Council areas A, H and J at the price of £200,000 subject to the condition that the

[8] Letter from UGC to Secretary General, dated 17 Aug. 1967.

University retained pedestrian right of way to the Uxbridge Road in area H. The sale of area B was not to be proceeded with unless additional funds had to be raised to complete the agreed purchases. Also no further action was to be taken 'for the time being' on areas F and G.

Negotiations dragged on; over a year later in December 1968 the Borough had not formally acquired the railway line land and remained unwilling to purchase areas A and B unless the University first obtained planning permission that would enable the land to be used for housing. At this time (27 November 1968) the UGC wrote blocking the grant of £65,000 for the railway cutting 'until the position with the local authority had been clarified'. Reluctantly the University Council agreed to apply for planning permission for residential purposes which in due course the Planning Authority refused to grant. As to areas H and J however planning permission for staff housing had been given earlier, and the New Buildings Committee turned to these with more confidence, but there was considerable further delay as will be recounted later (page 373).

CHAPTER 19

The Years of Separation, 1968–71

THE three years 1968–71 may be grouped together, for September 1968 saw such a considerable transfer of staff and students to Uxbridge that the move of the University to its new site seemed to become effective then, while 1971 marked the completion of the move. Throughout this period the science departments (Biology, Chemistry, Physics and Polymer Science) had to continue in the Acton Buildings, where they felt a disturbing sense of separation from the new and growing centre of activity. Building delays and cuts in grants added to the frustration and, more important, reduced the momentum of the University's development; marking time is not a very satisfactory activity for long. There were evidences of growth, however, 'not only in the occupation of finished buildings and the start of other new construction, but in the development of the University as a community and in its greater involvement in affairs outside'.[1]

The Mathematics Building and the Lecture Centre became available in September 1968, and the School of Mathematical Studies moved into its new accommodation and was able to offer rooms to the School of Social Sciences and the Department of Education 'until separate provision could be made for them elsewhere on the campus'. The Engineering Departments had full use of the laboratories and workshops in the Engineering Complex, and the abundance of lecture-rooms seemed unbelievable.

By the end of the session 1968–9 the second stage of the Communal Building and the second Hall of Residence were nearing completion, and starts (the revised 1969–70 programme) had been made on the Biology-Chemistry and Physics Buildings (see

[1] Annual Report, 1969, 5.

chapter 18). The UGC had also provided additional funds to allow a wing to be added to the Physics Building to accommodate the Department of Polymer Science and Technology. In October 1969 a third Hall was started, designed on the lines of the second Hall and made possible by the Appeal Fund supplemented by a grant from the UGC to cover the costs of furniture, equipment and professional fees. Messrs William Willett Ltd were awarded the contract. If everything went well the Hall would be finished by March 1971.

Discussions with the UGC had continued throughout 1968 concerning the Library and the Students' Union Building, which earlier (see page 270) had been allocated to the 1968–9 and 1969–70 programmes respectively. Reluctantly the New Buildings Committee accepted the UGC view that the library must be built in two phases, but it became increasingly clear that it would be well-nigh impossible and certainly costly to build half the library and satisfy the local authority's fire regulations. Moreover experience of two-phase buildings was not reassuring and in this case the construction of the second part in the inaccessible middle of the campus would have been difficult. The more the problems were argued the more I was convinced that a one-phase contract was essential and finally the UGC officers capitulated; a contrary decision would as things turned out have affected the development of the library adversely for a decade or even longer, and the University would have been saddled with half a library for a long time. It was a critical battle to win.

The proposed Students' Union Building proved at least as difficult and went through even more vicissitudes. The original schedule of accommodation presented by the students totalled 37,000 square feet but in the lean times of 1968 the UGC thought that with the extra accommodation made available in the second stage of the Communal Building 17,000 square feet was adequate and funds could not be provided for more. A Sports Barn, so-called from Acton days, was also high on the list of desiderata, as well as a Pavilion on Site 5. After discussions with the students in and out of the Council/Students' Union Committee I presented a programme to the New Buildings Committee in March 1969 which received general assent. In a letter dated 31 January 1969 the UGC had informed the

University that the allocation for building starts in 1970-1 was only £0.67 million and in 1971-2 a mere £0.09 million for site works; in neither year was there any allocation for minor works. (The University had requested £1.0 million for each year, before it was known that Government had limited the UGC to a total sum of £28 million for 1970-1 and £24 million for 1971-2 for distribution among all the universities.) Of the £0.67 million in 1970-1 the Library and Students' Union Building had been apportioned £0.51 million, there was £0.07 million for the playing fields and pavilion and another £0.07 million for site works. The remaining £0.02 million was for a Vice-Chancellor's house. Clearly other funds would have to be found, and there were grounds for confidence that the Appeal would yield sufficient money not only for the third Hall of Residence but for some student amenities as well. (By October 1969 the Appeal Fund reached the figure of £385,000.)

I therefore proposed and the New Buildings Committee agreed that the best policy to pursue would be (a) to build the complete Library Building in one contract (at a cost of about £0.48 million), (b) to prepare plans for a permanent pavilion on Site 5 with some further development of playing fields, (c) to plan a Students' Union Building (for 3,000 to 5,000 students) and a Sports Barn, and (d) to build as much of the Students' Union/Sports Barn complex as was possible from the 1970-1 funds, from interest received on short-term deposit investments and from Appeal Funds in excess of those required to build the third Hall of Residence. The Council gave their support but the UGC had still to be convinced.

So that the Students' Union could have some additional accommodation immediately a prefabricated hut was moved from Acton 'as a temporary measure'—a decade later it was still being used; also to augment the playing field facilities some new pitches on Site 5 were sown and came into use in September 1970 (page 314).

In due course the UGC agreed that the whole of the library could be built, but on the understanding that two of the four floors of the building be used initially to house the School of Social Sciences and the Department of Education—a reaction to the University's insistence (see chapter 17) that these two growing areas of activity could not go on indefinitely occupying rooms in the Mathematics Building; indeed they sorely needed buildings of their own. Reluctantly the New Buildings Committee accepted the dual use proposal but this presented the architect, Richard Sheppard, with almost insuperable difficulties. Preparatory work on the planning of the library had been going on throughout 1968 and into 1969; Richard Sheppard and C. E. N. Childs, the University Librarian, had visited other libraries, notably those of the Universities of Edinburgh and Warwick, and after protracted discussions with the UGC agreement had been reached on a library that would house ultimately 300,000 volumes and have 1,000 reader places and 50 carrels. It was December 1969 before the Council learnt that 'UGC approval had been given for a Library Building of 54,825 usable square feet. The cost limit for the building was £497,000 including £40,000 for alterations to accommodate the School of Social Sciences.'[2]

To effect the reduction in size from that originally approved the Architects felt compelled to modify their plans in two ways; to take 'a slice from the middle of the building' and 'to cut down the ground floor area by reducing the perimeter of that floor'.[3] The latter was undesirable for aesthetic reasons, nor could such a permanent reduction in the size of the library, which would have been impossible to remedy later, be accepted readily. I suggested to the New Buildings Committee that they might consider reinstating the ground floor area in the plans; the sum involved amounted to only £12,000 and it seemed likely that the UGC would agree if the University were willing to meet the additional cost. This was accepted and the design of the ground floor reverted to the original plan making it equal in area to each of the other three floors—another critical decision.

To modify the plans further to provide for the School of Social Sciences needed more extensive changes than first seemed likely, and the high cost (about £100,000) of the conversion and of the reinstatement of the two floors later for Library purposes finally convinced everyone that such joint use was not viable. Simpler changes that would allow the temporary use of part of the building 'for Complementary Studies activities and allied academic purposes' were however feasible to which the UGC

[2] Minutes of Council, Dec., 1969.
[3] New Buildings Committee, Dec., 1969.

agreed. With this agreement went the acceptance that a separate
building for the School of Social Sciences and the Department
of Education would have to be provided as soon as possible.
'Tenders for the Library were received in December 1970 and as
the lowest was higher than the UGC cost limit there was further
delay; the happy ending of the story however is that construction started in April 1971.'[4] The contractors were William Moss
and Sons, who were already on the site having been engaged on
the Physics Building since July 1969. The UGC approved a total
expenditure of £543,341 including a sum of £5,689 for built-in
furniture.

Writing in the Brunel Bulletin of July 1971 the University
Librarian commented:

The fact that Brunel is only now starting to put up a library building
does not mean that it is at present without library services. Housed
temporarily in parts of the Engineering Centre and Lecture Centre,
our library has about 65,000 volumes and subscribes to 1,600 periodicals. In the course of 1971 it will lend over 80,000 items to Brunel staff
and students, including more than 8,000 borrowed from elsewhere
through a very active inter-library loan service. In addition to books
and periodicals, a start has been made on introducing lectures on half-
inch videotapes to library users. These can be viewed by individuals on
a simple relay apparatus. Liaison with the Brunel Television Service,
which produces these videotapes, is close and there is also close liaison
with the University's Computer Unit, which is actively co-operating
in the application of computer techniques to various library processes.

Interesting examples of the videotapes produced by the Television Service for the library were two named 'Introducing the
Library' and 'How to use the Catalogue'.

The Acton Branch of the library was moved during the
summer of 1971 and its books, periodicals and catalogues inter-
filed with those already at Uxbridge. 'Every volume in the
collection was re-arranged, the books being housed in accommodation temporarily partitioned off at the south end of the
Lecture Centre and the periodicals in the part of the Engineering Centre already occupied by the library [see page 342].
Although space was very restrictive and the circulation aisles too
narrow for convenience, there were seats for 250 readers.'[5]

Of the proposed Students' Union Complex only one part was

[4] Annual Report, 1970, 5.   [5] Annual Report, 1971, 31.

built. 'There were sufficient funds available to erect a Sports
Barn costing not more than £75,000 and to provide limited
changing room facilities on Site 5, at a cost of £25,000'; so the
New Buildings Committee reported to the Council in December
1969. 'The provision of a Students' Union Building would
depend upon either the receipt of further grants from the
U.G.C. or money from the Appeal Fund.' The students found
some difficulty in deciding priorities but agreed that a Sports
Hall should be built first; the change of name from Sports Barn
reflected its greater size and the extended facilities, such as squash
courts, which in the earlier Acton days when the Sports Barn
was first mooted were not envisaged. Who could have guessed
how popular squash was to become? Evidence of its popularity
came in a proposal that a private company should build squash
courts on land leased from the University, and though ultimately turned down the scheme was seriously considered.

The UGC agreed early in 1970 that a Sports Hall could be
built with a cost limit of just over £0.1 million (partly provided
from the 1970–1 allocation), which meant that the proposed
expenditure of £25,000 on extra facilities on Site 5 would have
to be postponed. Within the prescribed cost limits, so the UGC
suggested, a single-court multi-purpose Hall could be provided,
with ancillary rooms and squash courts, adequate for 3,000
students. Richard Sheppard was commissioned to design the
Hall and was asked to allow for the construction in the future
of an additional hall alongside. In April 1970 his first sketch
plans were available which were readily accepted by the
Students' Union, and two months later he displayed the second
stage sketch plans, whereupon the New Buildings Committee
instructed him to proceed with the Schedule II submission to
the UGC. The Hall was to be constructed in red brick and
positioned to the east of the River Pinn, opposite the Mathematics Building and alongside the footway to Kingston Lane,
with sufficient space, so the New Buildings Committee insisted,
between the end of the Hall and the river to allow for landscaping developments. The Architects had in mind a link with
a future Students' Union building that would, it was hoped, be
erected between the Sports Hall and the third Hall of Residence.
Discussions with the UGC went fairly smoothly though some
reduction in size was insisted on; 'the building had had to be

re-designed,' reported Adlington, 'and would now be square rather than rectangular in shape but the playing areas would remain unchanged.' Tenders were invited in January 1971; the lowest tender, even after a number of savings had been made, turned out to be £22,000 over the cost limit set by the UGC, but fortunately the University was allowed to accept it. The contractors were Messrs William Moss and Sons, and by June 1971 work on the Hall was going well. Mr M. C. Brightwell was appointed Director of Physical Education and took charge of the Department of Physical Education in September 1971.

The University Grants Committee arranged a visit to the University on 21 May 1969, only a few months after Sir John Wolfenden had been succeeded as Chairman by Mr Kenneth Berrill. The event followed similar lines to those of the first visitation in June 1965 (see p. 294) but it was a less momentous occasion; the discussions included some new themes but all were played in a minor key; no one was inclined to be rapturous about the economic scene or about prospects further ahead. Inevitably there were discussions about buildings and land and the further development of the University, and these helped to expedite decisions about the Library and its partial use by the School of Social Sciences. The visiting party suggested that the University might be expanding too rapidly and should consider a slowing-down of its rate of growth which had exceeded that anticipated by the UGC (see p. 324). By 1971-2 the undergraduate numbers were likely to reach 1,800, some 20 per cent above the UGC figure, and the number of postgraduate students would also be higher than expected, in fact double the UGC figure of 160 if allowance were made for the relatively large number (500) of part-time post-graduate students. So caution was advised; there should be some restriction on new courses and on the number of options; the University might strengthen its full-time research but there was a danger of too much emphasis on short postgraduate courses. A plea that the UGC might provide a special grant for the purchase of books when the new Library Building became available was met by the suggestion that the University should use its unspent balances for this purpose; shrivelling financial winds were blowing. However, the Committee expressed pleasure that the University 'had remained firm in its decision to follow the sandwich mode of education', and was complimentary 'about the relationship between staff and students in these difficult times', and commended the work done by the Student Counsellors and Lodgings Officer.

By mid-1969 the University was well embarked on a number of new ventures; one was in cybernetics which started in March 1968 when through the good offices of Dr Stafford Beer I was able to inform the Council that 'the International Publishing Corporation might be willing to raise money from industrial and other sources with which to endow an Institute of Cybernetics'. In fact IPC wrote expressing the wish that the Institute should be located at and be part of Brunel University and that they would give £10,000 per annum over a period to endow a Chair and would in addition contribute to the cost of a building. A first estimate of cost was about £300,000. To make a special appeal for funds of that magnitude at the moment when the University was poised to launch its own general Appeal was a matter of some delicacy about which the Council expressed reservations but the proposals about the Institute were readily welcomed and further negotiations agreed. The Chancellor with some members of Council met Cecil King and other Directors of IPC, and it was possible at the next meeting of Council on 29 May 1968 for the Chairman to express his confidence that 'the IPC appeal would not be injurious in any way to the University Appeal'. Further I confirmed that IPC would donate £10,000 for five years (later changed to seven) for the establishment of a Chair and would contribute £25,000 towards capital costs, while other funds depended on the success of an appeal which was to be inaugurated at a dinner in London at which Lord Mountbatten was to be Chairman. I therefore suggested that a post of Professor of Cybernetics be instituted and advertised immediately; Senate and the Academic Advisory Committee had expressed their support and the UGC had been kept informed. Council agreed and an Appointments Committee was later set up by Senate.

In October 1968 Council noted that Dr F. G. George of the University of Bristol had been appointed Professor of Cybernetics and would become Director of the Institute of Cybernetics 'when this was established'. Council further accepted the recommendation of the Appointments Committee that Dr Gordon Pask be appointed as a part-time Professor of Cybernetics for a period of one year in the first instance. Both men joined the University at the beginning of the 1968–9 session, when a start was made on building up a Department of Cybernetics. The future of the proposed Institute was still in doubt; 'meanwhile teaching and research in this developing field of knowledge', commented the Annual Report for 1968, 'has been introduced in the University; it is likely to have a pervading influence in the future, particularly in control engineering, computing, biology and the social sciences'. Without the timely and generous help of the International Publishing Corporation no such development would have been possible. It was an innovation that attracted the sympathetic interest of Anthony Wedgwood Benn who was then Minister of Technology.[6]

The *raison d'être* of an Institute within the University or in association with it was examined in some detail by Senate, sparked off by a proposal to set up an Institute of Organization put to Senate in May 1969 by Professor Jaques. The many social research projects in which the School of Social Sciences was increasingly involved could not, in his view, be 'forwarded within the normal UGC-financed university framework. They were essentially self-financing services of the University to the community and need to be independently organized'. He suggested[7] that the Institute should be a separate university institution under a Board appointed by the Council of the University; it would conduct a full-time programme of post-experience courses financed wholly by fees, and conduct consultancy-research and other systematic research financed by the bodies concerned or by grant. It would have its own teaching and research staff and would require a new building. Many of the proposed activities were accepted as essential to the proper functioning of a university and were normally associated with a Department; the question arose as to when or at what stage the volume of commissioned research and teaching justified a separate organization such as an Institute. It was a question to which a fully satisfactory answer was never formulated. Senate expressed concern about two particular aspects of the proposals; firstly the relationship between the Governing Board of the Institute and the organs of University

---

[6] See *Brunel Bulletin*, No. 5, Apr. 1969, 5.
[7] Council Paper, CO/104.

government, and secondly how decisions on priorities were to be made having in mind the financial implications and the possibility of similar developments arising from other areas of work in the University. Council gave its approval in principle, asked Senate to study the proposals further and sought the advice of the Finance and New Buildings Committees. The Finance Committee agreed to find £75,000 from the Appeal Fund as soon as possible, the New Buildings Committee approved the erection of prefabricated buildings on Site One, and the UGC made a pump-priming grant of £5,000 for three years beginning in 1969–70. (During 1968–72 pump-priming grants were made for 56 projects in 39 universities and colleges, and totalled nearly £200,000 in 1969–70.) By March 1970 a revised constitution had been worked out by Senate, the Academic Advisory Committee had given its approval, and Council decided that an Institute of Organisation be established forthwith as an academic section of the University within the School of Social Sciences. Professor Jaques became Director of the Institute while continuing as Head of the School.

A change of name to Brunel Institute of Organisation and Social Studies (BIOSS) came later and the Institute's research activities expanded with increasing financial support from government departments and other public bodies. A number of research units were grouped within it; they included the Health Services Organisation Research Unit set up in 1966 (see page 318) and the Social Services Organisation Research Unit founded in 1968, both supported by the Department of Health and Social Security. A Community Development Project research team was established in 1969 on a grant from the Home Office. The Health Services and Social Services Organisation Research Units ran regular programmes of conferences on organization and management for senior members in the health and social services, conferences that served as a means of communicating research findings from the field projects. In addition the Institute organised a programme of short courses, seminars and conferences on management topics called the Brunel Management Programme.

At the meeting in March 1970 Council also agreed on the recommendation of Senate to establish an Institute of Industrial Training with effect from 1 September, 1970; it was to take over

the work of the Department of Industrial Training (a department in name only) and be closely linked with industry; representatives from Industrial Training Boards and from industrial
firms were to be invited to take an active part in its affairs. With
this broader base it would have extended responsibilities. Its
main tasks were to be, as with the Department before it, to
co-ordinate industrial training arrangements throughout the
University and to seek training places appropriate to the
courses, but in addition it would carry out research into
industrial training and assessment of training, organize short
courses in industrial training and maintain a close liaison with
the Training Boards, government departments and industry
generally. These functions were embodied in the report of a
Working Party established by Senate in October 1969.[8] The
Board of the Institute was constituted to consist of the Director
of the Institute, the Vice-Chancellor, two members of Council,
six members of Senate, three members nominated by the Training Boards and three representatives of industry. S. A. Urry was
appointed the first Director of the Institute—'a full-time member of the academic staff of the University, of professorial status,
and a co-opted member of Senate'. He continued to have the
advice of the Senate Committee on Industrial Training of which
he was Chairman. The number of industrial placements grew
and grew (1,056 in 1969 and 1,133 in 1970); a few students were
placed abroad, some of them under the IAESTE scheme (International Association for the Exchange of Students for Technical
Experience) which had been used by Imperial College and
other institutions for some considerable time.

So by the beginning of the 1970–1 session the University had
two new Institutes and the future of a third, Cybernetics, was
still in the balance depending on the acquisition of further funds.
The University Appeal had slowed down and in September
1969 the Appeal Committee had advised that in the economic
conditions then prevailing the total was not likely to exceed
£0.5 million; much of this was in the form of covenanted
subscriptions and consequently not immediately available.
Council had earlier agreed that a number of projects should be
funded from Appeal monies, in particular the third Hall of
Residence the cost of which turned out to be about £365,000,

[8] Doc. Sen., No. 316.

while another £75,000 was needed for buildings for the Institute of Organisation. I had also proposed that the cost of the animal house for the Department of Biology, about £20,000, should be met from the Appeal Fund as the UGC allocation for the Science Building, of which the animal house was an indispensable part, did not cover this addition. For similar reasons the proposed Sports Hall and Students' Union Building depended on University money.

Fortunately payments for buildings in process of construction stretched over a few years, but it was estimated that the University might have to face by July 1971 a deficit of about £200,000 and arrangements would have to be made to borrow any necessary sums. A deficit of this magnitude was however unlikely and looking further ahead 'Council noted that by 31 July 1979 the credit balance in the Appeal Fund would be £18,907, after all expenditure on the Third Hall of Residence and the payment of interest (on bank borrowings) had been met'.[9] In fact in May 1971 the Appeal Fund was £85,442 overdrawn; three years later (July 1974) however the total income received had reached £345,765, and there was a surplus of £12,270.

Besides the formation of the new Institutes there were a number of other academic developments in which Senate was closely involved. Working parties reported and others were set up during the summer term of 1968. One concerned with devising an undergraduate course in Biochemistry, in which the Departments of Biology and Chemistry were both interested, had the invaluable help of Professor A. L. Greenbaum of University College, London, Professor C. H. Gray of King's College Hospital Medical School, K. Durham of Unilever Research Laboratory, Sharnbrook, and Dr R. J. C. Harris of Imperial Cancer Research Fund. The working party reported in May 1968, and Senate agreed to the introduction of a course in Applied Biochemistry to which the first group of entrants was admitted in September 1970. At that time Dr T. F. Slater, Deputy Director of Chemical Pathology at University College Hospital, was appointed to a new Chair of Biochemistry and joined the Department of Applied Biology. Other recommendations of the working party concerned possible links with Hillingdon Hospital and postgraduate work in Biochemistry.

[9] Minutes of Council, May 1970.

A second Senate working party (which also included a number of outside experts) was set up in May 1968 to consider the introduction of an undergraduate course in Building Technology, conceived as linking civil engineering, construction and architecture. It was an innovation that for a long time had awaited the availability of resources; but delay at least helped to ensure that a carefully considered scheme of some novelty and originality was prepared. Senate[10] accepted the working party's report which was presented in May 1970 and agreed that a course in Building Technology should be started as soon as practicable. The working party saw little point in trying to introduce a specialist course in civil engineering (in spite of the name of the University) having in mind the strong centres already established, nor were there overwhelming arguments for a course in architecture even with some unorthodox elements to distinguish it, but there seemed a real need for a course different from any already in operation that would cater for the 'architect-engineer' or 'building-technologist'. Three 'models' were isolated, called Building Services Engineers, Building Constructions Engineers and Building Planning Engineers. 'We have given more attention to the first two kinds of building technologist, not that we think the third is less important, but simply because we found the task more difficult, there being less expertise in the University in this field.' Nevertheless courses were devised to afford a suitable sequence of education and training for the three kinds of building technologist, and the scheme gained the ready, even enthusiastic, support of Senate. In March 1972 a Division of Building Technology was established within the School of Engineering and S. A. Urry was asked to take charge. It seemed specially appropriate that he should be given the responsibility; ideas about the course had grown out of the work of the Planning Group and the experience of building the University including the many contacts with architects, consultants and advisers, quantity surveyors and contractors, in all of which Urry had been deeply involved. The new course flourished from the start.

Senate also approved a new undergraduate course in Computer Science which was introduced in September 1969 and expanded quickly, so that by September 1971 there were 82

[10] Doc. Sen., No. 347.

students following the course. A related joint course in Computer and Social Sciences was also approved in principle. A new computer, an ICL 1903A, was installed in September 1969 with the support of the Computer Board, and Senate extended its own structure by creating a Computer Services Committee with Professor Hogarth as chairman 'to advise on all matters concerned with the efficient operation of the Computer Unit and to ensure the proper provision of computing services throughout the University'. It was later decided to separate the Computing Unit from the Department of Computer Science, in order to allow the Department to concentrate on developing its academic work, and in April 1971 C. C. Ritchie became the first Director of the Unit under the new arrangements. A year earlier (in July 1970) a new Department of Statistics and Operational Research had been established within the School of Mathematical Studies, with Dr P. Macdonald who had been appointed Professor of Statistics in January 1970 as Head.

Changes were made too in Chemistry and Biology. Two new Schools were created with effect from September 1971; a new Department of Applied Biochemistry, with Professor T. F. Slater in charge, was linked with the Department of Applied Biology to form the School of Biological Sciences of which Professor J. D. Gillett became Head. In similar manner the School of Chemistry was set up with Professor K. S. W. Sing as Head. Professor Bond who had been appointed in 1970 to the Chair of Applied Chemistry was made Head of a new Department of Industrial Chemistry within the School, and an undergraduate course in Industrial Chemistry was established and started in September 1972.

A number of additional professorial appointments were made; some were to new posts, others gave recognition to a few members of staff of appropriate standing. Maurice Kogan became Professor of Government and Social Administration with effect from 1 October 1969; R. W. New was given the rank of Professor as Head of the Department of Production Technology, and Dr P. Feltham was made Professor of Applied Physics (April 1970). In July 1971 Council approved the Senate recommendation that the personal title of Professor be conferred upon Dr S. C. Bevan in the Department of Applied Chemistry and on S. A. Urry, Director of the Institute of Industrial Training, who was to be transferred to the Department of Mechanical Engineering (and was later appointed to lead the new Division of Building Technology). Another new post was that of permanent Head of the School of Engineering and it was agreed that it should carry the rank of Professor; Dr T. O. Jeffries was appointed with effect from 1 September 1970, and a year later Dr A. W. Crook joined the School as Professor of Mechanical Engineering. A. Daniels succeeded S. A. Urry as Director of the Institute of Industrial Training in April 1972. Careers Advice and Appointments Services which had developed under Urry's direction were formally included in the responsibilities of the Institute.

The greatest expansion of the University's work occurred in the post-graduate field, particularly in the part-time advanced study courses leading to the degree of Master of Technology and to a new award, styled the Certificate of Advanced Study, the requirements for which were the same as for M.Tech. study courses but without the dissertation. The Certificate courses were instituted by Senate (with the approval of the Academic Advisory Committee) to satisfy the needs of some students who could clearly benefit from a part-time M.Tech. course but were excluded because they did not possess a first degree or its equivalent. The total number of post-graduates rose from 416 in 1968 to 729 in 1969, and of these 383 were following part-time courses and 60 registered for the Certificate. New part-time courses included Applied Immunology, Metallurgical Quality Control and Environmental Pollution Science, and there were full-time courses in Management and Administration, Applied Social Studies and Production. In 1971 were added courses in Economics (on both a full and part-time basis), Statistics (part-time), Non-destructive Testing of Materials (part-time), and Power Electronics (replacing the part-time course in Electrical Engineering). By 1971 the number of post-graduate students had reached 1,207.

Undergraduate numbers which were 1,336 in December 1968 rose to 1,614 three years later. As noted earlier (page 360) this exceeded the UGC forecast of 1,490 by the end of the 1967-72 quinquennium; moreover, considerable further expansion seemed likely. I wrote in the Annual Report for 1969: 'As we enter the nineteen-seventies we face with the other universities some major problems mainly associated with the possible doubling of the undergraduate population by 1980.'

In the autumn of 1969 some members of the Committee of Vice-Chancellors and Principals, together with the Chairman of the UGC, met the then Minister of State of the Department of Education and Science, Mrs Shirley Williams, to discuss some of the problems of university development in the next decade. Basic to the discussions were the new DES projections (September 1969) indicating that the number of school-leavers qualifying for entry to higher education in the nineteen-seventies would be much higher than previously estimated.

Indeed, the estimate of 481,000 given by the Robbins Committee as the number of full-time higher education places required in England and Wales in 1981, has been revised upwards to 727,000. This means that if universities were in 1981 to take the same proportion of all school-leavers with two or more A levels as they do now (about 53 per cent), and if we allowed for entrants with other qualifications and included the Scottish universities, the number of university entrants in Great Britain in 1981 would rise to 450,000. This is double the number now, and four times that in 1960. In the same way there would be greatly increased numbers of students in the other institutes of higher education, in particular in Polytechnics and the Colleges of Education.[11]

Little wonder that the Minister and the universities were concerned about the financial provision needed to make such an expansion possible; could there be a matching increase in public funds? Was it possible to reduce the cost per head of university education? Merely to enumerate some of the factors is enough to indicate the quality and scale of the problem; fuller utilization of buildings; extent of residential accommodation (housing associations, loan finance) and numbers of home-based students; student grants and/or loans; staff–student ratios; wastage rates; regional organization; relations with public sector of higher education. The Committee of Vice-Chancellors and Principals commented on some of these matters in a statement with the title 'University Development in the 1970s' issued in April 1970. 'About a year ago the Committee instituted an informal enquiry among vice-chancellors to obtain an approximate indication of the overall student numbers which might reasonably be possible

[11] Annual Report, 1969, 9.

by the end of the decade, assuming that expansion were not fettered by inadequate finance,' and it was found that the estimates amounted in aggregate to a figure approaching 400,000 full-time student places by 1981-2. The Committee went on to express the view that it was reasonable to regard such an expansion as being within the capability of the existing universities, but added: 'An expansion of this order of magnitude would imply an average growth rate of some 6% per annum. This would be in excess of the likely rate of growth of resources nationally and would thus imply a government decision to devote a higher proportion of the national product than hitherto to higher educational purposes. Such a decision would, we believe, be both right in the interests of the nation, and inescapable in view of the prospective demand.' It was an optimistic conclusion that few politicians would have been able to accept, having in mind all the other demands on national resources.

Senate had been exercised for some time about annual student intakes. A working party was set up in January 1969 which reported two months later, and a second working party followed in December 1969; the presentation of its second interim report[12] in June 1970 coincided with the arrival of a communication from the UGC about student numbers in the next quinquennium.[13] Senate's decisions were incorporated in the quinquennial submission to the UGC which is discussed in detail in chapter 21. Immediate decisions had to be made about the associated accommodation problems, especially in view of uncertainties in the building programme, and another working party was asked in November 1970 to conduct a survey of the use of space in the University.[14] Meanwhile decisions on the introduction of new courses, such as those in Building Technology and in Computer and Social Sciences, had to be postponed. The Building Technology course was in fact introduced in September 1972 (see page 366).

Senate gave some further consideration to student participation in University government following the report of another working party[15] set up in June 1968 and again in December 1968. It was agreed that four students should be elected to serve

12 Doc. Sen., No. 373.   13 Doc. Sen., No. 393.
14 Doc. Sen., No. 409.   15 Doc. Sen., No. 258.

on each Board of Studies (except at meetings concerned with examination results and degree recommendations), two on each School Board and three on the Industrial Training Committee. Additionally students served on the staff–student liaison committees which were established in every Department, on the Library Committee, and also on the Council/Students' Union and Senate/Students' Union Committees which continued to function well although an overlap in the interests of the two committees became increasingly apparent. In October 1969 Council decided to co-opt two students as members—C. Watkins, President of the Students' Union, and P. Hunter who was elected by the students—and they attended their first Council meeting in December 1969.

I had expected to leave the University in the summer of 1970, by which time I would have reached the normal retiring age. When this was announced by the Chairman of Council at the meeting in June 1969 some members of Council were taken by surprise; I had of course told the Chairman of my intentions considerably earlier and there had been prior discussions in which the Chancellor and Pro-Chancellor had been involved. Under Statute 5.1 a Committee had to be established to report to the Council on the appointment of a successor; it was laid down that there should be seven members of which the Chairman of the Council was a member ex officio and Chairman, and the others were three members of the Council not being members of the Senate appointed by the Council and three members of the Senate appointed by Senate. Council appointed Lord Brown, E. R. Davies and Professor J. D. McGee; the Senate nominees were Professor J. D. Gillett, Professor E. Jaques and Dr A. J. Reynolds. The deliberations of the Committee were inevitably lengthy, and it was May 1970 before an announcement was made. At an Extraordinary Meeting of Council held on 13 May 1970 the Chairman presented the Committee's report which was accepted 'in its entirety'. Stephen Lawrence Bragg, M.A., S.M., Hon.D.Eng., was proposed as the University's second Vice-Chancellor and his appointment was announced at the meeting of the Court of the University held later that day (13 May 1970). Because of Mr Bragg's commitments with Rolls Royce, where he was General Manager (Engineering) of the Aero-Engine Division the Committee had agreed that he should take up his Brunel appointment in September 1971 and I was invited to remain in office until that date.

Fifteen months or more was a long hand-over period which went off well enough but had its attendant difficulties. To continue to carry the full responsibilities of the post and yet be aware that someone else would be involved in the consequences of almost every decision was never easy and became increasingly difficult as the summer of 1971 approached. However, I found satisfaction in concentrating on the work of the New Buildings Committee, on trying to finish some of the projects to which I had devoted much thought and effort, and on ensuring that the move from Acton was accomplished by the summer of 1971. Stephen Bragg at first spent about a day a week at the University, attended meetings of Council and Senate and as many of the meetings of committees as possible. After February 1971, on being released from his Rolls Royce post earlier than expected, he was able to spend more time at the University and to have discussions with Heads of Departments and other staff, so that by September 1971 he had become conversant with much of the University business and knew many of the senior staff. Professor R. T. A. Howell who had served as Vice-Principal since September 1969 was invited to continue in that post for a further period. His sudden death in June 1973 was a great loss to the University.

Council had agreed to purchase a house at Gerrards Cross, only a few miles from the University, as a Vice-Chancellor's residence into which Stephen Bragg and his family were able to move. The idea, which had long been accepted of having such a residence on or near the campus, was given up. The earliest plans had been to build a house adjacent to the Communal Building and indeed linked to the staff dining-room at the north-western corner, but other proposals prevailed. Attention turned to the periphery of the campus, perhaps influenced by my own experience of living near the first hall of residence surrounded by student activities of all kinds. Be that as it may, the New Buildings Committee spent much time, extending over three years or more, trying to acquire land around The Grove, referred to as areas F and G (see Figure 11.1), which adjoined Site 3.

20. First Hall of Residence (Clifton)

21. Second Hall of Residence (Saltash)

22. Third Hall of Residence (Chepstow)

23. Some student flatlets on Site One

The University had in mind to build a Vice-Chancellor's Residence on area F and being unable to raise the money attempted initially to acquire a lease on the plot with an option to purchase later. However, the Hillingdon Borough Council, who had taken over the property, generously suggested in March 1969 that the University should purchase it outright for £25,000 'which was the price paid by Hillingdon Council for its acquisition'.[16] UGC approval was sought but was refused on the grounds that the total cost of land and erection of a new house, £45,000 in all, was more than could be met from Treasury funds for such a project even if other land were sold in exchange. The University therefore decided it would buy the land using its own funds 'when they came available', and concentrated its efforts on negotiating a lease with Hillingdon Council with the option of purchase within five years. At one stage such an arrangement seemed achievable and Richard Sheppard was instructed to design a Vice-Chancellor's residence that would cost not more than £20,000, a sum that was acceptable to the UGC and was in fact included in the allocation for Building Starts for 1970–1 (see page 356). Planning permission had been obtained (November 1968) but agreement about the lease proved more difficult and the project was ultimately abandoned. The University would have been glad to have gained ownership of the land for purposes other than the erection of a Vice-Chancellor's residence; it seemed to offer opportunities for closer association with Hillingdon Hospital, but the possibility of the Iver Link Road going through the middle of the area was always a deterrent to purchase. Another site for a Vice-Chancellor's house in Station Road, adjacent to Site 1, was considered by the Committee but nothing further was done.

Other negotiations for land exchanges were proceeding at the same time—just as slowly and in some cases as fruitlessly. Those concerning areas A, B, H and J, as noted earlier (see chapter 18), seriously held up the construction of the causeway across the railway cutting. The legal processes associated with the purchase of the railway land by the Borough dragged on until the summer of 1969 and uncertainty as to how areas H and J could be used went on even longer. Indeed in September 1968 the New Buildings Committee decided to take no further action

[16] Council Paper, CO/94.

374 *The Years of Separation, 1968–71*

with respect to these areas on learning that the District Valuer was doubtful whether 'planning permission would be granted for residential purposes because of access difficulties' even though the University already held planning permission on these areas 'for residential purposes for staff and employees only'. Six months later however following a report that the Borough Council had expressed renewed interest in acquiring H and J, the Committee 'confirmed that negotiations for the sale of areas H and J should continue'; the valuation was £90,000. In April 1969 came the further news that 'the UGC had agreed to arrange for the District Valuer to negotiate sale to the Local Authority of these two areas. It was intended that the sale should coincide with the acquisition of the Railway Cutting'. Another six months elapsed before the University Council was informed that 'the railway cutting was now owned by the Local Authority', that negotiations were proceeding for the acquisition by the University of part of the cutting in exchange for other land, and that a causeway would be constructed at the first opportunity.[17] It looked as if all the major difficulties had been surmounted, but a number of complicating factors arose which A. L. Stuchbery and I tried to sort out with the Leader of the Hillingdon Council (Alderman Charles) and the Town Clerk. The use of areas H and J for housing impinged on the Council's commitments with respect to playing fields for the Greenway School and this took time to resolve. The University too had to reconsider radically its own policy, for there was pressure to build flatlets for students and it was suggested that areas H and J could well be used for this purpose, in which case a part of Site 1 abutting on Station Road might be offered instead of H and J in exchange for part of the railway cutting. These problems were still unresolved when the University Council met in December 1970, at which meeting it was made known that planning permission for the construction of the causeway had been granted and that the University had requested permission to start work on 1 January 1971 (even before the formal transfer of ownership had taken place).

The outcome was that the UGC finally approved the purchase of 3.37 acres of land in the railway cutting at a cost of £59,200. The University acquired not the whole of the cutting

[17] Minutes of Council, Sept., 1969.

'between the two bridges' (one to the north at the Greenway and the other to the south at Station Road), but only enough for the causeway and to allow buildings to be erected later from the Biology/Chemistry building across into Site 1. Niggardly it seems to some of us with our eyes on the future but to others the economic facts were compelling. I tried unsuccessfully to persuade the UGC to allow the University to buy the whole of the cutting. The contract for the causeway, totalling £54,716, was signed early in 1971 and construction started; from my room in the Administration Building I looked down on the railway cutting and watched the arrival of the first load of in-filling with a mixture of relief and disbelief.

When completed the causeway afforded vehicular and pedestrian access to and from Cleveland Road and became the main entrance to the University (see Fig. 20.1); with remnants of railway cutting stretching to the north and south it was much less attractive than was hoped and to provide some relief if not distinction the centre of the causeway was filled with water from which a jet could be projected heavenwards. Unsatisfactory and unattractive it still is and will remain until the railway cutting areas are transformed; I had hoped to see a theatre built in the northern part and the other portion as far as Station Road cleared and planted with trees and shrubs to afford at once a pleasant public space and an attractive approach to the University. The only change the Local Authority made was a widening of the Station Road bridge to ease access to and from Cleveland Road along which two-way traffic was allowed to continue; a one-way system had been proposed but the many repercussions on the surrounding traffic flow were found unacceptable.

The Borough Council acquired areas H and J, the University retaining a strip of land alongside the River Pinn where a footway was constructed giving access to the University from the Uxbridge Road. The northern limit of the University's land was agreed after some discussion with the Borough, and the Greenway School's playing fields were extended to this boundary, which was marked by an unattractive wire fence. No further houses were erected and a part of the area became unfortunately a desolate waste-land. The changes in the boundary reduced the selling price of H and J from £66,500 to £55,000, but this exceeded by about £5,000 the purchase price of the portion of the railway cutting acquired by the University, which in turn had been reduced. The balance, such as it was after interest charges and professional fees had been met, was returned to the Treasury.

The future of Honeycroft and the Football Club land adjoining Site 1 had not been decided. The owners still wished to acquire the right to develop the land for residential purposes and towards the end of 1968 made a second application for outline planning permission which was refused. In April 1969 they offered the property to the University at a price of £130,000 but the District Valuer's estimate of its value (without planning permission) was £31,000, and the University could not acquire land from public funds at a value higher than that agreed by the District Valuer. However, the University decided to offer £35,000, but the owners continued with an appeal against the refusal of planning permission, which was heard by an Inspector of the Ministry of Housing and Local Government in July 1969 and was in due course rejected; thus for the second time the University's objection to the proposed development was upheld. When this became known (in July 1970) Council decided to raise the matter again with the UGC in the hope that purchase by the University might be permitted or facilitated but no headway was made; the final blow[18] was the renewed refusal of the Planning Authority to grant planning permission for residential development on areas A and B which removed the basis for the sale of these pieces of land and made any exchange impossible.

Ideas about acquiring Site 4 had to be given up too; for the UGC was adamant that the University had enough land and could only buy Site 4 provided some part of the campus were sold. Such an exchange, even if it had been acceptable to the Council, would have been well-nigh impossible as experience with areas A, B, H and J had amply demonstrated.

A large hall or theatre had been included in the building programme for many years; indeed at Acton a large hall had been accepted as part of the 'next phase' but was never built (see chapter 7). At Uxbridge with the largest lecture theatres having seating capacity for about 180 there was a real need for a hall

[18] Minutes of Council, Dec., 1971.

seating 500 or more, and the earliest schemes included an assembly hall to be sited in the space between the Administration Building and the Library; to justify a hall in economic terms bearing in mind its occasional use was difficult, as colleges everywhere found. There were stronger arguments however for a multi-purpose theatre that could be used not only for large gatherings of one kind or another, but for plays and films and music, for special lectures and particular occasions, by the Students' Union and by groups and societies in Uxbridge and the area around. Such a theatre could contribute significantly to the cultural life of the University, could strengthen its academic programmes particularly complementary studies, and be an important influence in the society around the University. At the time, which was before the centre of Uxbridge was re-built, there was no large hall available near the University and no theatre.

The proposal gained the support of the New Buildings Committee and the Council, and I was encouraged to try and raise the necessary funds, a task to which I devoted much of my last year at the University. It was no easy assignment; the University Appeal had been less successful than was hoped and only about £0.5 million of the target of £2 million had been raised. I had some confidence that with a theatre as a particular objective a special approach to certain Foundations and to the Borough of Hillingdon might yield a substantial response; about £150,000 was needed. The Gulbenkian Foundation had helped other universities; there was a Gulbenkian Theatre at the University of Kent which some of us visited.

When I approached the Director of the Foundation I discovered I had to present a much more detailed case than had been prepared, whereupon the New Buildings Committee asked Richard Sheppard to examine further the possibility of siting a theatre in the railway cutting to the north of the concourse and to design a multi-purpose building that would seat about 350. In December 1970 report was made to the Council that 'the Foundation might support the project to a quarter of the cost but it would want to know what measure of support would be given by Local Authorities and the Arts Council'. It looked as if the Borough of Hillingdon 'might be prepared to help the University by way of a covenanted gift', but the Borough's involvement was adversely affected by the decision to include a hall and associated facilities in the new Civic Centre in Uxbridge. Other neighbouring local authorities were unable to make a contribution towards the cost of a university theatre, a lack of support which weakened the University's case.

The New Buildings Committee and the Architect found it was far from easy to satisfy in one building the minimum needs of a theatre, a cinema and a concert-hall and to keep the cost within reasonable limits. Regulations were stringent too; the Gulbenkian Foundation required the approval of the Association of British Theatre Technicians, to which body the first draft plans were submitted and considerable modifications had to be made. Other changes were necessary if the building were to serve as a Regional Film Theatre. When I submitted my last report to the Council, in July 1971, I simply stated that after the Architect's revised plans had been submitted to ABTT and approved 'it would be possible to make a formal application to the Gulbenkian Foundation'. Contacts with the Foundation were continued as were discussions with the Borough of Hillingdon, and hopes were revived from time to time, but by the end of the nineteen-seventies a theatre had not been built; saplings and weeds continued to flourish in the railway cutting. Fortunately when the Sports Hall became available, as it did in late 1972, musical events could be arranged there, the Brunel Orchestra was able to use it, and there was a lively extension of interest and participation in music generally, including opera presented by a group known as 'Opera at Brunel'.

The musical life of the University suffered a grievous blow in January 1972 when Niso Ticciati died. Ten years earlier he had joined Brunel as a part-time contributor to general studies, but his work quickly extended beyond the lecture-room and he became conductor of the orchestra and choir with a charm and enthusiasm that were compelling. He was later appointed to the full-time staff. Someone wrote of him: 'He established a precedent for general involvement in music, firstly by engendering enthusiasm through his brilliant lecturing style, secondly by making it possible, not just by the experts, but also for the novice to have a go.' He was succeeded as Music Director by Derek Fraser who helped to found the Brunel Philharmonic Society and organized very successful concerts in the Sports Hall.

For the New Buildings Committee 1970–1 had been a hectic year. By the summer of 1971 the Science (Biology/Chemistry) and the Physics Buildings were nearing completion, the third Hall of Residence was ready for occupation, the Library and the Sports Hall had been started, and the concourse across the railway cutting was nearly finished. On Site 1 the temporary buildings for the Institute of Organisation and Social Studies were complete, and much preparatory work had been done on loan-financed flats for students. The University owed a great debt of gratitude to the New Buildings Committee and particularly to its Chairman, Professor J. D. McGee, who had guided the deliberations of the committee throughout.

The third Hall of Residence (later named Chepstow) was occupied at the beginning of the autumn term having been finished in good time. Built in brick like the other two it filled part of the space on the east side of the Pinn between the Sports Hall and the second Hall of Residence, and was in many ways a repeat of the second. There were 230 study-bedrooms, which raised the number of residential places in the University to over 600 at a time when the undergraduate population was about 1,600. Some of the earlier ideas of a students' village, akin to those that had been developed in countries abroad, seemed to be taking shape.

The summer of 1971 was notable for the move of the science and education departments from Acton. 'It is a tribute to all the staff of these Departments that the move was achieved so smoothly', wrote S. L. Bragg in the Annual Report for 1971. 'Inevitably there were problems, largely due to the late completion of the buildings; nevertheless by the beginning of the autumn term most teaching and research had re-started.' There was a little further delay in the completion of the nuclear science unit, a separate structure to the north of the main Science Building, but its laboratories were brought into operation by December 1971.

The buildings at Acton were handed over to the Ealing Borough Council, which had become the local education authority after the demise of the Middlesex County Council in 1965, and Huxley College of Education moved in.

So at last the whole University was established at Uxbridge; the years of separation were ended and a new era began.

The new Science Building housed the School of Biological Sciences and the School of Chemistry. It was a simple concrete structure of rectangular form; the external frame was left as exposed concrete from Wrot shutters and infilled 'with precast concrete exposed aggregate panels of Wally flint', so harmonizing with the materials used in other teaching buildings on the site. There were three floors with storage tanks on the roof. Construction had taken 27 months; 12 months for the basic structure and 15 months for fittings, services and finishing, thus reflecting the complexity of the interior provision. The net usable areas were initially 3,120 sq. metres for Chemistry (in the eastern part of the building) and 2,350 sq. metres for Biological Sciences, with about 450 sq. metres devoted to common use. The School of Biological Sciences had a separate animal house to the north of the main building. At the outset a decision was taken to integrate the research and teaching laboratories, an arrangement that enabled storage, preparation and ancillary service rooms to be planned as areas common to teaching and research. Moreover an open plan was adopted for the laboratories leading to greater flexibility in their use. Standardisation and a basic simplicity of fittings helped to create a feeling of unity in the building. By common acclaim it served staff and students well.

The other building, known as the Physics Building, was designed in the form of a U with the arms pointing roughly to the north; the east wing housed the Department of Polymer Science, and the Department of Physics occupied the remainder of the building—about 3,000 sq. metres of usable space, except that some of the laboratory and office accommodation was temporarily allocated to the Department of Education, which still had no home of its own. Some additional accommodation was also made available for it in the Science Building. 'It was an immense relief', wrote Professor Furneaux in the Annual Report for 1971, 'to have everyone together on one campus. It will be an even greater relief when they can all be accommodated in the Department's own properly designed building.'

The Physics Building completed the north side of a paved court with the Lecture Centre opposite and the Mathematics Building to the east. It was a concrete structure with three floors but Blindel brick was used liberally, mainly on the south front where a broad flight of steps led to the main entrance at first floor level. There were laboratories associated with the teaching of several branches of applied physics, as well as general research and project laboratories. Workshops were available for use by undergraduates during a period of workshop training in the first year and for the construction of items used in fourth year projects. As in other buildings on the campus each member of the academic staff had a separate room (office) large enough to accommodate small groups of students for tutorial purposes, a facility which all staff appreciated highly.

The Science and Physics buildings came into use in September 1971 and were officially opened[19] during the session 1971–2.

The University had to wait another two years for the new Library; it opened in September 1973 and proved in the opinion of many the most attractive building on the campus and certainly a worthy monument to all the effort that had gone into the planning. It dominated the buildings around and gave distinction and finish to the central area that had seemed empty for so long. Some lawns and a few trees completed the transformation. The Library was officially opened on 10 December 1973 by Heinrich Böll, a distinguished German writer, who had been awarded the Nobel Prize for Literature in 1972.

Parts of the Library Building had to be used initially as seminar rooms, for examinations and to provide accommodation for the Careers Service and the Education Liaison Bureau. 'A large area on the main entrance floor was handed over to the University Arts Group', wrote the Librarian,[20] 'and there have been arranged a succession of exhibitions which have been one of the unforeseen attractions of the new building.' But much else was foreseen.

The Library was not built in the middle of the campus by chance and its main entrance did not face the exit from the main Refectory by chance. Nor was it by chance that the interior was cheerful and colourful and with a wide variety of seating to suit different tastes, and practically every book is on open shelves. The Architect, Librarian and Brunel administration had put much thought into providing a library which would be convenient and attractive to students and staff.

---

[19] See booklets on the School of Biological Sciences, School of Chemistry and Department of Physics published at the Official Openings.
[20] Extract from a memorandum written by the Librarian to the Author.

It would have been disappointing if, after waiting so long for a proper library, they had not used it. In fact, in the first year of operation, 230,000 visits were made to the Library.

As to the Sports Hall it was completed in October 1972 five months behind schedule, and was used virtually to capacity from the day it opened. A year later Dr Roger Bannister, Chairman of the Sports Council of Great Britain, performed the formal opening ceremony. The Hall became known as the Sports Centre and activities of many kinds prospered in which staff as well as students took part. The main hall provided for most indoor games; a special feature was the climbing wall, built along one face using natural limestone, gritstone and granite rock; it served not only the University Climbing Club but was used by local climbers who made the Centre their home-base. The three squash courts were soon insufficient for the needs of the University and there was an abnormal demand from members of the public to help satisfy which four new courts were built later (opened in May 1979) through a self-supporting loan-financed scheme.

The Sports Pavilion and the playing fields on Sites 3 and 5 continued to be well-used; inter-departmental sport flourished and playing standards soared. The Director of Physical Education could rightly claim that since 'the completion of the Sports Centre in 1972 the University has made rapid progress in all aspects of Physical Education, Sport and Recreation'.

CHAPTER 20

Developments on Site One

EARLIEST developments on Site One were associated with the
School of Social Sciences, and the first buildings were a group of
pre-fabricated huts for the Institute of Organisation and Social
Studies (BIOSS); they provided rooms for research and other
staff and a few teaching spaces. The huts were erected opposite
the Administration Building with access from Cleveland Road
and formed the four sides of a rectangle with an open centre;
their disposition relative to the proposed causeway over the
railway cutting and the pedestrian way through Site 2 is shown
in Figure 20.1. The Architects had in mind that the street would

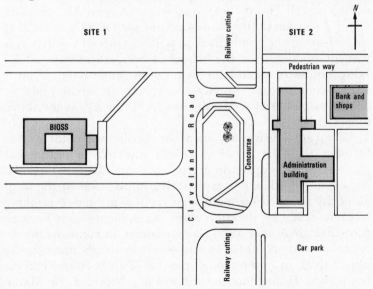

FIG. 20.1. The BIOSS building and the Cleveland Road entrance to the
University.

be continued across Site 1 to the Cowley Road boundary. In the aerial photograph of the University in 1971 (Plate 18) the BIOSS buildings appear in the left-hand bottom corner and are incomplete, as is the causeway. The Uxbridge Football Club ground and Honeycroft show up clearly immediately to the right. The three halls of residence are at the top right-hand corner.

The positioning of the BIOSS buildings had been a matter of some controversy in the New Buildings Committee. The Architects were strongly opposed to the erection of temporary buildings as the opening development on Site 1 and feared that this would inhibit or adversely affect the ordered growth of permanent buildings. Their fears proved well-grounded. Alternative temporary building spaces on Site 2, one in particular alongside the Mathematics Building, were canvassed but in the end (March 1970) the New Buildings Committee decided to 'open up' Site 1; such a step, the Committee thought, would give 'strength to the University's case that the UGC be persuaded to allow the causeway to be included in the building programme commencing 1 April 1970'. There would be some savings as well. Not that everyone was convinced that spending about £100,000 on the causeway and site works was the best way of using the funds then available, especially when permanent buildings for the School of Social Sciences and for Education were urgently needed. On the other hand, if Site 1 were to come into use considerable expenditure, about £30,000, on the extension of services across from Site 2 was inevitable sooner or later.

After a good deal of argument the decision was made, and in October 1970 the Buildings Officer was able to report that planning permission for the erection of temporary buildings had been granted (that it was the third application to the local authority reflected the many changes of plan) and 'everything was now ready for the contractors to commence work on site'. Moreover there was to be no more delay in constructing the causeway and permission to start was to be sought immediately (see chapter 19), even though the sale of areas H and J to the Borough of Hillingdon had still not been decided. By March 1971 the UGC had approved the planning of road access to Site One and associated work commenced in mid-September 1971.

It was at the meeting in October 1970 that the New Buildings Committee noted the revised building programme for 1970–1 which had been agreed as shown in Table 20.1. The increase in the total from £0.67 million allocated earlier (see p. 356) was made possible by the transfer of certain funds from 1969–70 to 1970–1.

TABLE 20.1

Project	Programme Grant Estimate (£ million)
Library	0.510
Sports Hall	0.102
Vice-Chancellor's House	0.020
Science Building (Animal House)	0.029
Site works—Sports Hall	0.030
—Causeway	0.060
Site 1—road works	0.030
Landscaping and general site works	0.100
Total	0.890

The BIOSS building is not included in the above list; it cost £30,000 from University funds, was started in November 1970 and became available in September 1971. Even at the start the building was 'not big enough to accommodate all the events— notably the Management Programme seminars'.[1] However, the activities of the Institute continued to expand, the Development Fund began to build up, and by the end of 1971 the Institute managed to pay about £8,000 as a contribution to University running costs. Later a scheme was agreed whereby the Institute paid a regular all-in rental to the University.

The School of Social Sciences needed permanent accommodation (see page 357), as did the Department of Education, and a single building was proposed—with no great enthusiasm from either 'partner'. The News-letter of November 1967 recorded that preliminary work had started 'on a building which we have asked the UGC to include in our 1970–71 programme'. The needs of the Department of Education seemed likely to remain fairly modest, but the School of Social Sciences had more ambitious aims, encouraged by the support accorded

[1] Annual Report, 1971, 5.

to BIOSS and justified later by the phenomenal demand for courses in the social sciences, a development that characterized the early seventies not only at Brunel but throughout British universities.

When the Mathematics Building was occupied in September 1968 the School of Social Sciences and the Department of Education were given some temporary accommodation there. Later a second temporary home was suggested in the Library Building, a costly proposal that would have satisfied nobody and which fortunately was not carried through (see p. 357). Attention then turned again to the planning of a separate building, on Site 1, for which the UGC was likely to provide the sum of £0.2 million. Indeed the UGC later[2] confirmed that such a figure would be included in the 1972-3 building programme.

When serious discussions with the Architects began it was immediately apparent that the schedules of accommodation proposed by the School and the Department far exceeded the facilities that could be provided in a building costing about £0.2 million; at least twice that amount was needed. Should not a first instalment be erected with all possible speed? Much as I disliked two-phase contracts I supported a proposal to plan a building in keeping with the schedules requested by the School and Department (there were a few controversial items including a crèche on the roof), and to build as a first phase such parts of it as made academic sense for both users of the building, and yet within the £0.2 million limit. In December 1970 the New Buildings Committee was informed that the UGC had approved the University's submission for the first stage of the building, that the Architect was continuing discussions with the School and Department, and that 'arrangements were being made for visits to other universities with similar departments'. But progress was slow; at the last meeting of the New Buildings Committee that I attended (in June 1971) the Buildings and Estates Officer reported that 'second stage sketch plans were being prepared'. Later the Annual Report for 1971 recorded that 'The first phase of the Social Sciences Building is now likely to be started in April 1973 with a planned completion date of February 1975—though the architect indicated that partial occupation in August 1974 was a possibility'.

[2] New Buildings Committee, 14 Oct. 1970.

To my great disappointment permanent buildings were never started. I would have preferred half a building to no building at all, but others (in the School of Social Sciences) feared that an instalment would saddle them with an inadequate and inefficient building for years ahead and postpone indefinitely the creation of a centre from which the School could develop on the scale it should. Nothing that happened afterwards caused me to change my mind; I continued to regret that the opportunity was missed.

During 1972 a temporary centre was provided for the School by the erection of two more prefabricated buildings on Site One adjacent to the BIOSS building; they cost jointly about £70,000 provided from the Minor Works allocation. This additional space greatly improved the working conditions of staff and students, but the Economics Department and half of the Psychology Department continued to use rooms in the Mathematics Building. As to a permanent building the difficulties were not surmounted and a UGC letter dated 6 December 1972 'advised the University to suspend further planning on the Social Science Building as now designed.'

However, discussions went on throughout 1973. 'Extended negotiations took place with the UGC on the cost limits for the Social-Science-Education building and the Students' Union building,' wrote the Secretary-General in the Annual Report for 1973. 'By the end of the year tenders had been invited from four contractors for the former building in the hope of starting on site in March 1974. The contractors concerned had barely begun their examination of the building specifications when a moratorium on all major building projects until 1 July 1974 was announced by the UGC. The invitations to tender were withdrawn.' In the event neither of the buildings was started and the Annual Report for 1974 sombrely recorded that 'a start on the construction of accommodation for Social Sciences, Education and the Students' Union has been postponed sine die'. Decisions followed to make changes in the Communal Building to accommodate the Students' Union and to redistribute the 'social space', while in the Engineering Centre provision was made for some of the needs of the School of Social Sciences. The temporary buildings for the School on Site One had become quite inadequate. The Department of Education continued to use the rooms in the Biology-Chemistry and Physics Buildings it had been accorded in September 1971, and some of its associated activities were accommodated in the Library Building when that was opened.

Happily there were other developments on Site One that were more successful. Towards the end of 1970 the New Buildings Committee was involved once more with housing association proposals, this time concerned with housing for students. Ideas about the type of provision had changed; earlier the Planning Group had thought mainly of halls of residence on the lines of the first two halls, which housed about 400 students—roughly a quarter of the student population in 1970–1. A third hall was being built and was expected to be ready in September 1971, but the Architect's original vision of eleven halls covering the area between the River Pinn and Kingston Road had faded. There was a demand for accommodation of a different kind; some students wished to live independently in flatlets either alone or in small groups and possibly off the campus. To this end the Students' Union put forward proposals to the Council in December 1970 for off-campus student residences that required the setting-up by the Union of a Housing Association. The initiative was given a general blessing but there were obvious difficulties, some of which had been rehearsed at length in 1964 (chapter 14); others were inherent in any housing association scheme emanating from a body like a Students' Union, and proved insuperable.

About this time the UGC adopted new policies about Halls of Residence and in July 1970 the New Buildings Committee learned that capital grants for student residences would no longer be made except under loan-financed schemes for which the UGC undertook to contribute one-quarter of the cost up to a maximum of £250 per place. (This sum was later raised to £300.) Money would be available from 1 April 1972 for any scheme submitted and approved. It seemed certain that any new hall of residence would have to be of much lower standard than those already built which had cost about £1,600 per place. This figure was exceptionally high, because of various unusual constructional difficulties, and £1,300 was a more reasonable estimate. The New Buildings Committee's first reaction was to ask for UGC help under the scheme to provide two residences in 1972, one in 1973 and one in 1974, while other types of accommodation were being considered (see chapter 21).

A number of universities embarked on loan-financed projects of one kind or another, and at Brunel it was ultimately decided to build houses which would accommodate groups of four or more students. There had been a good deal of discussion with the students and in the various Committees of Council not only about the size of each unit (whether for four or six or ten students), but about the position of the houses, the facilities they would offer, the rent to be charged and the general financing of the whole scheme. Initially the UGC indicated that a weekly rental of £4 would be regarded as reasonable, and later agreed to increase their contribution to the capital cost. Some members of Council were strongly in favour of arranging a package deal with a building firm. Areas H and J seemed to offer a very convenient location (see page 374), but the southern end of Site 1 abutting on Station Road was finally chosen and it was there that Messrs Wimpey & Co. Ltd. were asked to erect the first group of houses to accommodate about 200 students. Of a number of proposed schemes Wimpey's was found acceptable 'because of its value for money, durability, lower maintenance costs, acceptable grouping of students and adequate communal facilities'.[3] The tender figure was £248,000, an average of £1,240 per student place—higher than was first assumed.

There was uncertainty as to how many residential places would be needed as the University expanded, but Senate adopted a planning figure of 3,390 full-time students by 1976-7, the end of the quinquennium, and of these it was estimated that some 1,400 would be in residence. With over 600 students in the three halls of residence, about 800 new places would have to be provided through loan-financed schemes. Even assuming that the 3,390 figure was an over-estimate one could be fairly confident that another hall of residence, with 200 places, and student flatlets with 300 places would be needed, leaving the Students' Union free to pursue their own proposals for off-campus acommodation.

To finance the project, whatever might be its ultimate form, Council agreed to accept the Midland Bank's offer of loan finance and directed that 'sufficient land in the Station Road

[3] Council Meeting, Oct. 1971.

enclave be mortgaged to the Midland Bank as security for the
'loan'. The Bank later 'confirmed its willingness to lend the
University £0.75 million for loan-financed residences repayable
over 30 years at an interest rate of 2% above base-rate'.[4] The
Wimpey scheme was started on 1 January 1972 and the first ten
flats came into use in September 1972, a very speedy and satisfactory start to the scheme. The remainder of the first block
which contained in all 25 flats for individual students and 8 flats
for married couples was handed over in December 1972 and
occupied in January 1973. Each of the single flats had five study-
bedrooms, and a kitchen/dining room, one bathroom, one toilet
and a store-cupboard; there was a common room on each
landing. The flats proved to be extremely popular with the
students.

The first buildings were restricted to 2–3 storeys in height, but
later 3–4 storeys were permitted, and the contractor started
work on the next two blocks immediately the first was finished.
Wimpey News[5] recorded:

When construction started [on the next two blocks] permission
had not been received for them to be four storeys; however the University—in need of the extra accommodation—authorised that the
blocks should be built in such a way that they could either be roofed
over at three storeys or extended for the extra floor. To do this the
foundations and walls were made as if for four storey buildings even
though there was a possibility that they might only be three [storey].
By the end of September permission for the extra floor was obtained
and work began immediately on the additional floors. The timing was
almost perfect as by then the second block had just reached first floor
and the University had made plans to put a temporary roof on so that
the building could be used for accommodation rather than left empty
until permission was granted for the extra floor. Plans for the
temporary roof were scrapped and Wimpey was able to start the
permanent roofing in November 1972.

One car-parking space was provided for every two students
and the whole site was landscaped. 'The landscaping was carefully designed to break up any barrack-like effect the blocks
might create. Undulating lawns, scattered with shrubs and trees
and meandering paths contrast well with the squareness of the

[4] Council Meeting, Dec. 1971.
[5] *Wimpey News*, July 1973.

blocks'—a well-intentioned plan more successful with the first block than with the later ones.

Some of the general development is shown in Plate 23.

In the Annual Report for 1972 the Vice-Chancellor reported that the whole project would be complete by November 1973 at a total cost of £984,000, and would provide 102 flats with single study-bedrooms, 32 flats for married couples, 1 caretaker's flat, 41 common rooms and 289 car-parking places. The building costs per place were £1,355, excluding site works. With the completion of the programme the number of residential places on the campus would have reached about 1,200, distributed as in Table 20.2.

TABLE 20.2

	Single places	Doublets
Clifton Hall (First)	236	
Saltash Hall (Second)	174	
Chepstow Hall (Third)	232	
Isambard Close (Flats)	510	64
Total	1152	64

Excellent progress was maintained on the buildings and the last block was occupied on 19 October 1973. 'The Contractors, George Wimpey & Co. Ltd were as pleased as the University with the progress achieved in this "design and construct" contract,' wrote the Secretary-General in the Annual Report for 1973. 'In spite of delays occasioned by the local planning authority on whether the blocks should be 2/3 storey or 3/4 storey, the final account showed only a marginal increase over the agreed contract sum. The success of the building contract was due to the very close liaison with the contractor, and the contractor's efficiency in pre-planning all stages of the work.' Robert Adlington had a major responsibility for the development.

There were however some unexpected financial troubles. When the scheme was first examined for viability, the interest rate agreed with the Midland Bank was only $5\frac{3}{4}$ per cent, base rate being 4 per cent. 'The entirely unforeseen escalation in the base rate to 13%, taking the interest rate on the loan to $14\frac{3}{4}$%, brought with it very serious problems of capital/interest repayment over the 30 year period of the loan.'

Brunel University was not alone in this. The UGC's Annual Survey for 1971-2 drew attention to the serious difficulties that were encountered from the summer of 1972 over loan-financed schemes in all parts of the country as a result of the sharp increases in building costs and interest rates. These difficulties continued throughout 1972-3, and the Annual Survey for that year commented:

In December 1972 the Committee increased their standard rate of subsidy from £300 to £350 per place. In April 1973 the rate was increased to 25 per cent of the total capital cost, the maximum permissible under the agreement with the Government of June 1970, provided that the cost per place did not exceed a reasonable maximum, set initially at £2000. It soon became evident, however, that with building costs and interest rates both increasing fast, even this was insufficient; and in June the Committee put forward proposals to the Government for major changes in the loan financed residence system. No agreement on these proposals had been reached by December, and consequently during the latter part of 1973, although special factors made it possible for a small number of schemes to be started, the residential building programme as a whole was coming to a standstill.

As some indication of the difficulties at Brunel it might be noted that the Bank Interest item in the Loan Financed Account for the year ending 31 July 1974 was almost £100,000. Further, the University Council was informed in July 1974 that the Residence Account cumulative deficit at 31 July 1975 was likely to be of the order of £150,000 including a budgeted deficit for the 1974-5 year of £74,000 (later reduced to £56,000) provided rents were £6 per week in that year. If rents had remained at £4 per week a further deficit of about £70,000 would have resulted. However, universities were expressly exempted from the application of the 'rent-freeze' order, which Government extended to 31 March 1975, and rents at Brunel were increased to £6 per week with effect from 1 January 1975—a decision not very acceptable to students, but at least the blow was softened by the increase in student grants that had been made. It was a problem that universities and students had to live with while inflation and high bank-rates prevailed.

The University continued in its efforts to acquire Honeycroft and the Uxbridge Football Ground alongside Site One, but the owners, the Cleveland Investment Trust, were ultimately given permission by the planning authorities to develop the land. Honeycroft was demolished, construction fronting on Cleveland Road was started in July 1973 and a small group of houses was completed, but the rest of the development was held up for lack of finance. Six years later the neglected football pitch had a forlorn air.

CHAPTER 21

The Quinquennium 1972–7

THIS chapter does not give a comprehensive survey of the whole of the period 1972–7; to attempt it would be to include events well beyond the summer of 1971 when my involvement came to an end, and one chapter would in any case be quite inadequate. I have preferred to restrict the account to the special activity that marked the end of one quinquennium and ushered in another, and so in essence it provides, like chapter 20, an appendix to chapter 19 which covers the period 1968–71. To afford a measure of completeness and to avoid too abrupt an end the story is carried into the new quinquennium so as to include the decisions on the estimates made by the UGC and the policies they devised to cope with changes precipitated by the grave economic difficulties that government had to face. The full impact on the development of the University merits a more detailed assessment.

The UGC wrote to universities in May 1970 concerning submissions for the quinquennium 1972–7, and gave an indication of the student numbers in 1976–7 which the UGC thought might be adopted by each university as a guide for the consideration of its development over the years 1972–7. A broad indication was also given of the building priorities for the three building years 1972–5 which the UGC regarded as likely to be consistent with reaching these numbers, in the light of the University's prospective capacity on completion of its building programmes to 1971–2. Further, the UGC included a Preliminary Memorandum of General Guidance on Quinquennial Planning for 1972–7, supplementary to the Memorandum of General Guidance issued by the Committee in November 1967.[1]

As to student numbers at Brunel in 1976–7 the UGC suggested

---

[1] *University Development, 1967–72*, HMSO, 14.

a planning figure of 3,500 (full-time equivalents), divided into 850 Arts-based and 2,650 Science-based, estimates that would have raised little comment had not the UGC added the very important proviso that 'where full-time students spend substantial periods outside the university (e.g. on sandwich courses or periods of study abroad) the number of full-time registered students ought normally to be greater than the full-time numbers included in the stated figures.' This was a serious departure from previous practice. Hitherto a sandwich course student had been regarded as a full-time student; the new proposal meant that the number of full-time equivalents was to be determined by multiplying the number of sandwich course students by a factor less than unity. The value of this factor was critical; did Brunel's figure of 3,500 full-time equivalents imply a sandwich course population of about 4,000 or even more? Moreover Brunel was likely to be affected more seriously than any other university because *all* its undergraduate students were on sandwich courses. There might be justification for the factor in the case of 'thick' sandwich courses, but courses of the 'thin' variety had a teaching year not very different in length from that at Oxbridge and in addition teaching staff had involvements as tutors during the industrial phases of the courses. When the proposal was first mooted some of the Vice-Chancellors of technological universities argued against it with the Chairman of the UGC but had little success. My very last letter to Kenneth Berrill pleaded 'that you drop the weighting factor proposal for sandwich course students. I can think of no decision that is likely to do the technological universities more harm'. The UGC instruction in the May 1970 letter was: 'It will be for the university to indicate in their proposals for the next quinquennium the way in which the number of full-time places which their Estimates imply are built up from full-time and part-time students and take account of the extent to which the stated full-time figures represent less than the registered numbers in the case of sandwich students and others spending periods away from the university.' The UGC suggested that the weighting factor should not exceed 0.85; Brunel used a factor of unity.

Preparation of the Estimates extended over a year. They had to be submitted to the UGC by 30 September 1971 and in a form described in detail in the notes for guidance issued by the

Committee; they were to incorporate figures for 1971–2 together with the proposed increase in expenditure for developments by 1976–7. Senate, the Finance Committee and the New Buildings Committee were all involved.

The starting point of the calculations was the number of full-time equivalent students. The Senate, after considering reports from a Working Party set up in December 1969, estimated and agreed student admissions for the years 1972 to 1976 as well as the student load by Departments. Some of the figures are given in Table 21.1, where the total number of full-time students in 1976–7 is shown as 3,650, for after representations from the University about the likely expansion in the social sciences the UGC agreed to increase the estimated number of arts-based students from 850 to 1,000.

TABLE 21.1

Estimated Total Student Load

	1971–2		1976–7	
	Dept. Load	Academic Staff	Dept. Load	Academic Staff
Biology	133	17	240	27
Chemistry	135	20	220	24
Physics	90	17	200	22
Polymer Science	63	8	100	11
Metallurgy	100	13	160	18
Engineering School	—	1	—	—
Electrical	190	21	350	39
Mechanical	210	21	370	41
Production	120	13	210	23
Mathematics	187	18	330	37
Statistics	95	8	150	16
Computer Science	90	9	180	20
Psychology	196	12	360	40
Social Institutions	169 ⎫	22	320	
Economics	66 ⎭		120	49
Education	55	8	110	12
Complementary Studies	113	8	190	21
Cybernetics	21	3	40	4
Total	2033	219	3650	404

Using the Departmental student load figures the teaching staff establishment was calculated on the basis of one member of staff for every 9 full-time equivalent students. Thus the total number of academic staff in 1976-7 was estimated as 404, that is 43 Professors, 93 Readers and Senior Lecturers, and 268 Lecturers. In 1971-2 the corresponding numbers were 23, 38 and 158 respectively, a total of 219.

It might be interpolated here that the actual student numbers in 1971-2 and over the quinquennium turned out as shown in Table 22.1. The full-time equivalent total for 1976-7 was about 2,740, three-quarters of the estimated figure of 3,650. It was clear in September 1973, when the intake fell far below the estimated figure of 670, that the 3,650 figure would not be reached.

Other items of expenditure were difficult to estimate and it was decided to base them all on the total of academic staff salaries, calculated in accordance with the UGC notes for guidance. An exception was the estimate of library expenditure which had to anticipate the opening of the new library building. An analysis of expenditure over the years 1966-70 showed that about 33 per cent of the total was devoted to academic staff salaries, and this proportion was used for extrapolation purposes through the quinquennium 1972-7. The total expenditure in 1976-7 was thus estimated at £4.590 million. The figures for 1971-2 and 1972-3 were £2.758 million and £3.096 million respectively. (The actual allocations are given later on page 401.)

The draft quinquennial estimates reached the Finance Committee and the Council in June 1971, and were submitted to the UGC in September along with a statement of academic policy which Senate had discussed and agreed.

Decisions had had to be made too on Building Priorities for the period 1972-5. Taking as a starting point the capacity of the buildings which would be available on completion of the building programme up to 1971-2, the UGC came to the conclusion that the estimated capacity in 1973-4 was adequate for 3,500 full-time equivalent students (the original figure). No further building work was therefore necessary (in the years 1972-3, 1973-4 and 1974-5) 'to bridge the difference between the 1973-74 capacity figures and the suggested total of places for 1976-77'. The UGC's only suggestions for Building Priorities for 1972-3 and the two following years were 'Sports Hall and social space'—meagre indeed.

It has to be recalled that the UGC granted a sum of £0.67

million (later amended to £0.89 million) for starts in 1970-1
and only £0.09 million in 1971-2 (see page 356). After considerable discussion with UGC officers about the use of these
grants agreement was reached on building the Library, started
in April 1971, the Sports Hall, started in March 1971, and the
causeway, started in January 1971. A Students' Union building
was left in abeyance but the provision of 'social space', for staff
and students, was still being actively debated.

The UGC asked the University to 'let the Committee know as
soon as possible what building starts they consider necessary in
these years (1972-73, 1973-74 and 1974-75) in the light of the
Committee's comments and to put them in an order of priority'.
This the New Buildings Committee decided immediately at
its meeting in June 1970 and presented the list shown in
Table 21.2—formidable by any standards.

TABLE 21.2

Year starting April	Building	Completion July	Cost (guesses)	Total Starts
			£ m	£ m
1972	Social Sciences and Department of Education	1974	0.35	
	Two residences	1974	0.70	
	Building Technology	1974	0.20	
	Students' Union	1974	0.25	
	Assembly Hall	1974	0.35	
	Car Parks & Site Works	1973	0.06	1.91
1973	Electrical Engineering	1975	0.35	
	Residence	1975	0.35	
	Staff House		0.10	
	Car Parks & Site Works		0.10	
	Development of playing fields		0.06	0.96
1974	Extensions to existing academic buildings	1976	0.50	
	Residence		0.40	
	Extension to Sports Barn		0.12	1.02

The inclusion in the proposed 1972 programme of a building
for the School of Social Sciences and the Department of Education anticipated a decision against making alterations to
two floors of the Library Building. The proposals about residences were made before the UGC's decisions on loan-financed

buildings had been promulgated (see chapter 20). The Students' Union (1972) and Staff House (1973) were 'social space' proposals which staff and students were discussing. The Assembly Hall (1972) was linked with the idea of a University Theatre.

Discussions with the UGC ensued and the University was granted £0.35 million for starts in 1972–3 which included £0.2 million for the School of Social Sciences and Department of Education building and £0.15 million for 'social space'. This was followed by an allocation for 1973–4 of only £0.10 million for alterations to buildings, development of playing fields and landscaping, with the addition of £22,000 for minor works. It looked as if many of the items included in Table 21.2 would have to be postponed indefinitely, and as the quinquennium proceeded the prospects deteriorated considerably.

The Government's decision on quinquennial grants to universities for 1972–7 was announced in the White Paper *Education: a Framework for Expansion*, presented to Parliament by the Secretary of State for Education and Science, Mrs Margaret Thatcher, in December 1972. For expenditure on recurrent items and on equipment the grants were to be as in Table 21.3. They were quoted at 1972 Survey prices, but before they were allocated to the universities by the UGC they were to be revalued to take account of subsequent price increases.

TABLE 21.3

Academic Year	Recurrent Grant	Equipment Grant
	£ m.	£ m.
1972–3	252.0	23.5
1973–4	263.0	24.5
1974–5	276.0	25.5
1975–6	292.0	27.0
1976–7	309.0	29.0

The recurrent grant of £252.0 million for 1972–3 compared with the provisional allocation of £250.3 million (£248.5 million announced in November 1971 plus £1.8 million for vacation and field study courses). In addition, compensation of £7.4 million was to be paid during 1972–3 for price increases which occurred in the previous academic year.[2] Other changes were made subsequently.

[2] *UGC Annual Survey, 1974–75*, HMSO, 13.

In 1971–2 there were 236,000 full-time students in the universities and part-time students equivalent to an additional 13,000 full-time students. The grants shown above were intended, so the White Paper explained, to enable the universities to reach a total of 306,000 full-time students by 1976–7 and at the same time to increase the number of part-time students to the full-time equivalent of 15,500, making 321,500 in all.

Most of the places needed were already available 'or are being provided in building programmes up to and including that for 1972–73', claimed the White Paper. 'The 1973–74 building programme, which the Government announced last year, is expected to provide some 9,000 further places. In order that the remaining requirements for places may be met the Government have decided to allocate £29 million for the building programme for 1974–75.'[3]

The confidence of the White Paper was shattered by the mounting inflation in the national economy. During 1972–3 universities experienced increasing difficulty in planning; 'despite increases in building cost allowances of 15 per cent in December and 22 per cent in April 1973, some £11.4 million worth of work remained unstarted at the end of March 1973'— a tragic situation. The UGC Annual Survey for the academic year 1972–3 (published in November 1974) showed the size and progress of the Committee's building programme as in Table 21.4. No major building project was started at Brunel in any of these three years.

TABLE 21.4

Building Programme Year (April–March)	Original Allocation	Revised Allocation	Carried forward from previous building programme	Total Programme	Total Starts
			£ m		
1971–2	24.0	28.8	3.0	31.8	25.1
1972–3	25.0	32.5	6.7	39.2	27.8
1973–4	27.0	31.6	10.5	42.1	18.5

There were adverse effects too on the building of residential accommodation by loan-finance, to which reference was made

[3] White Paper, Dec. 1972, HMSO, 39.

in chapter 20, although Brunel successfully carried through its own scheme.

Recurrent grants to universities were announced by the UGC in a letter dated 15 January 1973. They were higher than those quoted in the White Paper (see page 400), having been adjusted to mid-1972-3 prices and based on academic salary scales as at 1 October 1972 (see Table 21.5). The grant for the year 1972-3 was fixed but the grants for further years were to be supplemented to take account of any further increases in salaries and costs in accordance with prescribed arrangements. For example, the recurrent grant for 1974-5 in the event was nearly £413 million.[4]

TABLE 21.5

	Recurrent Grants	Equipment Grant
	£m	£m
1972-3	295.5	25.5
1973-4	311.5	27.0
1974-5	327.75	28.0
1975-6	346.75	29.5
1976-7	367.0	32.0

Brunel's allocations are shown in Table 21.6. From 1973-4 an addition had been made to the allocations to replace minor works capital grants, a change that applied to all universities. The actual sums received yearly by the University took cognizance as mentioned above of the rise in price levels; for instance, a supplementary recurrent grant of £0.227 million was received for the year 1973-4 with similar increases for each of the remaining years; nevertheless strict economy measures had to be devised and applied.

TABLE 21.6

	Recurrent Grant	Equipment Grant
	£m	£m
1972-3	2.847	0.220
1973-4	3.061	0.257
1974-5	3.309.	0.270
1975-6	3.580	0.313
1976-7	3.863	0.368

[4] *UGC Annual Survey, 1974-75*, HMSO, 13.

The target number of full-time students in universities in 1976-7 was kept at the White Paper figure of 306,000, including 254,000 undergraduates and 52,000 post-graduates. The corresponding figures for 1971-2 were 191,000 and 44,000 respectively, so that there was a projected increase of 33 per cent in undergraduate numbers but only 17 per cent in post-graduates. The UGC letter commented:

Over the past decade the numbers of postgraduates have increased faster than those of undergraduates. The numbers assumed in the Government grant for 1976-77 give a rate of growth for postgraduates only about half that for undergraduates. By contrast the universities in their submissions for 1976-77 asked for a continuation of previous trends with postgraduates rising faster than undergraduates. This means that, whereas the Committee will, broadly, be able to finance the number of undergraduates which universities proposed in their plans for 1976-77, they will only be able to meet 40 per cent of the desired increase in postgraduates

—a considerable blow for universities generally.

'These undergraduate numbers are needed to achieve the national figures,' the UGC commented, 'and, because of the implications for qualified school-leavers, every effort must be made to reach them. This purpose should not be frustrated by substituting postgraduates for undergraduates. The numbers given are consonant with the agreed academic capacity of the University buildings and with the plans for the quinquennium which the University submitted, and it is assumed that the University in endeavouring to achieve them, will be guided by those plans.'

The student numbers (full-time equivalents) for 1976-7 at Brunel were given as 2,882 undergraduates and 692 post-graduates, 3,574 in all, with the undergraduate numbers divided into 898 Arts and 1,984 Science. The proposed post-graduate numbers were set out in precise detail for each section of the University, with full-time students totalling 432 and part-time students contributing 260 in equivalent numbers.

The UGC made some comments on the trend of academic developments across the country; for example,

Within the technologies, they would encourage the development of Electronic, Electrical and Production Engineering and Engineering

Design, and would favour broad-based research training and under-graduate courses.

The Committee would strongly discourage the establishment of any new schools of Architecture.

The Committee would not wish to see the development of new schools or departments of Education based on courses leading to a professional teaching qualification. They would, however, welcome the development of undergraduate courses with an Education component combined with another subject; combinations of Education with mathematics or sciences would be specially welcome.

The Committee retain their confidence in sandwich courses and universities providing such courses have been given the weightings for sandwich courses requested in their submissions.

The Committee also commented on a few of the developments in each university's quinquennial submission. Brunel was informed that in Mathematical Sciences 'provision has been made to improve the staff-student ratio. The Committee wish to encourage the establishment of a Chair in Computer Science.' In Social Studies 'provision has been made for a postgraduate course in Economics. No provision has been made for the setting up of a degree course in Law'. For Business and Management Studies: 'The Committee have allocated funds for 100 post-graduate students in Business and Management Studies, as requested in the supplementary submission of 27 June 1972.' And as to central expenditure 'in view of the existing level of expenditure no additional provision for Educational Technology has been included in the grant'.

A UGC party visited the University in March 1973, only two months after the receipt of the quinquennial allocation letter. The outcome was a great disappointment to the University; indeed the Vice-Chancellor in reporting to Council summed up the general reaction to the UGC's comments and suggestions as one of astonishment. 'In the 1968 visitation the UGC had commended sandwich courses; in the quinquennial allocation letter the University's proposal for the Arts/Science split had been accepted. In the latest visitation UGC had asked whether sandwich courses were necessary, particularly for Social Scientists, and moreover had suggested that in any further expansion the provision of extra places should be in the ratio of 2 Arts:1 Science instead of the Brunel proposals of 1:2.' The Committee had also stressed that growth in post-graduate work should be restrained, particularly in the natural sciences, but that was not unexpected in view of governmental policy expressed in the White Paper.

The end of the year was even more depressing; the University was informed of the latest cuts in government expenditure, that the recurrent grant for 1974–5 would not be compensated for inflation, that the grant for purchase of equipment would be halved, and that the target number of students for 1976–7 would be revised; 1973 was not a good year.

Nor was 1974 any better. In March 1974 the Secretary of State for Education and Science announced that the UGC's revised building allocation of starts for 1974–5 would be reduced from £30.6 million to £11.5 million at 1973 prices, and would apply to a building year running from 1 July 1974 (instead of 1 April), following the nine months' moratorium on building starts running to June 1974. 'The end of 1974 finds us exactly half-way through the 1972–77 quinquennium,' wrote the Vice-Chancellor.[5] 'It started with a government white paper proposing a decade of expansion in numbers and of increases in annual expenditure on higher education. During the last three years, however, the total number of applications by British students for university places has hardly increased at all. At the same time, accelerating inflation has made a mockery of long-term financial planning and threatens the quinquennial system itself. The confidence of expansion has been replaced by an anxiety about even maintaining what we have.'

Academic developments were inevitably affected; the Academic Registrar[6] commented:

Financial restrictions also laid a heavy hand on academic matters in 1974. The most ominous expression of this was the UGC's request in June for a revised estimate of the University's undergraduate population in 1976–77, so that the recurrent grant for 1975–76 and 1976–77 could be adjusted accordingly. After many calculations and discussions, the UGC was informed that it would be realistic to assume an undergraduate population of 2,000 in 1976–77—against the 2,882 assumed in the quinquennial settlement in January 1973. This reduction was proportionally more than the average national shortfall in undergraduate numbers, but in line with the shortfall in the particular

[5] Annual Report, 1974, 3.   [6] Annual Report, 1974, 6.

fields of science and technology. It was a special irony that in October 1974 the University had—at 598—its largest ever undergraduate entry.

The total undergraduate numbers reached 1,954 in 1976-7, as shown in Table 22.1.

The Registrar's report continued: 'Financial stringency led to Senate deciding not to allocate any of the six new teaching staff posts created by Council for 1974/5, nor to fill three other posts that became vacant through a retirement and resignations. As a result our student/staff ratio rose in December 1974 to 10.2/1— one of, if not the, highest in England.' Nevertheless some new courses were approved,

including BTech Physics with Education (to start in 1975), MA in Sociology and Law, MEd in Education, and MA in Management Studies. The latter course was to be conducted at the Administrative College, Henley, the institution with whom the University established a special relationship in 1972. During 1974 the relationship was formalised by the 'recognition' of 13 teachers at Henley as preparing students for the University's awards, including research degrees. Senate also agreed to start a Master's course in Digital Electronics and Telecommunications Engineering in co-operation with the University of Manchester Institute of Technology, and entered into formal 'exchange' arrangements with the University of Compiègne (France) and the University of Azarabadegan (formerly Tabriz, Iran).

Chandler added characteristically: 'In addition, that hoary academic football—first degree titles—was brought out for its triennial airing, and given a good kick around. The only goal scored in 1974 was a decision to institute Bachelor of Laws for the honours Law course—but the ball remained in play at the end of the year.' Another goal was scored the following year; the degree of Bachelor of Science for other courses in the School of Social Sciences was instituted.

CHAPTER 22

Retrospect

In 1976 the University celebrated the tenth anniversary of its founding and published a special issue of the *Brunel Bulletin* with the title 'Brunel University—the first ten years'.

One of the contributors was Stuart Maclure, Editor of the *Times Education Supplement*, who as described in Chapter 16 wrote about the new Brunel University in the *Listener* of 2 December 1965. He was invited to come back a decade later and one outcome of that visit was his article 'Brunel Revisited—ten years on'. He wrote:

It is, in fact, salutary to look back on the first 10 years, and compare the University now with the confident expectations of 1965, when I included Brunel in a mammoth series on 'Britain's New Universities' which appeared in *The Listener*. Brunel was number six, chosen as an example of an ex-CAT making the transformation to university status, and seeking to breathe life into the idea of a technological university within a system dominated by a quite different tradition.

I remember spending some hours with Dr Topping at Acton, and discussing with heads of departments and lecturers and students, their plans, hopes and fears for the brave new world which was to be built at Uxbridge.

It was a time of hope: Robbins had crystallized expectations in a form which politicians could understand and had offered what seemed like an acceptable long-term development plan. There was no shortage of economic danger signals, but the plans still included big spending on universities and advanced further education.

This was the time when opening up higher education was discussed in terms of social mobility, and philosophical webs were weaved around the meaning of equality of opportunity. But more important, perhaps, than the ideological superstructure was the underlying pressure of numbers: the big post-war age groups were emerging from the sixth forms. Higher education had to expand or else the competition for places would become intolerably keen. Moreover, the proportion of each age group obtaining the minimum qualification for university entrance rose steadily. And just as it was necessary, philosophically, to hold on to the belief that more need not mean worse, it was essential politically to satisfy the expectations thus created.

Against this background, Topping was articulating his vision of Brunel. The sandwich principle was to be the guarantee of its individuality, its technological approach, its concern for the application of knowledge. Science and engineering would predominate over social science and arts. The University and its staff would develop close links with industry. Brunel would take with it two legacies from its technical college origins—first, a tradition of solid and conscientious, if pedestrian, teaching, and second, a respect for the world of work and the needs of the factory and the market place—and elevate them to the level of excellence demanded by its new role as a university.

I suppose the first question the returning traveller asks, 10 years on, is how much of this vision has remained. The key element was all along seen to be the sandwich course, and this has so far survived triumphantly. Periodically it is reviewed and argued about. There is talk of changing the layers of the sandwich altering the thickness of the bread and the filling. But the Topping doctrine survives. It is accepted that if there is to be a sandwich arrangement, all departments have to operate the same sandwich for the sake of the University as a whole. As there is no unanimity about an alternative to the present pattern, which involves six months' job placement in each of the first three years, plus a fourth academic year spent wholly in the University, the Brunel sandwich continues, warts and all, because it still has more friends than enemies.

The critical choice is between insisting on the sandwich course for all, and allowing some departments to run full-time, conventional three-year degrees as an alternative. So far Brunel, alone among the ex-CATs, has resisted this temptation. Professor S. A. Urry, now Professor of Building Technology, who for many years headed the Department of Industrial Training and built up the number of training places as the University grew, speaks of 'puritanical zeal' and 'fanatical determination' in defending the sandwich idea.

What has happened to the sandwich course idea at Brunel, however, is typical of what has happened to Brunel generally during the first 10 years: it has been developed in circumstances quite different from those originally envisaged.

Almost as soon as buildings began to appear on the Uxbridge site, the balance of student demand began to swing away from science and technology towards the arts and social sciences. The Dainton Report (1964) confirmed the trend towards arts and social science, and considered ways in which the school curriculum might be altered to avoid premature subject choices which restricted later options. It is not quite true to say that nothing has happened as a result: the School Council's long-drawn-out and so far inconclusive efforts to reform the 'A' level system date from about this time. But the strength of the Dainton arguments has been largely ignored; the trend away from the hard sciences and technology in the sixth form has continued. University expansion, based on hopes of a technological revolution, became unbalanced. Empty places in science and technology went with overflowing demand for arts and social sciences. Later, the rising trend of 'A' levels, generally, levelled off, and the demand for cuts in public spending on higher education was reinforced by evidence of a faltering in demand. From a relatively early stage Brunel's plans were affected by the changing student balance, and the need to develop the sandwich principle for the growing number of social science students who, by 1976, accounted for more than a quarter of the undergraduate population (585 out of 1,916).

In the process, the University found that it had to go further and further afield for job placements. Original hopes to place a high proportion within 15 miles of Brunel (and thus keep the student residences occupied) were disappointed. Now, as then, the quality of the training received by students in their work period is highly variable. In the social sciences many of the first job placements have no training component, but are valued simply as a new experience for students who have come to university straight from school.

A reporter gets the impression that the rationale has changed significantly: the value of the sandwich principle is now seen in what it does to the student's attitude to his work and to his post-university expectations. It enables him to place his academic work in some sort of context; saves him from the hazards of study in a vacuum; puts money in his pocket, and teaches him the connection between work and pay. It may also provide industrial work experience which is of direct bearing on his academic study—if so, this is a bonus but, in any case, exposure to the world of work has proved its value in keeping his feet on the ground.

In the highly charged political atmosphere in which some students (and some staff, too) live and move and have their being, all this begins to sound a bit manipulative, and implies a hidden curriculum which it would be embarrassing to spell out. So it isn't spelled out, it is accepted as a self-evident good—for social scientists, no less than for scientists.

For those whose courses are leading towards social work, it has been fairly easy, till this year, to find work in the social services, which bears at least a superficial relevance, and may in some cases be of direct value. It is always easiest in the case of students who are sponsored by employers before they start at Brunel, but this fraction of the under-graduate body has been falling steadily. This year, the squeeze on local authority spending and unemployment generally, have made it more difficult than ever before to place students, particularly social scientists. At the end of June 1976 there were 17 unplaced, and the University may eventually have to review the degree requirements for the handful of social science students who were left at the end of the day with no approved assignment.

Did this year's experience portend the breakdown of the sandwich system? Is it all becoming too difficult? Will the jobs which people have to take be so diverse that the pretence that there is a training link between work and study becomes untenable? Nobody would like to take 1976 as typical, with unemployment at record levels. 'It's uphill going at the moment,' said Professor Urry. 'We simply have to pedal harder.' So more staff are engaged, full-time, in sniffing out training places. But some doubts must remain about the immediate future, especially if public employment is being curbed, thereby restricting not only the training places for sandwich students, but the job oppor-tunities for graduates too.

To talk to the Student Union leaders is to be drawn into fruitless comparisons between left and right and the intricacies of student politics, which of all kinds of politics is the most boring. All sorts of morals can, no doubt, be drawn from the domination of the Brunel union by the minority of social scientists, and what this means about the majority of the students who are in science and technology departments.

I didn't penetrate to the level of student activity where life is actually lived—only that of the Students' Union and its interesting commitment to large-scale commercial enterprise. If you take the Union—at Brunel or anywhere else—at its face value as the barometer of student consciousness, it would only be possible to take a very jaundiced view of the student body, and the cultural inheritance it is being offered.

There are, however, no more stolid defenders of the sandwich principle than the fourth-year students. The proportion of Brunel students going straight into permanent employment on leaving the University is much higher than that for British universities as a whole (67.3% compared with 39.3%). There can be no doubt that the sandwich principle helps many students to make up their minds about how they want to earn their living, and also helps them to do some-thing about it.

This must be an asset to any university in the hazardous years ahead. It might help students decide to put Brunel down on their

UCCA forms. It gives the University a strong distinguishing characteristic which students can choose or reject according to taste. Professor Maurice Kogan summed up the sandwich argument by saying: 'Sandwich courses do very well for the students they attract. But they probably don't attract the "scholarly undergraduate".' But then, presumably, one of the reasons for starting technological universities was to promote other ideals of excellence than that presented by traditional scholarship.

Echoes of this are not difficult to pick up. Professor D. W. Lewin, the head of the Department of Electrical Engineering, spoke of the uphill task of building up a strong research activity since 1972 when he returned to Brunel. The absence of a research tradition in engineering was the other side of the coin which advertised conscientious teaching and vocational orientation. Ten years after Brunel became a University, it was still possible to hear people talk, inelegantly, of the need for the passage of time to flush out members of the pre-university staff whose contribution to research was nil. Research and scholarship require a particular attitude of mind and a particular atmosphere, which takes time to create. It also requires staff and studentships which can only be accumulated in a period of confident expansion. This, of course, is a constant complaint in new universities whose planned build-up in numbers has been stunted. If all had gone according to plan, Brunel would now be moving towards the 5,000 mark; more departments would be able to create second chairs and to sustain sizeable PhD programmes. With a full-time equivalent student body of 2,650 now, expected to rise to 3,500 by 1977, the Vice-Chancellor, Mr S. L. Bragg, talks about the need to specialize—to take advantage of Brunel's geographical location, and the links with industry and the public services which have been built up from the beginning.

Thus, Dr B. R. Jennings' unit in the Physics Department is on the reporter's itinerary, and he is duly impressed with research into the electro-optics of macromolecules and its important medical and industrial applications. In the biological sciences he learns that the concentration is on 'activity of a biomedical nature, ranging from cancer research, immunology, parasitology to the physiology of insect transmitters of human disease'. And so on, through the gamut of the University's research programme to such obviously romantic, Jules Verne examples, as Professor I. Aleksander's work on 'intelligent digital systems'.

In Mr Bragg's view, the University has no option but to capitalize on being small—with Stirling, City and Essex, at the small end of the university scale—and on the good things which should follow from easy interdepartmental communication. Much of the most interesting work going on in the science and engineering departments is taking e trospect   411

place at the interface between different specialisms, so Brunel ought to be well placed to take advantage of this.

Another of Brunel's distinguishing badges is the postgraduate studies programme, and in particular to part-time arrangements which are made for part-time students. Some 20 courses are offered, attended by 1,500 students—the full-time equivalent of 400. Their courses seem to fit perfectly into what the Americans would understand by 'the service function of the University'—providing industry and the public services with specialized courses for men and women who need to extend their expert knowledge within a narrow field. The part-timers spend one day a week at the University over a period of two years, and follow this up with another year devoted to a dissertation.

A much-quoted example is the Master's Course in Immunology, which recruits mainly from graduates in medical research and the pharmaceutical industry. Students attend from all over the country and commute from as far afield as Scotland and Holland. The Brunel ego swells at the evidence of such metropolitan attractiveness. The University's location, close to London Airport and midway between two motorways, is a big help. (The closeness to London Airport, it seems, can damage Brunel's reputation unjustly, too: there is a wide-spread belief that schoolmasters, looking at the map, jump to the conclusion that it must be intolerably noisy. In fact it isn't—it suffers remarkably little from aircraft noise because it is out of the main flight paths.)

From the University point of view, these postgraduate students are eminently welcome. They help to maintain the science-engineering preponderance, in spite of the Dainton drift which constantly threatens to swamp the University with social scientists. They also reinforce the emphasis on the application of knowledge, thereby helping to keep the University on its toes. They ensure that the University maintains contacts at the middle management level in industry and industrial research, and this becomes important when it comes to finding work places for sandwich students. Nobody claims they are unique to Brunel, but they have become one of Brunel's 'things'.

Important as it has been to find ways of countering the Dainton effect, it has been even more important to make a success of the expansion of the social sciences. The school founded by Professor Elliott Jaques in 1965 has blossomed as the numbers have increased, and now consists of Departments of Economics, Psychology, Sociology, Government and Law. The circumstances have been favourable: the same recession which hit science and technology brought a boom in government and in the social services in particular. With government and the public services as the major consumer of social science graduates, Brunel has had no difficulty in developing an approach which is oriented towards the application of knowledge, and to back this up with a formidable research and postgraduate effort, too. Here again, the postgraduate studies programme has been important, and helped to build up Brunel's reputation and influence.

The Institute of Organization and Social Studies (BIOSS), Professor Jaques' brainchild within which an important range of policy research studies has been developed, has proved a brilliantly successful adjunct to the social sciences school. Through BIOSS, Brunel has been one of the beneficiaries of a succession of new government policies. Whatever the faults or merits of the reorganization of the National Health Service, it has made a great deal of work for Brunel. So has local government reorganization, and the reorganization of the social services. Again Brunel seems to have been aided by geography—it is near London, has the largest health authority on its doorstep—and by guessing right at the right moment about where to push, and who to get to do the pushing. (It now even has a professorial representative in the House of Lords to prove its respectability.)

The present phase sees the attempt to extend the range of subjects studied—a reflection, among other things, of the popularity of law, and the arrival of students of history and modern languages. As the arts struggle finally to shed the last remnants of their 'general studies' origins at Brunel, and seek to establish their own identity, they too are seeking to give their own meaning to the sandwich course, and to prove (against the odds, maybe) why Brunel should be a good place to read history and European studies.

Part of which comes back again to Brunel itself, as a university, a community, not just a set of separate departments or schools. New universities are desperately dependent on their architects, who in turn are dependent upon the sites they are given, and the resources at their disposal. It will be some years before Brunel is complete—the repeated changes in university building programmes which have long delayed the social sciences buildings, the Students' Union and the construction of any large hall except the sports hall, have not helped the University to develop a warm environmental personality. It would be churlish to quote the more critical comments of members of the faculty themselves, but it must make the task of building a strong university community extremely difficult to be set down on the nondescript edge of London's western sprawl. For the geographical 'benefits' of which mention has been made earlier, the University has to pay dearly.

Was I right in detecting a slightly frenetic note in the earnestness with which I was assured of the vigour of the cultural life—the excellent work done by the University Arts Group, the Theatre Arts and the Brunel Philharmonic Society? If so, it was no doubt because of the obvious importance in developing this side of the University's life, and the difficulty of doing so somewhere which is neither a Baedecker City, nor yet the Scunthorpe long beloved of radical university reformers.

At the end of 10 years, Brunel is a very different place from the university its progenitors expected. It has received less support from government, less support from industry, both of which have become increasingly hard up, and have, to some extent, lost their nerve where higher education is concerned.

It has justified its creation by the flexible, entrepreneurial attitudes which have been forced on it by the instinct to survive. Brunel is more innovative and quicker on its feet than most long-established universities—and so it most certainly should be. It is too small. No amount of whistling in the dark can make this a virtue. It could yet be obliged to think sensibly about linking up with another institution—say, City University—which is probably in the same boat, or to mention the unmentionable, when the inevitable rationalization of polytechnics and universities eventually takes place, with a poly. When that day comes, its capacity to improvise, triumphant in the first 10 years, will really be put to the test.

Perhaps no planner would deliberately have placed Brunel College/University in the most westerly borough of the Greater London Council, whatever advantages nearness to Heathrow Airport might confer. (Our first reaction was to despatch staff to the site armed with noisemeters; that they found the place unbelievably quiet seemed an amazing stroke of luck.) However, the small borough of Uxbridge was well-disposed and welcoming, but it soon (April 1965) gave way to the new Borough of Hillingdon, a bigger composite authority that was too new and perhaps too fragile to give much support to the growing institution within it—that was to become its second largest ratepayer, after Heathrow. Both the University and the Borough were too new; it was in some ways unfortunate that they were born almost at the same time and so in the early years much concerned with their own development and less outward-looking than they might have been.

Elsewhere the new universities were closely associated with cities of some strength and tradition, and most of the techno-logical universities, notably Aston, Bath, Bradford, City, Salford and Surrey seemed assured of civic backing. For Brunel there was some compensation in that the Metropolis, with all that it had to offer, was not many miles away but students found it distant, thus repeating the experience of earlier generations at Royal Holloway College, similarly placed to the west of London at Egham and Brunel's nearest university neighbour. As an institution Brunel had to seek its civic involvements, not in London, but with the communities and local authorities near at hand—the Borough of Hillingdon, the Buckinghamshire County Council and more tenuously the Hertfordshire County Council. If it looked to them for support it had of course some-thing to offer, and from the earliest days tried to fulfil its social responsibilities adequately, both locally and nationally.

This found expression in its academic policy, including the nature of its undergraduate courses, its post-graduate arrange-ments and the character of its research activities, and was reflected in such special agencies as the Educational Liaison Centre and the Industrial Services Bureau.

The former owed much to the co-operation of the Bucking-hamshire County Council. It was opened in 1972 to promote contacts between the University and schools and colleges working in the field of secondary education. Malcolm R. Mander, formerly Senior Science Master at High Wycombe Grammar School, was appointed Director and guided the early work with great skill and enthusiasm. The origins of the Centre were rooted in the close relations the University had established with schools in Hillingdon and Buckinghamshire through the work of its Department of Education and the initiative of some members of staff of the Departments of Chemistry, Physics and Mechanical Engineering. A Chemistry Teachers' Centre that owed much to the drive of G. M. Saul, with the encouragement of the Royal Institute of Chemistry, was established in 1970. A joint Standing Conference with Hillingdon had at that time been formed which brought together informally a group of members of staff of the University and representatives of other educational activities in the Hillingdon LEA area. Further the Chief Education Officer of Buckinghamshire supported moves by Professor G. Jackson to continue the work of the Project Technology Centre (page 336) at the University after the Project came to an end in 1972. The help of the County Council was critical and made possible the opening of the Liaison Centre; accommodation was later made available for it in the new library building. By 1975 seven Teachers' Centres were in operation—chemistry and technology to start with, to which were soon added biology, mathematics and physics, and later social sciences and modern languages. In-service training courses for teachers were well supported, and conferences and sixth-form lectures were regular features of the Centre's work.

In similar fashion the Industrial Services Bureau grew out of earlier work with industrial firms. G. L. Burkitt who was first appointed as Industrial Liaison Officer in 1968 (page 336) became the first Director of the Industrial Liaison Bureau when it was formally set up in 1973 (its title was changed a year later). The Board of the Bureau included three representatives of industry and three members appointed by Senate. The Bureau's objects were to assist teaching and research staff in 'broadening and strengthening contacts with industry and business in the fields of research, development and consultancy; publicising the research activities of the University and the experience and knowledge of the academic staff; seeking support for research projects in the University', and similar associated activities. The Bureau also provided an administrative service to the University in the organization and arrangements for short courses, conferences and meetings of various kinds. A fruitful development was the Chief Executive's Club which brought managing directors to the University to share mutual interests over a meal and to take part in discussions introduced by speakers from a wide field. The Club grew rapidly from the start and soon reached a membership of a hundred.

Another local institution with which the University became intimately involved was Hillingdon Hospital. Liaison with the Hospital went back to about 1964. A Joint Committee was set up in 1966 (page 296) and a few years later active steps were taken to establish a Postgraduate Centre at the Hospital, which it was hoped would satisfy some of the needs of consultants in the Hospital and of general practitioners in the area, as well as provide a place where joint researches with the University could be undertaken. A number of investigations had already been carried through and several University departments had contributed. The Department of Mechanical Engineering had become increasingly involved in bio-medical engineering, notably through the work of one of the staff, M. J. Bennett, on

neonates; the Department of Computer Science had co-operated
in dealing with some problems in gynaecology and cardiology,
and much of the research activity in the Department of Biochemistry was medically-oriented and of great potential value
to consultants in the Hospital. Equally interesting was the
significant number of projects undertaken by students in the
final year of their courses (chapter 9), particularly in Biological
Sciences and Mechanical Engineering, that were connected
with medicine and medical matters and indeed arose from
practice in the Hospital. A few students spent one of their
training periods there. It was a development of great value and
of immense promise.

Another close link between the University and the Hospital
concerned hospital administration, and in particular the contribution of Professor Elliott Jaques to investigations of the
working of the National Health Service which culminated in its
reorganization in April 1974, when the new Area and Regional
Health Authorities started to function. Professor J. D. Gillett
had earlier served on the Hospital Group Management Committee and I was Chairman from 1971 to 1974.

General confidence prevailed that financial support would
be such that a Hillingdon Hospital/Brunel University Post-
graduate Centre would be built. The next step would be a
Postgraduate Medical School affording facilities for teaching
as well as research.

Was Brunel too small, as Stuart Maclure suggested? Ideas of
size changed dramatically with the expansion of university
education. When Lord Lindsay founded the University College
of North Staffordshire at Keele in the late nineteen-forties the
projected size was some 600 students, no bigger than a single
Oxford College (see page 317). Small was beautiful. And at
Brighton plans for the University of Sussex started (in 1954)
with 'a college for 800 in the first instance'; W. G. Stone wrote 'it
was natural to think of a small university'.[1] The Robbins
Committee however had larger institutions in mind; they
envisaged the student population of the existing universities and
colleges of advanced technology expanding to 300,000 by 1980,
which implied that apart from London six universities would
have 10,000 or more students and seven would have at least

[1] *The idea of a new university*, edited by David Daiches, André Deutsch, 1964, 180.

7,000. By then the new universities would have reached totals of at least 5,000, so it was surmised, and the technological universities would have 3,000 to 5,000 students each. Brunel had almost attained the lower figure by 1976. Lack of resources rather than small student numbers was its main deficiency. Fortunate it was to have been born in the flush of support for higher technological education, but its growth was stunted by the financial blight of later years. If only the University Appeal for funds had received greater support and the target of £2m had been reached the development of the University would have been significantly changed.

Amalgamation with City University was a bizarre suggestion. Links of other kinds had been canvassed earlier; one with a college later designated a Polytechnic, another with a neighbouring College of Technology, but they proved impossible. However an association with the Administrative Staff College at Henley was successfully achieved in 1972 (page 405), a relationship which allowed students of the College to qualify for degrees of the University, such as the MA degree in Management Studies and the M.Phil. and Ph.D. degrees by research. (The University introduced the M.Phil. degree in 1973, awarded on the basis of research training—in all Schools and Departments.) The number of students involved was not large, some full-time and some part-time; by 1975 these totalled 50 in equivalent full-time terms. Another interesting development was with the Shoreditch College of Education at Egham about which negotiations were in progress throughout 1979; a close association with the College seemed an appropriate extension of the University's interest in the teaching of design and of technology in schools (page 414).

Brunel's outstanding growth by the end of the first decade was in post-graduate courses and research. The study courses leading to a Master's degree (M.Tech., MA or M.Sc.) or a Certificate of Advanced Study (page 368) proved specially attractive, and grew in number from 4 in 1966 to 28 in 1975. Many of the students attended part-time, a facility that was clearly appreciated by those residing or working relatively near to Uxbridge, but it was surprising how many came from far afield. The full-time courses also attracted students from all parts of the country and in 1975 more than a third came from overseas.

The total numbers of students in the University over the first ten years are shown in Table 22.1. The figures in brackets in the last column refer to full-time students in the Department of Education taking the course leading to the Postgraduate Certificate in Education.

TABLE 22.1

Year	Under-graduates	Postgraduates				Postgraduates
		Research		Courses		
	Total	Full-time	Others	Full-time	Others	Total
1966	1,051					145 (1)
1967	1,190					279 (26)
1968	1,336					416 (43)
1969	1,523	64	179	103	383	729 (43)
1970	1,547	90	168	110	427	796 (41)
1971	1,614	121	294	120	672	1,207 (43)
1972	1,713	145	347	160	788	1,440 (54)
1973	1,641	181	367	196	911	1,655 (44)
1974	1,813	190	426	205	1,069	1,890 (38)
1975	1,916	222	458	239	1,102	2,021 (52)
1976	1,954	223	499	237	1,130	2,089 (48)

The main changes in the student population arose from developments in the social sciences; by 1976 the proportion of students following undergraduate courses in these subjects had risen to 30 per cent of the total from only 9 per cent in 1966 (see page 326). The main body of students entered with A level passes but in the School of Engineering many of the entrants— 37 per cent in 1976—had an ONC/HNC qualification. This latter figure was about three times the average figure for entrants to engineering and technology departments in United Kingdom universities. The number of mature students was small—13 in 1976, but was expected to increase. Students came from a very wide area, with a little over half[2] from the Greater London Area and the South Eastern Region. About a fifth of the undergraduates in 1976 were women, as against a tenth in 1966.

Research activity expanded and notably in the newer departments as for example in biochemistry, and there were interesting

[2] This is a rough estimate as detailed figures are not available. The UCCA Statistical Supplement for 1977–8 indicates that 55 per cent of the entrants to the universities in the South Eastern Region, including Brunel, were domiciled in the two areas referred to.

developments in bio-engineering and production technology. Biology, chemistry, mathematics, physics and engineering all had extended programmes, and the School of Social Sciences received a fillip from the creation of BIOSS. The number of full-time research students remained small compared with many other universities, but financial support for research grew satisfactorily.[3] The University in 1966 attracted slightly more than £20,000 from external sources, and by 1976 this had reached £400,000, a rise that reflected the high inflation obtaining at the time but in terms of the UGC recurrent grant there was an increase in research expenditure from about 4.5 per cent in 1966 to 12 per cent in 1976; of the latter figure only 3 per cent came from the Research Councils. Much of the research was sponsored by industrial firms and other external organizations. Members of staff were also encouraged to undertake consulting work. Deliberately the University took the view that its main research drive should be directed towards the sort of problems which society, and industry in particular, had to face. This was not to restrict the freedom of individual members of staff wishing to pursue their own special interests, or to make the mistake of drawing a rigid boundary between applied and pure research; there was a wide awareness that the two areas overlapped considerably, and that some investigations in which industrial laboratories were involved could only faintly be labelled 'applied'. Nevertheless it seemed important that the University should stress where its main research interests lay, an essential counterpart to its attitudes on undergraduate education. It was disappointing that early ideas of establishing industrial units on the campus in close association with the University came to nothing.

The higher degree regulations were framed so that research workers in industrial laboratories could qualify for a higher degree of the University. The growth in the number of part-time research students, shown in Table 22.1, owed much to the recognition by the University of projects carried out in industry or government-sponsored laboratories, provided certain conditions were satisfied such as appropriate supervision by someone of standing. This was in part an acknowledgement that many research workers outside the universities were contributing

[3] *Brunel Bulletin*, 'The first ten years', 1976, 24.

significantly to the advancement of knowledge. The higher
degrees awarded in the year 1975 are shown in Appendix E.

The special characteristic of the University however remained
the sandwich courses for all its undergraduates. That these
courses had survived the tests of over twenty years and remained
vigorous was no mean achievement. That they had been
extended, not without some opposition, to non-technological
courses and particularly those in the social sciences, was almost
a miracle, especially as the winds of change had not all blown
favourably.

An early disappointment was the discovery that industry in
the area around Uxbridge though 'the largest industrial
concentration south of Birmingham', and including many large
firms sympathetic to the University's educational aims, could
not possibly provide enough training places for the numbers of
students the University had in mind. Not only had training
places to be found further afield but the idea, admittedly rather
utopian, that students could continue in residence during the
training periods had to be abandoned—reluctantly on my part.
The educational possibilities were very attractive, linked as they
were with the vision that some at least of the academic staff
would be living on the campus—another idealistic hope that
was not fulfilled.

It was of course always realized that the support of industry
and business, on which the university critically depended,
would be subject to the cycles of economic change. No one
was surprised therefore when the numbers of industry-based
students followed the decline of industrial activity. If one elected
to live in the real world one had to accept its buffetings. The
numbers of industry-based students fell as industry withdrew
or reduced its financial support, and the numbers of those
who were university-based, and for whom industrial training
places had to be arranged, correspondingly increased. To help
rationalize the provision of places, and to avoid or even reduce
the competition between colleges, I had hoped that agreement
would be reached on the setting-up of some national agency
that would bring order into the processes, in the same way as
the creation of UCCA had eliminated the disorder in the
applications for entry to universities. Why could not entries
for places in industrial firms and in other training institutions

be dealt with in similar fashion? There was no easy or quick answer.

Brunel had fortunately set up its own Department of Industrial Training in 1964, the first college to do so; the responsibilities of the Department grew, and by 1970 when it became the Institute of Industrial Training the number of industrial placements had risen to over 1,100; about 55 per cent of the students were then university-based. Anticipating greater difficulties in finding appropriate training places the Institute appointed four administrative officers—attached to the various Schools—to supervise the training arrangements (Appendix F). It was a wise move for there were 1,254 placements in 1972, some of them in European countries. The next few years were very difficult.

All the technological universities, to the extent to which they had retained their allegiance to sandwich courses, were faced with similar difficulties. The Vice-Chancellor's Committee[4] maintained close contacts with the Confederation of British Industries (CBI) and a Universities Committee on Integrated Sandwich Courses was established. Earlier a link with the CBI was provided by the Universities and Industry Joint Committee, but in 1972 the Universities, Polytechnics and Industry Committee (UPIC) replaced it and a tripartite relationship was developed. As one of its many responsibilities UPIC examined the future of sandwich courses and set up a working party which reported in 1975. This report expressed the belief that 'the sandwich system of education and training has an important and growing part to play in the future provision of highly educated man power at a wide range of levels in industry and commerce'; at the same time there was concern that any expansion should be at a rate compatible with the provision by employers of appropriate training for students, and the working party recommended that 'machinery should be established at national level to undertake a continuing and comprehensive review of the supply and demand'. It was suggested that 'the DES and the Scottish Education Department, acting in conjunction with the Training Services Agency (TSA), might take an initiative in this respect'. A measure of Government help

[4] Report on the period 1972–76, The Committee of Vice-Chancellors and Principals of the Universities of the United Kingdom, 37.

seemed assured, and somehow Universities and Polytechnics struggled through.

In fact some financial aid came through the Industrial Training Boards. In the Annual Report for 1975 the Director of the Institute commented: 'The economic situation was generally bad and there were serious set backs in Government expenditure followed by cuts in Local Government Support Grant.' Nevertheless in industry placement problems were not too difficult, partly because 'the Department of Employment, through the Training Services Agency (TSA), provided extra funds to enable companies through the Industrial Training Boards to maintain their commitments'. But placements in Law, Sociology, Psychology and Government Studies were severely affected, especially as the Local Government Training Board suffered cuts in its own funds and was unable to help. In 1977 however Government departments made available about £3 m to all Industrial Training Boards as an emergency measure. This financial support covered 'the training overheads of the organisation together with a basic salary of £30 per week for the student.'[5] The term 'industry-based' student lost some of its original significance.

A further concern of UPIC related to the employment prospects for graduates, another problem exacerbated by the prevailing economic difficulties. University careers advisory services had for some time had to face greater demands and the need for central arrangements for all universities had become imperative; in 1972 the Central Services Unit (CSU) came into being, with its offices located at the University of Manchester, and a year later the Polytechnics started to participate in its work. CSU was involved in the publication of vacancy lists and the collection and distribution of statistical material relating to graduate employment, including the annual survey of the first destination of graduates.

At Brunel the Careers Advisory and Appointments Service within the Institute of Industrial Training expanded its work and responded to the changing demands for graduates. Initially a high proportion of graduates, higher than in other universities, went into industry—68 per cent in 1970. The pattern changed with the deterioration in the prospects of employment; '1976

[5] Brunel University, Annual Report 1977, 97.

was a difficult year for graduate recruitment' reported the Careers Advisory Officer; 'The final prediction was of an overall 10 per cent decline in graduate demand. This drop was mainly concentrated in the public sector, encompassing the Civil Service, Local Authorities and public utilities. Whereas in 1971 we suffered from a sudden curtailment of graduate vacancies in the private sector, in 1976 it was the public sector and this will have serious repercussions as it is likely to continue.' In such a year it was a source of satisfaction that the proportion of new graduates who gained permanent employment remained at 63 per cent. One year later it was 65 per cent. These figures were much higher than those for other United Kingdom universities, the average being around 40 per cent—for arts-based graduates about 30 per cent and for science-based about 50 per cent.

Inevitably graduates had to look beyond the areas where their predecessors had found employment. Fortunately there was evidence of a growing demand to increase the graduate entry to a number of professions and services, 'notably the legal professions, executive ranks of the civil service, public services and accountancy.'[6]

The Report on the period 1972–6 of the Committee of Vice-Chancellors and Principals (CVCP) commented on the universities' contribution to economic development through research and other work relevant to industry, and also noted the increasing emphasis on degree studies as the main route to professional qualification. 'The Universities' commitment to professional education has always been a substantial one,' the Report continued, 'since they have the sole responsibility for the education and training of the country's doctors, dentists, veterinary surgeons and agriculturalists and also for that of most of the highly qualified engineers, technologists, lawyers and architects. There is also their major contribution to the teaching profession.' The Report went on to mention that the Committee had also taken an active interest 'in matters affecting the initial training of teachers, legal and accountancy education, degree studies for nurses, and the provision by universities of education and training for civil engineers and social workers.'

The use of the words 'education and training' in combination is striking, as is the emphasis on education for the professions.

[6] *University Development, 1967–72*, HMSO, 27.

There are many who would react by saying that this did not mean mere vocational training. One of my concerns at Brunel was to raise vocational education and training to a proper level, and to ensure that it realized the aims of a liberal education in the fullest sense. This found expression in the complementary studies which were an essential element of the undergraduate courses, in the attempt to reform teaching methods and to make use of the students' widening practical experience, and in the general broadening of the content of the courses (see chapter 9).

Broadening courses is alas not very acceptable to many specialists; naturally they enjoy teaching their specialism to students of that specialism, but unfortunately find it unrewarding, even irksome, to teach students of another specialism. Until teachers accept readily this latter responsibility a broadening of university education will not be achieved. Service teaching as it is called is too often made the responsibility of the latest arrival on the staff, whereas it demands all the skills and experience of the best teachers. To help social scientists, economists and lawyers to be numerate and to gain some insight into natural science demands teaching of a high order. It also requires an imaginative approach to the selection of what is taught; a unit taken from some established mathematics or science course is more than likely to be completely inadequate. By the same token courses in social studies or economics for mathematicians or natural scientists need to be carefully selected and imaginatively taught.

The concern of the UGC about the dangers of over-specialization and the importance of general education was referred to in chapter 9. It was a recurring theme; the terms specialist and generalist re-entered the vocabulary of educational discussions through the Swann Report[7] published in 1968. A working group on Manpower for Scientific Growth, with Professor Michael Swann as Chairman, had examined in depth the education and employment of technologists; not surprisingly many of their comments and recommendations could be applied to a much wider area of university education, to the arts and social sciences.

The Group looked at what scientists and technologists actually do, and quoted findings that suggested 'high level

[7] *The Flow into Employment of Scientists, Engineers and Technologists*, HMSO, 1968.

specialist occupations may amount, at most, to 40 per cent of the total employment of scientists and technologists', the main requirement in the future would be for science-based generalists in occupations such as school teaching, general management and administration. On the other hand specialists are needed for research, both in universities and elsewhere, but the extent of specialization in university education exceeds that in employment; therefore 'British universities should consider the possibility of making the first degree course in science, engineering and technology broad in character.' The Report added, 'Adaptation to future needs requires a shift towards a more general scientific or technological education with specialism grafted on later, as and when appropriate.'

The grafting on of specialisms later was relatively easy, as Brunel's experience with taught courses leading to a Master's degree well testified; they seemed to provide satisfaction for the specialist yearnings of the staff. To get agreement on wider undergraduate courses however was much more difficult; even to suggest that materials science should be taught throughout the science and engineering courses divided the academics; to propose a common science course in the first two years was revolutionary and quite unacceptable. Even when a start was made with a broad course in Psychology, Sociology and Economics (PSE), it had to be accompanied by a specialist course in Psychology to which later were added a specialist course in Economics and others in Sociology and Government Studies.

It seemed inevitable that most if not all the undergraduate courses had to be specialist and one was limited to trying to ensure that some generalist elements were included. Other academics saw a solution to some of the problems through modular courses but I found them unattractive, preferring a course designed as an entity. Thinking was often bedevilled by the idea that a general course was an easy option, whereas in fact the broader the course the more difficult students found it. Perhaps a distinction should have been more carefully made between the general courses that weaker students have often been offered and generalist courses that have adequate depth as well as breadth; 'the term generalist has become almost indissolubly stuck to the low-level generalist'. I was concerned that science and engineering students should be introduced to a study of men (as well as of materials and machines) for science and technology not only have profound effects on the society in which we live, but science has something to do with scientists and the relations of scientists with others. There is a web of human relationships which science teaching often overlooks. Science and engineering courses should include a fair measure of social science, not simply or mainly because of the particular content of subject matter, but to give students a glimpse of the methods social scientists have to use in dealing with the many-parameter problems that abound in society—with incomplete and uncertain data. They might then be all the better prepared for the technological problems of industry which unlike those in the text books are not provided with just enough data or have unique solutions. Students should more often be working on open-ended questions and on the frontiers of knowledge, the aim being to help develop their physical insight, a quality which distinguishes outstanding scientists and engineers—not least Isambard Kingdom Brunel.

A broad education would, one hoped, also encourage flexibility, even versatility; that is graduates would have not only the skill to acquire other skills but would be prepared to do quite a different job. Too often to be educated in a specialism means to be educated to be a specialist—and nothing else. The Swann Report commented: 'Education must also instil into graduate scientists and technologists the idea they they must be prepared to use their ability in a variety of employment, where they are most needed. That the typical British education for scientists and technologists does so little to generate these qualities is, in our view, largely a consequence of its specialised nature.'

How was a change to be made? If British universities do not educate generalists as well as specialists, how do we advance? I had always hoped that Brunel University might make a move forward.

Whatever success the University might have had is for others to assess; only those who took part in trying to forge a new mode of university education will know the excitement and satisfactions it generated. In an article 'The Vice-Chancellor looks back' which I wrote at the request of the Editor of the students' newspaper *Isam*[8] I made the point that 'sandwich courses were

[8] *Isam*, Feb. and Mar. 1971.

not, as some seem to imagine, an acceptance of a training scheme appropriate to technicians, but for me they were a revolt against university education as I had known it as a student and a lecturer. (It is strangely amusing to ponder that students cannot believe or seldom surmise that a Vice-Chancellor may be opposed to the educational conservatism of his day and even of some of his staff and students.) The sandwich mode was adopted in order to provide a vocationally-oriented education, that whilst making an appeal to practical things and providing experience of the real world yet offered that training of the mind and development of the whole man which we associate with education at its best.' Sandwich courses were certainly no easy option; they could have been discarded because they were too demanding, too exacting; that they were maintained redounds to the credit of the staff—and of many from outside the University who encouraged and helped. Among them must be included the lay Governors of Brunel College and Brunel University, the directors and education officers of many industrial firms, and the Middlesex County Council.

Someone[9] has written: 'The old, now defunct, Middlesex authority could have a worse epitaph than that it helped to create Brunel University.'

[9] T. Burgess and J. Pratt, *Policy and Practice*, The Penguin Press, 1970, 171.

APPENDIX A

Brunel College of Technology

Governing Body
1957–58

CHAIRMAN

Sir Miles Thomas, D.F.C., M.I.MECH.E., M.S.A.E.

County Alderman J. W. A. Billam, B.SC.
County Alderman Mrs. K. M. St. P. Crump, B.SC.
County Councillor Mrs. M. R. Forbes, J.P.
County Councillor C. Furber, M.I.T.
County Alderman Capt. O. J. Galley
County Councillor R. E. Gundry, M.A.
County Councillor Major A. Jardine
Councillor L. Marchant, B.SC.
Alderman T. W. Newson, J.P.
Councillor M. C. Nokes, M.C., M.A., B.SC.
County Councillor Miss J. L. Scott, B.SC., A.R.I.C.
L. A. Jordan, Esq., C.B.E., D.SC.
E. Alexander, Esq., A.M.I.E.E., A.M.I.PROD.E.
R. Beeching, Esq., B.SC., PH.D., A.R.C.S., D.I.C., F.INST.P.
W. B. D. Brown, Esq., M.B.E., F.I.I.A., F.B.I.M.
A. Hallworth, Esq.
O. W. Humphreys, Esq., C.B.E., B.SC., F.INST.P., M.I.E.E.
Major C. Johnson, M.B.E., M.A.
Sir John Paget, Bart., M.A., M.I.MECH.E., M.I.PROD.E.
D. Heron, Esq., M.A., D.SC.
R. C. Chirnside, Esq., F.R.I.C.
Professor D. G. Christopherson, O.B.E., D.PHIL., A.M.I.C.E., M.I.MECH.E.
E. R. Davies, Esq., O.B.E., B.SC., F.INST.P.
D. P. Sayers, Esq., B.SC., M.I.E.E., M.I.MECH.E., M.AMER.I.E.E.

PRINCIPAL

J. Topping, M.SC., PH.D., D.I.C., F.INST.P.

Diploma in Technology Courses
Numbers on 31 March 1960

(figures in parenthesis refer to 31 March 1959)

	Colleges	Courses	Students
Colleges of Advanced Technology	9 (8)	61 (44)	2,876 (1,899)
Regional Colleges	11 (10)	25 (20)	831 (554)
Area Colleges	2 (1)	2 (1)	79 (50)
Royal Aircraft Establishment Technical College	1 (1)	1 (1)	28 (15)
	23 (20)	89 (66)	3,814 (2,518)
Brunel College of Technology (included in Regional Colleges above)	1 (1)	8 (7)	333 (250)

On 31 March 1960 of the 89 courses 74 were sandwich courses with 3,342 students in all; the others were full-time.

Brunel College
of Advanced Technology

GOVERNING BODY 1962

NOMINATED BY

The Minister of Education
W. B. D. Brown, Esq., M.B.E., F.B.I.M. (*Chairman*)
Sir John Paget, Bart., M.A., M.I.MECH.E., M.I.PROD.E.

Council of the Administrative County of Middlesex
County Alderman J. W. A. Billam, B.SC.
County Alderman Mrs. M. R. Forbes, J.P.
Dr. C. E. Gurr, M.SC., PH.D., F.R.S.A.
County Councillor Miss J. L. Scott, B.SC., F.R.I.C.

Regional Advisory Council
Mrs. Margaret Cole, M.A.

London University
Professor J. D. McGee, O.B.E., PH.D., M.SC., HON.A.R.C.S., F.INST.P.

Federation of British Industries
R. G. Beldam, Esq., M.A., F.C.A.

Trades Union Congress
L. J. Sapper, Esq., LL.B.

Institution of Electrical Engineers
D. P. Sayers, Esq., B.SC., M.I.E.E., M.I.MECH.E., M.AMER.I.E.E.

Institution of Mechanical Engineers
A. W. Manser, Esq., B.SC., M.I.MECH.E., M.I.E.E., M.I.LOCO.E., F.R.S.A.
(*Vice-Chairman*)

Institution of Production Engineers
A. L. Stuchbery, Esq., M.I.MECH.E., M.I.PROD.E.

Royal Institute of Chemistry
R. C. Chirnside, Esq., F.R.I.C.

Institute of Physics and the Physical Society
  E. R. Davies, Esq., O.B.E., B.SC., F.INST.P.

Academic Board of the College
  Dr. S. C. Bevan, B.SC., PH.D., F.R.I.C.
  Dr. J. Crank, M.SC., D.SC., F.INST.P.
  L. H. Hancock, Esq. A.M.I.MECH.E., A.M.I.PROD.E.
  Dr. R. T. A. Howell, B.SC. (ENG.), PH.D., M.I.E.E.
  E. E. Robinson, Esq., M.SC.

Principal
  Dr. J. Topping, M.SC., PH.D., D.I.C., F.INST.P.

Co-optative Members
  Sir Joseph Latham
  Dr. A. T. M. Wilson, B.SC., M.D.
  H. J. Bunker, Esq., M.A., F.I.BIOL.

Brunel University

COUNCIL MEMBERSHIP 1966

(i) The Chancellor

John Anthony Hardinge
Earl of Halsbury

The Pro-Chancellor

Lord Brown of Machrihanish

The Vice-Chancellor and
Principal

J. Topping, M.SC., PH.D., D.I.C.,
F.INST.P., F.I.M.A.

The Vice-Principal

G. C. Shipp, M.A., PH.D., D.I.C.,
C.ENG., A.M.I.CHEM.E.

(ii) Seven persons nominated by the
following Councils:

  (a) Two by the Greater London
      Council

Mrs. M. R. Forbes, C.B.E., J.P.,
G.L.C.
Miss J. L. Scott, B.SC., F.R.I.C.,
G.L.C.

  (b) One by the Council of the
      Administrative County of
      Buckingham

J. R. Ireland

  (c) One by the Council of the
      Administrative County of
      Berkshire

J. S. Cook, B.SC. (LOND.), A.R.C.S.

  (d) One by the Council of the
      Administrative County of
      Hertford

Alderman H. E. Fern, C.B.E., J.P.

  (e) One by the Council of the
      Administrative County of
      Surrey

Capt. G. R. G. Allen, C.B.E., D.S.O.,
R.N.

  (f) One by the Council of the
      London Borough of
      Hillingdon

Alderman A. J. Beasley

(iii) Seven persons nominated by the
following Bodies after consultation
with the Council:

(a) Four by such professional
Institutions or Associations
or learned Bodies as may be
determined by the Council

    (1) Institute of Physics and   E. R. Davies, O.B.E., B.SC., F.INST.P.
the Physical Society

    (2) Institute of Electrical   L. Drucquer, C.ENG., M.I.E.E.
Engineers

    (3) Institute of Mechanical   A. W. Manser, B.SC., M.I.MECH.E.,
Engineers   M.I.E.E., M.I.LOCO.E.

    (4) Royal Institute of   R. C. Chirnside, F.R.I.C.
Chemistry

(b) One by the Confederation of   R. G. Beldam, M.A., F.C.A.,
British Industry   M.I.MAR.E.

(c) One by the Trades Union   L. J. Sapper, LL.B.
Congress

(d) One by the Graduates   M. F. Brittain, B.TECH. (Oct. 1967)
Association of the University

(iv) Five members of the Senate   Professor J. D. Gillett, O.B.E., D.SC.,
nominated by the Senate   PH.D., F.I.BIOL.
                                 L. H. Hancock, B.TECH., C.ENG.,
                                 A.M.I.MECH.E., A.M.I.PROD.E.
                                 Professor C. A. Hogarth, B.SC.,
                                 PH.D., F.INST.P.
                                 Professor G. Jackson, M.A., D.I.C.,
                                 C.ENG., A.M.I.MECH.E., A.F.R.Ae.S.
                                 Professsor Elliott Jaques, M.A.,
                                 M.D., PH.D.

(v) Two members of the non-   R. Borger, M.A., B.SC.
professorial staff elected from   R. H. Creamer, M.SC., A.INST.P.
among their own number by the
Readers, full-time Senior
Lecturers and Lecturers of the
University

(vi) Two members of the Academic   G. Templeman, M.A., PH.D., F.S.A.
Advisory Committee (while that   Sir John Paget, Bart., M.A.,
Committee exists) appointed by   M.I.MECH.E., M.I.PROD.E.
that Committee

(vii) Such other persons, not exceeding   A. L. Stuchbery, A.M.I.MECH.E.,
ten in number, as may be   A.M.I.PROD.E.
co-opted by the Council

Higher Degrees Awarded in 1975

	Ph.D.	M.Phil.	M.Sc.	M.A.	M.Tech.	Cert.	Total
Biology	11	2	16	—	—	1	30
Chemistry	7	1	—	—	1	6	15
Physics	6	1	—	—	14	4	25
Engineering	3	1	—	—	32	12	48
Materials	3	—	—	—	6	3	12
Maths	3	1	18	—	25	17	64
Social Sciences	2	4	—	88	—	5	99
Education	1	—	—	—	—	36	37
Cybernetics	5	1	—	—	—	—	6
ASC Henley	1	—	—	—	—	1	2
Totals	42	11	34	88	78	85	338

APPENDIX F

INSTITUTE OF INDUSTRIAL TRAINING   BRUNEL COLLEGE

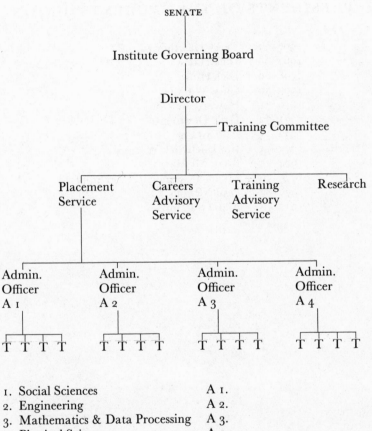

SENATE

Institute Governing Board

Director

Training Committee

Placement Service   Careers Advisory Service   Training Advisory Service   Research

Admin. Officer A 1   Admin. Officer A 2   Admin. Officer A 3   Admin. Officer A 4

T T T T   T T T T   T T T T   T T T T

1. Social Sciences   A 1.
2. Engineering   A 2.
3. Mathematics & Data Processing   A 3.
4. Physical Sciences   A 4.

   T = Academic Tutor.

Brunel University

PRESIDENTS OF THE STUDENTS' UNION

1966–67	Terry Hawthorn
1967–68	Dick Hales
1968–69	Dick Hurst
1969–70	Chris Watkins
1970–71	Howard Newton
1971–72	Dave Dewhurst
1972–73	Pete Swain
1973–74	Jim Doel/Nick Warren
1974–75	Brian McAlley
1975–76	Michael Chappell/Philip Stopford
1976–77	Paul Nicholls
1977–78	Alan Graham

APPENDIX H

This list is not intended to be comprehensive, but merely includes histories of some Colleges of Advanced Technology and Polytechnics, and other related writings.

A Technological University: an experiment in Bath.
   Edited by Gerald Walters. Bath University Press, 1966.
Chelsea College—a history.
   S. J. Teague and H. Silver. Chelsea College, 1977.
1866-1966: One Hundred Years of Technical Education.
   A. Harvey. Welsh College of Advanced Technology.
Loughborough: from College to University.
   Leonard M. Cantor and Geoffrey F. Matthews. Loughborough University of Technology, 1977.
The Foundations of the University of Salford.
   Colin Gordon. John Sherratt & Sons Ltd., 1975.
Pioneering in Education for the Technologies. The Story of Battersea College of Technology, 1891-1962.
   H. Arrowsmith. University of Surrey, 1966.
The Borough Polytechnic Institute.
   Edric Bayley. London. Elliott Stock, 1910.
Borough Polytechnic, 1892-1969.
   F. G. Evans. Borough Polytechnic, London, 1969.
Traditions and Controls in the making of a polytechnic; Woolwich Polytechnic, 1890-1970.
   Michael Locke, Thames Polytechnic, London, 1978.
From Technical College to University; a case study of Brunel College.
   Janette Faherty; M.Phil. thesis, Brunel University, 1976.

Universities and General
A New University; A. D. Lindsay and the Keele Experiment.
   W. R. Gallie. Chatto and Windus, 1960.
Keele; An Historical Critique.
   Sir James Mountford. Routledge & Kegan Paul, 1972.
The idea of a new university: An experiment in Sussex.
   Edited by David Daiches. André Deutsch, 1964.

The New University.

Edited by John Lawlor. Routledge & Kegan Paul, 1968.
Four Hundred Years of English Education.

W. H. G. Armytage. Cambridge University Press, 1964.
South Kensington to Robbins.

Michael Argles. Longmans, 1964.

Index

Abercrombie, M. L. J. 172
Academic Advisory Committee 229, 233, 239, 240, 287, 299, 310, 327, 363
— Board 129, 186, 190, 206, 231, 241, 286, 299
Acton Borough Council 136, 139, 152
— Divisional Executive 112
— Junior Technical School 15, 19, 23, 73
— Technical College, 1, 7, 15, 19, 21, 22, 27, 44, 102, 124, 162
Adlington, R. vii, 328, 360, 392
Administrative Building 265, 269, 312, 340
— College, Henley 405, 417
Advisory Committees 51
— Council on Scientific Manpower 278
— Panels 116, 155, 168, 206, 208, 210, 273
Allanson, J. T. 229, 327
Anderton, R. S. 21
Andrew, E. R. 229, 327
Annan, Noel 229, 244, 290, 327
Annual Reports, Acton TC 32, 74, 77, 79, 92, 98, 100, 103, 105, 116, 124
— — Brunel College 127, 130, 142, 155, 208, 222
— — University 304, 332, 340, 348, 362, 379, 392
Appeal Fund 356, 363, 364, 365, 377, 417
Appointments Committees 191, 211
Architects, Brunel College 189, 202, 203
— Middlesex County Council 132, 135, 136
— Ministry of Education 135
Architectural Association 203
Arts Council of Great Britain 25
Ashby, Sir Eric (Lord) 175
ASLIB 131
Assembly Hall, Acton 133, 136, 141
— — Brunel 311, 316

Assessment 211, 212, 302, 303
Association of British Theatre Technicians 378
— of Education Committees 181
— of Principles in Technical Institutions 69, 112, 114
— of Teachers in Technical Institutions 86, 128, 211, 240
— of Technical Institutions 69, 84, 112, 114
— of University Teachers 211, 240, 246
Atchison, J. 101
Atomic Energy Research Establishment 225
Audio-visual aids 334, 335
Aylett, P. D. 124, 156

BACIE 5
Bacon, Francis 99
Bannister, R. 382
Barlow Report 64, 69, 110
Battersea Polytechnic/CAT 90, 149
Beecham 11
Beeching, Lord 337
Beer, Stafford 361
Benn, A. Wedgwood 362
Bennett, M. J. 415
Berrill, Sir Kenneth 360, 395
Bevan, S. C. vii, 367
Billam, J. W. A. 188
Biochemistry 365
Biological Sciences, School of 300, 367, 380, 416
Biology, Applied 88
— Department of 154, 314, 320, 354
Biology/Chemistry Building 314, 347, 348, 349, 379, 380
BIOSS 363, 383, 385, 412, 419
Birmingham College of Technology 83, 90

Bishop of London 310
Bishop, J. S. & Co. 253
Board of Education reports 1, 7
— of Studies 129, 159, 191, 287, 300
Bodsworth, C. 293
Boiler-house 308
Böll, H. 381
Bond, G. C. 367
Borger, R. 119, 316
Bosworth, G. S. 303
Bragg, S. L. 371, 379, 410
Brightwell, M. C. 360
British Association for the Advancement
    of Science 174
— Psychological Society 218
Broadbent, R. W. 21
Brosan, G. S. 140, 150, 151, 152
Brown, R. 225
Brown, Wilfred (Lord)
    Glacier Metal Co. 13
    Chairman, Acton Governing Body 47,
        84
    Chairman, Brunel Governing Body 186
    Appointment of Architects 189
    Planning Group 196, 250
    Conditions of Service 211
    New Brunel 227
    Statutes Committee 232
    Life Peerage 242
    Academic Advisory Committee 243
    Letter to Staff Association 245
    Pro-Chancellor 248
    Rubber Technology 257
    Maiden Speech 266
    Resignation as Chairman 286
    School of Social Sciences 290
    D.Tech. 309
    Appointment of Vice-Chancellor 371
Brunel, I. K. 98, 197, 339
Brunel Bulletin 304, 320, 338, 349, 358,
    406
— College 98, 107
— Orchestra 222, 378
— Players 222
— University 231
— — Act 308
Brynmor Jones report 334
Buckinghamshire County Council 414
Building Bulletin No. 5 134, 136, 137, 141
— Contracts 249
— Crown 208, 275
— plans, Acton 132
— — Brunel 189, 251

— Technology 366, 370
— starts 262, 265, 266, 269, 270, 279, 314,
    349, 356, 398
Buildings Officer 328, 384, 386
— Superintendent 328
— temporary 152, 207, 275, 356
Bunker, H. J. 210
Burgess and Pratt 185, 207, 215, 427
Burkitt, G. L. 336, 415
Burnett, J. vii, 193, 221, 222, 291, 292, 338
Burningham, D. J. 225, 227, 301
Bursar 340
Butler, R. A. (Lord) 25, 58
BX Plastics, Ltd 225

C. and E. Organisers Ltd 311
Careers Advisory Service 422
Carr-Saunders, Sir Alexander 65
Car-parks 261
Catering Manager 341, 348
C.A.V. 11, 12
C.B.I. 303, 310, 421
Certificate of Advanced Study 368, 417
Chambers, T. P. 159
Chambers, W. R. M. 111
Chancellor of the University 309
Chandler, E. R. vii, 158, 187, 191, 204,
    312
Chaplains 332
Chapman, S. 339
Charter and Statutes 213, 230, 246, 329
Chelsea Polytechnic/College 90, 325
Chemical Engineering 140
Chemistry, Applied 88, 96
— Department of 230, 314, 320, 354
— School of 367, 380
— and Biology, Department of 73, 101,
    154
Chepstow Hall 379
Childs, C. E. N. vii, 316, 322, 357
Chirnside, R. C. 210
Chiswick Polytechnic 8, 9, 99
Chromatography 321
City and Guilds Institute 20, 21, 29
— University 149
CLEAPSE 256, 333
Clerks of Works 264
Clifton Hall 340
Cogan, C. V. Camplin 45
College of Advanced Technology 89, 142,
    143, 146, 204, 249, 279, 284, 304, 306,
    334
— — — assesssor 187

College of Advanced Technology designation 184
— — — interim award on salaries 213
— — — trust deed 182, 186
— of Technologists, Membership of (MCT) 147, 225, 236
Collop, A. D. 186
Committee of Principals of Colleges
— of Advanced Technology 211, 216, 278, 306
— on Scientific Manpower 108, 109
— of Vice-Chancellor and Principals 306, 307, 369, 421, 423
Communal building 309, 313, 330, 340, 341, 347, 348, 354
Complementary Studies 169, 292, 357 (*see* General Studies)
Computer Science 367, 370
— Services Committee 367
— Unit 346, 367
Computers 105, 157, 319
Conditions of Service 211, 212
Contract procedure 260
Cooper, F. W. 156
Cooper, S. R. 331
Cotgrove, S. F. 5
Council for National Academic Awards (CNAA) 237
— Room 340
— of University 231, 310
Council/Students Committee 247, 310, 331, 332
Counselling 331, 361
Course, K. W. 316
Course Board, *see* Board of Studies
Court of University 231, 330, 340
Crank, J. vii, 124, 152, 157, 236, 300, 318, 329
Crook, A. W. 368
Crook, J. M. 187, 205
Crosland, C. A. R. 4, 285
Crowther report 4, 21, 87, 102, 179
Cybernetics, Institute of 361

Dainton Committee 298, 407, 411
Daniels, A. 368
Davies, C. 124
Davies, E. R. 210, 232, 310, 371
Day Continuation Schools 2, 3, 5, 45
Degree congregations 310
— courses 236, 237
— titles 299, 405
Deighton, H. S. 331

Department of Education and Science 252, 277, 279, 320, 399
— of Scientific and Industrial Research 117, 220
Departments, Acton TC. 72, 74
— Brunel College 122, 123, 192, 221, 223, 226
— and Schools 153, 287, 289, 300, 303, 317
Diploma in Education 238
— in Management Studies 219, 220
— in Psychology course 218
— in Technology (Dip. Tech.) 61, 88, 94, 105, 124, 127, 193
Director of Physical Education 360, 382
District Valuer 252, 374
Doctor of Technology 309
Dore, J. 316
Drever, J. 117
Durham, K. 365
Dyson, Sir Frank 98

Ealing Borough Council 379
— Technical College 8, 9, 18, 99, 133, 136
Eccles, Sir David (Lord) 181, 188
Economies 318
Eden, J. 261, 264, 271, 328
Education Acts (1902) 44; (1918) 2, 45; (1944) 16, 26, 46, 48, 58; (1948) 48
Education Department, Brunel 257, 292, 305, 320, 335, 354, 414
— and Teacher Training 238, 325
— and Training 78, 92, 127, 163, 423
Educational Development Panel 126, 128
— Liaison Bureau/Centre 381, 414
— Method, Division of 221
— Technology 334, 343
E.M.I. 11, 88
Electrical Engineering, Department of 72, 80, 88, 96, 123, 124, 156, 224
— Research Association 88
Electronics, Department of 122, 123, 156
Enfield Technical College 7, 27
Engineering, School of 289, 317, 368
— Building, Acton 132
— — Uxbridge 254, 268, 309, 313, 315, 322, 330, 340, 344
— Cadets 24
— Centre 344, 345
English Electric Valve Co. 88
English, C. R. 83
Equipment grants 322
Estimates 115, 272, 279

Evans, E. S. G. 222
Evening Institutes 1, 106
Examinations 173

Farrant, D. 344
Farrer-Brown, L. 319
Fassnidge, Son and Norris, Ltd 347, 349
Federation of British Industries 186
Feltham, P. 367
Ferguson, I. K. 127
Field, H. V. 93
Fielding, J. T. vii
Finance Committee, Brunel College 189, 272, 280
— Officer 340
Firestone Tyre Co. 11, 14
Forbes, Muriel 188, 309
Ford and Walton 314
Foster, D. B. 156
Fraser, D. 378
Fundamentals of Design 221
— of Science 82, 104, 148, 169, 171
Fund Raising (*see* Appeal Fund) 282, 308, 311, 312, 316
Furneaux, W. D. 293, 320, 380
Further Education and Training Scheme (FETS) 110

Gavin, M. R. 84
General Assembly 329, 332
— Education 424
— Electric Co. 83, 88
— Studies (*see* Liberal Studies) 148, 172, 221, 291
— — in Technical Colleges 179
George, F. G. 361
Giddings, W. F. 21, 101, 124
Giles, G. T. C. 32
Gillett, J. D. 154, 193, 236, 296, 300, 320, 367, 371, 416
Gillette, Ltd 11, 14
Glacier Institute of Management 220
— Metal Co. 11, 13
— Project 220
Glaxo, Ltd 11
Glossop, W. J. & Co. 263
Gluckman, M. 117
Governing Body, Acton TC 45
— — Brunel College 112–18
Governors, Specialist 210
Gracie, J. J. 83
Graduates Association 310
Grant, L. A. 205, 328

Gray, C. H. 327, 365
Great Western Railway 99, 337
Greenbaum, A. L. 365
Greenway School 198, 200, 374
Gribble, F. D. 306
Griffin, G. J. L. 225, 294
Grove, The 352, 372
Guinness 11, 13
Gulbenkian Foundation 378
Gurr, C. E.
    Attitude to sandwich courses 83
    Clerk of Brunel Governing Body 113
    Nuffield Foundation application 119, 120
    College of Advanced Technology 180, 181, 188
    Uxbridge site 184
    Specialist Governor 210
    Letter to seconded staff 213
    Cleapse 256

Hailsham, Lord 111, 248
Halcrow, G. R. vii, 126, 331
Hale Committee 167, 176
Hales, R. J. 332
Halls of Residence 260, 262, 266, 271, 282, 308, 311, 312, 314, 330, 340, 347, 354, 355, 364, 379, 384, 388
Halsbury, Earl of 309, 310, 338, 361
Hammersmith Town Hall 309
Hancock, L. H. 155, 156, 316
Harcourt, R. A. F.
    Acton TC, Head of Department 74
    Brunel College, Head of Department 101, 154
    Centre for Psychological and Social Research 118, 155
    Application to Nuffield Foundation 119
    Conference Room 123
    Advisory Panel for Production Engineering 156
    Head of Department of Management 192, 219
    Liaison with Glacier Institute 221
    School of Social Sciences 291
Harris, R. J. C. 365
Harrison, G. B. 335
Hawkins, P. J. 316
Haywood, Sheila 202
Health Service 331
Heathrow 413
Hebenton, J. 303

Heinz 11
Hendon Technical College 7
Heriot-Watt College 231, 276
Heron, D. 48
Hertfordshire County Council 414
Hetherington, J. A. 225
Heywood, J. 196
Hillingdon, Borough of 259, 269, 310, 311, 333, 351, 352, 373, 378, 384, 413
— Hospital 198, 200, 296, 365, 415
Hinton, Sir Christopher 112
H.M. Inspectors' Reports, Acton TC (1928) 10; (1934) 16, 18, 22; (1952) 34, 36, 42, 53, 72, 80, 86
Hives, Lord 71, 93
Hogarth, C. A. 124, 236, 321, 361
Holden, G. A. 135
Holmes-Walker 294
Honeycroft 353, 376, 384, 393
Hooker, S. G. 339
Hoovers 11, 14
Hornby, F. R. 94, 97
Horner, G. S. 158
Hotel and Catering School 31, 132
Hostel, Brunel College 137, 138, 139, 152
Houghton, J. 124, 156
Housing Association/Society 257, 258, 267, 268, 388
— Policy 250, 388, 389
Howell, R. T. A. 124, 157, 231, 236, 289, 372
Hughes, Athol 146
Hunter, P. 371

Ibbetson, J. F. R. 316
Imperial College 68, 225, 226, 364
Industrial Liaison Officer 336
— Services Bureau 414, 415
— Survey Committee 225
— Surveys 227, 301
— Training 127, 166, 224, 228, 264, 287, 364, 408, 421
— — Act 166, 302
— — Boards 166, 302, 364, 422
— — for the Diploma in Technology 224
— — Working Party/Committee 302, 364
In-service training courses for teachers 415
Institute of Industrial Training 363, 421, 435
— of Organisation 362
— of Physics 87, 88, 113, 186

Institution of Electrical Engineers 113, 186
— of Mechanical Engineers 113, 186, 335
— of Production Engineers 113, 186
Instrument of Government (Brunel College) 113, 114
International Nickel Co. (Mond) Ltd 225
— Publishing Corporation 361
Isaac, J. D. 82, 148, 171, 221
Isam 426
Iver Link Road 197, 198, 200, 201, 264

Jackson, G. 206, 236, 302, 336, 414
Jackson, Willis (Lord) 83
Jahoda, Marie
    Joined Brunel College 118
    Nuffield project 120, 121
    Progress reports 145
    Education of Technologists 147, 162
    Liberal Studies working party 148
    Education and Training 163, 165
    Fundamentals of Science 171
    Head of Department 192
    Survey of Uxbridge 196
    Student failures 216
    Report on first sandwich course 219
    Meetings concerning Charter 232
    Appointment as Professor 236
    Resignation 238, 288
Jaques, Elliott 13, 221, 288, 289, 290, 362, 371, 411, 416
James, A. T. 154
James, A. H. 296
Jeffries, T. O. 368
Jennings, B. R. 410
Jones, M. D. R. 320

Kelly, F. H. 332
Kilburn Polytechnic 8
Kings Norton, Lord 93, 309
Kingston Lane 264, 346
Kitchener, R. 124, 157
Knaggs, J. H. 197
Knox, A. N. 229
Kodak 11, 13, 88, 321
Kogan, M. 318, 367, 410

Lacey, A. J. 139, 331
Lamb, D. A. 312
Lambert, E. V. 331
Languages, Division of 292
Large, J. H. 339
Latham, Sir Joseph 189, 272, 290

Lawson, D. 332
Lecture Centre 250, 267, 269, 308, 313, 340, 342, 354
Leff, I. 127
Legg, R. 332
Levy, H. 172
Lewin, D. W. 316, 410
Liberal Studies 82, 127, 144, 148, 160, 168, 169
Liberal Education in a Technical Age 178
Librarian, University 316, 322
Libraries 178, 296
Library
  Acton T.C. 73
  Brunel College 130, 133, 134
  Plan for new library 141
  Temporary buildings 152
  NCTA comments 207
  Additional hut 207
  Library at Uxbridge 267, 315
  Special non-recurrent grant 321
  Use of Engineering Centre 342
  Use of Lecture Centre 342
  New Library 350, 355, 356, 358, 381
Lindsay, Lord 416
Linstead, Sir Patrick 174
Listener, The 406
Lister, H. 316
Lloyd, F. C. 225
Lloyd, G. 111
Lodgings 295, 317
— Officer 294, 361
London Passenger Transport Board 11
Loughborough College of Education 335
— College of Technology 90, 257
Lowe and Shawyer 198
Lowery, H. 60

MacAdam, R. W. 18, 30, 66, 72
Macdonald, P. 319, 367
Maclure, S. 304, 406, 416
McGee, J. D. 197, 371, 379
McNair Committee Report 36
Maintenance Building 267, 269, 314
Maitland, R. J. 293
Malcolm Committee 5, 16
Management, Department of 74, 117, 122, 291
Mander, M. R. 414
Manser, A. W. 210
Maria Grey College 138, 139
Marsland, D. 291

Master of Technology degree (M.Tech.) 368
Materials Science and Technology 154
— Department of 293
— School of 315, 319
Mathematical Studies, School of 300, 317, 326, 354
Mathematics, Department of 72, 123, 124, 157, 300
— Building 267, 309, 314, 317, 340, 346, 354
— Courses 123, 223, 318, 326
Mechanical Engineering, Department of 72, 80, 96, 103, 124, 206, 208, 224, 415
Medical Centre 331
Medical Officer 331
Metal Box Co. 11, 14
Metallurgy, 125, 140, 154, 224, 226
— Department of 293, 294, 315
Metropolitan Vickers Electrical Co. 83
Middlesex County Council 7, 75, 102, 111, 112, 121, 135, 185, 186, 213, 266, 275, 427
Midland Bank 252, 261, 262, 309, 389
Mill Hill Road, Acton 120, 139, 208
Miller, D. R. 290
Milton Hutchings 352
Ministry of Aviation 225
— of Education 182, 186, 195, 249, 251, 292
— — Circulars 46, 67, 89, 135, 178, 192
— — Reports 1, 25, 35, 40, 58, 70, 92, 93, 180, 181, 190, 193
— of Health 318
— of Housing and Local Government 249
— of Technology 336
— of Transport 249
Morris, D. F. C. 193
Morris, Sir Philip 163
Morton, John 196, 258, 261
Moss, William & Son 349, 358, 360
Mountbatten, Lord 361

Napier, D. and Son, Engineers, Ltd 10, 11, 88, 89
National Advisory Council (NACEIC) 62, 66, 92, 151
— Certificates and Diplomas 5, 17, 18, 29, 33, 193, 294, 298, 320, 418
— Coal Board 88, 255
— Colleges 257
— — of Rubber Technology 257

National Council for Technological Awards (NCTA) 71, 93-6, 125, 147, 160, 161, 206, 215, 218, 224, 237
— Health Service 416
— Incomes Commission (NIC) 213, 284
— Institute of Adult Education 178
— Union of Students 131, 246
Nelson, B. 214
New, R. W. 156, 193, 316, 367
New Brunel 226
New Buildings Committee 269, 282, 314, 353, 357, 372, 379, 384, 385
New College Committee 203, 249, 250, 254, 262, 263, 266
Newsletter 313, 337
Nimmo, R. D. 316
Noordhof, G. H. 333
Northampton Polytechnic 90, 148
Northern Polytechnic 257
North-West Metropolitan Regional Hospital Board 318
Nuclear Engineering 106
— Science 314, 379
Nuffield Foundation 118
— Research Group 144-6, 165

O'Day, C. 48
Official Opening of University 337
On-site generation of electricity 255, 260
Open days 339
Operational Research 367
Owen, V. G. 312

Paget, Sir John
   Acton Governing Body 48
   Napiers 89
   Brunel College Governing Body 113, 116
   Nuffield Foundation 119
   Industrial Training 127
   Chairman Brunel Governing Body 140, 183, 186
   Appointment of Architect 189
   Academic Advisory Committee 327
Palmer, W. 45
Parliamentary and Scientific Committee, 69, 70
Parsons, J. 144, 145, 291
Part, Sir Anthony 309
Part III Authorities 44, 46
Pask, G. 361
Percy, Lord Eustace 4, 5, 58, 61
Percy Report 3, 54, 59, 64, 110, 306

Perkin, W. H. 98
Phase One 253, 256, 259, 261, 268, 271
— Two 262
Pinn, River 198, 201, 263, 346, 375
Pippard, A. J. S. 229, 239
Pitteway, M. L. V. 300, 319
Physical Education, Department of 360
— — Director of 360
Physics, Applied 88, 96
— Department of 122, 158, 224, 320, 321, 354
— Buildng 315, 347, 355, 379, 380
— and Mathematics, Department of 73, 123
Planning Group 200, 203, 249, 250, 253, 255, 259, 261, 264
Playing fields 197, 250, 252, 253, 311, 316, 356
Polymer Science and Technology, *see* Materials Science
Polytechnics, New 90, 307
Postgraduate Courses 226, 411, 417
— — Committee 228, 287, 299
Principal's fund 252
Privy Council 240, 241, 245, 247, 327
Production Engineering 74, 123, 155
— Technology 125, 143
— — Department of 156, 193, 289, 367, 419
Project Technology 335, 414
Projects 166
Psychology and Social Science 192, 290
Public relations 250, 259
Puckey, Sir Walter 48, 161
Pump-priming grant 363

Quinquennium 1967-72 283
— 1972-7 394

Radford, J. F. A. 89
Radio-chemistry 321
Railway line/cutting 198, 256, 269, 338, 351, 352, 374
Readers 193
Recurrent grants 323
Refectory building (*see* Communal Building) 348
Regional Advisory Committee 54, 55, 186
— Colleges 90, 114
Regulations for higher degrees 236
Research 117, 225, 418
Reynolds, A. J. 371

Rice, G. H. 21
Richardson, P. 341, 348
Richardson, W. A. 42, 45
Ritchie, C. C. 193, 319, 367
Robbins Committee on Higher Education 184, 215, 216
Robbins Report
  Overloading of courses 176
  New Universities 195
  Technological Universities 204, 296
  Wastage rates 217
  University Government 231
  National Colleges 257
  Department of Education and Science 277
  Student numbers 284, 297
  Size of universities 416
Robens, Lord 255
Robinson, E. E. 128, 148, 221
Robinson, G. A. 18
Rodgers, W. 74
Rootes 11
Rotax 11
Royal Colleges of Technology 306
— Institute of British Architects 203
— — of Chemistry 22, 113, 186
Russell, J. D. D. 316
Russell, Sir Lionel 151
Rutherford Technical College 90

Salford Technical College 90
Saltash Hall 347
Sandwich courses 60, 78, 88, 91, 236, 294, 360, 395, 407, 420
— — End-on 149, 150
Sapper, L. J. 233, 296
Saul, G. M. 316, 331, 414
Sayers, D. P. 189, 210
Schofield, H. 195
Schools 153, 287, 289, 303
— Council 335, 336
Science Building, Acton 32, 33, 57, 73, 100, 121, 130, 208
— — Uxbridge, *see* Biology/Chemistry Building
— Research Council 321
Scientist, The Complete 174
Scott, Sir G. G. 13
Scott, J. L. 188
Senate of University 231, 239, 310
Senate/Students Committee 247, 248, 311, 332
Shearman, Sir Harold 277

Sheppard, Richard
  Appointment as Architect 189, 270
  Master-plan 195, 201, 202
  First meeting with Brunel Governors 196
  Sussex Seminars 203
  Students' Union dinner 223
  Nominated Contractor 249
  Planning applications 251
  Sketch designs 253
  Changes in plan 255
  Hall of Residence 260
  Planning Group 261
  Biology/Chemistry building 314
  Council Rooms 340
  Lecture Centre Panels 343
  Article in Brunel Bulletin 349, 351
Shipp, G. C.
  Head of Department 156
  Planning Group 196, 264
  Vice-Principal 206
  Meeting with Staff Association 212
  Survey of Uxbridge 227
  Phase one equipment 271
  Hospital Joint Committee 296
  Industrial Training and Assessment 302
  Resignation 328
Shoenberg, I. 12
Shops 261, 262, 309, 340
Shoreditch College of Education, Egham 417
Shrigley, G. F. 47
Sing, K. S. W. 294, 321, 367
Site Engineer 264
Site One 198, 251, 252, 254, 255, 256, 267, 276, 316, 341, 351, 375, 383
— Two 197, 251, 252, 254, 256, 257, 276, 346
— Three 197, 251, 252, 276, 314
— Four 198, 251, 252, 262, 352, 376
— Five 251, 252, 261, 262, 314, 355
Skellon, J. H.
  Head of Department 101, 154, 294
  Acton Science Building 99, 135
  Tutors 127
  Planning Advisory Committee 196
  Meetings concerning Charter 232
  Resignation 230
  D.Tech. 339
Slater, T. F. 365, 367
Smart, J. Ewart 47
Smith, J. D. 126

Snow, Lord 266
Social and Psychological Research Centre 155
— Sciences 238, 265, 267, 326, 396, 418
— — School of 288, 290, 291, 317, 346, 354, 357, 362, 363, 383, 419
— Sciences/Education Building 316, 356, 358, 385-7, 398
Sofer, C. and Hutton, G. 32, 75, 125
Solicitor 251
Southall Technical College 7, 9, 97
Sparkes, S. R. 189, 196, 250, 261
Sparks, J. A. 111
Spence, R. 154
Sperry Gyroscope 11
Spink, N. O. 101
Spooner, J. R. 333
Sports Barn/Hall 311, 316, 355, 359, 378, 382
— Turf Research Association 269
Squash Courts 359, 382
Staff Association 75, 85, 104, 125, 144, 211, 212, 240, 241, 246, 295
— secondment 213
Statutes Committee 232, 241, 242
Stillman and Eastwick-Field 203, 255, 344
Stillman, J. 203, 253, 260, 268, 315, 344
Stuchbery, A. L. 156, 190, 210, 286, 310, 374
Student numbers 105, 106, 128, 193, 224, 226, 278, 324, 360, 368, 370, 395, 400, 402, 418
— participation 371
Students' Union
  Acton T.C. 74, 98, 100
  Brunel College 130, 131, 222, 223
  Union fees 190
  Playing-fields 227, 276
  Sports Barn 227, 316
  Student participation 246, 247, 332
  Premises 267, 295
  Joint Committee with Council 248, 310, 332
  Joint Committee with Senate 248, 311, 332
  Building 315, 350, 355, 356, 359
  Sabbatical Years 332
  Comment by Stuart Maclure 409
Sturgess, M. 332
Surveyor 252
Swann Report 424

Tait, J. S. 214
Taylor, A. J. P. 11
Tavistock Institute 75, 103, 196
Teachers' Centres 414, 415
Technische Hochschulen 60
Technology 149
Technology and the Academics 175
Telegraph Condenser Co. 88
Television 333, 338, 342, 358
Templeman, G. 229, 327
Terry, R. J. 320
Theatre 376
Thomas, J. B. 320
Thomas, L. F. 119, 126
Thomas, Sir Miles 113, 140
Thompson, Alan 189, 252, 265
Ticciatti, N. 378
Todd Commission 296, 300
Topping, J. 113, 172, 179, 233, 306, 406
Tottenham Polytechnic 8
Trades Union Congress 186, 310
Training Services Agency (TSA) 421
Trist, E. L. 196
Turner, Sir Mark 272
Tutor, Industrial 164
— System 163
Tutorial days 165.
Twickenham Technical College 7, 17

UCCA 298
Ultra Electronics 11
Unilever Ltd 225
United Kingdom Atomic Energy Establishment 321
Universities, Polytechnics and Industry Committee 421
— Student numbers in 38, 110, 297, 298
— and Industry Joint Committee 421
University Development (1947-52) 39, 177; (1952-7) 177; (1957-62) 177, 217, 277
University Grants Committee
  Note on Technology 64
  Expansion of technological institutes 68
  Student numbers 110, 297, 324, 394
  Postgraduate numbers 325
  Over-specialization 174
  Failure rates 174, 217
  Academic Advisory Committees, 229, 240
  Draft of Charter, 241, 245
  Building Starts 262, 266, 270
  Brunel in Grant List 276
  Quinquennial visits 277, 294, 360, 403

University Grants Committee (*cont.*)
 Halls of Residence 311, 347
 Difficulties of planning 315
 Phase One furniture and equipment 322
 Courses in Education and Teacher Training 325
 Deferred Starts 346-7
 Biology/Chemistry Building 348
 Physics Building extension 355
 Pump-priming grant (Social Sciences) 363
 Land exchanges 374
 Loan-financed schemes 392
 Memorandum of General Guidance 324, 394
 Recurrent grants 401
University of Bath 325
— of East Anglia 195, 303, 304
— of Edinburgh 357
— of Essex 195, 303, 317
— of Keele 317, 416
— of Kent 195
— of Lancaster 195
— of London 113, 186, 217
— — external degrees of 18, 21, 28, 36, 38, 80
— of Manchester (UMIST) 250
— of Strathclyde 231, 304
— of Sussex 195, 203, 231, 238, 287, 303, 304, 317, 416
— of Warwick 195, 303, 357
— of York 195, 304
Urry, S. A.
 Planning Group 196, 261
 Department of Industrial Training 228, 264, 287, 302
 Editor Brunel Bulletin 304
 Planning Assistant 328
 Director Institute of Industrial Training 364
 Division of Building Technology 366
 Professor 367, 407, 409
Urwick Committee 66
Uxbridge 138, 142, 182, 258, 259, 414
— Football Club 261, 352, 376, 384, 393
Uxbridge-Brunel 259

Vaizey, John (Lord) 67, 293, 316, 318
Venables, Sir Peter vii, 83
Vice-Chancellor, Appointment of 371
— Powers of 231, 233

Vice-Chancellor's residence 265, 316, 352, 372, 373
Vice-Principal 206, 329

Walker, B. G. 316
War of 1939-45 24
Warden 294, 331
Warren, G. W. 127
Wastage rates 215, 217
Watkins, C. 371
Weedon, B. C. L. 327
Weekes, Sir Ronald 62
Wells Organisations Institutional Ltd 282
West Middlesex Productivity Association 339
Westman, R. 225
Wheeler, T. B. 47
White Paper on Better Opportunities in Technical Education (1961) 179
— — on Education: a framework for expansion (1972) 399
— — on Technical Education (1956) 89, 90, 106, 107
Whittaker, R. C. J. 156
Whittle, Sir Frank 112
Whitworth, C. 83, 135
Wilkinson Sword Co. 11, 12
Willesden Technical College 7, 17
Willett, William Ltd 355
Williams, F. J. 124, 126
Williams, Shirley 369
Wilson, A. T. M. 75, 197, 210, 288, 290
Wimpey, G. & Co.
 Site 5 200
 Previous owners of university sites 259
 Phase One contract 264, 265, 268, 271
 Decision not to tender 309
 Labour troubles 312
 New completion date 313
 Reaction of other contractors 348
 Flatlets on Site One 389, 390
Winkler, M. C. 104, 148
Winstanley, B. H. vii, 205, 235, 242, 253, 312
Wolfenden, Sir John
 Academic Advisory Committee 228, 235
 Draft Charter and Statutes 240, 242
 Letter from Lord Brown 243
 Representation from Governors concerning allocations 266
 Letter to Principal 282

Quinquennial Visit 294
Successor 360
Woodhouse, C. M. 67
Woodlands Building 17, 30, 130, 133, 152, 181
Worboys, Sir Walter 229, 235, 242, 243, 246, 290, 327
Working parties
Tutor system 206, 215
Materials Science 206
Laboratory work 206
General courses 216
Examinations 218, 303
General Studies 221

Structure of courses 228
Regulations for higher degrees 236
Student participation 332
Industrial Training 364
Biochemistry 365
Building Technology 366
Annual student intakes 370, 396
Use of space 370
Wyatt, R. W. P. 322

Yates, A. 343

Ziseman, Bowyer and Partners 254